FOCUS ON THE FAMILY®

PARENTS' GUIDE TO THE

# Spiritual Mentoring of Teens

GENERAL EDITORS

## Joe White

## Jim Weidmann

Tyndale House Publishers,
WHEATON, ILLINOIS

Heritage Builders®

A Focus on the Family book published by
Tyndale House Publishers, Wheaton, Illinois.

**Library of Congress Cataloging-in-Publication Data**
Parents' guide to the spiritual mentoring of teens / Jim Weidmann and Joe
White, general editors.
     p. cm.
Includes bibliographical references and index.
   ISBN 1-56179-948-3
1. Parenting—Religious aspects—Christianity.  2. Parent and teenager—
Religious aspects—Christianity.  3. Christian teenagers—Religious life.
I. Weidmann, Jim.  II. White, Joe, 1948-
   BV4529 .P35 2001
   248.8'45—dc21

                                    20001003116

Editor: Larry K. Weeden
Front cover design: Peak Creative

Printed in the United States of America

01 02 03 04 05 06/10 9 8 7 6 5 4 3 2 1

# CONTENTS

# Introduction to Heritage Builders

Parenting a teen can be a lot like pulling on a rubber band. You pull and pull and wait in fear for that moment when the band will snap. Your relationship with your teen is stretched and tension builds as you confront his desires that run counter to your better judgment, rules, or beliefs. You stand in fear that your decision will cause your relationship to snap and your teen to blatantly rebel.

However, parenting a teen can also be like pulling on a bungee cord. You can pull and pull but not break it because of its strength. If you develop a healthy relationship with your teen day by day, then when those tense moments of challenge occur, your relationship will hold firm.

The vision of the Heritage Builders ministry is to motivate, educate, and equip parents to be intentional about passing on a rock-solid spiritual heritage to their children. And as you'll see in this book, the key to doing that in their teen years is to have a quality relationship with them. Every aspect of the heritage you pass on—obedience, respect, *and* spiritual training—comes from the relationships within your home.

Immerse yourself in the pages of this book. As you do, you'll gain the confidence, insights, and practical ideas you need to cultivate a healthy, God-honoring relationship with your teenage children and to prepare them for a full life in Christ.

*Jim Weidmann*
*General Editor and Executive Director, Heritage Builders*

# Introduction to This Guide

Being a daddy has been wild, fast, furious, and fulfilling. With two boys and two girls, our home was filled with emotional and spiritual highs and lows that only a parent can begin to understand. My children, Jamie, Courtney, Brady, and Cooper, have brought fulfillment, challenge, heartache, and—most of all—immeasurable joy to the past 25 years of my life.

With each of my kids, God allowed many foggy days into the testing and refining process of making them into the adults they would one day become. We cried and counseled through anorexia, rejection, rebellion, depression, and a whole smorgasbord of related adolescent issues. Some days the sun shone brightly and laughter flowed from the doors and windows of our Ozark Mountain home. But on many other occasions, being a parent was gritty, challenging work. My wife, Debbie-Jo, and I learned over and over that it is *never* too late to help teens become the people whom God intended. I hope part one of this book will convince you that, no matter what you're dealing with at home now, there is hope! Despite what you may feel, God has made you able for the task.

■ ■ ■

Now, I admit I was not feeling very able the day before my last child, Cooper, left for college and closed the book on phase one of my role as a parent. This day was supposed to be the pinnacle of my life. I had fallen head over heels in love with my kids' mom 28 years before, and this empty nest was about to become the home

3

of two lovebirds who were going to date and fall in love all over again. Moreover, my "grown-up kids" and I were polishing a friendship that had been 25 years in the making. However, for a long time I'd had an intuitive feeling that I was in serious medical trouble, and the moment had come when I'd have to tell Cooper and the rest of the family what I'd just found out.

For the past few months, I had been noticing unusual bruises on the back of my legs. I brushed my curiosity aside until the closing days of a demanding summer, during which my wife and I hosted 17,000 kids and 2,300 summer staff in our Christian sports camps, which God has built over the previous quarter century.

When I slipped into the lab for the results of the telltale blood test, the look on my doctor friend's face could have written a Broadway tragedy. He didn't need to tell me that the most feared words in the English language are *leukemia* and *cancer*. I knew from his scowl that both were now mine to wrestle with, though I wouldn't be doing so alone. My five best friends in the world would be stunned and perplexed when they heard the news.

■ ■ ■

Cooper and I had spent an exhilarating previous four weeks together, as he gave me the privilege of being his personal trainer for his debut as a college football player. What a capstone to a friendship intentionally hewn out of 19 years together those days had become! We had run 40 wind sprints the day before the doctor gave me the dreaded scoop. It was the movie *Brian's Song* all over again. I was Brian Piccolo; he was Gale Sayers. We would race to each finish line, pouring perspiration, panting for oxygen, laughing and jeering, arms and elbows and personalities intertwined. How prophetically the classic movie scene played out before our eyes. We were two best friends, neither knowing that a dreadful diagnosis lay just beyond the sunset. As I left the doctor's office, I sought my "best buddy's" soft heart.

Tomorrow, his long trek to college would change his life and the personality of our home forever. Though he wore a happy-go-lucky veneer, his insides were as soft and squeezable as a teddy bear. Throughout his childhood and until his graduation from high school, I had made it a firm habit to lie down next to Cooper each night before his bedtime prayers so we could memorize a Bible verse together. (When the peer pressure years came crashing into his life, those scriptural treasures we had tucked into his heart kept him from disaster.)

Tender sentimentality had crept into my friendship with Cooper, and we both knew that the 400 miles soon to separate us would be a trail of tears. He didn't need the news report he was about to receive.

"Cooper, uh, there's something wrong with my blood," I began as I squelched back tears and time stood still.

"What is it, Daddy?"

"It's cancer. Your Pops has leukemia."

"What does it mean, Daddy? What's going to happen?"

I could almost read his mind as we pondered the eerie silence that surrounded us. *Will you be there for my wedding day? Daddy, will you help me raise my children and be their granddad the way we dreamed it would be?* After I explained what little I knew at that point, Cooper and I hugged and cried. Then he asked me the hardest question I have had to deal with in my 28 years of marriage: "Have you told Mom?"

I could hardly bear the thought. She had already lost her father and stepdad. She has a loyal, "one man" heart and is the type of lady who would probably never marry again. How could she handle the news of one more tragedy in a span of so few years? But I brushed aside my tears and made a beeline for her. She was 30 miles away at our winter home, busily packing Cooper's necessities for college.

■ ■ ■

Debbie-Jo had been through so much in our 28 whirlwind years together. My wife is a pillar of fortitude, integrity, and sheer class. Proverbs 31 describes her well: "A wife of noble character who can find? She is worth far more than rubies. Her husband has full confidence in her and lacks nothing of value" (verses 10-11).

After I gave her my health report, we sat on the floor and melted in each other's arms. The roof over our heads and the walls that surrounded us had been a petri dish for intentional disciple making with our kids, built on a foundation of two very different personalities with two different backgrounds working like crazy to be a fulfillment of Philippians 2:2: "Make my joy complete by being like-minded, having the same love, being one in spirit and purpose." Countless apologies like "I'm sorry, honey, I let you down" and "Please forgive me; I blew it" had permeated our relationship. We were not naturals at building an exemplary marriage, but years of work had made the effort feel natural.

The walls around us were covered with happy 8-by-10-inch photographs of the kids. The bookshelves were stacked with scrapbooks that Debbie-Jo had carefully assembled through their growing-up years—chronicles of family vacations we had squeezed into our busy schedules, junior high and high school sports events too numerous to count, and prom dates and homecomings where home was the number-one stop for final instructions and pictures taken by Mom.

I had always thought that the sacrifice it took to create those thousands of photogenic moments was well worth it, but now the pictures seemed more than ever to deserve the frames that in our minds were studded with diamonds. The value of everything else that Debbie-Jo and I had ever invested ourselves in paled in comparison to what we'd done as parents.

■ ■ ■

I dreaded my next assignment that night. Jamie would be joining Debbie-Jo, Cooper, Brady, and me for Brady's 22nd birthday dinner.

Jamie was our first child, "Daddy's little girl." When her heart was broken, mine was the lap she'd run to. When my words and cuddles healed her, she'd say, "Daddy, thanks for tying my heart back together." Daddies are supposed to be good at that.

Jamie taught me to be a father first and a friend second. During her eighth-grade year, we were like two rails heading in the same direction but separated by the four-foot cross ties of the pressures of adolescence. Though communication broke down during those challenging days, as we traveled farther down the track, we eventually came back together. Her heart was always pure inside. Like the golden retriever that she is, Jamie was now my most loyal companion and friend, directing one of our Christian camps and giving us our first grandchild. That night, her tears flowed like spring rain.

Listening, too, was Brady, our older son. At six feet, three inches tall, his exterior manliness was dwarfed only by his heart. In preparing Brady for music ministry, God had entrusted him with a marathon of emotional hurdles to get over in his formative years. We had spent hundreds of hours together during his days of testing, using his dreams for basketball as our common bond. Brady didn't reach his wonderfully naive fourth-grade goal of playing in the NBA, but that tan leather ball had given me the opportunity to spend hundreds of hours under a 10-foot goal, catching over 100,000 of his shots in the evenings after work, and had cemented a friendship between us that made me the "go to" guy when counsel was needed.

To this day, Brady's and my favorite meal together is breakfast. I'm not much of a cook, but I have mastered blueberry pancakes, and Brady can put away as many as I can cook. This wonderful ritual began when our kids were young. Cooking breakfast was my excuse to get the kids around the breakfast table for a devotional time from Scripture. My kids and yours should never go to school without food in their tummies and a fresh taste of God in their hearts.

■ ■ ■

Courtney, though now 23, would be the most fragile. Far away at seminary in Seattle, my little buddy would need someone to hold her when I told her my news. I had been her security blanket, confidant, and best friend since seventh grade, when life piled a load on her shoulders far too difficult to carry alone. As with the rest of my kids, I'd tucked her into bed at night and captured those priceless, quiet moments right before sleep to listen, just listen, as she spilled out her tears, fears, and cheers of each day. What we couldn't conclude at night, we'd readdress at dawn, during our long jogs down the hilly country roads that lead to our home.

Courtney's highs were the highest and her lows were the lowest. A phone call to Seattle would have been disastrous, so I boarded the plane for a long, dreaded flight. After I arrived, we talked and cried into the wee hours of the morning. Finally, as I slipped wearily into bed, Courtney hit the Internet to study the disease and work through her emotions with God.

■ ■ ■

Why have I told you so much about the bond I have with my wife and kids? Because even though relating to my teenagers was often difficult and I made too many mistakes to number, I wanted nonetheless to illustrate one of the most important principles covered in this book. Part two will introduce you to many aspects of one central truth, namely that being an effective spiritual mentor to your teen begins with a strong parent-child relationship. Without that, you can do nothing. *The relationship is everything.* Write it down! Even when an awkward adolescent veneer says, "I'm on my own now, and I don't need you," the relationship is everything!

Before teenagers want to hear what you have to say, you first have to earn the right to be heard by spending lots of "friendship hours" together developing a common bond around things they like to do. Your teen must first enjoy hanging out with you. Only then will he or she desire to follow your example, share your values, and obey the same Lord who rules your life. Faith, you've no doubt heard it said, is caught rather than taught. For your teen to catch anything of value from you, the two of you must first be close.

To help you develop such a friendship, part two will cover such things as mentoring, having fun together, cheerleading, and becoming a great listener. You'll also pick up tips on how to overcome the conflicts that may be getting in the way.

As I open the pages of this book with you, I turn and look back at the years to which you can look forward, and I urge you to keep your camera handy! Every single day in the next few years holds a boxcar full of moments waiting to be captured. Lightning doesn't travel as fast as the hands of your wristwatch will. The destination is glorious, but oh, so is the journey!

For you that journey may be a solo adventure, as it was for the moms of the two best women I know, my mother and my wife. They were both successfully "trained up" in single-parent homes. Or perhaps you're fortunate to travel this road as part of a two-some. Maybe this book finds you trying to get a fresh start after some turbulent years of preadolescent training, or perhaps you want to shift into a higher and more effective gear as the parenting years become more critical and challenging. Regardless of your track record or circumstances, I pray and believe that this book will become one of your greatest companions. With God it's never too late, and it's so true that "all things are possible with God" (Mark 10:27).

■ ■ ■

I have no idea what's around the corner for me. I'm entered in a testing program with a promising new drug for leukemia. Whether the final curtain will drop in a year or five years or after I get to see my grandkids grow up, only the Father of us all knows. But there is one thing I'm sure of: The days when I was called "Daddy" were the best days of my life! And the most satisfying part of all was being used by the Lord to help my kids grow stronger in their walk with Jesus.

What vision do you have for your teen? What sort of person do you see him or her becoming in Christ? Do you have dreams for the long haul, for the immortal creature whom God had in mind when He first brought your child into the world? Travel back with me for a small example of a parent who set his sights on a short-term, thrilling target with lifelong implications for one of his kids.

One bedtime, when Cooper was in ninth grade and sailing in turbulent waters, I told him about a vision I had for his high school graduation. "Coop," I began, "in my mind's eye I see you going across the stage, receiving your diploma one beautiful spring evening in the not-too-distant future. And as you take off your cap and gown, your buddies are going to come up to you and, half choked up, thank you for your lifestyle and words that led them to Christ."

Cooper listened carefully but dozed off without much comment.

Night after night, as I lay beside him to conclude his day with "God time," we would pray for his friends. We would pray through his stumbling. We would confess our sins together, since his life and our relationship were peppered with an array of good times and bad. We would go to the Word for strength during those turbulent high school years, reading large chunks of the Bible together.

All this was part of an attempt to do intentional discipling, something I worked hard on with all my children. Part three of this book covers this topic in depth, including such things as having media discernment, learning to focus on others, and measuring the results of your parenting efforts.

During the middle of his junior year, something amazing happened to Cooper. One of his free-spirited friends named Jared went through a painful breakup with his girlfriend and found himself in a pool of tearful despair. On what would become the most significant night of his life, Jared came looking for Cooper. And there, in the privacy of Cooper's room, a fascinated 17-year-old led his best buddy into a personal, eternal relationship with the living Savior.

In subsequent months, Coop's other friends either took their first steps on a personal pilgrimage to the cross or were guided into a deeper, more abiding walk with God. Dozens of down-to-earth, Christ-centered counseling sessions ensued. When a friend was in emotional trouble, Coop would be his "go to" guy for a listening ear and a scriptural viewpoint.

After Jared asked Jesus into his heart, Cooper came to my bedroom in a state of wonderful bewilderment. "Dad," he said, "do you remember the vision you had for me in the ninth grade, about my graduation night?"

"Yes, son, I do."

"Well, in the ninth grade, that was about the *last* thing I wanted to hear. But now, after tonight, that's exactly what I want to happen. Dad, leading Jared to Christ was better than any football game I ever won or anything else that has ever happened in my life."

■ ■ ■

Nothing on this earth is as exhilarating as seeing your teen grow into a mature and lifelong disciple of our Lord. What that will look like may be different for each of your children. But you can't beat the challenge and experience of becoming your teen's best friend and then, on that foundation, being able to lead him or her into a closer walk with Christ. This book will provide you with some tools you need to have that kind of influence on your teen.

As I did, you may discover that adolescent struggles are many. Tears will flow. Disappointments will take you to your knees. But by God's grace, graduation night can be a grand occasion when the pride of the diploma pales in comparison to the inner joy you share with your graduate. You will both know deeply that your days as a parent have been fruitful, that God has used your home to graduate a godly man or woman. And you'll know that, for the rest of your life, you will have not only a son or daughter but also a treasured friend.

*Joe White is a general editor for this book and runs the Kanakuk Christian youth camps in Branson, Missouri. He is also cohost of Focus on the Family's* Life on the Edge LIVE! *radio broadcast for teens.*

# PART 1

■ ■ ■

# Catching the Vision

*Believe it or not, your child's teen years can be the best time of your parenting life. And God will enable you, day by day, for the vital task of instilling a love for and devotion to Him in your teenager.*

CHAPTER 1

# Why You Need This Book

It's great to have a teenager! In fact, while your child's teen years can be among the most challenging you'll face as a parent, they can also be the best years of your parenting life. Let's look at why that's true.

First, raising a teenager will give new depth and fervency to your prayer life, drawing you closer to God! You're likely to be reminded every day that, by yourself, you're not up to the task. That's okay; it means you're just like the rest of us. But it also means you'll want to speak often to the One who has promised to supply every need, to give wisdom generously if we only ask, and to provide His strength when we're weak.

*Passing the baton of faith successfully to your teenage child will, at the end of the process, give you a tremendous sense of victory and satisfaction.*

As you do so, your trust in and dependence upon Him will grow, as will your love for Him and your appreciation of His love for you and your family.

Second, passing the baton of faith successfully to your teenage child will, at the end of the process, give you a tremendous sense of victory and satisfaction.

As a loving and responsible Christian parent, you want to see your child develop a solid faith of his or her own, a faith that will give purpose and joy to life for the rest of your child's days. Passing your faith on to your child is like passing the baton in a relay race—it's the most vital part of the contest. Former Olympic running great Madeline Manning Mims explains, "I've had batons slip, drop, slide, and even bounce off the track back into my hand on the way to victory. But of all the crucial moments in an Olympic relay race, there is none so crucial as the pass. It is the approach, the timing, the grip, the exchange, the power, the pressure. It is the all-important transfer. It is where the race is won or lost. Period."

Clearly, the stakes are high in passing the baton of faith successfully in your child's teen years. Yet when you've done so, you can experience the thrill of victory—the incredible joy of having an adult child who knows, loves, and serves the Lord—that is a parent's greatest reward.

Let's change the word picture for further insight. The Colorado River, which starts in its namesake state and eventually flows through the majestic Grand Canyon, has long stretches of calm water or water with only slight gradients and occasional small ripples. Even a novice canoeist or rafter can handle those parts with no problem. The paddling is easy, and whatever obstacles arise are relatively simple to avoid.

Those stretches of the river are like parenting a younger child. You're building the relationship, which is generally good (even with a strong-willed child). Your word and values are accepted without question. You are clearly the dominant influence in your child's life.

If you're that beginner canoeist on the Colorado, you might hope that the calm

*"My God will meet all your needs according to his glorious riches in Christ Jesus."—Philippians 4:19*

*"If any of you lacks wisdom, he should ask God, who gives generously to all without finding fault, and it will be given to him."—James 1:5*

*"[The Lord] said to me, 'My grace is sufficient for you, for my power is made perfect in weakness.' . . . When I am weak, then I am strong."—2 Corinthians 12:9-10*

*"Even youths grow tired and weary, and young men stumble and fall; but those who hope in the LORD will renew their strength. They will soar on wings like eagles; they will run and not grow weary, they will walk and not be faint."—Isaiah 40:30-31*

stretches of water will continue indefinitely. But often they don't. Suddenly, out of nowhere, the river drops 10 feet in 100 yards and you find yourself in the middle of raging rapids. The water's white and fast and splashing around, over, and into the boat. Boulders loom everywhere, and you've got to dig in like crazy with your paddle, making split-second steering decisions, to keep from crashing into the rocks and being thrown into the river.

That's what it feels like to parent a teen. All of a sudden, the waters are turbulent. Your daughter goes to her first middle school social and comes home enthralled with someone of the opposite sex and with the earsplitting music that was played. Or your son comes home feeling totally rejected and worthless because nobody wanted to spend time with him, and nothing you can say will console him. It will blow your mind.

Then, when you realize that the influence of your child's peers is rivaling your own, and that the values of Hollywood are supplanting yours in your child's world, the waters are crashing down on you and the boulders are everywhere. You're jolted into the understanding that you'd better grab the paddle *now* and dig

## Teens' "Traits of Great Parents," Part 1

- ■ "True listeners. Always available and let their children know that they are a top priority. Let your children *see* your love for God, and let them see you struggle with spiritual issues. Don't be afraid to say, 'I don't know the answer to that question—let's try to find one.' "
- ■ "Demonstrating through words, quality and quantity of time, as well as touch (hugs, etc.) that teens are intrinsically special and loved no matter what they do or don't do. Encourage them in their relationship with Christ (model what that means), and help them see their God-given talents. Also, honesty and forgiveness are crucial."
- ■ "Constant, open, not clingy, adventuresome, friendly toward the teen's friends."
- ■ "My parents always said, 'If your friends won't tell you your socks don't match, then who will? That's our responsibility.' If a parent can learn to critique in a healthy way, that's a great asset."
- ■ "Understanding, listening, bold, confident, intentional."

in with all of your might before you and your teen are overwhelmed.

The ride through this part of the river is thrilling and terrifying, energizing and draining. It takes your best effort to get through safely. But when you do, you thrust your arms into the air and cheer with all your

> *At the end of this process, you will have a treasured friend who will bless your life for the rest of your days.*

might. You're exhilarated as you enjoy a tremendous feeling of accomplishment. Part of you wants to do it again as soon as possible, and part of you vows never to risk another rapids.

In parenting, there's a similar sense of elation when you see your child finish adolescence in victory, with a solid faith that will stand against any trial or temptation. "We did it! We did it!" you want to shout aloud. And the sense of accomplishment is all the greater because of the challenges you had to overcome and the realization that there were times when the outcome was in doubt.

A third reason your child's teen years can be great is that, as you continue to build the relationship and invest in his or her spiritual development, you get to see your girl blossom into a woman or your boy grow into a man—a mature young adult ready for independent living. At the end of this process, you will have a treasured friend who will bless your life for the rest of your days.

A teenager named Alma illustrates both the lowest lows of this period and the highest highs that can await a parent who sees a child safely through. Here's what she wrote:

> Last night my mom and I were shopping. We'd had the worst argument the day before, and I was feeling bad. The store had a little teddy bear that said, "Mom, you're #1." I just had to get it.
>
> When I gave it to Mom, the glow that went across her face made my eyes fill with tears.
>
> Just to think that one year earlier I had wanted to kill myself! I'm so glad I didn't die. I would have missed so much. God has blessed me with so many good things, starting with my parents' love. Now that I'm a year older, I realize how fortunate I am.

> I bought a [contemporary Christian] CD for my birthday. The artist sings about wanting to make a difference for God. I know he will. And now I know that *I* will, too.

Parenting your child through the teen years, especially in the area of his or her spiritual growth, is a divine calling, a challenge that will demand the best you've got to give, and a wonderful privilege. You don't face this task alone, however. In the pages of this book, you'll find practical, parent-tested advice to guide you each step of the way:

- You'll see that no matter what your situation, and no matter how good a job you have or haven't done before now, *you can be the effective mentor your child needs.*
- You'll gain a clear understanding of the fundamental change that takes place in the parent-child relationship during the child's teen years, along with what that means for influencing your teen's faith.
- You'll learn that the key to influencing your teen is having a great relationship with him or her, and you'll acquire

---

## Teens' Advice to Parents About Nurturing Spiritual Growth, Part 1

- "I always have something to say, but not many of my friends 'actively listen'! Some teenagers need that parental affirmation at home—to have someone to be there and listen to all of their emotional whims and convictions."
- "Nurturing makes me think of affection. Parents need to be lovingly vulnerable with hugs, kisses, sitting on laps, smiles, and just general eye contact."
- "If parents live out daily their excitement about serving Christ and show teens their identity in Christ, teens notice and desire that."
- "Parents need to ask their teens questions about what they are thinking and struggling with. Listen, and take them to Scripture for the answers."
- "Develop a relationship with your teen in which he or she will feel free to share with you and seek your counsel. Don't preach, or you will be immediately tuned out. Even when your teens stumble, discipline them but love them. Show them that you believe Christ has a purpose for them."

crucial insights into how to build and maintain that kind of relationship.

■ You'll discover a wide variety of ways in which to intentionally disciple your teen, allowing you to tailor a plan to fit your family's unique situation, personality, and schedule.

■ Finally, you'll review a series of "measuring sticks" to help you evaluate the progress you're making and identify areas that may need special emphasis at a given point in time.

Most important, as you face the challenge of mentoring your teen, you have the Lord of heaven at your side. He loves you, He loves your child, and He is committed to your success. As He encouraged Joshua, who faced the daunting challenge of leading Israel into the Promised Land, so He encourages you: "Be strong and courageous. Do not be terrified; do not be discouraged, for the LORD your God will be with you wherever you go" (Joshua 1:9).

CHAPTER 2

# You Can Do It!

If you're like most parents of teens, the biggest question on your mind as you consider the task of being a spiritual mentor to your child is probably "Can I really do this?" Or you may have already concluded, "I really wish I could do this, but I don't think I'm cut out for it!"

Fueling those doubts may be thoughts like these:

- *My child is already 17 and will be gone in a year. It's too late for us to get started now.*
- *I'm a single parent (or I'm married but going it alone spiritually because of my spouse's lack of interest), and I just don't have the resources (time, energy, money) for the job.*
- *I've blown it with my child in the past, leaving our relationship in a shambles, so he's not about to start listening to me now.*
- *My parents didn't do a good job of training me spiritually, so I don't even know where to begin with my own child.*
- *I made sure my child was taught well in her younger years. There's not much more that I can do now, when she seems to listen to her friends more than she does to me.*
- *The truth is that I'm far from being a model Christian myself, and if I try to start mentoring my child spiritually, he'll blow me off as a hypocrite.*

If you can relate to one or more of those concerns, you've got a lot of company. In fact, we'd be surprised if there's a Christian parent alive who doesn't feel inadequate in at least one of those areas. Yet it's also true that, in spite of those understandable and often well-founded feelings, millions of parents are exerting a positive influence on their teens' spiritual development every day, and *you can too.*

To show you how that's possible, let's consider each of the above concerns in turn.

### Too Late to Start

Perhaps, for whatever reason, you've never been very intentional about, or personally involved in, your child's spiritual training. Now your child is 16, 17, or 18; busy with school, a job, and friends; pretty set in his ways of thinking and relating to God; and deep into planning for college and independent living. Haven't you missed your opportunity to be a spiritual mentor in his life? What could you hope to accomplish in the little time you have left with your child at home?

The answer is that in only a year, or even in just a few months, you can still make an eternal difference.

> *Just 10 minutes a day, wisely and intentionally invested in your child's relationship with the Lord, can plant a love for Him and His Word deep in your teen's heart.*

If your teen is beginning her senior year of high school, for example, and you start today to invest yourself daily in her spiritual growth—studying the Bible together, praying together, memorizing Scripture together, talking about what God is doing in your lives, serving side by side in your church or a soup kitchen—you can share 365 potentially life-changing experiences.

Even if you have only 30 days left before your child goes off to college or joins the military, that's long enough to help him establish the habit of making time to meet with God every day. And there's no better habit you could hope to see him take along as he leaves home. It will give him a much better chance of living a morally upright and God-pleasing life.

VISION

Nor does starting late mean you've got to spend an hour a day feeding the Bible to your teen (we all know *that* isn't going to happen). Just 10 minutes a day, wisely and intentionally invested in your child's relationship with the Lord, can plant a love for Him and His Word deep in your teen's heart. In section three of this book, we're going to show you just how to do that.

Even if your relationship with your teen is rocky, or if it seems awfully late in the game for you to take such an active interest in her spiritual life, your sincere desire to have these daily times together gives you a reason to meet and a foundation on which to begin rebuilding the relationship. (Later on, we'll say a lot more about how to build or, if necessary, to reconstruct a great relationship with your teen.)

## Going It Alone

There's no doubt that parenting in general and spiritual mentoring in particular are more difficult when you're going it alone. Whether you're a single parent or you're married to an uninvolved spouse, your challenge is multiplied. But as countless other single parents have proved, you *can* succeed in this all-important assignment.

Effective single parenting has been a reality for a long time. Look at the example of Timothy, the young pastor and protégé of the apostle Paul in New Testament times. Paul wrote to him, "I have been reminded of your sincere faith, which first lived in your grandmother Lois and in your mother Eunice and, I am persuaded, now lives in you also" (2 Timothy 1:5). We know little about Timothy's father and grandfather, but this verse suggests that, at least when it came to the spiritual training of their children, his grandmother and mother had functioned as single parents. And they had each done such a superb job that Paul now called Timothy his son in the Lord.

Yes, your load will be greater than if you had a spouse to help carry it. But here are some encouraging things to remember:

■ First, you're not alone. Most importantly, God is on your team and at your side. He's ready and eager to provide strength, wisdom, and hope as you need them; all you have to do is ask. Scripture identifies Him as a Father to the fatherless (see Psalm 68:5), and He cares even more about the spiritual growth of your teen than you do.

People in your local church and community are almost certainly willing to help as well. They just need to be asked. Since they're busy too, and they don't want to seem to interfere, they probably won't approach you and volunteer. But if you ask for their support, you're likely to be pleasantly surprised.

■ Second, take advantage of that willingness of others to help by connecting your teen with good Christian role models who can at least partially "replace" your missing spouse. Since most single parents are moms, this usually means finding strong male role models. Be proactive in seeking out a youth leader, a teacher, a coach, a counselor at a summer camp, or some other man who loves teens and is willing to become involved but just needs to be made aware of your need. Such a mentor can do wonders for your child's emotional and spiritual health.

■ ■ ■

## A Faithful Mother

Shawn, a Christian teenager, was adopted as a baby by a couple in which the wife is a Christian but the husband is not. Throughout Shawn's childhood, her mom faithfully took her to church and Sunday school, even when Shawn complained, "But Dad isn't going!" Mom also prayed with her when she put her to bed every night.

When Shawn got in trouble for drinking early in her teen years, Mom responded, "Shawn, I love you, and there's nothing we can't handle with God's help." Today, Shawn is close to her mom and often asks for her advice.

What about Shawn's dad? Shawn says, "I think I was put in my adoptive family to show God to my dad." She's praying and trusting that her father will eventually put his faith in Christ. And for herself, she adds, "I've learned that I want to have a husband who is godly."

VISION

■ Third, with God's help, commit yourself to the daily nurturing of your teen's faith. As hectic and demanding as your life may be, you can still join with the thousands of other single parents who grab a few minutes at breakfast or bedtime to open the Bible and pray with their kids; who use times in the car together and other casual opportunities to talk about what's happening in the child's life and apply biblical principles; who include in their teen's sack lunch, along with the fruit and cookies, a little note that says, "I love you and God loves you." Consistent planting and watering of faith seeds can yield an overflowing harvest of faith.

As a single parent, you have a lot to provide for your teenager. But like all of us, you manage to make time for the things you deem most important. And while responsibilities like preparing nutritious meals and keeping the house clean are obviously important, none is more significant than your calling to help your child develop a personal relationship with the God who made and fiercely loves us all.

## Blew It in the Past

Perhaps you've blown it somehow earlier in your teen's life—you were an absentee parent, emotionally if not physically; you were ruled by a spirit of anger that hurt your child and destroyed the relationship; you struggled with an addictive behavior that caused your child to lose respect for you; you tried to force-feed your faith to your child, and now he wants nothing to do with Christianity. Those are just a

> *Relationships can be rebuilt. Hardened hearts can be softened. Closed minds can be opened.*

few of the ways in which we can blow it as a parent and close a child's spirit to the values and faith we would like to instill.

If you have damaged the relationship or in some way made your child unreceptive to the things of God, there's good news. Relationships can be rebuilt. Hardened hearts can be softened.

Closed minds can be opened. There is realistic hope for you to become the kind of spiritual mentor to your teen that God has called you to be.

How can you bring about such a turnaround? Begin with prayer, confessing your mistakes to God. Then ask Him to open your child's mind and heart, heal the hurts, and give you wisdom, grace, and love for the task. There's no substitute for His active intervention.

## Teens' "Ways in Which a Parent Was Spiritually Influential," Part 1

- "My mom and I had many late-into-the-night discussions while sitting on my bed. She was not afraid to answer any of my questions, and no concern or frustration was too silly for her. She laughed with me, cried with me—she made me feel valuable by just wanting to be with me. These times laid a foundation of trust that made me want to ask about more spiritual matters."
- "Before I got my driver's license, Daddy used to drive me about 10 minutes to school every morning. During this time, we would listen to Chuck Colson's *Breakpoint* commentary on the radio and then discuss the day's topic. These times helped me begin to understand the importance of having a Christian worldview, and I saw my daddy's passion for God's truth and how that relates to our culture."
- "My dad, brother, and I went to breakfast together at least once a week throughout high school. We didn't always have a serious discussion, but it was nice to know we would have that time together to talk or even just to laugh."
- "Even though my dad was not the most spiritual influence growing up, I remember the few times that were instrumental. When I was in about second grade, we owned a country store out in the middle of nowhere. In order to have the Sunday morning paper on hand for customers, my dad had to leave about half past four in the morning to pick them up. He asked each of us children at different times to go along with him, and then he would take us out to breakfast."
- "My dad would always talk to me man-to-man anytime we rode together, even when it was only six minutes to get home."

Next, go to your child and admit that you blew it. Be specific about what you did wrong. This may well be one of the hardest things you've ever done, and you may come up with a hundred reasons why you don't think it's really necessary. Do it anyway. It *is* necessary.

One of the main reasons we resist admitting our shortcomings is that we think doing so would make the other person respect us less and so move further away emotionally and relationally. What usually happens, though, is just the opposite. As relationship experts Gary Smalley and John Trent point out, "When we own up to our limitations and frailties—our humanity—we find that people [including our teen children] actually draw closer to us. . . . For some strange reason, most folks seem to identify with someone who doesn't know it all and can't do it all!"[1]

Because that's true, admitting our failures can open lines of communication and understanding that might otherwise remain closed indefinitely.

After acknowledging the ways in which you've fallen short, ask for your teen's forgiveness. Let him know that you're sincerely sorry for your mistakes and for whatever hurts you've caused him and that receiving his forgiveness is important to you. Yes, this means making yourself vulnerable and, in a sense, putting yourself at his mercy. It can be a scary and insecure place to be. But when your child extends forgiveness, you will enjoy an unmatched feeling of freedom and release from guilt. And you will also be free to start rebuilding the relationship.

Don't be surprised, however, if your teen is unwilling or unable to forgive you right away. If the hurts caused by your past failings are deep, forgiving you may take time and hard emotional and spiritual work. Be patient, be encouraging, and continue to show your teen, day by day, that you're serious about overcoming past mistakes and becoming a better, more godly parent.

Above all, continue to pray. If you have honestly asked for forgiveness, you can trust that God's Holy Spirit is working in your teen's heart and mind to heal hurts and open the door to reconciliation. Pray that your child will respond to the Spirit's prompting. As teen specialists Stephen Arterburn and Jim Burns write, "No matter how many mistakes we parents make, there is still hope that a . . . child will respond to the power of the Holy Spirit. . . . [W]e encourage you to never lose hope, never give up, never stop praying."[2]

If you've blown it with your teen in the past because of some repetitive behavior, it will also help greatly to make yourself accountable to your child for overcoming that failing. Doing so will show your teen how serious you are about changing, and it will help you to conquer the habit as well.

Suppose, for instance, that you tend to get so caught up in your own duties and interests that the end of a typical day arrives and you haven't made the time to have a promised period of devotions with your teen. Give her your permission (and blessing!) to come to you during the evening and ask, "When are we going to get together for devotions tonight? I'll be done with my homework in half an hour."

One dad realized he had developed the habit of letting loose a profane expletive whenever he got upset. Wanting to break the habit, and also concerned about the impact his example was having on his children, the father told them one day, "From now on, every time one of you catches me swearing, I'll give you a dollar."

Needless to say, the kids thought this was a great idea! From that point forward, they paid even closer attention than usual to what their dad said, especially when he seemed to be getting riled. But they also knew that Dad was serious about changing. And sure enough, after having to open his wallet in embarrassment a handful of times, this father quickly learned to say a short prayer for help and get his tongue under control before he uttered something that he would regret and that would leave him the poorer for the experience.

Sadly, in some cases where a parent has blown it badly in the past, the hurt is so deep and the relationship is so damaged that no amount of effort and patient persistence seems capable of restoring it. What's a parent to do then? The best answer may be to seek help from a qualified Christian counselor. Such a person can assist a parent, from an objective and biblical perspective, in dealing with guilt issues, changing behaviors, and rebuilding relationships. If you've tried the other ideas in this section for a while and things are still not going well, don't be afraid to get this kind of help.

## Own Parents Didn't Mentor Well

Your own parents might not have been Christians. Or maybe they were, but for some reason they didn't make your spiritual training a personal priority. Either way, if your own parents weren't good spiritual mentors to you, it's understandable that you might feel insecure about trying to mentor your teenager. After all, unless someone else stepped in to fill the void, you don't have firsthand experience with the process, and you probably haven't even seen it modeled.

Your parents' shortcoming in this area, however, doesn't mean you can't succeed with your own child. You are *not* doomed to repeat their mistakes.

To mentor your teen well in spite of a less-than-perfect background, you first need to understand that God has called you to fulfill that role and to accept the responsibility. The fact that you're reading this book indicates that you're already serious about this aspect of parenting.

Next, you need wisdom and insight into the principles of mentoring a teen. Keep working through this book and you'll be well on your way, because that's what it's all about!

Then you'll need practical, tested tips for making effective mentoring a part of your family's daily life. Again, the book you now hold in your hands is a great starting point for just that kind of help.

Would you be better off if the priority and the methods of spiritual mentoring were already ingrained in your mind through having received them from your own mom and dad? Would that have given you a big head start in doing it well yourself? Of course. But if you want to learn how to mentor your teen in spite of your background, you can and you will.

What if your personal experience with spiritual mentoring was not just poor but actually painful? In such a case, do you need to get healthy emotionally before you can begin to properly mentor your own teen? In a word, no. We all carry some hurts from the past, but we can and do choose to move ahead in spite of them. Complete healing comes only when you get to heaven. And a lot of healing can be gained here and now when you love and serve others, starting with your children.

If the thought of trying to mentor your teenager brings up painful memories or unresolved issues, by all means seek help. Just talking things out with your spouse or a trustworthy friend can bring tremendous relief. A good Christian counselor can also be of great assistance. But whatever help you may need, resolve that your past will not keep you from being an effective mentor to your own child.

## Already Done All I Can

Some Christian parents feel that, having raised their children in church and in programs like AWANA or Christian Service Brigade, they've already finished their training job by the time the kids reach adolescence. Other parents feel that their church's youth pastor and ministries like Young Life and Fellowship of Christian Athletes understand teens better than they do, so they're content to leave the further training of their teens to such "experts." And some parents, when they consider the powerful influence of peers and the culture on their teens, throw up their hands in despair of having much ongoing impact on their children's spiritual lives.

> **Now is not the time to coast.**

If you find yourself tempted to think along those or similar lines, concluding that your role in the spiritual training of your teenager is already over, let us hasten to say that nothing could be further from the truth. *Now is not the time to coast.*

Christian camp director Joe White tells of the undersized and undertalented college football team on which he played. Despite their shortcomings, they were a group of hardworking over-achievers, and at the end of the season they found themselves in a bowl game facing the mighty Oklahoma Sooners. Joe's SMU Mustangs were heavy pregame underdogs, but based on their conditioning and their determination, they had a conviction and confidence that the fourth quarter of every game belonged to them. At the start of that final quarter, all the players and coaches would raise a hand high into the air with four fingers extended, signifying their resolve to do whatever was necessary in those last 15 minutes of play time to gain or to seal a victory.

And sure enough, though Joe's SMU team was trailing the fast and powerful Sooners as the fourth quarter of that bowl game began, the Mustangs felt a giant surge of energy come off the bench and out onto the field. With their "never give up" confidence and tenacity, they shot past Oklahoma and went on to claim one of the great upset victories in bowl history.

Joe goes on to point out that parenting in general and the spiritual training of a child in particular are like playing a football game. The first three quarters are the child's preadolescent years. You work hard, following a carefully devised game plan, scoring some touchdowns along the way as your child comes to faith in Christ, learns biblical truths, begins to consider what it means to think and live as a believer, and so on. You try to hold back the opponent, which is any bad experience or un-Christian set of values that might hurt or mislead your beloved child. By the time the third quarter draws to a close, you hope that you (and your child) are so far ahead in the score that there's no way you can lose the game now.

But you still have to play the fourth quarter—your child's teen years. And no matter how well you've done up to this point, this is the period when the game is either won or lost. Your child will either hold tight to the "ball" of faith as the opponent tries to tear it loose with various temptations, or he will fumble it away with one compromise after another.

The teenage years are the time when, if you press on in mentoring your child, adjusting your strategies as needed but never letting up while the game clock is still running, you can enjoy the sweet smell of victory. You can see the fruits of your labors displayed in your scrapbook, in family videos, and in joyful memories that will last a lifetime.

But your child's teen years can also be the time when, if you become lethargic and start to coast, thinking the game is already won, your nose can wrinkle up with the sour smell of defeat. Lethargy in your God-given role can lead to devastating tragedy as worldly influences take sway over your child's thoughts and feelings and decision-making processes.

Remember that the fourth quarter is the time when the opponent is also more determined than ever. Peers are speaking the loudest. Hollywood is offering its most appealing and misleading enticements. Our "anything goes" culture is pressing home its most convincing arguments.

The final quarter of your parenting career can be your finest hour—or it can be the time when you see everything you have worked for come undone. Resolve to keep working for and with your teen all the way to the last tick of that game clock.

## Not a Good Example

Maybe you're concerned that you are not setting an example of the kind of Christian life you'd like your teen to lead. That's a valid concern, for at least two reasons.

First, you can't give your child what you don't have yourself; you can't expect him to grow above your own level of spiritual maturity. If the quality of a person's spiritual life could be measured on a scale from 1 to 10, and you're at 3, you can't expect your teenager to develop a 4 or higher quality of life under your influence. It just won't happen.

It's the same principle behind the safety instructions given by the flight attendant on a commercial airliner at the beginning of every flight. Should the cabin lose pressure while you're traveling with a young child, you're told, you must first put on your own oxygen mask and make sure it's functioning properly. Only then should you help your child to put on her mask. Why? Because if you try to help her first—if you try to give her oxygen before you're getting any yourself—you may pass out from oxygen deprivation before your child is safe. Then you're both in trouble.

> For good or bad, children imitate what they see their parents doing.

Helping your child grow spiritually is a similar experience, and this is never more true than in the child's teen years. You can't help your teen "breathe" spiritually unless you've got adequate "oxygen" for your own needs. That is, you can't teach him truths about God that you haven't learned yourself.

VISION

A second valid reason to be concerned about your example is that what you *do* is far more important than what you *say*. For good or bad, children imitate what they see their parents doing. Joe White offers clear examples of both sides of this coin.

On the negative side, he wrote, "As I counsel America's hurting teenagers, I so often find that their bad habits and major failures were learned from the example of their mom and dad. . . . *Sixteen-year-old, brown-eyed Mary had an abortion*. Her mom has a boyfriend. *Eighteen-year-old Andy went to jail with two DWIs*. His daddy caps every evening with martinis. *Martin has a hard time telling the truth*. His dad evades the IRS with falsified financial reports."[3]

On the positive side, Joe tells of two nephews who learned in an unforgettable way what it means for a husband to fulfill the biblical mandate in Ephesians 5 to love your wife self-sacrificially, as Christ loved the church and gave Himself for her. They learned this lesson not so much from the words of their father—Joe's brother Bob—but more significantly from his actions. Here's the story:

> *"Parents could have the best relationship with their teen, but if they do not 'practice what they preach,' kids will not take their words seriously. For me, making the right decisions seemed logical because my parents demonstrated that it worked for them."*
> *—a 20-year-old college student*

My big brother Bob has always been my hero. He married his first and only love, Mary Evelyn, after college. He's loved her and she's loved him for well over 30 years. But we as a family knew that at about age 51—in the glory of their marriage, just as their children were getting ready to leave college and go into their own careers—Mary Evelyn's life would probably end because her mom's life had ended there due to a congenital condition called polycystic kidney disorder.

Right on schedule, at age 51, Mary Evelyn's kidneys quit. They didn't quit slowly; they quit instantly. The poisoning in her blood accelerated beyond the charts of danger. Dialysis wasn't going well. No donor kidney was available to match her unique blood type and needs. Little Mary Evelyn's body was quickly dying.

Bob pleaded with the doctors to test him and his

kidneys. The doctors rebuffed him, saying, "The husband's kidney never matches the wife's. It's impossible."

"Please test my kidney!" he kept insisting.

Finally, to appease him, they tested him. To their amazement, they found that his kidney *was* a match for Mary Evelyn's. Since her condition was by now critical, they immediately wheeled those two lovebirds into surgery. There they opened my brother's side, cutting that dear man from his belly button to his backbone, taking out three ribs to get at a healthy kidney—as if Adam and Eve were having surgery themselves. After removing the kidney, they slipped it into his little bride's abdomen and connected the tubes and blood vessels.

The next morning, when Mary Evelyn woke up from the operation, her blood was being filtered perfectly by her husband's kidney.

Now, I know my brother Bob, and I know that in this case he had two healthy kidneys and gladly gave his wife one. But I also know that if she had needed his one and only healthy heart, he would have happily given her that as well. That's how much he loves her. And that's the quality of love that their boys saw demonstrated that day and every day. They will never doubt or forget what real love looks like.

As those illustrations show, your example as a parent will be far and away the greatest influence you have on your child's life. Whether you like it or not, your actions carry considerably more weight than your words. That's why your own walk with God needs to back up your words, to be consistent with what you're trying to teach.

So, for instance, if you tell your teen that things like prayer and Bible study and serving others are important, yet she never sees *you* doing any of those things, she will conclude (accurately) that you don't really think they're important. If you did, you would make time for them, just as you're asking her to do. And you'll find that she doesn't make time for them, either.

Teen expert Josh McDowell puts the situation like this: "If you want to pass on biblical values to your children you must model those values in your own life. . . . I can think of nothing that is more detestable to a teenager than a hypocrite. And they believe there are a lot of them. . . . [For example,] only 27 percent of our youth say their parents frequently 'admit when they're wrong or mistaken.' "[4]

If, then, you want to be a successful mentor to a teen who is growing steadily in his relationship with God, developing a mature and meaningful faith of his own, you need to have such a faith yourself, and you need to be living it out in front of your child day by day.

That's our challenge as parents, and it's a big one. It can appear daunting. But there's also good news. First, you don't have to be a perfect Christian (not that there really is such a thing anyway) in order to be a good role model. You don't even have to pretend. In fact, as we saw earlier in this chapter, your child will respect and trust and want to be like you more if you're honest about your shortcomings. He's probably already far more aware of them than you realize, so trying to pretend they don't exist is useless at best and will cause him to brand you a hypocrite at worst. On the other

## Teens' "Things I Wish My Parents Had Done Differently," Part 1

- "My parents have always encouraged me to be real and consistent in my social, academic, and spiritual walks, yet their 'encouragement' came across very forcefully, like it wasn't a choice. Things weren't suggestions but commands. Sometimes Christian parents have too many expectations and not enough understanding."
- "I wish I would have seen them reading their Bibles and praying. Although I believe they do those things, I never saw them doing so, and I think that's important."
- "Study God's Word together at home, not just at church."
- "We should have had a family devotion time on a consistent basis, or at least prayed together each night."
- "Step-by-step help in methods of Bible study and prayer would have better equipped me for life on my own."

hand, if you admit your failings and also show that you're sincerely trying to be a good Christian, committed to knowing, loving, and serving God better, your teenager will cut you some slack. He'll see that your faith is genuine, and he'll be attracted to the same God.

> *Becoming more like Jesus Christ every day can be a shared journey.*

Second, realize that you can grow *with* your child. Becoming more like Jesus Christ every day can be a shared journey. What should be happening is that you're on an exciting adventure of spiritual growth yourself—so exciting that your teen wants to join you on the way. Passion is contagious.

Remember that, now more than ever, adolescence is a time of stimulation, excitement, challenge, and passion. Teens are drawn to those things like moths to a flame. And just as kayakers are drawn to the thrill of a mountain river that offers raging rapids and whitewater, ignoring those streams that are slow-moving and even stagnant in places, so teens are looking for a way of life that offers the excitement and challenge they crave. Ask yourself, then, *Is my life in Christ one into which my teen would want to "put her kayak," or is she going to go looking for thrills with her peer group, on the Internet, in television, in music, or maybe even in drugs?*

But remember, too, that even if your own Christian life has been less than exciting up until now, you can start today to change things for the better with your teen. All you have to do is tilt the riverbed a little and then jump into your kayak side by side with your child.

Joe White tells of a time in his life when he had gotten so busy with work that his spiritual life had become a stagnant pool. His oldest child was 12 at the time, and he came to realize that she might soon start looking for excitement in the wrong places if he didn't have something better to offer. So he decided to tip the riverbed. Here's what happened, in his own words:

> Praise God, I found a mission trip to take that girl on. All of a sudden, that 12-year-old and I were in a foreign country, knocking on hundreds of doors, sharing Christ—way out of my comfort zone. Now the river was

moving—fast. I was more nervous about it than she was. But that's where that girl's faith became dynamic and her heart for world missions was born. She's involved in world missions today and will be until the day she dies.

Whatever it takes, tilt that riverbed in your own life of faith and get the water moving. When you do, your teen will want to get on board with you.

Finally, although the example you set has a powerful impact on your child's spiritual life, you're also supported by other positive influences. Some of these are or can be other people—your spouse, a grandparent, a pastor or youth pastor, a teacher, a coach, and so on. But most importantly, never forget that the One who cares infinitely more than all the rest is the God who loved your child enough to send His Son to be her Savior. By His Word and His Holy Spirit, He works without ceasing, day by day, to draw and guide and nurture your child. And He will never give up shaping her into the image of Jesus Christ (see Romans 8:29).

Knowing that to be true, commit your child to His care every day in prayer. Live out the Christian life to the best of your God-given ability, but also trust that He knows what your teen needs and can make up for your shortcomings in more ways than you could ever imagine. The Bible promises, "He who began a good work in you will carry it on to completion until the day of Christ Jesus" (Philippians 1:6). That is as true for your child as it is for you.

## God Has Made You Adequate

As you face the prospect of serving as a spiritual mentor to your teen, knowing your own weaknesses as well as the strong appeal of worldly enticements to your teen, it's easy to feel inadequate for the task. If you find yourself feeling like that at all, congratulations! You're right where God wants you.

Only those who know they can't do it on their own turn to Him for help. Only those who acknowledge their weakness will see His strength at work in their lives (see 2 Corinthians 12:9). Only those who realize they don't have all the answers will seek the wisdom He offers to give generously (see James 1:5).

If you have committed your life and your child to Jesus Christ, and if you're willing to do your best as a mentor, seeking God daily for guidance and strength, you *are* adequate for the job. He makes you so. He's committed to your family and to your success. Keep reading, keep working, and keep trusting Him for the results.

CHAPTER 3

# Never Quit on a Child

Is there a surefire recipe for raising well-adjusted, responsible, and conscientious teenagers? Probably not. But as Joe White discovered, there *is* an essential ingredient that no successful parent can do without:

> My father, now in his eighties, has always been a man of simple faith, sure convictions, and straightforward speech. He's also one of the wisest people I know. When I visited him one time, I asked, "Dad, what would you say is the key to successful parenting?"
>
> He squinted his green eyes and wrinkled his brow, then said, "Relentlessness."
>
> I waited a moment to see if he might elaborate, but he just stared at me as if his one-word answer needed no further explanation.
>
> Finally, I pressed for more. "So, what exactly does that mean to you?"
>
> He ran a rough hand over his whiskers and pushed back the cap he was wearing. "Relentlessness," he said, "you know, tenacity, stubbornness, perseverance, persistence. It means when your 16-year-old smashes up your brand-new pickup, you hug him and tell him you did the

same thing when you were his age. It means when your daughter tells you she hates you, you tell her, 'I'll always love you.' It means that when your son makes some boneheaded decision, you stand by him and support him through all the consequences. Basically, relentlessness means that you never, ever give up on your kid."

As a father who had guided two children through the teen years at that time—with another two in the midst of them—I knew exactly what Dad meant and I knew how right he was. So many times I've wanted to just let my kids "do their own thing" because my parenting strategies weren't working. But I didn't. I acknowledged where I had failed and redoubled my efforts to improve.

So many times I've wanted to say "See, I told you so!" when one of my teens ignored my advice and ended up in a mess. But I didn't. I held my tongue and simply listened without judgment as my son or daughter poured out his or her heart to me.

So many times I've wanted to give up because I was tired or frustrated or disappointed. But I didn't. I prayed for strength, reached deep within myself, and summoned the determination to do the best I could for my teenagers.

There may be a lot of things that go into effective, successful parenting, but right at the top of the list is the word *relentlessness*.

Since you have survived parenthood long enough to see your child reach the teen years, you probably know a thing or two about relentlessness. You needed that quality to make it through many sleepless nights when your child was an infant. You needed that quality when your son or daughter was young and said, "No, I don't want to!" a couple of dozen times a day. You needed that quality when your child got suspended from school or kicked off the team or caught shoplifting. And you

> *Now that you have a teenager living in your household, it's likely that your ability to be relentless will be tested like never before.*

may have needed that quality when your child was a middle schooler—when you were sure some alien had invaded his body and turned him into a creature with bizarre behaviors, habits, and mannerisms.

But now—now that you have a teenager living in your household—it's likely that your ability to be relentless will be called upon and tested like never before. Indeed, the apostle Paul could have been writing to parents of teenagers when he said, "Love is patient, love is kind. . . . It always protects, always trusts, always hopes, always perseveres" (1 Corinthians 13:4, 7). Clearly, Paul understood that love may sometimes involve warm, tender feelings, but it is more often a matter of choice and will—dogged determination, believing the best, never giving up, always persevering.

## Holding On for Dear Life

Jim and Gina Michaels learned the hard way what it means to love relentlessly. When their daughter, Amanda, turned 17, it was as if someone flipped a switch to turn her from a sweet, good-natured, all-American girl next door into an angry, troubled teen. Almost overnight, she became sullen, brooding, and withdrawn. Everything about her body language screamed, "Stay away from me—I'm mad at the world!"

What's worse, it wasn't only Amanda's attitude that soured; her actions and behavior became erratic and destructive. It seemed as though every other comment out of her mouth was a put-down, criticism, or attack. On several occasions her parents caught her sneaking out of the house late at night. She repeatedly skipped school, and she started spending time with a rough-looking crowd. More than a few times Jim and Gina smelled alcohol on Amanda's breath, although she always vehemently denied drinking.

Jim and Gina, both in their midforties at the time, were stunned by the abrupt turnabout in their daughter's attitude and behavior.

"We'd always had a close, fun relationship with Amanda," Jim recalled. "For the first 16 years of her life, parenting was a breeze. Gina and I often gloated to each other that we must have

**VISION**

done something right to be blessed with such an easygoing, compliant child."

"But our gloating turned to guilt, fear, and confusion," Gina continued. "We asked each other many times, 'What did we do wrong? What could we have done differently?' And we said even more often, 'I can't believe our wonderful little girl has turned into this angry adolescent who can't stand us.' "

One night, as Gina was putting away laundry in Amanda's dresser, she found a bag of marijuana. Though she was disturbed and disappointed, Gina was not entirely surprised. That was, after all, just the latest in a series of unwise choices Amanda had made. When confronted by her parents, Amanda insisted that the bag of pot was a friend's and that she'd never even tried the stuff. When Jim asked if she were being completely honest, Amanda screamed, "I knew you wouldn't believe me! You've never trusted me! How can I tell you anything when you don't believe me?"

As Amanda grew more and more defiant and deceitful, her mom and dad became increasingly concerned about where her choices might lead.

"Like most parents in a situation like that," Gina said, "we were heartbroken, confused, and worried—worried that our daughter would make a mistake with lifelong consequences, such as getting pregnant or seriously injuring herself while driving drunk."

With each passing day, Jim and Gina felt their daughter becoming more distant and withdrawn. Seeking some solutions, they met with their pastor and Amanda's youth pastor. Together, they devised a plan, including setting limits on Amanda's contact with friends who might be a negative influence and steering her toward positive experiences, such as church events and family outings. But underlying everything else was Jim and Gina's decision to be relentless in pursuit of their daughter.

"The number-one thing we decided was to persevere—to not surrender to our sense of hopeless-

*"Let us not become weary in doing good, for at the proper time we will reap a harvest if we do not give up."*
—*Galatians 6:9*

*"Let us run with perseverance the race marked out for us."*
—*Hebrews 12:1*

*"My dear brothers, stand firm. Let nothing move you. Always give yourselves fully to the work of the Lord, because you know that your labor in the Lord is not in vain."*
—*1 Corinthians 15:58*

VISION

ness, to tell and show Amanda how much we cared, to do whatever it took to bring her around," Gina recalled. "We resolved to communicate in every way possible that we wouldn't abandon her or give up on her. She could try as hard as she wanted to push us away, but we would remain involved in her life no matter what."

Jim and Gina also committed to praying together each morning and evening, as well as several times individually throughout the day, for Amanda. "We saw this primarily as a spiritual issue,

■ ■ ■

## *"I Will Always Love You!"*

Author and family counselor John Trent tells of the time when he came to understand his mother's relentless love:

> Late one night my mother and brothers and I were all sitting around the dining room table. Not because we were pretending to eat dinner at midnight in New York, but because the police had just brought us home for being out beyond curfew and for being rowdy.
>
> I remember sitting shamefaced, looking down at the table. And I remember mumbling, "I guess this means you won't love us anymore."
>
> That's when I saw my mother blow up at my words like a whole fireworks factory going up at once.
>
> "I will *always* love you!" she roared.
>
> Her words snapped my head up like a jolt to the chin. With her gray-green eyes riveted on me, she declared, "I will *always* love you . . . but I am tremendously disappointed in you."
>
> Even then, at the Death-Valley low point of my rebellious days, I knew she meant it. I knew that even though she would ground us and be terribly disappointed in us and struggle to sleep that night (and the next) from worry over us, she really would love us *forever*.
>
> And like never before, that thought—that promise—sank in. I was loved *forever*. No matter what kind of trouble I got into. No matter where my roaming feet would take me. No matter how I was transported home. Mom would *always* love me, and she insisted that I know it.[1]

■ ■ ■

## *Not All Teens Are Rebels*

We're bombarded with troubling news about teenagers. News magazines feature cover photos of sneering teens with multicolored hair, tattoos, nose rings, and ragged clothes. We hear statistics about ever-escalating teenage drug and alcohol abuse, out-of-wedlock pregnancy, and suicide rates. We see news footage, played over and over, of the latest school shootings. We glimpse a music video from the latest bubblegum pop singer (who couldn't be more than 13!) as she struts seductively and croons about the joys of sex.

Is it any wonder that most parents face the approach of their children's teen years with concern, wariness, alarm, or outright panic?

Okay, take a deep breath. It may not be as bad as you fear. The fact is, not all teenagers are rebels, rogues, and rabble-rousers. Not all teenagers experiment with drugs, guzzle booze, hate their parents, defy authority, and behave violently.

Although it's true that our culture presents many temptations and exerts tremendous pressure on teens, the majority of them are good kids who try hard to live according to the values they've been taught. When we hear statistics about the 20 percent of teenagers who are doing something illegal or immoral, we tend to forget about the other 80 percent who have resisted the temptation.

Researcher George Barna gives us more reason to be hopeful. In recent surveys of 13- to 18-year-olds, he found the following statistics to be true:

■ Seventy percent of teens have daily conversations with their mothers about an important issue in their life, and 53 percent have a similar type of conversation with their fathers.
■ The vast majority describe themselves as "happy" (92 percent), "responsible" (91 percent), "optimistic about my future" (82 percent), and "trusting of other people" (80 percent).
■ Seventy-seven percent say it's important to have a clear purpose for living, and 71 percent say it's important to live with a high degree of integrity.
■ Almost two-thirds (64 percent) describe themselves as "religious"; 56

VISION

percent feel that their religious faith is very important in their life; and 43 percent talk to family or friends about religious matters in a typical day.

- Over half of teens (56 percent) attend church on a given Sunday.
- The same percent of teens—56 percent—say they want to influence other people's lives and make a difference in the world.[2]

---

Will your teenager make dumb mistakes? Of course. Will he use poor judgment on occasion? Sure. Will she say hurtful things to you? Count on it. But will your child become rebellious? Not necessarily. Believe that your teenager will be one of the good ones—and he might just prove you right.

---

and we weren't about to let Satan win a battle for our daughter," Jim said.

Amanda tested her parents' resolve over the next several months. She refused to give more than yes and no responses to most of their questions. She did only the minimum schoolwork to avoid flunking out. And twice she "borrowed" the family car without permission to take friends cruising.

As the months passed and Jim and Gina remained steadfast, however, they noticed that Amanda began to soften. Progress was slow, but her attitude gradually became more positive, and she showed fewer and fewer signs of rebelliousness. She reconnected with a couple of friends from her church youth group, she conversed more freely with her parents around the dinner table, and she showed renewed interest in her schoolwork.

"It was like she slowly walked out of a dark tunnel and into the light," Gina said. "It was still a matter of three steps forward, two steps back. But after many painful months, we were thrilled by any progress at all."

The turning point for Jim came one Saturday afternoon when his daughter spontaneously threw her arm around his shoulder and said, "Pops, let's you and me shoot some hoops in the driveway." Jim admits he almost broke down crying when she said that. "Pops" had been Amanda's affectionate nickname for him since she was in grade school, and they had passed many hours together chatting about life while shooting baskets. It seemed to

Jim that his daughter was announcing that the "old Amanda" was making a comeback.

Still, healing took time. Amanda and her parents saw a family counselor for several months to sort out what had happened and to rebuild their relationships. All three of them had raw feelings that needed to be expressed and wounds that needed to be assuaged. Toward the end of their therapy sessions, it was Amanda who pinpointed what had turned her around after nearly a year of rebellion.

"Part of what I went through was trying to figure out who I was, and another part was testing Mom and Dad to see if they'd still love me and accept me if I wasn't the sweet little goody-goody I'd always been," she said. "The thing that won me over was seeing my parents not give up on me. I pretended not to care when they said, 'We'll always be here for you,' but deep down, those words sank in. And they proved it through their actions, too. I also thought, *If they still love me after the terrible things I've done, maybe there's something to this Christianity stuff they've been talking about all these years.*"

Score another victory for relentless parenting.

## This Is No Time to Coast

Fortunately, most parents won't have to go through the heart-wrenching experiences that Jim and Gina endured. After all, not all teenagers make destructive choices and act defiantly (see sidebar "Not All Teens Are Rebels"). But that doesn't mean relentlessness isn't needed with adolescents who are relatively trouble-free or with those who exhibit only normal mood swings and engage in only normal limit testing. In other words, it isn't only extreme situations that call for persistent parenting.

> **It isn't only extreme situations that call for persistent parenting.**

As we said in the last chapter, some parents are tempted to coast when their kids hit the teen years. They see the finish line—when their son or daughter will leave home—and decide, either consciously or subconsciously, to slack off a bit. Especially if their teenager is performing well in school and staying out of trouble, these moms and dads assume their child doesn't need much parental guidance or attention.

Listen to the lament of two parents who traded persistence for passivity:

*Steven, age 52:*
When our son, David, turned 16, he started driving and spending more and more time with his friends and away from home. At that point, my wife and I just—I don't know—*backed off.* No, we didn't just back off, we *checked out.* It seemed like David didn't need us anymore, so we gave him space. After all, he had always been a great kid—a straight-A student, an excellent athlete, very responsible. Now we realize we gave him too much space. We didn't ask where he was going or what he was doing. We didn't try to be involved in his world. . . .

In essence, we relinquished our influence to his peers. Thankfully, David never got in any serious trouble—he never got arrested or did drugs, at least not that we're aware of. But in his junior year of high school, his grades started slipping and he got in a few fights at school. He quit the basketball team when he didn't think he was getting enough playing time. And he all but dropped out of the church youth group, where he'd once been on the leadership team. We just chalked all this up as a "teenage thing," a phase or a stage that every kid goes through. But David never really came out of his funk. As a senior, he didn't participate in sports or any other extracurricular activities, and he graduated with a C average.

My wife and I wondered how a kid who had entered high school with so much potential could settle for just getting by. Now I'm pretty sure our lack of involvement, encouragement, and prodding had a lot to do with it. I really regret that.

*Lydia, age 44:*
As a single parent, I was relieved when my daughter, Ashley, hit the teen years and started being more independent.

I'd raised her by myself for 10 years—10 exhausting, drain-ing years. I was pooped out! So when she wanted to hole up in her room or hang out at the mall with her friends for hours on end, I was happy to let her. It gave me much-needed time for myself. I started pursuing my college degree, which I'd abandoned years before, and I thought maybe I could start dating again.

Ashley didn't get in any trouble—she'd always had a good head on her shoulders—but I lost touch with her. The closeness we'd shared for so many years slowly dis-appeared. I realize it's natural for kids to separate from their parents and learn to stand on their own two feet, but we became so distant from each other. Not angry or hostile, just sort of cool and detached.

In a few months, Ashley will be heading off to col-lege, and I feel like I hardly know her anymore. After that, she'll probably never be under my roof again. Now I think I missed some opportunities to deepen our rela-tionship and prepare her for adulthood.

As Lydia learned, the teen years pass all too quickly. Before you know it, your son or daughter will be out of the house, per-haps forever. This season in your child's life provides wonderful opportunities to begin developing an adult-level friendship. In a sense, the patterns you establish now will deter-mine the type of relationship you'll share in the years ahead.

*"When you're at the end of your rope, tie a knot and hang on."*
*—Franklin D. Roosevelt*

All moms and dads would do well to remem-ber the metaphor used by Dr. James Dobson, who likens the parenting process to letting out rope. He wrote, "Teaching your child to deal responsibly with indepen-dence and freedom is like lowering him out of a five-story window with a rope. You do it little by little, slowly, deliberately, hand over hand. If you let the rope out all at once, he may plunge to the ground in a disastrous tumble."[3]

Unfortunately, this is precisely what happens with some par-ents of teenagers—the moms and dads loosen their grip too soon or let go of the rope completely. Parents who are relentless, on the other hand, know that the teenage years are no time to coast, slack off, or check out. They must remain involved in, engaged with, and responsive to their teen's life.

## The Seven Habits of Highly Relentless Parents

We've talked about the principle of relentless parenting, but how can you apply this concept day in and day out with your teen? Let's look at seven practical ways you can demonstrate relentlessness:

### 1. Pray, Pray, Pray

This habit is placed first on the list because that's exactly where it belongs. The number-one strategy for guiding your child through the teen years is to surround him with prayer. Simply put, relentless parents are those who pray relentlessly.

Moms and dads of teenagers should heed Paul's admonition to "pray without ceasing" (1 Thessalonians 5:17, NASB). This means consistently, throughout the day, asking God to protect, guide, and direct your teen. And don't forget to include yourself in those prayers. Ask the Lord to give you strength, wisdom, and courage as you parent your adolescent.

### 2. Choose to Be Active and Involved

Clinical researcher Dr. Nick Stinnett has conducted extensive studies on what makes strong families. After interviewing thousands of successful families, Stinnett and his colleagues identified six traits of close parent-child relationships. One characteristic is regular participation and involvement with each other. Stinnett says: "Members of strong families are dedicated to promoting each other's welfare and happiness. They express their commitment to one another—not just in words, but through choosing to invest time and energy. Their commitment to each other is active and obvious."[4]

Those last two concepts are key to any discussion about relentless parenting. Your love and commitment should be *active* and *obvious*. Be involved in your teen's life whenever and however you can. Ask questions about her day. Play racquetball with him on the weekends. Go out to breakfast together. Consistently attend games, school plays, choir concerts, piano recitals, and speech competitions in which your teen participates. Be there for all the important events—and even the seemingly unimportant ones.

Naturally, choosing to be involved in your child's life means taking a keen interest in his spiritual life. Provide every opportunity—whether at home, through church, or elsewhere—for your teenager's faith to grow and flourish (part three of this book is full of practical ideas for how to do this). More importantly, present a model of spiritual maturity and passion by living out Christlike love, humility, and servanthood.

### 3. Don't Take No for an Answer Too Easily

Of course, you should respect your teen's boundaries, but some teenagers say "I don't want to talk about it" or "It's no big deal" because they're not sure their parents are really interested. Be persistent without being pushy. Assure your teen that you are genuinely interested in, and concerned about, her life and that you're always available to listen. (It goes without saying that you should, in fact, be accessible and listen attentively when your teen is ready to talk.)

### 4. Emulate Our Heavenly Father's Steadfast Love

God's love for each of His children is unchanging, enduring, and unwavering, regardless of how badly we blow it. Throughout the Old Testament, God declared and demonstrated His unyielding love for the Jews, His chosen people, even when they were rebellious and contemptuous toward Him.

- "Though the mountains be shaken and the hills be removed, yet my unfailing love for you will not be shaken" (Isaiah 54:10).
- "I have loved you with an everlasting love; I have drawn you with loving-kindness" (Jeremiah 31:3).

This same theme is repeated dozens of times in the New Testament as well.

- "Surely I am with you always, to the very end of the age" (Matthew 28:20).

- "I am convinced that neither death nor life, neither angels nor demons, neither the present nor the future, nor any powers, neither height nor depth, nor anything else in all creation, will be able to separate us from the love of God that is in Christ Jesus our Lord" (Romans 8:38-39).
- "Never will I leave you; never will I forsake you" (Hebrews 13:5).

Let this kind of faithfulness be your model as you express and demonstrate love for your teen. Say to your child often, "There's nothing you could do that would make me stop loving you."

### 5. Renew Your Mercies Every Day

Christians are fond of quoting the verse "Through the LORD's mercies we are not consumed. . . . They are new every morning" (Lamentations 3:22-23, NKJV). The promise here, of course, is that God's mercy toward us is ongoing, continual, daily. As we savor the reassurance offered by this verse, let us also extend this same sort of mercy to our teenage sons and daughters. Every morning should bring a clean slate, a chance to start anew. If last night's argument was talked out and resolved, leave it behind. If your daughter apologized for the lie she told last week, believe that she's going to tell the truth today and tomorrow.

### 6. Nurture Yourself as You Nurture Your Teen

The famous Green Bay Packers coach Vince Lombardi said, "Fatigue makes cowards of us all." We might amend his adage slightly to say, "Fatigue makes quitters of us all." The point is, parents who are chronically depleted and drained of energy can offer little to their teenager. Therefore, it's vital that you guard your spiritual, emotional, and physical health. Do whatever you must to recharge your batteries: Get plenty of rest, set aside time for fun, exercise regularly, pray, and meditate on God's Word.

One of the best ways to nurture yourself is by developing a network of supportive friends—ideally, other parents of teens—with whom you can share concerns, learn from one another's experiences, and pray for one another. If you aren't already part of a group like this or can't find an existing one to join, take the initiative and start one in your church or community.

### 7. Resolve to Never, Ever Give Up

Go the distance, never surrender, stick it out, finish the race, hang in there, be steadfast to the end—whatever terminology you prefer, decide now that you'll always, always be there for your teenager. No matter how angry, stressed out, frustrated, disappointed, or exhausted you are, resolve to be the best mom or dad you can be. Whether you are preparing for your child's teen years or are presently in the midst of them, make a commitment—an act of your will—to never give up on your son or daughter.

## Stages of Adolescence: What's Normal?

Some parents become needlessly alarmed by their teen's behavior simply because things are changing so rapidly. New and perhaps peculiar attitudes, perspectives, and activities crop up seemingly overnight, and parents are left to ask, "What's going on with this kid?" Moms and dads may mistake changes for signs of danger.

Psychologists Ken and Elizabeth Mellor provide help by identifying six typical stages adolescents move through and what parents can expect (use for comparison only—your teen's development may vary):

*The baby (13 years old).* Bodies are changing rapidly and hormones are stirring. Teens at this stage become focused on body image, appearance, and comparisons with peers. They're open, naive, vulnerable. This is called the "baby" stage because, when in it, teens often regain qualities of a baby—they are dependent, needy, and easily upset, their moods shift almost instantly, and their attention span becomes limited.

*The dissenter (14).* Kids in this stage are willful, argumentative, uncooperative, passionate, self-centered, and inclined to tantrums. Their moods go to extremes. The moment they've got what they want, they struggle over something else. Their bodies continue to change and develop. Some young teens are relatively mild in this phase, while others are quite difficult.

*The fledgling (15).* Typical qualities in this stage include calmness, availability, desire to help and cooperate, sensitivity to others, a high level of interest in the world and how it works. Fledglings move away from the earlier level of struggle and willfulness (sometimes quickly, sometimes gradually). These teens show intelligence and cognitive development, and they enjoy conversation and learning.

## "We're Going to Finish This Race Together"

British runner Derek Redmond had trained every day for four years to give himself a shot at Olympic glory. After an injury-plagued career that included five surgeries and a forced withdrawal from the 1988 summer Olympics two minutes before his first race, Redmond appeared encouraged about his chances at the 1992 Barcelona Games.

Putting earlier disappointments behind him, the 26-year-old believed he could bring home a medal. "We're going to come back with something," he told his coach.

In the semifinal round of the 400 meters, Redmond ran fluidly

---

*The sweet and sour (16).* Here, previously accepted values and thoughts are challenged and new approaches are tried. Outrage is common: "How dare you interfere with my life! I am the boss of me!" The I-know-everything attitude is acute. Sexuality is becoming a stronger and clearer issue. These teens are often sweet to people outside the family while sour toward parents and siblings. This is a time when you might be told by other parents that your teen is delightful to be around—and you wonder if you're talking about the same person.

*The romantic/novice (17).* Teens pass through a threshold into maturity at this age. They're full of good intent and want to be recognized as adults but are not quite able to *be* adults. They do much practicing in how to be grown up. Life takes on a romantic aura for them. They become more sociable, more inclined to connect with people. There's an increased awareness of others as individuals rather than as extensions of themselves. Boyfriends or girlfriends often make their appearance at this stage.

*The world leader (18 to 21).* These young people are concerned about the world and social issues—and are certain they know the answers and solutions. This is a time of taking on causes, exploring their world, and achieving the independence they have long desired. It is definitely a phase of increasing autonomy and responsibility taking. Here, the young person forms his or her identity, whether it be as a rebel, a revolutionary, a conformist, a crusader, a good citizen, a philosopher, an intellectual, or any of a hundred other possibilities.

(For more detailed information about the adolescent stages identified by Ken and Elizabeth Mellor, visit www.biamenetwork.net.)

**VISION**

for 250 meters. Then suddenly, shockingly, he felt his right hamstring tear. Falling to the track in excruciating pain, he watched the other runners sprint past him and into the distance. In one heartbreaking instant, his bright hopes of medaling vanished.

But Derek Redmond had no quit in him. Determined that years of hard work and sacrifice were not going to be for nothing, he resolved to limp to the finish line—crawl, if necessary. As the crowd roared its approval, he dragged himself to his feet and continued down the track, step by agonizing step.

From his seat in the stands, Derek's father, Jim, had witnessed the scene in horror. Now leaping to his feet, he rushed down the steps at Olympic Stadium, past security guards, and onto the track.

A heavyset man wearing a T-shirt and khaki pants, Jim Redmond put a supportive arm around his son's shoulder and said, "You don't have to do this. You don't have to put yourself through this."

"I've got to finish," Derek said.

"Okay," Jim said. "We started your career together, so we're going to finish this race together."

With arms around each other, Jim and Derek Redmond trudged down the track. Entering the final stretch, Derek sagged into his father and began sobbing.

At last they crossed the finish line as the crowd of 65,000 rose to their feet and cheered wildly. Millions of television viewers around the world also watched as father and son completed the race together. Derek Redmond—with the help of his dad—had become an Olympic hero even though he never won a medal.[5]

What a picture of relentless parenting! Whether your teenager is gliding fluidly toward adulthood or stumbling badly, keep on cheering, encouraging, and applauding. Keep on offering your support and assistance. Keep on believing the best. Keep on telling your son or daughter, "We're going to finish this race together!"

CHAPTER 4

# The Goal of Spiritual Training

Your high school senior is about to graduate. Can you imagine the scene? It may be five years or three years or one year in the future—or it may be just a few months away. Whatever the time frame, picture yourself sitting there in the auditorium as your teenager, looking proud and yet awkward in her cap and gown, chats and laughs with friends while you all wait for the ceremony to begin.

The high school band works its shaky way through its repertoire, getting ready for the endless replay of "Pomp and Circumstance" as the graduates walk across the stage to receive their diplomas. Around you, people are chatting and waving, and the parents with video cameras are setting up, preparing to capture every priceless moment.

Watching your child, you experience a flood of memories and emotions, a mixture of happiness and pride. You enjoy reminiscing for a few minutes. And then your thoughts turn to the future, to the hopes and dreams you hold for your child. As a Christian parent, you especially wonder again whether your teen is really prepared to take on a world—at college or in the workplace—that will be hostile to her faith and values.

The corners of your mouth turn down, and worry lines crease your forehead. *Is she ready?* you ask yourself. *Will her faith in God and her relationship with Him be strong enough to stand up to all the challenges that are coming?*

Our fervent desire, like yours, is that you would be able to answer those crucial questions with a confident yes, for instilling that quality of faith in your child is a Christian parent's most important responsibility. But just what does that kind of faith look like? As with any target you hope to hit, you need to know what you're aiming at if you're to have the best chance of achieving success.

In this chapter, therefore, we want to set the goal clearly before you. We want to give you a target that's worth all the prayers and tears and faithful, daily effort it will take for you to hit the bull's-eye. We want to give you a picture of the kind of faith you can help your teen develop between now and graduation day, a faith that will sustain and guide her for a lifetime and earn for you the Lord's "Well done."

Perhaps this picture will encourage you with the reassurance that you're already on the right track with your child. Or maybe it will help you identify areas in which you need to work. Either way, you'll be better prepared for the task ahead.

## A Personal, Vibrant Relationship with Jesus Christ

The kind of faith you desire to see growing in your teenager includes several elements, but first and foremost among them—the one out of which all the others develop—is a personal and vibrant relationship with Jesus Christ. That may seem to be a statement of the obvious, but let's look at just what it means.

Our high school graduates need to leave home with a *personal* relationship with Jesus Christ. That means it's real to them. It's theirs.

If a child has grown up in a Christian home, gone to church and Sunday school and then youth group all his life, taken part in a kids' program like AWANA or Christian Service Brigade, and maybe even attended a Christian school, it's easy to assume that at some point he placed his faith in Christ. Likewise, we want to believe that he loves God and desires to live in accordance with biblical principles. The fact is, however, that there are many such children who have never truly or fully committed their lives to Christ and who feel free to follow biblical principles or not, depending on the situation.

We simply can't take a teen's faith for granted. By probing gently with questions, and by observing the daily choices that make up his lifestyle, we can get an idea of how real belief in Christ is to him. We can gauge whether he truly has personal faith or is just doing what's expected of him.

> We simply can't take a teen's faith for granted.

In the same vein, is his faith vibrant and alive, or is he just mechanically going through the motions?

Sixteen-year-old Nikki had a personal faith in Jesus; she had trusted in Him as her Savior at the age of nine. However, because she and her family attended a church that emphasized things a "good Christian" shouldn't do, she grew up with the view that the Christian life consists mostly of trying to follow those rules. If you do well at obeying those restrictions, at least compared to other people, you're on the right track.

In this view (which is shared by a lot of Christians), God is more a stern judge than a loving heavenly Father. Sure, He loved us enough to provide a Savior, but once we're believers, we had better toe the line or else! That's the way Nikki usually thought of Him, and so she says, "It never occurred to me that God wanted a close relationship with me, that He wanted me to know Him and love Him as a friend and Father. When I read the Bible at all, which wasn't often, it was out of a sense of duty rather than any sense of wanting to do it for myself or of expecting Him to reveal Himself to me."

Anyone looking at Nikki's life and faith superficially would probably have concluded that she was, indeed, a good Christian. But a closer look and a candid conversation would have revealed that she was only going through the motions. She never sought to know and love God better, and she served only out of a sense of obligation.

In contrast, our goal as Christian parents is to send off a high school graduate who, with all her heart, mind, soul, and strength, loves God and desires to know and serve Him better every day of her life out of that overflowing love. *That* is the essence of the Christian life, the kind of relationship He wants with every person who calls Jesus "Lord."

## A Head Filled with Applied Wisdom from Scripture

The second basic element of the faith we aim to instill in our teens is a head filled with applied wisdom from Scripture. After all, the Bible is God's personally given love letter to mankind, the primary means by which He reveals to us His character and His will. The Bible says of itself in 2 Timothy 3:16-17, "All Scripture is God-breathed and is useful for teaching, rebuking, correcting and training in righteousness, so that the man [or woman] of God may be thoroughly equipped for every good work." Thus, if our kids are to grow in their relationship with Him, they need to study it, learn it, and know how to apply its truths to life's challenges and choices.

They also need to realize that when God gives guidelines for human conduct in the Bible, it's not because He is some kind of celestial killjoy, out to make them miserable or deprive them of the fun everyone else is enjoying. Rather, He is like a parent who knows some things His children don't and issues instructions for

■ ■ ■

One of the greatest truths you can share with your child . . . is that inherent within every negative command in the Bible there are two positive principles: 1) it is meant to protect us, and 2) to provide for us.

[For example,] God knows that if sex is going to be meaningful, it must be experienced within a loving commitment of marriage. His laws, restrictions, and commands are actually for our good (Deut. 10:12-13). They establish the boundaries and guidelines that define maximum love, relationships, and sex.

As much as possible, explain to your children this basic truth behind the restrictions God places upon them. Be sure to communicate that both you and God want only what is best for them. Eventually the point will get through; you love them and your loving limits—that come from a loving God—are to protect and provide for them.

—Josh McDowell in
*Raising Them Right*[1]

their well-being. A loving parent says "Eat your vegetables" and "Don't touch the hot stove" for the child's own good. Likewise, God tells us "Honor your father and mother" and says not to commit adultery because He knows this is a better, more peaceful and satisfying way for us to live.

Like the first faith element, this one may seem obvious, but the fact is that many of today's young Christians are woefully ignorant of God's Word and how it relates to them. Recent surveys have shown that even students planning to attend Bible college or seminary lack basic biblical knowledge. As a Christian parent, however, you can make sure this is not true of your teen.

The third section of this guidebook will provide specifics for teaching your teenager scriptural truths in

> *You need a plan, and you need to be working at it every day.*

a mentoring relationship. But for now let us reiterate a couple of themes that are at the heart of this book's message. One is that God has given you, as the parent, the primary responsibility for the spiritual training of your child. You can use the help of resources like Sunday school, church youth group, Young Life, Fellowship of Christian Athletes, and so on, but you can't just put your teen in the hands of such others and assume that the training is taking place. You need to be talking with her, training her, modeling faith for her, and assessing her spiritual condition for yourself.

Second, you need to be intentional and persistent about your child's training in the things of God. You need a plan, and you need to be working at it every day—studying the Bible together, memorizing it, and talking about how it applies in the nitty-gritty of life.

We'll admit this isn't easy; it calls for commitment and determination on your part, bathed in daily prayer. But it's the only way. And God will guide you and strengthen you for the task.

## Skill in Filtering Life through a Christian Worldview

Going hand in glove with a storehouse of applied biblical wisdom is skill in filtering all of life through a Christian worldview. Another way of saying this is that we want our ready-to-graduate teenagers to know how to "think Christianly" and to make a

**VISION**

habit of doing so. As they look at everything in their lives and all that's happening in the world around them—issues about how to work, how to spend their money, how to choose their friends, how to vote, how to assess the strengths and weaknesses of the surrounding culture—they should do so from an authentically scriptural perspective.

The wonderful nature of God's Word is that there are verses that apply directly to just about any event or situation a person might face. And even when there's not a passage that speaks directly to a given circumstance, there is almost certainly a biblical principle that applies. The beauty of that fact is that when our teens know those passages and principles, they can use them in analyzing situations and making the dozens of choices they face every day.

For example, a Christian teen who is offered a marijuana cigarette at a party and is told that "everyone else is doing it" ought to know what 1 Corinthians 6:19-20 says: "Do you not know that your body is a temple of the Holy Spirit, who is in you, whom you have received from God? You are not your own; you were bought at a price. Therefore honor God with your body."

Looking at the situation through that filter, the teen will

■ ■ ■

Teens are caught in a paradox. At the same time as three out of four assert that the Bible provides a clear and totally accurate description of moral truth, a large majority of those same individuals argue that there is no such thing as moral truth. . . .

Why is there this seemingly glaring and obvious discrepancy? . . . Many teenagers use the words 'moral' and 'truth,' but really do not know what they mean. Theirs is a vague understanding of truth and morality—'stuff that has to do with right and wrong.' Thus, when they talk about 'absolute' moral truth, they're not really sure what we're talking about, even when an explanation is provided. This speaks volumes to those of us who have become so comfortable with such language that we use it in our teaching and conversation with teens. Unfortunately, teens probably don't have a clue what we're babbling on about!

—George Barna in *Generation Next*[2]

understand that more is at stake in his decision than just "Will I get caught?" or "Isn't it okay to give it a try this once?" Having this perspective doesn't guarantee that he'll make the right choice, of course, but it will make him more likely to do so and to say a quick prayer asking for God's help to resist the temptation.

The mindset we want to see in our children is summed up in the recently popular WWJD bracelet fad. Christians who wear these bracelets want to be reminded, whenever they face a decision large or small, to pause and consider what Jesus might do in their place. They want, in other words, to make sure they are filtering the events of their lives through a Christian worldview. And whether or not our teens choose to wear such a bracelet, that's the way we want them to be looking at the world as well.

It also bears repeating that we want their willingness and even desire to filter all of life through a biblical perspective to be motivated primarily by their growing and vibrant love relationship with the Lord Jesus Christ.

## An Ability to Articulate and Defend the Bible

Besides being willing and able to live their own lives according to God's Word, our soon-to-be-on-their-own teens need to be willing and able to articulate and defend biblical standards to others. The

### Teens' "Traits of Great Parents," Part 2

- "Loving acceptance; concerned with all areas of the child's life; encouraging presence—encouraging not just with words but also by their time and presence."
- "One who is involved in teens' lives. One who truly cares about whether their children succeed. Cares enough to tell a child he is wrong."
- "Genuine and honest, full of love and truth; insightful in understanding where their teen is at; dedicated and committed."
- "They set rules and make clear to the teen the purpose of those rules. They also need to share the struggles they had as teens. The parents need to be there for support if the teen fails or has questions."
- "Parents who are real with their teens and show them that they are trying their best to walk with Christ also. Good communicators!"

Bible itself speaks to this aspect of faith when it says, "Always be prepared to give an answer to everyone who asks you to give the reason for the hope that you have. But do this with gentleness and respect" (1 Peter 3:15).

In a world where, increasingly, even professing Christians feel free to accept or reject the authority of scriptural teaching over their daily lives, this can be quite a challenge. A 17-year-old named Melissa recently found out just how difficult it can be.

One day Melissa and her mom went to a taping of the highly popular *Oprah* TV talk show in Chicago. They thought it would be fun to see how the show is done from behind the scenes. Before the taping began, the producer came out to the audience and said that Oprah Winfrey is a Christian who upholds the values of the Bible and the Christian lifestyle. The producer went on to explain that Oprah's guest that day would be Ellen DeGeneres, the comedienne and actress who had her own TV show at that time and who would soon be "coming out" on her program as a gay person.

"Does anyone in the audience have a problem with Oprah doing this show and voicing her support for Ellen?" the producer wanted to know.

Melissa, aware that the Bible says God loves everyone but condemns homosexual conduct, felt compelled to speak up. Calling in later to Focus on the Family's *Life on the Edge LIVE!* radio program, she continued the story: "I said that I thought that it would be wrong for Oprah to go on the show and support Ellen in her homosexual lifestyle if she [Oprah] professes to be a Christian and upholds those values and believes in Jesus Christ, and that would just be a double standard, and she couldn't do it."

From the reaction of other audience members, Melissa could tell that (except for her mom's support) she was standing alone. The rest either voiced their backing of Oprah and Ellen or stayed silent.

Shortly thereafter, Oprah came onto the stage and the show began. At one point, after Oprah had made her case for supporting Ellen's lifestyle, Melissa was invited to speak briefly. Then, she said, "Oprah just kind of shot things at me. . . . I didn't have a lot of chance to interject things that I wanted to. . . . What I wanted to say was that . . . God does love everyone, but we all have sin in our lives that needs to be reconciled, and that's why Christ came to save us."

As if standing up for biblical truth in front of Oprah and a hostile audience and the TV cameras weren't tough enough, Melissa also "got a lot of flak for it" when she went back to school. Yet this ordinary Christian teenager, knowing the truth of Scripture and being willing to defend it publicly, was able to do so gently and respectfully.

That's another element of the faith we aim to instill in our children.

## A Desire to Make Christ Known through Life, Work, Service, and Witness

Finally, a teen who has a personal and vibrant relationship with Jesus Christ, who knows the Bible and how to apply its truths to all of life, and who is willing and able to articulate those truths will also want to share the joy and hope of that relationship with others. Sometimes that will be done with words, but most often it will be done through the example of a life lived to the honor of his Lord and Savior.

> **When a teen treats everyone with politeness and respect, people notice.**

When a teen treats everyone—even the new kids at school and those whom others consider "weird"—with politeness and respect, people notice. When a teen works hard, does more than is expected, and volunteers to help others, people notice. And when that teen publicly thanks God for the good things in his life, people listen.

People also take notice when a Christian teen, for biblical reasons, turns down an opportunity that most kids would jump at without a moment's hesitation. Such was the case with a high school student named Charity Allen, who also told her story on the *Life on the Edge LIVE!* radio program.

In most respects, Charity was a typical teen. She and her parents and four siblings lived in a two-bedroom mobile home. And like a lot of kids, she had dreams of becoming a professional actress and Hollywood star. Unlike most teens, however, she got a chance to turn her dream into reality.

During her senior year, Charity came to the attention of NBC-TV executives who were looking for a new teen star for a popular soap opera. Her school principal, who got to break the news to her about the network's interest, told her the role was "the break of a lifetime." Charity was invited to do a cold-reading audition for the casting agent, and when she finished, the agent said, "Charity, how would you feel about moving to New York in two weeks and becoming a Hollywood star?"

It looked as if her dream were coming true!

But Charity, a girl who loves Jesus with all her heart, felt that she had to explain something before she walked out of the agent's office that day. So she looked the woman in the eye and said, "I know that this is a soap opera, and it's very important for me to be real honest with you about who I am. I'm a Christian. I have made Jesus Christ the Lord of my life, and I have given everything of my life to Him, and it's very important for me to know what kind of character this is going to be that I'm going to be playing."

## Teens' Advice to Parents About Nurturing Spiritual Growth, Part 2

- "Take a proactive role in your kids' lives. Start at an early age, because if you try to instill family devotion time at a late age (14–18), your kids will resist it."
- "Equip children and teens to study the Bible for themselves. Demonstrate how to extract biblical principles from the text directly and how to meditate on Scripture. If you don't know how to yourself, learn with your child."
- "Be a good example of Christ. Show that Christianity extends outside the church."
- "Time spent personally with your teens is required to nurture their spiritual development. Being genuine in where they are at spiritually will help them to grow."
- "You need to build up your teens and make them confident in what they believe to be true. Provide a good visual example for them, and be an encouragement without provoking them."

The casting agent replied that she respected Charity's position and that she didn't have to worry about anything her character would do or say.

Reassured, Charity nonetheless didn't feel right about making an immediate decision. "Let me pray about it for a week, while I'm on spring break," she requested. The agent agreed.

When Charity returned to the casting agent's office a week later, bad news was waiting. "Charity, I need to talk to you because you were so honest with me," the agent began. "There have been a few changes made in your character that I think you should know about. First of all, your character's going to be the lead singer of a rock band, and she's going to fall in love with another member in the band, and they will become sexually involved. But she'll cheat on her boyfriend and have an affair with an older, married man, completely destroying his family, and she gets pregnant by him.

"When her boyfriend finds out that she's had this affair and is pregnant by this other man, he threatens her that if she does not terminate the pregnancy in abortion, he will leave her. And so your character decides to have an abortion."

The agent concluded, "Charity, I know what you told me about your personal convictions, but I just want to encourage you. You're an actress. Actresses don't get paid to play themselves. They play other people. So I'm just encouraging you to act."

Now, to a lot of moral teenagers, including many Christian young people, that offer would have been an irresistible temptation. After all, Charity might have rationalized, she could take the part and then use press interviews to talk about how *unlike* her character she was in real life. But she knew that playing the part would have meant portraying immoral and unbiblical behavior in a positive light, and so her immediate response was "Ma'am, I am an actress, but I'm a Christian first, and I couldn't live with that."

With those words, Charity turned down "the break of a lifetime." But she doesn't regret it one bit. And she knows—from the thousands of letters she received, after her story came out, from other teenage girls, their parents, their older brothers, and pastors—that her desire to make Christ known and her willingness to hold loyalty to Him as her highest value have greatly encouraged the faith of people around the world.

Charity concluded her story, "That, in and of itself, has been more than enough payment for me for the stand I took."

## Faith Ready to Leave Home

As we parents look ahead to our children's high school graduation and their cutting of the proverbial apron strings, we want them to have a faith in Jesus Christ that's personal, vibrant, biblically informed and guided, and strong enough to stand up for the truth with gentleness and respect. That's our goal, the target at which we're aiming and toward which we're working daily.

It's a goal worthy of our best efforts. And, like most goals worth reaching, it will *require* our best efforts. But remember, you're not alone in this quest. Most importantly, God is on your side. As you keep reading this guide, you will also find many helpful insights and practical tools. God bless you as you give your best to build your teenager's faith.

# PART 2

...

# Building a Strong Parent-Child Relationship

*Without a strong, healthy relationship with your teen, you have little chance of making a positive impact. But with a good relationship based on grace and mutual respect, you can develop a teenager who is eager to learn the things of God.*

# CHAPTER 5

# The Role of a Mentor

Remember when your teenager was born?

Unless she became a member of your family later through adoption or other means, you probably took care of that child's every need from birth. You bathed, fed, dressed, and changed her. As time went on, even though she may have been able to dress herself, brush her own teeth, and take herself to the bathroom, your job wasn't done. You still had to prepare her food, tell her to bundle up in the winter, and make sure she took her vitamins.

In time her list of skills grew, but your "to do" list seemed as long as ever. You screened her friends, signed her up for ballet lessons or basketball, and told her when to practice the flute or feed the dog. You were still in control, more or less.

Those were the good old days, right?

Many parents wish the adolescent years were simply a continuation of the preteen process. They'd like to control everything their teen does.

As you may have noticed, few teenagers share that view.

It's only normal: As an adolescent struggles to form an independent identity, he pulls away from the "Yes, Mommy" approach to decision making. And as the young person's need to take on greater responsibility increases in preparation for adulthood, it's vital that the "control center" begins to move from parent to offspring.

Whether we like it or not, the relationship is changing—and *must* change. We can't influence our teens in the way we did when they were younger. But we *can* choose to work *with* the process and not against it. That's why the most successful parents of teenagers will recognize the change, accept the change, and plan accordingly, gradually transferring control and responsibility for choices and actions to their teens.

> *Whether we like it or not, the relationship is changing—and must change.*

## What's a Mentor For?

As your child matures, he needs you less as a governor and more as a mentor. And what is a mentor? Someone who leads by walking alongside.

Mentors major in guiding, encouraging, and teaching, not in controlling. The transition from governor to mentor is made by slowly letting go during the teen years, giving more and more free rein as the child proves himself trustworthy. Instead of maintaining a viselike grip on the youngster's life until the last possible second when he leaves home, the wise parent shifts responsibility and choices a bit at a time, a little more each year, onto the shoulders of the teen.

Making the transition from governor to mentor requires courage, as all battles do. In his book *Home with a Heart*, Dr. James Dobson described the "battle for control" this way:

> Everybody understands that teenagers are itching to get out on their own—to run their own lives and not have parents telling them what to do anymore. But this yearning for control actually starts much earlier. It's a fundamental dimension of the human personality.
>
> I remember one mother of a tough little four-year-old girl who was demanding her own way. The mother said, "Now, Jenny, you're just going to have to obey me. I'm your boss, and I have the responsibility to lead you, and that's what I intend to do!"

RELATIONSHIP

Little Jenny thought over her mother's words for a minute, and then she said, "How long does it have to be that way?"

Already at four years of age, this child was yearning for a day of freedom when nobody could tell her what to do. Something deep within her spirit was reaching out for control. She shares that yearning with millions of her age-mates—some more than others. The task for us as parents is to hang on to the reins of authority in the early days, even though little hands are trying to pry our fingers loose, and then gradually grant independence as maturity arrives. But this is the most delicate responsibility in parenting. Power granted too early produces folly, but power granted too late brings rebellion.[1]

That's why, when it comes to mentoring, timing is crucial. The parents of 13-year-old Derek, for example, know that he's ready to take on more responsibility for his own spiritual growth. He's so zealous, in fact, that kids at school call him "Bible boy." He even started an after-school prayer meeting in a classroom. Now is the time for Derek's folks to offer him a new challenge—a mission trip during spring break, perhaps, or a backyard Bible club for neighborhood kids in the summer.

By contrast, 15-year-old Brianna has always been more interested in surfing the Web than in searching the Scriptures. Her parents are helping her find Web sites that offer devotional readings, in the hope that she'll develop the habit of spending "quiet times" with God.

It wouldn't make sense for "Bible boy" Derek's parents to hover over his devotional life, planning his next 365 readings by chapter and verse and sitting on the edge of his bed to make sure he doesn't miss one. He's past that point. Nor would it be wise for webmistress Brianna's folks to simply hope that her lack of interest in Bible reading will somehow take care of itself. Demanding that Brianna muscle her way through Leviticus might foster only resentment and failure, but starting with her Internet enthusiasm just may work.

The parents of Derek and Brianna know these things because

■ ■ ■

## *For Example:*
## *One Mentor Who Mattered*

RELATIONSHIP

I was 16—and angry.

For health reasons, my father had just ended his career as a minister. My family had moved to a new town, seemingly without a future. My enthusiasm for church had evaporated, but the habit of going was so ingrained that I showed up at youth group anyway, frowning and hanging back at the edge of things.

Before long, the youth pastor—Pastor Ted, they called him—visited our house. It was one of those welcome-to-the-group calls I knew ministers had to make. But soon he was back, asking me to do him a favor. He wanted me to write funny announcements in the youth group's weekly newsletter.

Somehow he'd picked the one assignment that could have attracted me. I started using the newsletter to poke fun at the church, the other kids, and Ted himself. Instead of pulling the plug, Ted claimed that everyone looked forward to reading my work every Sunday.

Next, hearing that I liked to draw, Ted let me make posters to publicize youth events. It was a job he'd previously reserved for himself, having studied art in college. When I got a guitar, he allowed me to join a musical group in the church, even though my strumming was barely audible, my chord changes clumsy.

Before I knew it, I was one of the busiest kids in the youth group. Eventually the other kids, perhaps mistaking my perpetual scowl for spirituality, elected me president of the group.

As the end of my senior year approached, Ted came to me with a final project: an evangelistic "Youth Booth" at the state fair. I helped put together a slide show, made a sign for the booth, and wrote a low-key tract. Then, on a Saturday afternoon, I went to the church to paint the sheet of plywood onto which the slides would be projected.

The only sound in the empty hallway was the wet *skish, skish* of the paint roller—until I heard footsteps. Suddenly there was Pastor Ted, standing next to me.

As we talked, I began to see how, for the last two years, he'd always been there. He'd put up with my mocking and mumbling, feeling the effects of my anger but never responding in kind.

He'd ignored the way I was and focused on what I might become. In the process, I'd become a little less angry and a little more useful.

Years later, I worked as an intern at that church—right next to my old mentor, Pastor Ted, and the rest of the staff. At one of our meetings, the need for people to do projects was discussed. When talk turned to recruiting volunteers, Ted had a quiet comment.

"I don't believe in getting things done through people," he said. "I believe in getting people done through things."

He didn't point me out as an example, but he could have.

Thanks, Ted.

—John Duckworth

RELATIONSHIP

they understand that mentors must be clear-eyed observers of their kids. As Dr. Dobson concluded, "It is a wise mother or father who can let go little by little as the growing child is able to stand on his or her own. If you watch and listen carefully, the critical milestones will be obvious."

## The Mentor's Job Description

To better understand what a mentor does, let's consider some fictional stories about those who lead by walking alongside.

Every story is about a character's journey toward a goal. Along the way, the character faces challenges through which he or she grows. Many stories include a mentor—someone whose wisdom can help the main character to overcome those challenges.

In *The Lord of the Rings* trilogy by J. R. R. Tolkein, Gandalf is mentor to Frodo Baggins. Gandalf doesn't make Frodo's journey for him; he imparts wisdom, practical advice, and skill so that Frodo can complete his own quest.

In Focus on the Family's radio drama series *Adventures in Odyssey*, the mentor is John Avery Whittaker. "Whit" doesn't control the rest of the cast, most of whom are youngsters; he helps them make better choices or learn from their bad ones.

In the film *Karate Kid,* Mr. Miyagi is Daniel's mentor, teaching him how to control his temper, be strong, and deal with bullies. The martial arts master doesn't fight Daniel's battles for him; he cultivates the boy's self-discipline, preparing Daniel to face enemies on his own turf.

Author Christopher Vogler, in his book *The Writer's Journey*, has this to say about mentors:

> In story, the mentor's role is to motivate the hero and help the hero to overcome their fears. The function of the mentor is often to plant information that will be important later. . . .
>
> Mentors provide heroes with motivation, inspiration, guidance, training, and gifts for the journey. Every hero is guided by something, and a story without some acknowledgment of this energy is incomplete.[2]

In the real-life story of your teen, he or she is the hero on a journey. Yours is the role of mentor. To see how you've been playing that part so far, try asking yourself the following questions:

*1. Am I trying to fight my teen's battles for him, or am I arming him with the weapons of truth and character he needs to face his own foes?*

*2. Am I attempting to control my teen's choices, or am I giving her the information she needs to make her own decisions?*

*3. Am I pretending that my teen hasn't grown, or am I watching for milestones that show he's ready for more independence?*

*4. Am I ignoring my teen's weaknesses, or am I helping her to overcome them?*

*5. Am I only giving advice about the future, or am I helping my teen deal with his fears about that future?*

*6. Am I lecturing out of frustration or offering motivation and inspiration when my teen is open to receiving it?*

*7. Am I dealing only with crises of the moment, or am I planting information and values that will be useful to my teen later?*

*8. Am I trying to get my teen to conform outwardly to my expectations or to be transformed inwardly through personal interaction with God, the ultimate Mentor?*

If your answers to those questions indicate that you aren't a perfect mentor, join the club. In fiction

> **If you've learned from your mistakes, you have road-tested wisdom to offer the teen hero in your home.**

and in life, most mentors are flawed. Fortunately, imperfections—and your admissions of them—can make your teen more open to your guidance. And if you've learned from your mistakes, you have road-tested wisdom to offer the hero in your home.

This doesn't mean, of course, that your teen will always be eager to hear that wisdom. Even fictional mentors are often resented and their advice resisted—until the hero learns the hard way that Gandalf or Mom or Dad was right.

■ ■ ■

## All by Yourself?
## The Single-Parent Mentor

Can a single parent manage the task of mentoring?

As a single mom, I've found God to be full of grace and sufficient for what I need. That doesn't come easily, however. It takes conscious effort to reach for Him and to believe He can answer those needs in my daily reality.

One day I was at the end of my rope. I'd done all I could to discipline my teenager, and it didn't seem to be working. Having just moved to a new city, I had no close friends locally to draw upon.

Finally I dropped to my knees. I reminded God that I had no husband with whom to discuss this problem. Would He please be that husband and coparent? Would He please help me in this situation?

I went to bed with no answer. In the morning, though, it was clear to me what steps I needed to take. I proceeded through those steps. In return, my daughter still gave me tears, anger, and blame for everything wrong in her life. Yet I felt God telling me to hang in there. I did, and it proved to be precisely the right thing to do.

That was a turning point for me. I began to go to God with many issues that some would think only a husband or father could deal with. God continued to fill those gaps, provide those answers, and be there for me. Yet He never provided those things unless I went to Him for them.

There have still been many tears, many days of excruciating loneliness, and the profound need for a human partner to share the load of life. But God is always there through those times.

—Lissa Johnson

RELATIONSHIP

## The Mentor as Coach

Another way to understand your role as a mentor is to think of yourself as a coach.

When would-be athletes are young, a coach begins with the basics. He explains everything. He's not just on the field; he's positioning kids' feet and arms, showing them how to catch the pass or hit the ball. He's involved in every movement, every choice.

Later comes scrimmage time, when the coach moves from being in the middle of the play to being just behind it. He's still close, but he's not involved hands-on. He lets the players play, calling instructions as needed. At the end of practice, he's there to point out where things went right and where they went wrong.

When the day finally arrives for a real game, the coach stays on the sidelines. The players take the field. The coach can shout directions, but he doesn't hold the players' hands or demonstrate

### Teens' "Ways in Which a Parent Was Spiritually Influential," Part 2

- "My mom had me memorize a verse from the Bible a week. She told me about spiritual warfare."
- "My mother would kneel beside my bed at night and pray for me before telling me good night. It was often during the prayers that she was able to communicate her feelings or concerns to me. She also told me this often and wrote it down for me: 'I have great worth apart from my performance because Christ gave His life for me and therefore imparted great value to me. I am deeply loved, fully pleasing, totally forgiven, accepted, and complete in Christ Jesus.' "
- "My dad always made me go to sports practices when I didn't want to because he said I have to keep my commitments. This caused a lot of yelling, but I learned something very important about commitments."
- "My mom would have devotions with my sisters and brother and I as we were growing up."
- "When we were little, my mom read us Bible stories either after dinner or before we went to bed. Her way of making sure we were listening was to ask us questions about the story."

technique anymore. He waits for time-outs, halftimes, and the end of the game to offer detailed guidance.

It's the same way with parents who want to be spiritual mentors. In the early years, we may show our children how to pray, even giving them words to say and telling them to close their eyes. Later we might ask leading questions: "Are there any problems at school we should pray about? What happened today that you can thank God for? Do you want to pray first or should I?"

Eventually our kids are praying on their own, often silently. We might wish we could elbow our way into those conversations, but all we can do is make suggestions from the sidelines: "I keep a list of answered prayers; it reminds me to keep praying no matter what." "Please pray for Mrs. Logan next door; she just found out her husband has Alzheimer's." "If you'll pray about my sales presentation today, I'll pray about your geometry test."

Our shouts of encouragement may come at the start or end of a school day or in a note in a lunch bag. Our halftime pep talks may be delivered on a weekend or during a family vacation. Our postgame analyses may occur at bedtime or over pie at a coffee shop.

Sometimes we'll find ourselves sharing the coaching duties with others—camp counselors, youth leaders, or Sunday school teachers. But because we're the parents of our teens, we'll be their head coaches—their primary mentors—for better or for worse.

## The Mentor as Model

Mentors are role models, too.

Imagine Obi-Wan Kenobi, mentor to Luke Skywalker in the original *Star Wars* movie, trying to train his aspiring Jedi knight as follows:

*Obi-Wan:* Use the Force, Luke.

*Luke:* Why?

*Obi-Wan:* Uh . . . I'm not sure. Never used it. I hear it's very effective, though.

*Luke:* But—

*Obi-Wan:* Now, about this light saber. To turn it on, you just push this button. No, that's not it. Maybe this switch over here . . .

*Luke:* Haven't you used that, either?

**RELATIONSHIP**

*Obi-Wan:* Hey, smart mouth! What do you think you are, a Jedi master? You kids today! Why, when I was your age . . .

Mentors aren't perfect, but they need to practice what they preach. In fact, they may have to practice a *lot* before they offer advice to their apprentices.

Alex, 14, hears his father quote from Colossians 3:12: "Clothe yourselves with compassion." Two hours later, Alex watches his father kick the family dog for snatching a sandwich that fell to the floor. What has Alex learned?

Tracy, 16, receives frequent lectures about her "bad attitude" toward the church youth group. Yet every Sunday, in the car, she watches her mother stage a postservice roast of their pastor, the committee that chooses music, and the elders who draw up the church budget. Will Tracy change her attitude? Probably not for the better.

Being a role model may be an intimidating assignment, but it's ours nonetheless. Whether we want them to or not, our teens are watching. Regardless of our words, they will try behavior that seems to work for us. They're telling us, in effect, "Mom and Dad, who you are and what you do speak so loudly that I can't hear what you're saying."

Are you modeling behaviors you don't want your teen to imitate? For starters, ask yourself whether you'd be happy if your

## How to CONNECT:
## Seven Qualities of Effective Mentoring

To help you get the most out of the mentoring relationship, remember the word CONNECT. The seven qualities spell it out:

- **Consistent:** As a . . . mentor, you will need to be committed and dependable to meet together. . . .
- **Open:** Be authentic and honest about yourself. . . . Be willing to take some risks as you dive in and discuss topics you have never discussed before.
- **Nurture:** Be willing to provide an atmosphere of acceptance and willingness to grow. Both the mentor (parent) and the teen will be nurtured as they spend time in the process.
- **Notice:** Tune in to each other. Listen and observe cues. Spend more time

son or daughter adopted your *modus operandi* in the following areas:

- handling anger
- gambling
- driving
- alcohol use
- sexual behavior
- dress
- work hours
- credit card debt

Now ask yourself about behaviors you *want* your teen to imitate. What kind of example are you setting in the following areas?

- sharing your faith
- showing hospitality
- forgiving
- exercising self-control
- giving generously
- responding to the needs of the poor
- supporting missionaries
- praying

**RELATIONSHIP**

listening than talking if you have a tendency to talk too much. Notice how the other person feels and displays her emotions.

- **Encourage:** Pour courage into the other person by affirming, believing in, and supporting her. Create more encouragement by keeping certain discussions personal and confidential.
- **Care:** Demonstrate love by being patient, forgiving, understanding, and nonjudgmental. Mentoring is more about care than it is about imparting information.
- **Talk:** to God. Prayer is vital for effective mentoring. It keeps the focus right. It helps us remember that we are not in this alone. Talking to God is a resource that gives us balance, perspective, and strength.

—Tim Smith in *Life Skills for Girls*[3]

RELATIONSHIP

If that list makes you feel more like a muddle than a model, there's hope. Consider these biblical personalities:

- Abraham was a good example of faith—except when he tried to create a promised heir by having sex with his wife's servant (see Genesis 16:1-4).
- Elijah was a model prophet—except when fear sent him into a suicidal depression (see 1 Kings 19:3-4).
- Peter was a paragon of courage—except when he turned his back on his own mentor, Jesus (see Matthew 26:69-74).

God uses imperfect models, too.

Still, we're easier to use when we've practiced enough to know which end of the light saber is up.

## Are You Meant to Mentor?

In the world of fiction, there are characters known as "reluctant mentors." They'd rather not offer their wisdom. They may feel they have nothing to share or that it wouldn't make a difference if they did.

There are reluctant mentors in real life, too. Maybe you're one of them.

When it comes to guiding your teenager spiritually, do you fear you have nothing to share? Take this brief inventory to see whether you're as unqualified as you think:

- Do you know even a *little* more about any aspect of the Christian life than your teen does?
- Have you learned *anything* from a spiritual mistake that your teen hasn't made yet?
- Have you made even a *tiny* bit of progress since beginning your relationship with God?
- Could you *begin* to make such progress, perhaps as a project you and your teen could undertake together?
- Can you keep reading this book until you find a *small* nugget of truth to pass on to your teen?

"Okay," you say. "I may have something to share with my teenager. But what difference would it make? He probably wouldn't listen to me."

That's where the next step—relationship—comes in.

Whether you're bursting with spiritual wisdom or feeling like you left it in your other suit, you won't get far as a mentor unless you build a relationship with your teen.

As a longtime youth worker said, "The world of teenagers is by invitation only." Build a relationship and you'll get an invitation. It won't matter that you're "losing control" over your teen. Work on the relationship, and your influence will increase *because he or she will invite it.*

Want that kind of relationship? That's what the next chapter is all about.

**RELATIONSHIP**

# CHAPTER 6

# The Relationship Is Everything!

Janna, age 17, had been dating Tom for nearly two years. Like many teen couples, they spent most of their waking hours together. They liked laughing, listening to music, and exploring side roads off the interstate. Everything inside Janna and everything Tom told her indicated they'd probably spend the rest of their lives together.

But then he broke up with her.

In her room, Janna sobbed until her chest hurt and her throat was raw. She curled up into a ball.

How could she get through this? Having recently moved far away from her friends, she felt so alone. She supposed she could talk to her parents, but everybody knew how adults felt about teen romances. They were "puppy love," infatuation, foolishness. Janna knew, though, that this was real enough to break her heart.

Finally she pulled herself together and went downstairs, trying hard to pretend everything was okay. Her mother, knitting on the sofa, called her over and patted the cushion next to her. Janna sat, looking at her hands folded in her lap.

"It must be very hard," her mother said softly. "I know how much you loved him."

Janna couldn't believe her ears. Her mother understood! She

hadn't told Janna she was immature or that she wasn't capable of true love.

Because of that conversation, Janna was able to move forward through her grief. She also began to feel closer to her mother and to share more with her.

Janna's mom had made a crucial choice that day. She'd chosen to build a bridge to her daughter rather than deliver a condescending speech. As a result, Janna was more willing to accept her mom's guidance in matters of the spirit as well as of the heart.

As the parent of a teenager, you can make that choice as well. You can cultivate a relationship—even a friendship—with your teen that will last into adulthood. If you want to be a spiritual mentor to your young person, that relationship isn't a luxury. It can spell the difference between success and failure.

Veteran youth worker Joe White reports that in his 30 years of counseling troubled teens he has made a habit of asking boys who are rebelling or in serious trouble, "How is your relationship with your dad?" And almost always the answer comes back, "I don't know my dad" or "What dad? I never see my dad." Truly, when it comes to making a positive difference for God in a teen's life, the relationship is everything!

### Relationship: Don't Leave Adolescence Without It

Passing the spiritual baton to your child involves more than handing him a worldview at a specific moment in time. Just as a relay runner must practice and build trust with teammates for the handoff to be smooth and solid, so must you.

> *Without relationship, mentoring is merely a nice idea.*

Without a strong, healthy relationship with your teen, you have little chance of making a positive impact on her. Without relationship, mentoring is merely a nice idea.

"But I have *rules* to pass along to my teenager," some impatient parents might say. "Values and behaviors I want him to adopt. There isn't *time* for that touchy-feely stuff."

But rules without relationship lead to rebellion. As Josh McDowell has observed, "Simply occupying a position of authority, such as pastor, youth worker—even mother or father—by no means guarantees that you can effectively teach a young person right from wrong. Anyone who wishes to pass on biblical values to someone else must begin by developing a strong, positive relationship with that person."[1]

Rex, a father, found that out one evening when he turned down a request from his son Neil. Frustrated, the boy lashed out. "You only care about Mom, work, God, and Jesus!" he shouted and walked out of the room. Rex stood there, stunned. He knew what Neil was saying: "You don't care about me. Why should I obey you?"

The boy's outburst led Rex to ask himself some hard questions: *Have I been sending the wrong message? Do I give the impression that only the adult world and its rules are important? Does Neil think I don't love him? Am I turning him off to spiritual things?*

Rex resolved immediately to work on his relationship with Neil. He didn't want to lose his influence with his son—and he knew that might happen if Neil saw himself as being at the bottom of Dad's priority list.

When your teen knows you love her beyond all measure, when she knows you enjoy being with her, she'll be more willing to believe that your guidance is motivated by caring. She'll be more likely to accept the idea that the rules and values you want to pass along are in her best interest.

## Finding the Ties That Bind

Being a spiritual mentor to your teen doesn't require a *perfect* relationship. But the relationship must be genuine, caring, and reciprocating. That kind of bond doesn't come with the birth certificate. It requires effort. It's earned.

What does this kind of relationship look like? To envision it, think for a moment about *your* favorite relationships. With whom do you like to spend time? Most of us prefer to be around people who . . .

- love us
- see our strengths and compliment us on them
- listen to us and respect our opinions even if they don't agree with us

- are affectionate verbally and physically
- respect our boundaries
- are fun to be with
- honestly share themselves and their stories
- are interested in developing a genuine relationship with us
- would not ridicule us
- forgive us
- embrace all of who we are—good and bad, struggles and successes

That's the kind of relationship you need to develop with your teen.

If you're not there yet, take heart. Whether things are currently warm or chilly between you and your teenager, the following ideas can help you improve the relational weather in your vicinity.

### Relationship Builder 1: Empathy

There's a step you can take right now, this minute, to start building a bridge to your adolescent: You can remember what it was like to be a teenager yourself.

That may be a scary proposition, especially if your teen years were ones you'd rather forget. But recalling the feelings, pressures, and dreams of our own adolescence helps us to empathize with our kids. Remembering those years tells us when to back off and when to step in. It tells us when to be strong, when to share, when to speak hard truths, and when to listen.

Consider Katie, whose daughter Allyson is lying across her bed, sobbing her heart out. The problem: Allyson wasn't asked out this weekend. Katie can stand in the doorway and say with a shrug, "So what if you don't have a date? Life isn't over. There are plenty more weekends to look forward to."

Technically, she'd be right. But so would Allyson, who would be thinking, *Mom, you just don't understand.*

To build a bridge to her daughter, Katie needs to ask herself questions like these:

*RELATIONSHIP*

- *How did I feel when nobody asked me out?*
- *How did I feel when my best friend went out with the guy I had a crush on?*
- *How did I feel when I was teased about the surge of acne I could do nothing about?*
- *What did I do when I didn't make the team?*

Katie needs to remember that, when she was a teenager, she had only the present to rely on. She didn't have years of experience to tell her which problems were mountains and which were molehills. She had only the *now*.

Janna, whose story opened this chapter, was fortunate to have a mom who remembered what it was like to be a teenager in love. Janna's mom took her daughter's pain as seriously as she had taken her own—and their bond grew stronger.

■ ■ ■

## *Never Forget:*
## *How a Crisis Gave Me Empathy*

When I was just 22, I discovered a lump where no woman ever wants to find a lump. About a week before my biopsy—when I *knew* I would be found to have cancer and be lopsided the rest of my life—I received a letter from an old friend of my mother.

I didn't want to read it. I was sure the woman would have no idea what I was going through. I was sure she would offer only pat answers and "Christianese" jargon.

Finally, without bothering to sit down, I ripped the letter open and glanced over it. Then I sat down and read it again, slowly.

She didn't tell me not to be afraid. She didn't give me any pat answers. Instead, she wisely told me to *always remember this time*. She wanted me not to forget how terrified I was—and to know that one day, when I had children, their "childish" fears would be as real to them as this fear was to me now.

That piece of wisdom stayed with me throughout my child-raising years. No matter what my kids faced, I connected because I remembered a time when I shared those intense, undeniable emotions.

—L. H. J.

Need help to focus on your own adolescent ups and downs? Try writing your answers to these questions:

- When you were your teen's age, whom did you wish you were?
- Whom did you hope to become?
- What were your deepest hurts? How did they feel?
- What did you usually do when faced with a crisis?
- How did you feel when your friends were involved in something that you knew wasn't right? What did you do?
- If you could travel back in time and be a friend to your teenage self, what advice would you offer? What comfort? How might that advice and comfort be received?

## Relationship Builder 2: Respect

Imagine yourself walking into someone's house. On the wall are wooden plaques with sayings like these: "Friends are obnoxious," "Friends are the cause of my insanity," "Beware of friends!"

Would you want to visit that person? Or would you get the idea that you're unwelcome—someone to be ridiculed rather than enjoyed, liked, or appreciated?

Strangely enough, this is what happens with many teens. Some parents put up "cute" signs in their homes or bumper stickers on their cars that are disrespectful toward adolescents. Some fall into the trap of rolling their eyes when talking about their child. They tell other adults, even in the teen's hearing, how difficult their son is to live with or how foolish their daughter's latest tears were.

When we treat anyone with such dishonor, what should we expect? The disrespected person will respond in kind—or become so disheartened that he'll never fulfill his potential.

As parents who want to earn the respect of our teens in order to mentor them, we can't ignore this relational building block. We need to make sure our homes are havens where our teens are respected—where they and their opinions are valued.

Respecting teens also means allowing them privacy. Gail, a single mom, has made it a rule that she won't open her daughter's mail, notes, or journals. After all, she says, she wouldn't want anyone digging through her own purse, briefcase, desk, or clothing drawers. She wouldn't want anyone eavesdropping on her phone conversations or reading her private writings, either. (Gail allows, however, that if her daughter seemed to be involved in some sort of dangerous behavior, she probably would break the rule for the girl's protection.)

Dr. James Dobson, in his book *Solid Answers*, wrote that knowing a teen well is the key to the privacy question:

> There are some who would never do anything illegal or harmful. It's just not in them. In those cases, I would not recommend snooping through their room and private stuff. But in situations where a secretive boy or girl is doing suspicious things, running with the wrong crowd, and then demanding utter privacy at home, I would gather whatever information I needed in order to know how to respond.[2]

Regardless of where you must draw the line on your teen's privacy, it's critical to have and show respect for him or her. As a result, you may even find your teen doing the same for you.

■ ■ ■

## With All Due Respect: A Thank-You Note

The following is a real letter from a teen to an adult who treated him more respectfully than other grown-ups usually did:

> You treated me as I would assume you treat most of your children's friends: as adults. That's so hard for us to find. You understand that kids are smart enough to start making their own decisions about things and come to their own conclusions. Many adults look at them as know-it-all brats with little experience and patronize at best.

> Would your teen write a similar note about you? Why or why not?

**RELATIONSHIP**

### Relationship Builder 3: Honesty

Maybe you've heard this line in a TV show or movie: "I don't want a relationship based on lies!"

It's true—a relationship without honesty has no firm foundation. To forge and maintain an authentic bond with your teen, you'll need to tell the truth.

This doesn't mean you must divulge every secret in your life. If 15-year-old Jeffrey asks, "Dad, did you ever have sex before marriage?" Dad can choose to take the Fifth Amendment. Or he can say, "Jeff, I want to answer your questions about sex based on life in general, but I'd rather not talk about all the details of my personal experience." Or he can take the "full disclosure" route. No matter how Dad chooses to reply, he needs to (1) tell no lies and (2) get to the root of what Jeff really wants to know—which probably has more to do with Jeff's options than with Dad's past.

Usually honesty is a much simpler matter. Consider this conversation between 16-year-old Angie and her mother:

■ ■ ■

## *Quit Multitasking: Paying Attention to Your Teen*

Frustrated, my daughter told me that she felt I wasn't listening to her. The problem: I was often dusting or washing dishes when she was talking to me. She asked that in the future I sit and look at her.

Being a person who hates to sit still, I find it difficult to listen to anyone while staying in one place. I'd rather listen while doing mindless tasks. It's been hard for me to learn, but now I remind myself that nothing is more important than what my daughter has to say. So I sit, listen, and look.

Our relationship has improved. It seems she trusts me more; she certainly shares more with me. Most often it's the fun, daily stuff her life is made of. But on occasion, it's the deeper thoughts, hurts, and emotions that course through her.

—Lissa Johnson

"Mom, can I have some money for new tennis shoes?"

"No, I don't have any money."

Angie thinks, *She's such a liar. I saw $75 sitting on her dresser!*

Mom knows that money is earmarked for the electric bill, but Angie sees only a discrepancy between Mom's words and the cash on the dresser. Mom would be better off with a reply like "We don't have any money for that right now" or "All our money this month is designated for other things." By acknowledging that there is money but that the shoes will have to wait, Mom builds trust instead of suspicion.

Sometimes honesty is even simpler. It may boil down to saying those three little words many of us find hardest to choke out: "I don't know."

No matter what the issue, our teens need to know we'll never lie to them. After all, if you can't trust your spiritual mentor, who can you trust?

## Relationship Builder 4: Listening

Teens are notorious for not talking. Yet many say they don't talk to their parents because their parents don't really listen.

You'll find in-depth help on how to communicate with your teen in chapter eight. For now, try strengthening your relationship with the following pointers on being all ears:

1. *Take time to listen.* Are you working on your master's degree? Your golf game? If your teen hears time and again, "I'm busy; can we talk later?" he will eventually stop talking to you. When kids want to talk, it's often because a strong feeling has surfaced—and may soon resubmerge. If you wait, the opportunity for a relationship-building conversation could be gone.

2. *Just listen, period.* Listening isn't judging. It's not jumping in to "fix" things, lecture, or take care of our parental agendas. It's taking time to hear the heart and mind of your teen in order to get to know her better. If your teen expresses a view with which you disagree, ask why he feels that way or how he came to that conclusion. There will be time to offer your thoughts later, when the task of listening has been completed.

3. *Listen even when it's tough.* Listening may mean hearing things

RELATIONSHIP

RELATIONSHIP

> | *Listening may mean hearing things you don't want to hear.*

you don't want to hear—a scathing review of how you handled a situation, a disturbing hint that your teen isn't the innocent you thought you knew, or a rambling list of accusations. It may even mean that you'll need to respond with an apology. If you want to strengthen your relationship, listen anyway.

4. *Consider carefully what you hear.* Tim, a high school senior, wants to talk to his father about the 11:00 P.M. curfew he's had since his freshman year. "I think I should have a little more freedom," Tim says. "Some of my friends don't have a curfew at all."

Tim's dad feels himself tensing but resists the urge to panic. "What would you suggest?" he asks. As it turns out, Tim has some good ideas. He wants a midnight curfew, but he will call by 11:00 to let his parents know where he is and exactly when he'll be home.

Dad breathes a sigh of relief, glad that he didn't end the discussion too soon. He promises to think seriously about his son's suggestions and to talk again tomorrow. Tim feels respected and valued—and listened to.

## Good Times: 25 Fun Things to Do with Your Teen

1. Play air hockey
2. Bake cookies
3. Train a dog or horse
4. Go to a concert
5. Do crafts
6. Go on a "date"
7. Attend an English-style tea
8. Race go-carts
9. Go hiking or rock climbing
10. Go hunting, fishing, or camping
11. Take a missions trip together
12. Visit museums and art exhibits
13. Play table tennis
14. Attend school sports events
15. Go shopping
16. Ice-skate or roller-blade
17. Ski
18. Play volleyball, football, baseball, golf, or bowling
19. Star-gaze
20. Take a group of friends out for pizza or ice cream
21. Play laser tag or paintball
22. See a play
23. Take a weekend getaway
24. Play miniature golf
25. Shoot a video

Listening is a two-way street. The more we listen to our teens, the more they'll listen to us. That's vital for a spiritual mentor, who has some pretty important things to say.

*Bgin here*

## Relationship Builder 5: Fun

"I want my kids to like me," says Joe White. "I want them not to drink and hang out because I'm more fun than 'Miller time.' I want them to stay home on Friday nights because home is the funnest place to be."

Are you that committed to having fun with your kids? Good times with your teen will give you strength to face the hard times the relationship is bound to bring. Fun times together remind your teen that you're not just a disciplinarian—and that you're interested in many aspects of his life, not just his behavior.

In *Bound by Honor*, Gary Smalley tells how a priceless moment during a fishing trip with his teenage son provided a chance for relationship building:

## Table Talk: Fun at Family Meals

Dinner can be a good time to develop the fun side of your relationship as well as learn about each other on a deeper level.

- Have a box of thought-provoking questions available. Each person draws a question and answers it. No one is allowed to interrupt or ridicule an answer. Sample questions: What is your most ambitious goal? What was your most embarrassing moment? When have you felt that God was doing something through you? What would you ask God if you could see Him sitting at this table?
- Keep a "nasty jar" available. Anyone who makes a rude or derogatory comment during a meal must put a quarter in the jar. When the jar is full, give the money to missions or use it to do something fun as a family.
- Have each person say something nice about the one on his or her right. Or get into a circle after dinner, putting one family member in the center. Everyone in the circle gives a sincere compliment to the person in the middle.
- Ask each person to describe the highlight of his or her day.

Because our hotel was about 40 miles from the nearest town and we were surrounded by the Grand Canyon, the sky was lit up with stars that looked like millions of tiny diamonds. The scene was breathtaking and far more interesting than the thought of sleep. So, wanting the perfect place to watch the show, we decided to take our pillows and perch on the top of a big stone wall behind the hotel. . . .

At one point in our reverie, without any warning, a stray cat leaped up and landed right on Greg's chest. In sudden terror, with a high-pitched scream, Greg flung the cat at my unsuspecting head. We both tried to dodge the flying cat claws, but we lost our balance and fell off the wall.

Needless to say, we never saw that cat again. And after regaining our composure, we couldn't stop laughing as we watched the stars well into the next morning.[3]

Want to have some fun? Observe what your teen likes to do; then extend an invitation to go do it together. If your daughter likes to shop, invite her to the outlet mall. If your son likes to eat, rent a pig roaster and go "whole hog" (or just take him to his favorite spot for dinner). Don't try to become your teen's primary pal, but spend time enjoying each other's company often enough to strengthen the bond between you.

## Relationship Builder 6: Affection

If your teen doesn't get affection at home, he or she will go elsewhere for it. Teens often make poor choices because they're desperate for affection. Take, for example, the girls who have become sexually active with a boyfriend "because he was the only one who would touch me."

No relationship is complete without affection. Sadly, some parents feel that when a child becomes a teenager, the time for affectionate words and touch is past. Dads feel especially awkward when their girls blossom into young women, fearing it would be inappropriate to hug them. Ironically, such withdrawal can cause a girl to feel that the changes in her body are bad and that she has become repulsive. A father can always give his teen daughter "Daddy hugs"—brief, one-arm-around-the-shoulder squeezes.

How can you offer appropriate, sincere affection to your teen? Here are some suggestions:

1. *Touch caringly and carefully.* Some families make it a rule that one hug or kiss a day must be exchanged. Nevertheless, saying "You need one hug a day" can offend teens who don't want to be told what they need. So try saying something like "Mom needs at least one hug a day." Offer hugs when your teen has made you proud, when he is returning from a trip, during worship in church, after a good chat, or when you're saying good night.

> **Make sure your "I love you's" don't go unsaid, even if your teen fails to respond in kind.**

Hugs aren't the only way to express affection through touch, of course. When you speak with your teen, try touching her on the arm or shoulder. Give her a quick kiss on the top of the head (if she's taller than you are, just wait until she sits down). Moms can offer to braid a daughter's hair; dads can wrestle with a son.

*Never* touch your teen in an angry way. If you do, rebuilding trust can take a long time.

2. *Express affection in words, too.* One father never ends a phone chat with a family member without an enthusiastic "I love you!"—even when he's at the office. Other employees tease him

## Touching Moments: More Affection Options

1. Pat on the back
2. Arm around the shoulders
3. High-five
4. Handshake
5. Quick stroke of the hair
6. Pat on the knee (especially while driving, sitting in church, or watching television together)
7. Shoulder massage
8. Back scratch
9. Kiss on the cheek or forehead

**RELATIONSHIP**

about it, but they know his relationship with his kids is solid.

Make sure your "I love you's" don't go unsaid, even if your teen fails to respond in kind. At other times, include affirmations like these:

"You're sweet."

"I like who you are."

"You are so cute (or handsome)."

"I love your smile."

"I'm so fortunate to have you as my son (or daughter)."

Eye contact and a gentle tone communicate affection too. So does consistency between your words and your actions; teenagers are experts at discerning "double messages" or anything that smacks of hypocrisy.

3. *Don't push it.* If your teen would be embarrassed by displays of affection in front of his friends, wait for a better time. If he needs less affection than a sibling, tailor your expressions of love accordingly. But don't be fooled into thinking that a standoffish teen needs no affection at all.

If your teen resists your hugs for a time, try to determine whether she is expressing anger by withdrawing. Talk about the anger (see Relationship Builder 8). During this period, let your

## Double Messages:
## Matching Affectionate Words with Actions

Here are some common double messages you'll want to avoid sending your teen:

- Saying "I trust you" but continually asking probing questions, calling to make sure your teen is where she said she would be, or verifying her stories by talking with other parents.
- Saying "I like your choices" but not letting your teen follow through on any decisions that don't match your preferences.
- Saying "Intelligence is one of your best qualities" but encouraging your teen to stay away from advanced classes or challenging careers.
- Saying "I support you in whatever you choose to do" but telling "scare stories" to keep your teen from pursuing missions instead of banking, or music instead of computer programming.

kind words and a fleeting touch on the back or shoulder suffice as a sign of your love.

If you haven't been affectionate with your teen in the past, it's not too late to start. Avoid overwhelming him with sudden gushiness and bear hugs, though; begin slowly and increase the affection gradually.

## Relationship Builder 7: Vulnerability

Whether your story is one of God's faithfulness since you accepted Christ as a young child or a more recent saga of crisis and conversion, your teen needs to know how faith has worked in your life.

Or even how it *hasn't* worked.

Russell grew up as the son of a pioneer missionary in China. Russell's father was a godly man, but he wasn't given to talking much about his own spiritual struggles. As a result, Russell had a hard time relating to his dad. Even today, as a middle-aged man, Russell wishes he'd gotten a chance to know the human side of his father—a legend to whom he feels he'll never measure up.

Your teen needs to see the reality of God in your life, including how your relationship with Him has its ups and downs. It's okay, even beneficial, for your young person to know that you have questions and for the two of you to go to the Bible together for answers.

A great parent-teen session is for each of you to take turns tracing your spiritual pilgrimage on a sheet of paper in a game called "Mountaintops and Valleys." As you draw a mountaintop, representing a high point in your walk with Christ, or a valley, which represents a low point, you give a brief description of what happened and what you learned from it.

Telling your spiritual story isn't just a onetime event, either. Your teen needs to see how you walk with God daily. For example, do you try to have a quiet time? How does it work? What about it frustrates you? How do you pray about difficult things? What if God doesn't seem to answer? Do you ever get mad at God? Does He ever seem distant?

When your teen sees that your experience with God includes

doubts, euphoria, emptiness, fullness, satisfaction, grumpiness, failing, and forgiveness, she'll be more likely to understand that your experience has relevance to hers. It's tough to have a relationship with a legend, but all-too-human believers can make great parents—and spiritual mentors.

## Relationship Builder 8: Erasing Bitterness Daily

Garbage stinks. Nobody wants to leave it around the house and live with the stench. That's why we keep taking it out.

In the same way, the "garbage" that happens with your teen must be disposed of as soon as possible. Otherwise, your relationship will begin to take on an unpleasant odor.

The garbage is usually anger. It's caused by hurt feelings, misunderstandings, frustration, disagreements, and feeling unsafe. Unresolved anger—trash that isn't taken out—can distance you from your teen. The longer it's unresolved, the harder it is to restore the relationship. Perhaps that's why the Bible says, " 'In your anger do not sin': Do not let the sun go down while you are still angry, and do not give the devil a foothold" (Ephesians 4:26-27).

If you think your teen is angry with you, but you don't know why, ask him. Then take these steps:

1. Listen to understand, not to defend yourself.
2. Listen to discover how your actions made your teen feel.
3. Listen to fully hear your teen's point of view.
4. Allow your teen to be upset and to show it.
5. When you respond, do so gently, quietly, and slowly.
6. If you were wrong, admit it.

If your teen doesn't want to open up, give her time and space to work through her emotions alone while allowing her opportunities to speak with you. An exchange of letters at this point might be helpful.

Even if your teen refuses to deal with a problem promptly, you can erase your own part of the bitterness daily. The following may help:

■ physical activity—running, brisk walking, vacuuming, weightlifting

- prayer—going to God with your anger
- writing your feelings in a journal
- putting the problem in perspective by asking yourself how angry a response the incident really deserves

If, after taking these steps, you decide that your teen must be disciplined for something he said or did, calculate the consequences carefully. Let go of the anger before carrying out your disciplinary plan.

Taking out the garbage lets you start fresh the next day. When it comes to relationships, all of us could use a second chance.

## Relationship Busters

Every job has its list of don'ts. Forging a bond with your teen is no exception.

■ ■ ■

## *Risky Business: Sharing the Struggle*

During a difficult time in my life as a Christian, I wrote a note to my daughter about my struggles and questions. This would, on the surface, seem stupid since my daughter was seriously questioning her own faith. Wouldn't it be smarter to keep silent on those issues? Might I blow her fragile faith right out of the water?

Don't ask me why I sent her a three-page journal of my struggle, but I did. Her note in response took me by surprise:

I am so honored that you would share something like this with me. It amazes me that we can have this kind of relationship where you feel okay in sharing something so personal. . . . Here I am, in the throes of questioning all the areas of my faith, and hearing your struggles with yours only makes me feel stronger in mine. . . . I've often told people that if I could model my faith after anyone, it would be you. Thank you for that.

—L. H. J.

### Relationship Buster 1: Attacking Your Teen

Never attack your teen verbally or physically. Instead of condemnation, she needs guidance to move from a bad choice to a better one.

Never discipline your teen in front of his peers. His humiliation will likely lead him to return the "favor" with belligerence. If an issue needs to be dealt with immediately, take him to another room and speak quietly there.

### Relationship Buster 2: Giving Up Your Parental Role

Having a good relationship with your teen doesn't mean you stop being a parent. If you've established a boundary and your teen deliberately crosses it, the boundary must be enforced. Rules without love lead to rebellion, but so also does love without rules.

As a parent, avoid responding to your adolescent's behavior in an adolescent way. Don't trade insults. Don't chase a sullen, stomping son and deliver a tirade to his retreating back. It's not

■ ■ ■

## *Typical Teen?*
## *There's No Such Thing*

One day when my daughter was a senior in high school, we were in the grocery store. We ran into an adult friend who asked what her plans were. My daughter expressed excitement about going to Wisconsin for college, even though she'd never been there and knew no one who lived there.

The friend said, "You'll miss your family so much."

"No, I won't," my daughter replied. "I'm excited to be on my own."

The friend snickered and said, "Oh, you'll change your mind pretty quickly. Teenagers always do."

I could almost see steam curling from my adventurous daughter's ears. "Not me!" she declared. "I'm not like other teenagers."

I was angry to see her so easily dismissed, to have her feelings and decisions pooh-poohed as though she were foolish.

It turned out that my daughter was right. She wasn't like other teenagers (who also aren't like one another). She did *not* miss her home, family, and friends terribly as the adult friend had predicted. She thrived in her new environment.

—Lissa Johnson

worth ruining a relationship just so you can have the last word. Disengage from the battle, if necessary, and tell your teen that you'll discuss the subject later.

Your teen needs you to be a parent. On the other hand, being a parent doesn't mean you have to be unlikable. Based on his years in youth work as well as parenting, Joe White says, "When you like someone, you obey him because you *want* to. Likable parents don't scold; they speak with grace. They don't lecture; they serve. Likable parents don't act bitter; they discipline and forgive. They don't give kids a list when they come home from school; they give them hugs."

**Relationship Buster 3: Treating Your Teen as a "Typical Adolescent"**
"Teenagers are all alike."

Do people lump all adults together in that fashion? Of course not. It's a laughable idea:

"Oh, you adults are all alike. All you ever do is buy and sell stocks."

"All adults are obsessed with their jobs."

"All adults are on a diet."

"All" teenagers aren't rude, wild about sports, growing like weeds, quiet, loud, in love with rock stars, or wearing a particular brand of jeans. Each teen is unique and needs to be treated that way.

Do you relate to your teen as an individual? Do you allow her to be shy or prod her to be the life of the party? Do you suspect him of lying because "all" kids lie? Do you keep her uniqueness in mind when you discipline, when you plan a vacation, and when you choose a church?

> *Each teen is unique and needs to be treated that way.*

We can't build relationships with "types," only with people. Give your teen a chance to reveal who he is and you can enjoy a relationship that's unique and genuine.

**Relationship Buster 4: Resisting Outside Help**
If your relationship is struggling, you'll find help in this book. But if the problems persist, don't be afraid to seek assistance from your pastor or a counselor.

Many parents fear revealing family problems to "outsiders" or are ashamed to admit their "failure." The truth is that a trained counselor can often see the roots of a problem more clearly and quickly than most family members could and so can provide invaluable help. If you do see a counselor, resolve to work on yourself and your relationship with your teen, whatever it takes.

## The Bottom Line

A poll of 5,000 adults found that, when they were teenagers, they most appreciated these five things from their parents: (1) love and affection, (2) encouragement, (3) independence, (4) trust, and (5) security.[4]

To give your teen these gifts, you need relationship. As Joe White says, "With no relationship, none of this is going to happen. With a great relationship, *all* of this is going to happen."

## Teens' Advice to Parents About Nurturing Spiritual Growth, Part 3

■ "Talk with your kids openly about your faith, especially if you are strong in your faith. Allow your kids to see you dive into the Bible together and alone."

■ "Set boundaries, speak the truth in love, and take your teens' hands even though they are trying to slip away. They still want to be guided."

■ "Be active in your children's development. Ask them what they are learning. Take a moment to teach an object lesson. Have family devotions on a regular basis. Be real with them."

■ "Pay attention to what your teens are saying to you. It may not seem important now, but they will be more likely to come to you with the important issues later if they know you care."

■ "Parents need to realize the value of being an example to their children. They also need to communicate with them about their walk with the Lord. Depending on the relationship, parents should offer to help their children grow (for example, accountability, intentional activities to talk about spiritual growth)."

# CHAPTER 7

# Becoming Your Teen's Biggest Fan

It's near the end of the football game. The home team is behind by two points, thanks to a series of fumbles. It's third down and 16 yards to go. The home players' shoulders slump.

Suddenly a string of perky girls appears in front of the grandstand. The young ladies put their energy into motion, chanting, getting the crowd to shout with them: "Our stupid team does its best to make us scream! Losers! Losers!"

No, wait. That's not how it happens.

Instead, the cheerleaders are there to encourage the team no matter how far behind it is, no matter what mistakes it has made. Even if the game is lost, the cheerleaders will be back next week, cheering the team on as though the last defeat had never occurred.

Spiritual growth is a little like football. Your teen may gain yardage one week, only to lose it the next. There will be plenty of fumbles. Through it all, your adolescent needs someone to keep calling from the sidelines, "You can do it!"

> It's hard to cheer your teen on if you're absent when he takes the field.

You are that someone. As a parent, you've been elected head cheerleader.

**RELATIONSHIP**

That may not seem to come naturally, at least not at first. Most parents find it easy to be members of their babies' and toddlers' fan clubs, but many lose their enthusiasm by the time their children reach the teen years. Yet kids, especially those in today's world, never outgrow the need for regular shots of praise that send them into the day with hope.

As a parent who wants to be an effective mentor, you need to equip yourself with big, colorful pom-poms every day. Whether or not you shook any pom-poms in high school, you can excel as a cheerleader now. Here are six ways to get started.

## Cheer 1: Don't Miss the Game!

It's hard to cheer your teen on if you're absent when he takes the field. Are you around when your son competes in the speech tournament or runs the cross-country race? Are you there when your daughter sings in church or leaves for the youth group retreat?

Finding time to "be there" may not be simple in a world of pagers and personal digital assistants. But cheers for a victory you didn't witness can ring hollow. To make things easier on yourself, regularly ask your teen for his schedule, and immediately put key events on your calendar. Whenever possible, make sure that non-family events—even good, spiritual things like a Bible study—take second place to these.

If you find your teen is involved in so many events that you can't begin to attend them all, consider withdrawing her from one or more activities. Too many events are a good sign that your teen is overcommitted.

When you face multiple events at the same time with more than one child, send Mom to one and Dad to the other. Next time, alternate. If you're a single parent, ask a close relative or friend to attend the other child's activity. Be sure to switch for the next event.

After the activity, take time to tell your teen how proud you are of him. If there's a tangible memento of the event (a program from a school play, a trophy, a photo, a certificate), display it on the refrigerator, mantel, or other prominent place in the house.

## Cheer 2: Encourage Their Socks Off!

First period: geometry. Sam's test is returned with a large, red D at the top. He studied, but he just doesn't get this stuff about radius and circumference.

Second period: physical education. The other guys razz Sam for missing an easy fly ball that would have been the winning out for their team.

Third period: chemistry. Sam's lab partner spills a chemical, and the teacher yells at them both.

Lunchtime: The girl Sam's had his eye on looks at him, smiles, then whispers to her friends, who all giggle. He's beginning to think she likes him; then one of the friends comes up to him. "You have something green stuck to your face," she says and bursts out laughing.

### The Encouraging Word: Biblically Boosting Your Teen

Let your teen know God loves him. The Bible is full of encouraging passages. Try writing some of them on slips of paper and placing them on your child's pillow once a week. Or tape them on a mirror your teen uses.

Here are a few encouraging verses to get you started:

- Psalm 52:8 (God's unfailing love)
- Psalm 91:14-16 (God is with us in trouble)
- Psalm 117:2 (Great is God's love toward us)
- Isaiah 43:1-3 (Fear not)
- Isaiah 43:18-19 (Forget the former things; God is doing a new thing)
- Jeremiah 29:11-14 (God has a plan)
- Jeremiah 31:3 (God's love is everlasting)
- Jeremiah 33:3 (Call and God will answer)
- Lamentations 3:22-23 (Great is God's faithfulness)
- Habakkuk 1:5 (God is doing something amazing)
- Romans 5:8 (God demonstrates His love toward us)
- Romans 8:38-39 (Nothing can separate us from the love of God)
- Ephesians 3:17-18 (Christ's love is wide, long, high, and deep)
- 1 John 3:1 (We are children of God)

Fourth period: study hall. This is the only "class" that seems to move pretty smoothly.

Fifth period: art. Sam has been working for three weeks on a plaster sculpture of a dolphin. He's about to put on the finishing touches when the teacher walks past and says, "Interesting. I've never seen a bird like that before."

Sixth period: English. It starts out okay, but then Sam realizes he has picked up the wrong book from his locker.

Seventh period: history. When the teacher asks Sam where Napoleon was defeated, all he can think of is Neapolitan ice cream.

After school, Sam walks home, feeling the weight of the day on his shoulders. He opens the back door and drops his backpack onto the kitchen table.

"Sam! Take your backpack all the way to your room," his mother chides. "You know I don't like my kitchen messed up when I'm trying to get ready for dinner."

## Cheers!
## 25 Phrases That Communicate Enthusiasm

1. You are so thoughtful!
2. This is a tremendous improvement.
3. Good for you!
4. You are such a joy to us!
5. I never did that well when I was your age.
6. You handled that beautifully.
7. That's incredible!
8. You're really special to me—and getting more special every day!
9. I really enjoy being with you.
10. What a super effort!
11. The guy (girl) who marries you will be so lucky.
12. Your mom and I are so grateful to be your parents.
13. I really enjoy your smile.
14. That's fabulous!
15. There you go. That's it!
16. You're so helpful! Thank you.
17. You're going to make it.
18. I wish I could have done it that well.
19. I'm impressed!
20. I know you worked very hard on that. Wonderful job!
21. I love to hear your laugh.
22. I really like that.
23. I believe in you.
24. Excellent! That's the way to do it.
25. I love you.[1]

Without a word, Sam picks up the pack and starts to move through the kitchen.

"Oh, and Sam," his mother calls after him, "don't forget to take out the trash and vacuum the living room."

"I won't," Sam says sullenly.

"Don't talk to me like that."

Sam takes his pack into his room and drops it onto his bed. His mother appears in the doorway. "So, how was school?" she asks.

Sam shrugs.

"I don't know why you never talk to me," Mom says and returns to the kitchen.

Chances are that your teen has a lot of days like Sam's. After getting his ego ripped apart or slowly eroded away, he needs to know that he can come home and find encouragement. He needs to know that in spite of peer cruelty and embarrassing goofs, he *is* special. He's a welcomed member of the family.

What if Sam came home to the following?

Opening the back door, he drops his backpack onto the kitchen table.

"Hey, sweetie!" Mom says. "I'm so glad you're home. I missed you." Walking over to Sam, she can tell by his demeanor that he needs a hug but will probably resist one. So she ruffles his hair and touches him briefly on the shoulder. "Need anything to eat?"

Sam shrugs.

Mom grabs his favorite snack from the refrigerator—a jar of peanut butter and an apple. She puts it in front of him, along with a knife and cutting board, then sits at the table. "How'd you do on that geometry test?"

"Terrible, Mom," Sam blurts out. "I studied so hard, and I just didn't get it."

"I know. Geometry was really hard for me, too. What do you think we could do that would help? We could call Sue, if you like. She used to teach math. Or we could see if Dad remembers his geometry better than I do."

"Mr. Nagy said we could go in after school for help."

"Is that what you want to do?"

"I guess."

RELATIONSHIP

"You *can* learn this, Sam. It might be a little harder for you, like it was for me. But your father and I will do whatever we can to help you through this."

After the talk and snack, if Sam forgets the backpack on the table, Mom gently asks him to take it with him. Before the evening is over, other pieces of Sam's day have tumbled out in conversation. By starting with encouragement, Mom has counteracted seven periods of discouragement and kept the lines of communication open.

Encouraging your teen can happen in a variety of ways:

1. *Speak your encouragement.* This is especially effective when you praise your teen to someone else within your teen's hearing. Tell others what you like about your child—not just good grades or tennis skills but also character traits like integrity and faithfulness. Avoid gushing or exaggerating; be truthful and your teen will be more likely to believe you when you tell her other positive things about herself.

2. *Write your encouragement.* Tuck a note into a lunch sack or binder. Sneak a greeting card into a backpack. The message can be as short as "I'm proud of you," "Have a good day—I'm praying for you," or "I love you like crazy." When your teen goes to camp or on a mission trip, write letters whenever possible. Let him know he's always on your mind.

Your adolescent also needs to know she's special to

---

## Cheer Up:
## Five More Ways to Encourage Your Teen

1. Lovingly wipe a tear from a sad face.
2. Have a personal evening Bible study with him.
3. Go to the game even when she is sitting on the bench.
4. Help clean up the mess as you affirm the embarrassed teen who made it.
5. Throw a special birthday party with customized cake and decorations that reflect his uniqueness.[2]

others who aren't "obligated" to love her. If you have a friend who knows your teen well, ask that person to also write an occasional encouraging note to your teen.

3. *Touch your encouragement.* When your teen is happy, give him a hug. When he's had a bad day, a hug, pat, or touch will reinforce the verbal encouragement. See the "Affection" section of chapter six for more tips on this subject.

4. *Look your encouragement.* In some homes, eye contact is made only when a child is being reprimanded or given instructions. But it's also an important component of encouragement. If your words say "Good job" but your eyes say "Couldn't you do better than that?" your teen won't hear the verbal cheering. You can also use eye contact to encourage your teen when you can't talk or touch—when you're across the room from each other, for example.

## Cheer 3: Catch Them Doing Good!

One mother says, "I adored the son God gave me. He was so sweet, darling, and good-tempered—until he turned three. By the time he was four, I wondered what in the world I'd ever seen in him. My mother gave me a blank book with the instructions that every day I must record four wonderful things about my son. It didn't take long for me to again see the good in him."

Sometimes it takes extra effort to notice a teenager's plus side, too. But it's vital to watch our kids in order to catch them doing something good or using their God-given gifts and talents—and to let them know when that happens. For example:

> *It's vital to watch our kids in order to catch them doing something good or using their God-given gifts and talents.*

- "I noticed that you showed mercy to your sister when you complimented her new haircut instead of making a joke about it."

RELATIONSHIP

- "I liked the way you brought Dad the sports section of the paper this morning."
- "Thanks for feeding the dog today. I appreciate it when you use your gift of service to help me."
- "I saw you pick up the little boy down the street when he fell off his scooter. I can tell you care about people."

Being observant in this way does two things. First, it helps your teen see that the small, good deeds he does are valuable and worthy of recognition and praise—and this makes their repetition more likely. Second, it shows that you're paying attention and that you care.

Imagine 15-year-old Kerri, who always has to be reminded to do her chore of cleaning the family bathroom. Then, one Saturday, she decides to do it on her own. Instead of getting the praise she hopes for, she hears her father say, "Why should I give you a medal for something you were supposed to be doing all along?"

Given a response like that, Kerri may not remember to clean the bathroom on her own again anytime soon. But imagine Dad saying, "I noticed that you remembered to clean the bathroom. I appreciate it very much. It looks nice. You've done a good job." With words like that, she's likely to clean the bathroom again—without being asked.

## Cheer 4: Point Out the Positives!

Have you noticed that it takes far more to fill our emotional bank accounts than it does to deplete them? In only a moment, a teen's fragile self-confidence can be ripped apart—even by a parent. Here are some common ways in which parents do this:

- finding humor in making cutting remarks to a teen, or using such remarks when correcting or disciplining
- laughing at a teen's failures
- comparing their own strengths with a teen's weaknesses
- punishing too harshly
- making behavioral demands of a teen that are inconsistent with their own example

- refusing to say, "I'm sorry"
- being too proud to submit to and serve each other or their kids
- offering encouragement *only* for such externals as looks, clothing, and athletic skills[3]

Avoiding these "self-image bombs" is a step in the right direction, but the wise cheerleader goes further. If you really want to build your teen's self-concept, try making five positive comments for every negative remark you make. A positive comment might be a compliment or a word of thanks or praise or appreciation.

Why should you try this? Because researchers have found that husbands and wives who follow this formula have a 94 percent chance of marital happiness. Applied to parent-teen relationships, the principle builds self-respect and mutual admiration that can fortify an adult and adolescent during the toughest times.

To see how you're doing at this, keep an actual count for a week of both positive and negative comments you make to your teen. You're likely to be surprised, discovering that your normal ratio is closer to the reverse of the ideal. And changing that for the better,

■ ■ ■

## Condemnation: The Opposite of Cheerleading

The other day in a store, I overheard a conversation between a mother and her young daughter. The little girl, who seemed well behaved and sweet, desperately wanted to own a pair of toy dress-up, high-heeled shoes. She politely asked her mother if she could buy them.

The mother said, "I'll think about it—*if* you're good."

The little girl said in a small, plaintive voice, "I'm good."

The mother snapped back, "When? When you're asleep? Because it certainly ends the minute you wake up!"

How will this child ever believe she can do something right? And if she can't, why bother trying?

Chances are, this girl will fulfill her mother's beliefs about her. That's what happens when parents condemn instead of cheering.

—Lissa Johnson

**RELATIONSHIP**

noticing and commenting on positive things more than negatives, may take a concentrated, persistent effort.

Whatever it takes, however, keep at it. The effort will be worthwhile. This one change in your behavior toward your teen is almost guaranteed to improve your relationship dramatically.

If you must say something negative to your teen, do so with respect, kindness, and concern. Try the "sandwich" approach, preceding and following criticism with words of love and affirmation. This, along with the five-to-one ratio of positive comments to negative, can cement a good relationship or revitalize one that has been struggling. Encourage other family members to use the "sandwich" approach as well, banning ridicule for any reason.

### Cheer 5: Let Your Teen Be an Expert!

Hopefully, by the time your child is a teenager, you've helped him to identify one or more things that he can excel at and that aid him in gaining a positive sense of identity. Letting him use those talents to benefit the family is a concrete way to cheer him on. Is your son an eagle-eyed map reader? Make him the navigator on

## Teens' "Ways in Which a Parent Was Spiritually Influential," Part 3

- "Mom was always there for me. She was always willing to talk when I had problems or questions about God or anything else."
- "My parents always encouraged me to be active in my youth group as well as Bible studies, Young Life, etc."
- "Just talking with my mom in the afternoon about what went on in my day or was going on in my spiritual life."
- "Having a daily 'conference' with my dad really gave me guidance and accountability in my life. Being able to share with him what God was saying to me that day and hearing his wisdom and advice shaped my Christian walk and grounded it in Christ."
- "At any time, I could and still do sit down with either of my parents and talk with them about spirituality."

your next vacation. Is your daughter a math whiz? Ask her for help with your taxes.

Author Al Janssen tells how this approach has worked with his son:

> One Saturday morning, I logged on to my computer. Instead of responding, it froze. Nothing I tried got it working. Finally I pushed the power button and shut down the machine.
>
> A few minutes later I tried to reboot, but the screen froze again. I was locked out.
>
> I called in my 17-year-old son, Joshua. He posed like a doctor examining X-rays, and I knew the news would not be good. I headed upstairs to try to escape the possibility that I'd killed this machine. A few minutes later, Joshua reported his diagnosis. "The hard drive memory is full," he said. The culprit: a virus that had entered through an E-mail attachment.
>
> "Can you fix it?" I asked.
>
> He'd have to reformat the hard drive, he said—but promised to back up my precious files first. He went to work.
>
> It was a six-hour procedure. Every hour or so, Josh came upstairs to give me an update. The surgery was going well. "I was able to save all the files you needed," he said, handing me a disk.
>
> Just before dinner, Josh came upstairs a final time to tell me the patient was recovering nicely. He led me down to see the results. The computer looked completely normal. "I've divided the hard drive into two sectors—so hopefully if one crashes again, we won't lose it all." I nodded my head appreciatively.
>
> This time when I logged on, it worked perfectly. All our files had been restored. Nothing was missing.
>
> I find that when I interrupt my son's activities for computer help, I am met with a huge grin and an eager attitude. I appreciate the fact that my son knows something I don't. (It also saves me a lot of money in computer

consultation bills!) He obviously feels good about being an expert, and that his parents are the students.

We wonder what we'll do when he leaves home, though. How can we possibly survive without his tech support?

## Cheer 6: Seek Your Teen's Input!

Just as teens have expertise, so they also often possess insights that could be helpful when making family decisions. Including them in that process lets them know they're needed and wanted, and it gives them a chance to develop their own powers of decision making.

One couple asked their son, an electronics enthusiast, to help them decide which cordless phone to buy. Here are other examples of choices on which you might consult your teen:

- which church to attend
- where to go on vacation
- which restaurant to eat in
- how to arrange living space when a grandparent comes to live with you
- what kinds of devotions would work best in your family
- how to decorate your home
- whether to repair or replace an old appliance
- what kind of family car to buy
- what to do with a tax refund
- whether you or your spouse should accept a job offer, especially if it would require a family move

## Is Cheerleading for Everyone?

Cheering your teen on is always a challenge. For some parents, however, the challenge may seem insurmountable.

This is especially true of single parents, who often desperately need cheerleaders themselves. Yet many solo parents have discovered that cheerleading is possible—and rewarding—even when there's no squad to back them up. Longtime youth mentor Joe White tells what happened to a good friend of his:

> One of my close friends, Keith, had an alcoholic father who left home early in the boy's life. But Keith had a star for a mom, and he's turned out to be one of the finest Christian men I know.
>
> A talented athlete, Keith recently told me about the greatest event in his sports career. It was Dad's Night at his high school, in his senior year. All the fathers were lined up on the sidelines with their sons' numbers fastened to their shirts. Keith felt alone and depressed as the special observance got underway.
>
> Then suddenly he noticed someone standing in the line wearing his number. His heart skipped a beat: *Has Dad come home?*
>
> Looking closer, Keith felt a tear enter his eye. There stood his mom, stately as any dad in the line, her hair tucked under her work hat, jeans pressed neatly—and number 24 displayed proudly on the back of her shirt.

Cheerleading is more difficult for a single parent. But it's well worth the effort. One single mom offers the following ideas for making it work:

- Occasionally bring a friend along when you attend your teen's events, to help ease the loneliness and the feeling of awkwardness among the married parents.
- Ask friends and fellow church members to observe your teen's strengths and remind you of them.
- Don't forget God's role. Scripture says God will be "a father to the fatherless" (Psalm 68:5). It also declares, "Your Maker is your husband—the LORD Almighty is his name" (Isaiah 54:5). Remember that God cares and wants to help be a parent with you. To read more about this, see the sidebar "All By Yourself?" in chapter five.

### Cheerleading: The Results

What happens when parents neglect their cheerleading function? Just ask Joe White, who has received notes like the following from teens whose parents failed to cheer them on:

> If I ever have a question, I'm scared to ask it at home. I hate being yelled at. Now, if you were in my shoes, wouldn't you hate yourself too? Well, I do. I hate life.
> —Amy

> You told me you were proud of me. Thanks for making my day. No one ever said that to me before. My dad used to tell me I would never amount to anything. It took a long time to get over that.
> —Andy

> My mom hurts me so bad. She says one of the reasons she doesn't like me is because I'm dumb. . . . My grades are six F's and one D. Maybe I am stupid like my mom tells me.
> —Sharon

## Teens' "Things I Wish My Parents Had Done Differently," Part 2

- "One-on-one dates would have been awesome."
- "I would have liked them to take me to a church with a strong youth group and a church where I could grow spiritually."
- "I wish Mom and Dad had emphasized family night or family devotions. We had devotions as a family for a time every morning, and family meetings where we would discuss rules, budgets, etc., but my brothers and I always hated them and thought they were corny."
- "I wish they had sat down with me and studied the Scriptures, showing me how Scripture fits into the tough issues I was dealing with . . . self-image, peer pressure, etc."
- "I would have loved for them to talk to me about issues, model a love for Christ, ask me about my life, and have family devotions or a special time at night together."

RELATIONSHIP

Contrast those stories of pain with that of a teen girl who approached Joe at a youth rally. As they talked, he could see that her faith was solid, her morals sound, her standards high. "What makes you different?" he asked. The next week, she wrote him her answer:

> I am proud to say I don't drink, smoke, etc., and that I am completely accepted by my peers. Whenever I am offered anything, I firmly reply "No," and they accept it. I've found that some of my friends feel insecure or that they won't be accepted if they don't go along. You really need to feel confident and sure about yourself so that you don't have to go along to be accepted. I credit all confidence I [have] now to my great parents. I don't know where I'd be without them building me up and telling me how much they love me, not for what I do but for what I am.
>
> Love, Maria
>
> P.S. Here's a quotation I read today: "Parents need to fill a child's bucket of self-esteem so high that the rest of the world can't poke enough holes in it to drain it dry."[4]

It's a rough world out there, especially for a teen with a desire to follow God. But pressing on toward the goal is a lot easier when you've got a cheering section. You can make sure your child hears and feels that priceless affirmation clearly and regularly.

RELATIONSHIP

# CHAPTER 8

# Learning to Be a Great Communicator

"Patrick, how was youth group tonight?"

"Okay, I guess."

"What did you do?"

"Nothing."

"What was it about?"

"Stuff."

"Did you get anything out of it?"

"No."

"Why not?"

Shrug.

"Your sister always got something out of the small groups."

Grunt.

"Don't you?"

"Sometimes."

"What's something you've gotten out of the small groups?"

"It's personal."

"If you won't tell me, maybe I should ask your small-group leader."

Hard glare.

"Don't give me that look or you'll be grounded."

"Fine."

Ah, the joys of spiritual mentoring.

Communicating is crucial to giving spiritual guidance, but trying to communicate with teenagers can be a good way to jump-start a headache. Many parents are baffled by one-word responses from a son or daughter who routinely spends three hours a day on the phone with friends.

To make matters worse, real communication involves far more than just talking *at* someone. It's even more than listening to someone convey information. Communication is part of the relationship-building process.

> *Every teen is unique; what might work for one won't work for another.*

Perhaps that's why the *American Heritage Collegiate Dictionary* defines communication this way: "To be connected, one with another."

There's no magic pill for communicating with adolescents. Every teen is unique; what might work for one won't work for another. Trying the following suggestions won't guarantee that a quiet, withdrawn teen will suddenly become talkative and eager to share. But they are a good place to begin.

## How to Start a Conversation with Your Teen

When you want to get your teen talking, ask questions.

Starting a conversation with an adolescent is often like trying to get bread to rise in the cold. It's not going to happen unless you add a bit of yeast and warmth—and wait patiently. Ask your teen some well-thought-out questions (yeast), position yourself to listen attentively (warmth), and often you'll get a response.

If your teen seems to have something on his mind, ask, "Do you want to talk about it?" This leaves the door open for him to decide whether or not to open up. A "no" needs to be respected. You can ask the question again later.

Plan your icebreaker questions ahead of time. If you don't, you're liable to talk only about things that interest you, which probably will cause your teen to listen to you for about five minutes with a glazed look in her eyes.

Here are some conversation starters worth trying:

- "How was your day?"
- "How'd the test go?"

- "What was the best thing that happened to you today?"
- "What's going well?"
- "What's not going well?"
- "What's coming up in your schedule?"
- "Is there anything you need my help with?"

In his work with teenagers, Joe White gets them to open up by asking three questions:

1. "What's wrong?" (Or "What do you want?")

2. "How are you feeling?"

3. "What are you going to do about it?" (Or "What are you doing about it?")

Depending on the answer, he repeats the question or goes on to the next. Sometimes he rephrases the questions and asks them again. He finds that this method gets teens to talk things out, often discovering answers to their struggles on their own.

The following, abridged from Joe's book *What Kids Wish Their Parents Knew About Parenting*, is an example of one of these conversations. Talking with a girl who'd had an abortion, Joe starts the conversation:

"What's wrong?"

"I'm hurting really bad."

"How do you feel?"

"Terrible."

"What are you doing?"

"Talking to you."

"What's wrong?"

"I'm just so awful."

"How do you feel?"

"Sad."

"What's the sadness?"

"I don't know. Things are so bad, I cry every day."

"What's wrong?"

"I killed my baby. I had an abortion last month."

"What do you want?"

"I want to like myself."

"What's wrong?"

"I'm not being me. I've turned into someone I hate."

"Who do you really want to be?"

"I want to be the girl God wants me to be."

"What do you need to do to get what you want?"

"I need to give my life to Christ. I need to get forgiven."[1]

## When, Where, and How to Talk

One key to successful communication with your teen is knowing the best times, places, and ways in which to talk with him. Is your child more relaxed and open in the morning or in the evening? That may be the time to talk about feelings.

When does she tend to be most alert? That may be the time to discuss facts, worldviews, and rules.

## Communicating About Sensitive Subjects

How can you talk with your teen about difficult topics like sin, proof of God's existence, sexuality, death, and divorce? Here are some general tips for approaching big subjects:

1. Before tackling tough topics, it's best to establish rapport by discussing easier ones. If you discuss only difficult subjects with your teen, he'll run every time he sees you coming. If your discussions about mundane items are casual, non-threatening, and respectful, it will be easier to discuss more sensitive issues.
2. Shifting into lecture gear shuts off communication quickly. Try to stay in conversational mode. Remember that a mentor comes alongside rather than making pronouncements from above.
3. Avoid condescension or oversimplification. Your teenager wishes to be treated as an adult and will respond better if you discuss issues on that basis.
4. Keep lesser issues in perspective. If you nag a teen too much about less serious matters, she will be used to tuning you out when the time comes to discuss more weighty topics.
5. Don't bite off more than the two of you can chew. When the subject is a big one, it's usually wiser to use many small, teachable moments rather than a couple of marathon sessions. A resource like the book *Letters from a Skeptic*, by Gregory and Edward Boyd (Chariot Victor Publishing, 1994), can also help to stimulate and focus productive conversations.

Is your teen rushed during certain times of the day or week? Avoid starting complex conversations at those moments.

Taking your teen's mood into account is also critical in deciding whether to address a topic now or later. If he's in a funk, it may be best to postpone conversation. If your teen tends to have month-long funks, however, you may need to warn him in advance that a conversation on a particular topic is pending. Asking him to set the time for the chat within the next five days might help him to feel more prepared and cooperative.

As for the best place to talk, think about the spots in which you feel most comfortable chatting. Jodie recalls the house across the street, where she often went to talk with a friend. During their visits, the two of them would talk as they folded laundry or did the dishes. When they tried to talk in the living room at Jodie's house, however, things felt too formal. Sitting on the sofa felt like entertaining company, not embracing a confidante.

So it is with your teen. Different kinds of discussions should happen in different places. Sitting on your teen's bed may be the best spot for sharing emotions or bringing up prayer requests. The living room might feel too open for a private, heartfelt conversation, but it could be the right place to review what was discussed at the youth retreat.

> *If you're having a hard time getting your teen to talk, changing locations can help.*

The kitchen could be a great venue for casual chatting about the school day or memorizing a Bible verse together. Restaurants are also popular places to talk, especially if your past conversations in such places have been casual and safe.

If you're having a hard time getting your teen to talk, changing locations can help. Go shopping or to a favorite restaurant together, or take a drive or hike. Or stay at home and try an activity that allows you to talk but doesn't require that you look at each other constantly, like playing table tennis, air hockey, or chess, helping him develop a skill or hobby, or putting together a puzzle.

And how should you talk? Tone of voice can be a conversation booster or a conversation breaker. Do you tend to whine, screech, growl, or mumble? If you dare, record yourself talking and analyze the result. Or ask your spouse or a friend to review your typical manner of speech and its possible effects on your teen.

Body language is also important. Next time you're talking with your teen, try keeping the following in mind:

- Leaning forward, making positive eye contact, and nodding occasionally show that you're eager to hear what your teen has to say. Slumping in your chair, folding your arms across your chest, and staring to one side of the speaker show the opposite.
- Looking at the floor as you talk indicates that you're probably embarrassed, nervous, or afraid.
- Wild, broad gestures can express excitement or agitation; small gestures or clutching your hands in your lap can send the message that you're withdrawing due to shyness, fear, or sadness.
- Watch your teen's body language. Does it match her words? If not, you may need to ask some gentle questions. Do his posture and gestures hint at apprehension? If so, you may need to allow more time for him to open up.

## Eight Things Your Teen Wants from Communication

When your teen talks with you, chances are that he or she has a wish list—consciously or not. Here are eight things kids generally want from a conversation with a parent.

*1. To get your full attention.* Teens want to know that their parents love them, and attention is one of their favorite units of measure. The book *How to Get Your Teenager to Talk to You* tells how youth speaker Josh McDowell had 42 personal appointments with students at an evangelical church's week-long conference. He asked each one, "Can you talk with your father?" Only one said yes. The most common question he got from these students was this: "Josh, what can I do about my dad? He never talks to me; he never takes me anywhere; he never does anything with me."[2]

*2. To be listened to, from beginning to end, without interruption.* Luis is a father with a habit of interrupting. He can't understand why his daughter Carmen won't talk to him anymore. He doesn't realize he tends to jump in after hearing a few facts from Carmen about a situation. He never waits to hear the most important part of what Carmen wants to reveal—her feelings.

Luis needs to listen to the whole story. He can ask a question or two to clarify something Carmen has said. And when Carmen finishes saying something, he would do well to repeat it back to her in his own words so they both know that she was heard and understood. But he must resist the temptation to break into the middle of her statement with a lecture on what to do or what should have been done.

*3. For you to care about what he or she says.* The splinter in the finger, the nasty look he got from a former friend in the cafeteria, the agony of tripping in the 50-yard dash, the beloved character who was killed off in the season finale of her favorite TV series—they all matter to your teenager. Do they matter to you?

If someone shrugs at the things that are important to us, we don't talk to that person about important things anymore. We can't afford to treat lightly the problems that our kids consider serious. Communication is endangered when we laugh at, belittle, or minimize their experiences and feelings.

To make sure your teen knows you care about his concerns, try matching emotion for emotion. If your teen is describing an incident, opinion, or feeling with sadness, let your face mirror that sadness; talk softly. If she is speaking with great enthusiasm, lean forward and reply with excitement. If he's angry, express understanding of that anger even as you respond as a loving, guiding adult.

> *To make sure your teen knows you care about his concerns, try matching emotion for emotion.*

To show further that you care, follow up on your conversation. Ask later whether a problem was resolved. How did the teacher react to your son's request for a deadline extension? Is that former friend still refusing to speak to your daughter?

*4. For his or her secrets to be kept.* All of us need a place to be open and honest, a place to reveal intimate details and emotions that no one else will hear. Your teen wants to know that what he shares with you will be safe with you. If you bring up the information later in a list of grievances, he'll avoid candor in the future. If she cries in front of you and hears about it later from a friend of hers or yours, she'll keep a lid on her emotions in your presence.

There may be situations in which sharing information with authorities, preferably with your teen's permission, is necessary to protect someone from physical harm. But in general, if your teen tells you something in confidence, keep it that way. Say (and mean it), "Son, I give you my word that I will hold this conversation in strictest confidence."

5. *To express his or her feelings.* Our God-given emotions are meant to be expressed in healthy ways. As Charles Stanley wrote in *How to Keep Your Kids on Your Team*, "Parents, please do not restrict your kids from expressing their feelings. When you do, you are only cheating yourself. By cutting short their expressions of frustration and even anger, you are cutting short your relationship with them."[3]

Be sympathetic, then, and lend a caring ear. When your teen is hurting and wants to talk about it, respond with things like "How did your friend's words make you feel?" or "I'll bet it really hurt

■ ■ ■

## *Benefits of Blowups: Looking Beyond Emotional Outbursts*

For a variety of reasons, including hormonal ones, emotions are volatile during adolescence. Your teen may suddenly feel angry and not know why. You may get caught in the crossfire.

When your teen explodes emotionally, try to read the feelings as an indicator of an inner problem rather than simply reacting to the outburst. Ask gentle questions without attacking, judging, or belittling. Fitting the puzzle pieces together will take time and patience.

If the problem is more complicated or frightening than you can handle, find a good counselor who supports Christian values. Be sure to choose someone with whom both you and your teen are comfortable.

to hear your friend say those uncomplimentary things about you." Let your child know that you share her pain.

This isn't always easy. When a daughter is sobbing over something that seems foolish to you, it's difficult not to say, "Just wait until you grow up—then this won't seem like anything." And when a teen wants to express feelings about *your* errors or decisions, it takes strength to truly listen without retaliating.

*6. To be asked his or her opinion.* One of the many tasks of adolescence is to form personal opinions, values, and beliefs. It's important to encourage your teen to voice these views, even if they change daily. As Charles Stanley wrote in *How to Keep Your Kids on Your Team*, "Nothing builds communication barriers faster than taking away a child's right to express an opinion at home."[4]

This doesn't give a teen the right to express an opinion rudely, of course. When that happens, you can take the opportunity to show how to air a view without denigrating the views of others. This is done by example as well as through gentle verbal direction.

*7. To hear about your own failures.* Like it or not, your kids notice when you mess up. If you're honest about your current and past

■ ■ ■

## *True Confessions: Telling Your Teen About Your Past*

My friend's 15-year-old son asked me if I had done drugs as a teen. I told him that I had.

He said, "Well, drugs must not be too bad, because you turned out okay."

I responded that it is true that I am one of the lucky ones. I turned my life around, and now I have a good job, a beautiful home, and a nice car. I also told him that I wasted the best years of my life destroying precious brain cells and often wonder how much further I might have gone in life if I had not taken drugs. I looked him in the eye and said, "It's not worth the risk to see if you, too, can be as lucky as I was. It was only by the grace of God that I survived."

—Diane Bedell

RELATIONSHIP

**RELATIONSHIP**

failures and how you've worked through them, your teen may feel more free to tell you about his own defeats.

But what about embarrassing, long-ago choices that you regret? Should you reveal those? Beth Levine, in an article for *Reader's Digest,* suggested that if your teen asks whether you've indulged in premarital sex, drugs, alcohol, or illegal behavior, it helps to ask, "Why do you want to know?" If he's trying to find help for himself or a friend, it might be wise to tell your story. If the motivation seems more confrontational, a way for your teen to get out of consequences for his own actions, you need to keep the focus on your teen, not on your own past mistakes.

*8. To hear an understanding of his or her world.* Once upon a time, Chevrolet built a car called the Nova. The car had some nice features, but when Chevy tried to market it in Latin America, sales were dismal. Why? Finally someone told the company: In Spanish, *no va* means "doesn't go."

Understanding the culture is important when you seek to communicate with your teen, too. Today's adolescent lives in a different world from the one in which you grew up. If your teen is to trust you as a mentor, he needs to know that you have a clue about the way things are for him.

Want to find out how well you know your teen's world? Ask yourself questions like these:

- *What are my teen's favorite stores? What would she buy there if she could?*
- *How easy would it be for my teen to get illegal drugs?*
- *How many of his friends drink alcohol?*
- *What are my teen's three favorite songs? What are the lyrics?*
- *How many murders has my teen seen on movie and TV screens in the last year?*
- *Has my adolescent viewed pornography on the Internet?*
- *What video games are most popular right now, and what does my teen think of them?*
- *Does my teen worry about what she would do if someone opened fire at school?*
- *How much pressure does my young person feel to cheat on exams?*

- *Does my teen know anyone who's been sexually abused?*
- *Does my teen have more "virtual" friends in chat rooms than in the real world?*
- *If my teen defended the idea of absolute truth in front of his friends, would they laugh?*

To learn about your teen's world, you may need to step out of your comfort zone. Watch his movies, read her books (or graphic novels), listen to his music. One dad listens to every new CD that comes into the house, not necessarily to condemn it but to understand where his kids are. He and his kids discuss each song.

> *To learn about your teen's world, you may need to step out of your comfort zone.*

Without "spying," try to observe your teen with his friends. You might do this at school events or parties as well as in your own home. Let yours be the place where your teen's friends are always welcome and you'll better understand his world.

## Eight Things Your Teen Doesn't Want from Communication

Just as your adolescent has a wish list when it comes to communication, so she also has a "bad list." To avoid getting on that list, stay away from the following things no teenager wants.

1. *To be talked down to.* Here's how the authors of the *Focus on the Family Complete Book of Baby and Child Care* put it:

> Adolescents despise being treated like little kids. They hate being talked down to. They shut down if they try to express a heartfelt thought and no one listens or someone ridicules it. More often than not, their tempers flare and feelings are hurt because of the *way* something is said— disrespectfully—rather than because of the actual issue.
>
> In other words, they are just like adults.
>
> Even though your teenager may be light-years away from grown-up maturity and responsibilities, you will build strong bonds and smooth your path over the next

few years by talking to them as you would to another adult you respect.[5]

2. *To be pushed away.* When they've finally gathered enough strength to talk to you, teens want you to be available and to listen.

Gordon McLean, author of *Too Young to Die,* wrote that he once saw a report on the three things college students most remembered their fathers saying:

- "Don't bother me; I'm tired."
- "No, we can't afford it."
- "Go ask your mother."[6]

That doesn't mean, of course, that teens want you to force communication on them when they aren't ready. If you ask a question and get a grunt for a response, it might be best to try again later.

3. *For you to get in his or her face.* Jenny has severe mood swings when she suffers from premenstrual syndrome (PMS). Mom has encouraged Dad to be especially understanding at these times—to just acknowledge Jenny's presence with a kind hello and keep walking.

■ ■ ■

## *Providing Space:*
## *Knowing When to Back Off*

Discern when to pursue an issue and when to leave it alone until a later date. Growing up in a Christian home, I honestly would get tired of hearing about God as the solution to all things. My mom would let me cool down, but then she'd find an article to cut out for me to read and lay it on my desk.

My pride would not allow me to talk about the issue with her for a while, but her gentle nudgings in the right direction helped. Even when she knew I needed to sort through some things, she offered encouragement, not always with words.

—Angie I.

Instead, Dad marches up to her, gets almost nose to nose, and says, "What's wrong? Talk to me!"

Jenny doesn't want to talk. She wants to be left alone. Her relationship with Dad is becoming more and more strained because he won't respect her boundaries and her need for "alone time."

This desire for "space" also applies to sons who resist talking about emotions. Don't invade their territory or prod with endless questions. If their body language is crying out, "Give me space," grant them that courtesy.

4. *To be blasted with Bible verses or a sermon.* In *How to Get Your Teenager to Talk to You,* Josh McDowell stated, "A teenager said to me recently, 'You know, I try to share something with my parents and as soon as I open my mouth, they start quoting the Bible. I don't want the Bible quoted; I just want them to listen to me.' "[7]

A wise spiritual mentor knows when to cite Scripture and when to just listen. Sometimes it's more appropriate to write a pertinent verse on a card and slip it under a teen's pillow with an explanation like "I was thinking of what we were talking about earlier and thought this verse might be helpful." Avoid bringing it up again unless your teenager does.

5. *To be judged or ridiculed for what he or she says.* Kids whose verbal offerings are scorned won't take the risk again.

If your teen tells you about a teacher who has been "unfair," listen. Resist the urge to automatically side with the authority figure.

If your teen hurts because friends made fun of her new hair color (a color you advised against), listen. Resist the urge to say, "I told you so."

If your teen takes a political stand that makes no sense to you, listen. Resist the urge to lay down

> *A wise spiritual mentor knows when to cite Scripture and when to just listen.*

the law; instead, ask how he or she has come to these conclusions, and then listen some more.

6. *To hear unsolicited advice.* Unless your teen asks for it, advice is likely to be resisted. Kids don't always want advice when they bring up a dilemma; sometimes they just want to be loved and heard. And they would almost always prefer to work things out for themselves.

RELATIONSHIP

**RELATIONSHIP**

Fortunately, a teenager's resistance to advice can work to her advantage. Too much advice too soon can hinder the development of a young person's decision-making skills. Letting your teen talk about a situation can help her to clarify options. Try asking questions that will help your teen make wise decisions on her own. For example, you might ask, "What will be the likely consequences of choosing option A? How about the consequences of picking option B?" Or you could ask, "How do you think you'll feel about this decision 10 years from now?"

■ ■ ■

## Free Advice: Talking to Teens as Friends

My daughter had a best friend we'll call Laura. They'd been friends since early elementary school, but now Laura was going through a tough time. Her clothing and makeup were seductive, she sported purple marks on her neck, and she was involved in other destructive behaviors.

I knew my daughter was at her own rebellious point, not wanting to do what I asked. How could I tell her not to spend time with Laura anymore? If I laid down the law, I felt, my daughter would only become defiant and see Laura secretly.

Instead of preparing a lecture, I decided to speak to my daughter as though she were a friend I was concerned about.

With that in mind, I talked with her about Laura's behaviors. I told her I could see her beginning to slip in her own convictions by hanging out with Laura. Did she really want that? Was it really helping Laura to continue to hang out with her? We talked about how to be Laura's friend from a distance for the time being—still loving her and not snubbing her.

I told my daughter to think about it and get back to me. A day or two later, she reported her conclusion. She had decided that Laura was a bad influence on her, and she was going to distance herself from Laura for a while.

In time, Laura came back around—and the two were close friends again. Meanwhile, I'd discovered a way to give counsel and stay close to my daughter, too.

—L. H. J.

If you aren't sure what your role should be when your teen brings up a problem, ask, "Do you want advice?"

7. *For you to freak out.* Try not to show shock at what a teenager tells you. As Gordon McLean wrote in *Too Young to Die*, "A teen's approach is to tell you a little of the story, see how that goes over, and then decide whether to divulge the rest. If you blow up at the first hint of trouble, you may never get the whole story. Stay calm."[8]

The more fully you know your teen's world, the better prepared you'll be for the things you hear.

8. *To hear adult clichés.* Here are some time-worn phrases your teen could do without:

- "How could you do this to us after all we've done for you?"
- "Back when I was your age . . ."
- "As long as you're under my roof, you'll follow my rules."
- "You don't know how easy you have it."
- "You kids today don't know the meaning of (insert the word of your choice here)."

## Communicating During Conflict

Sometimes communication is more than hard—it's practically hopeless.

When family therapist Carleton Kendrick speaks at parenting seminars, he tells the story of an adolescent girl who'd been sullen toward her parents for months. One day she was on her way out the door to go to the movies with her friends.

Mom said, "Have a good time!"

The daughter turned around and snapped, "How dare you tell me what to do!"

No matter how hard you work at it, there will be times when communicating with your teen is virtually impossible. No matter what you say, you'll get a snarl in response. Or you'll find yourself delivering a monologue rather than having a dialogue.

Parents often respond to angry teens with anger of their own. "Don't you dare talk to me that way!" a mom might shout. A father might clamp down with punishment. Another might withdraw in

**RELATIONSHIP**

seething silence, washing his hands of any responsibility for "that kid."

It's hard to keep your cool during parent-teen conflict. But when your teen is in surly mode, try the following ways to show your love:

- Instead of insisting on conversation, be available to talk without pressuring.
- Respond to hurtful words by saying something like "When you act like this toward me, it hurts me. I was only trying to be nice (help, ask you a question, whatever)."
- To defuse the tension of face-to-face conversation, try communicating via a notebook or E-mail. Write a message and let your teen read it at his leisure. List things you appreciate about your teen; encourage him to write about questions, fears, frustrations, anger, and joy. Write for understanding, not to fuel a war.

■ ■ ■

## *Getting It Write:*
## *Communicating Without Confrontation*

During a particularly difficult time in my relationship with my daughter, the notebook method was the only way we could communicate. When she was angry, she tended to raise her voice and talk in circles, wanting me to admit that she was completely right. Her high-energy communication was confusing and caused me to withdraw from saying anything. I wasn't sure what the real issues were; if I answered, would I inadvertently answer the wrong thing?

With the notebook, I was able to ponder everything she said and validate her in the places where she was correct (and she did make some legitimate points). I would ask a simple question and get a page or more in angry response. Where I disagreed with her, I could take time to write down the precise words to state my disagreements. When she read my words, it was no longer in the heat of the moment, and she listened better.

It helped both of us say what we needed and fostered a relationship that eventually included face-to-face communication.

—Lissa Johnson

## Arguing Fairly with Your Teen

A gentle answer turns away wrath, but a harsh word
stirs up anger.

—Proverbs 15:1 (NASB)

Everyone must be quick to hear, slow to speak and slow
to anger; for the anger of man does not achieve the righteousness of God.

—James 1:19-20 (NASB)

Married couples find it important to learn how to argue fairly.
Some parents, on the other hand, seem to feel they should win all
arguments with their teens. The truth is that both parents and
teens are fallible, and both may have valid points that need to be
made when there's a disagreement.

> *"Arguments often exist because some-one doesn't have all the facts."*

Since you're probably more
experienced at conflict resolution
than your teen is, it's important that
you model fair fighting skills. To
start with, make sure the argument
is necessary in the first place. As
Gary Smalley and John Trent wrote in *The Hidden Value of a Man*,
"Arguments often exist because someone doesn't have all the
facts."[9]

## Elements for Resolving Conflicts Fairly

Once you've determined that confrontation is needed, be sure you
have the following four elements required for resolving conflicts
fairly:

1. *A willingness to admit your own role in the conflict.* Parents have been known to point fingers without
   acknowledging their own contribution to the dispute.
2. *The desire to work things out.* If you want to find a win-
   win solution, it's likely that you eventually will. But
   if your goal is to control your teen as you did when

he or she was a child, you'll find only increased conflict.

3. *A focus on the present and future.* Avoid bringing up the past; stick with the topic at hand. Aim for a more peaceful future.

4. *A commitment to listening.* As Greg and Gary Smalley observe in *Bound by Honor,* "Safety develops when your child trusts that your goal is to listen and understand, not to defend and challenge."[10] Commit yourself to listening even when it's painful. Decide to distinguish between anger and disrespect in your teen's tone of voice; forbid the latter, but acknowledge the former.

### Steps for Resolving Parent-Teen Conflict

Once you've assembled those four tools, you can interact constructively. The Smalleys recommend the following steps for resolving parent-teen conflict:

1. *Clearly define the issues.* Without getting lost on tangents, identify the problem and work on that.

2. *Let the other person speak without interrupting.* If it will help you to listen better, keep a piece of paper handy to jot points down so you don't forget them.

3. *Create solutions.* Listing all the pros and cons of each potential solution during your brainstorming is often helpful and can clarify the options.

4. *Agree on solutions.* Sometimes this means not following through on the solution that either the teen or the parent originally felt was correct. You may come up with a third course that combines both your preferences.

5. *Write down the agreement and have all parties concerned sign it.* This will avoid confusion later.[11]

### Argument Tactics to Avoid

Some ways of dealing with conflict have the power to maim a parent-teen relationship. The Smalleys advise staying away from the following:

1. *Withdrawing and never resolving the conflict.* Sometimes a time-out is needed if an argument is too heated. But issues need to be dealt with sooner or later, especially if they were raised by your teen. Short-circuiting the process tells teens that their problems are not important, and neither are they.
2. *Name-calling, ridiculing, making sweeping accusations, and button pushing.* In the heat of the moment, it can be tempting to cut a teen down to size with a scathing remark. But such comments, especially if they're about a trait that can't be changed (personality, appearance, intelligence), can be devastating for years to come.

   It can also be tempting to make broad generalizations ("You never . . ." "You always . . .") or to label your teen ("You're immature," "You're the most self-centered person I ever met"). In addition to warping a

## The Big C's: Four Communication Killers

Here are four common ways in which parents bring communication to a screeching halt: criticism, complaining, comparing, and condemning.

1. "You never sweep the patio very well. Look at all the dirt you leave behind!"

*Criticism* can slice to the core of a teen's being. Healing, if it ever comes, often leaves a scar.

2. "I guess it's just an impossible task to keep your room clean, huh?"

*Complaining* is unproductive. It only expresses a problem without acknowledging that the problem can be fixed. It does nothing to move toward resolution.

3. "Your brother is the star football player. Why can't you even make the team?"

*Comparing* leaves a teen frustrated, defeated, and devalued. If your sister is taller and more beautiful than you are, comparing yourself with her will not make you less short or plain.

4. "You're no good—and you never will be."

*Condemning* tells your teen there's no way out. It's hopeless; he or she is worthless.

**RELATIONSHIP**

young person's self-image, such statements do nothing to resolve the problem at hand.

Some parents, knowing their child's hot buttons, can't seem to resist pushing them during an argument. A mom whose daughter used to be afraid of the dark may bring that up when she feels the girl needs to be brave and sing a solo at church. A dad whose son once tried unsuccessfully to run away from home may remind the boy of that option when the boy resists following a household rule. But the Bible counsels, "Fathers, do not provoke your children to anger, but bring them up in the discipline and instruction of the Lord" (Ephesians 6:4, NASB). Button pushing is cruel as well as counterproductive.

3. *Assuming your teen is deliberately trying to frustrate, hurt, or scare you.* Suspicion poisons a relationship—and the communication process. "What we believe about our children may come true, good or bad," the Smalleys wrote. "Once we start developing a deep conviction that our teenager is stupid, clumsy, trying to drive us crazy, or going to get pregnant, we'll actually hear or

## Teens' Advice to Parents About Nurturing Spiritual Growth, Part 4

■ "Be an active part of it! Challenge them to daily spend time alone with God, and hold them accountable to it. Show them God through the things you do and say, and love them regardless of the outcome."

■ "Get involved. Don't rely on church or school."

■ "Develop a relationship with teens, and model, model, model what you want us to be. Be genuine. Set boundaries while letting teens grow."

■ "Spend time being open and honest with each other. Ask rough questions. Spend time in family devotions. (Make it fun!)"

■ "Be actively involved on a daily basis with your teens' lives. Come alongside them in times of difficulty. Be willing to give them independence, letting them find out for themselves who God is. Continue to be that nonanxious, influencing presence. Be their number-one example."

see signs of it even if it isn't true. The power of belief is so great that we see what we expect to see."[12]

If, during an argument, you believe that your teen is only trying to be understood, not to hurt you, and if you modify your response accordingly, you may find her calming down and speaking more respectfully.

During any conflict, consider the long-term outcome rather than the short-term "win." As Gary Dausey said in *How to Get Your Teenager to Talk to You*, "Flexibility, when it doesn't compromise spiritual, moral or ethical principles, may be the best policy."[13]

## Don't Give Up!

Maintaining the cables of communication with your teen is a never-ending task. But as the apostle Paul wrote in Galatians 6:9, "Let us not lose heart in doing good, for in due time we will reap if we do not grow weary" (NASB).

Good communication leads to heart connections that will never break. No loving parent—and no spiritual mentor—can do without those links. Years from now, when your teen has grown and left home but stays in touch, you'll be glad you made the effort to keep those cables connected.

**RELATIONSHIP**

# CHAPTER 9

# Finding Time for Your Teen

According to a recent Mayo Clinic study, the average time parents spend with their children in a given week has declined 10 to 12 hours since 1960.[1] Sounds a little ominous. But does it really matter? After all, your teen probably doesn't want you nosing around in his business anyway. And there's no need for 24/7 supervision anymore by the time he's reached the teen years. So what's the big deal?

> As a wise parent once said, "You never spend time with your kids; you invest it."

Veteran teen mentor Joe White discovered the answer when he asked teens a simple question: "What do your parents do to show they love you?" Consider their replies:

- "They spend time with me."
- "They pray with me."
- "They take time out of their busy schedules."
- "My mom talks with me when I have a problem."[2]

Teens, like everyone else, need love. They know they're receiving it when we invest time in their lives.

### The Investment of Time

As a wise parent once said, "You never *spend* time with your kids; you *invest* it." Investing time means using one of your scarcest resources. But there's a reward. The relationship, so vital to spiritual mentoring, increases in value. The idea of "spending" time might not be enticing, but if you're focused on investing it, you and your teen will find joy rather than obligation in the experience.

■ ■ ■

## *Thanks for Nothing:*
## *Quantity and Quality Time*

It's not the quantity of time that you spend with your children, it's the quality that counts. Or is it?

Maybe you've heard the argument that it doesn't matter how little time you spend with your children as long as your few moments together are especially meaningful. But the logic of that concept seems suspect to me. The question is, why do we have to choose between the virtues of quantity versus quality? We won't accept that forced choice in any other area of our lives. So why is it only relevant to our children?

Let me illustrate my point. Let's suppose you've looked forward all day to eating at one of the finest restaurants in town. The waiter brings you a menu, and you order the most expensive steak in the house. But when the meal arrives, you see a tiny piece of meat about one inch square in the middle of the plate. When you complain about the size of the steak, the waiter says, "Sir, I recognize that the portion is small, but that's the finest corn-fed beef money can buy. You'll never find a better bite of meat than we've served you tonight. As to the portion, I hope you understand that it's not the quantity that matters, it's the quality that counts."

You would object, and for good reason. Why? Because both quality and quantity are important in many areas of our lives, including how we relate to children. They need our time and the best we have to give them.

My concern is that the quantity versus quality argument might be a poorly disguised rationalization for giving our children—neither.

—Dr. James Dobson in *Home with a Heart*[3]

Lisa is a parent who knows the value of investing time in kids. Every weekend, she volunteers at the teen shelter downtown. "I've been here five years, and I've seen hundreds of miracles happen," she says.

> But the amazing thing to me is that these kids' problems always boil down to a need for a parent's attention. For whatever reason, Mom or Dad is not around. . . . I believe most of the parents we work with care for their kids, but something's gotten in the way: a job, a divorce, or whatever. And when these parents see their teen pull away, they think it's time to give them space. That's the real tragedy: These teens want attention, not space. And when attention isn't given, that's when these problems begin to pop up.
>
> What I try to get parents to understand is that no matter how their teen is acting, [he or she] doesn't really want to be 29th on the priority list. They desperately want to be the number one focus—and believe me, one way or another, they will be.

Actress Elisabeth Shue told *Movieline* magazine that she smoked marijuana and was "acting out sexually" during her teen years in order to get attention. "[Adolescent] rebellion is so obvious," she said. "When you're going through it you have no idea why you're doing it, but when you get older you look back and think, 'Oh, attention!' And nobody gives you attention, so you do worse and worse things."[4]

Her story doesn't have to be duplicated in the life of your teenager. By investing time, you can see to it that your child gets the kind of attention that leads him or her toward greater spiritual maturity.

## The Down Payment

Okay. You're ready to invest, but you're short on capital. How do you find time for your teen?

Experienced parents of adolescents have unearthed some jewels

■ ■ ■

## *Quick Studies: Three Teachable Times*

**RELATIONSHIP**

Jim Weidmann of the Heritage Builders ministry knows how to use those brief but potential-laden "God moments." Here are three examples he offers:

1. You're driving in the car. Your teen says, "Boy, this is a really nice day." You can reply, "Yeah, it is, isn't it? You know, God has given us this day to enjoy. The Bible says all good things come from the Lord."

2. Grandma's body is lying in the casket, and I'm sitting there, talking to my child: "You know, God promises us that we have life after death. He says that these bodies are nothing more than an old suit, an old pair of clothes that you'll grow out of. So Grandma's really not here. We know where Grandma is. Grandma's in heaven."

3. One Saturday, shortly after a family discussion on worry, I tucked my checkbook into my back pocket. My two sons and I climbed into the truck for our weekly trip to the hardware store.

   When we got there, I got out of my truck and reached into my pocket—and noticed I didn't have my checkbook anymore. Somehow, somewhere along the way, I had lost it. I said to the kids, "Guys, I messed up. Let's get back in the truck."

   We did. My son Josh said, "Dad, let's pray about it."

   I said, "Okay, Josh."

   Josh prayed a beautiful prayer that included this request: "God, will You please deliver our checkbook? It's important to us."

   That gave us an opportunity to talk about prayer. What is prayer? How can God answer prayer? What if He says "yes" or "no" or "wait"?

   Two weeks later, I got a package in the mail. I called my kids. I said, "Hey, guys, remember how God said He answers prayer?"

   After we reviewed the ways in which He might answer, I held up the checkbook, which had been returned in the package. I said, "This time God was telling us, 'No, not right now.' " We opened up the checkbook, and not a check was missing.

of wisdom on this subject. Those jewels polish up into eight principles for purchasing meaningful moments with your son or daughter.

**Jewel 1: Set Your Priorities**
"Priorities win wars," says Joe White in *FaithTraining*. "Priorities make CEOs successful. Priorities make good spouses. Priorities raise good kids."

Priorities are proved in action, of course. In Joe White's case, his priorities meant interacting with each of his children at bedtime, talking about the events of the day:

> Nine-thirty to 10:30 P.M. is my time to lie by the kids and visit one-on-one. The Dallas Cowboys might be playing San Francisco, but they'll have to play without me during that precious bedtime hour. I often have to excuse myself from guests in the living room. . . . They understand. The Cowboys can win and the conversation can go on without me.[5]

In the White household, family dinners were also a priority. Friends were often invited, but siblings were not allowed to skip

**RELATIONSHIP**

## Teens' "Traits of Great Parents," Part 3

- "They listen and ask questions. They're slow to speak—they model with actions, not always with words. Teens get tired of lectures. There is a time and need for correction, but great parents hear their teens more often than having to be heard. Also, they encourage and compliment a teen's character and person as opposed to actions and accomplishments."
- "Patience, open communication, intentional."
- "Open with love, intentional in actions, open about struggles, active in teaching children truth, willing to confront children about wrong (evil) in their lives. Growing in their own relationship with the Lord as well."
- "They are intentional in practicing what they say they believe."
- "Listening, unconditional acceptance. Those who are diligently seeking the Lord in how to guide their kids through the teenage years."

**RELATIONSHIP**

the dinner table. The kids' games were attended, too, even if the often-traveling Joe had to drive all night to get there.

Have you set your priorities? Or are you living in default mode, letting the latest crisis or squeaky wheel determine your schedule? Is your teen paying the price?

Being honest about what's most important in your life is the first step in setting priorities. Is it the World Series on TV? The big project at the office? The PTA, the dirty laundry, or the Wednesday night fellowship group? These things can elbow their way to the top of the list if you let them, but consider the expense. If you're not investing enough time in your teen, it's costing both of you. Making your teenager a top priority and shaping your schedule accordingly will prove to him that he is truly important to you. Besides, as speaker and author Barbara Rainey says, if you invest the time when your child is still at home, he'll spend time with you when you're older.

**Jewel 2: Neglect the Grass When Necessary**
Making time for your teen sometimes means forgetting about other worthy causes.

A former major league baseball player says that countless

## Teens' "Things I Wish My Parents Had Done Differently," Part 3

- "I wish my father could have had an impact on me spiritually. I still, at 22 years old, long for my dad to be a spiritual leader in our home. It's a defeating feeling to know that will probably not be the case."
- "I wish my dad would have been nicer to my mother. I picked a lot of this up. (He wasn't always building her up.)"
- "I would like my dad to have been more vocal. Talking was nonexistent regarding spirituality."
- "I wish they would have talked about God with me more often and prayed with me."
- "(1) More hugs; physical affirmation. (2) Prayer together. (3) Spiritual discussion and questioning. (I didn't *feel* like my parents were interested in my spiritual life. I felt it was a private thing.)"

hours of playing catch with his dad in the backyard led to his later success. But he vividly remembers one time when his mother, noticing that their daily practices were destroying the grass, became furious.

"She came out and yelled at us to look at the grass, and there really wasn't much left to look at," he says. "I thought, *Great. Big trouble.* But my dad just calmly turned to her and said, 'Linda, we're not raising grass, we're raising kids.' "

Our possessions, our hobbies, and our backyards will wait. Our teens will not. Wise parents, seeing how quickly teens grow, know that sometimes *things* have to take a beating to prevent the *relationship* from taking one.

### Jewel 3: See the Battle for Time as a Spiritual One

Let's say you've organized your priorities, mapped out your schedule, and resigned yourself to an ugly backyard. But the distractions seem to get stronger every day. Just when you feel you're making progress, something pops up—a forgotten commitment, a missed appointment. You're knocked back to square one.

Why is the battle to spend time on our kids' spiritual growth so difficult?

Maybe it's because this fight is about more than clocks and calendars. "Our struggle is not against flesh and blood, but against the rulers, against the authorities, against the powers of this dark world and against the spiritual forces of evil in the heavenly realms" (Ephesians 6:12).

In this battle, we need all the help we can get. When you're frustrated and want to give up, don't just blame the busy schedule. Kneel down and pray for divine defense. Get prayer support from family and friends, especially fellow parents who understand what you're going through. And invite someone, perhaps in your small group or Sunday school class, to hold you accountable for keeping the main thing—time with your teen—the main thing in your Day-Timer.

### Jewel 4: Buy Time

Believe it or not, you can buy time with your teenager. You can pay someone to wash your car, mow your lawn, make your dinner, buy

RELATIONSHIP

your groceries, walk your dog, or clean your house—and invest that time with your teen.

If money is tight, try bartering (trade that unused exercise bike for some fence painting) or taking turns (shovel your neighbor's driveway after every other snowstorm so he'll do the same for you).

The goal is to earn yourself some space to talk, to bond, to teach. Every asset you have, including money, can be applied toward that goal. And there is simply no better use of your money than to enable you to invest more time in your child.

> *To find activities that will motivate you and your teen to spend time together, try starting with your son's or daughter's interests.*

### Jewel 5: Choose Activities You Believe In

Which is easier: finding 15 minutes to savor a hot fudge sundae or finding 15 minutes to translate ancient hieroglyphics? That depends on whether you prefer eating or Egyptology. The point is that it's usually easier to make time for the things we really

## Something in Common: Parent-Teen Together Times

Can a parent and teen really find activities they both enjoy? Try this list to get your brainstorming started:

- hiking, fishing, hunting, camping
- biking, jogging, sunset chasing
- watching sports events—televised or live
- bowling, golfing, football, baseball
- watching and discussing movies
- making a video of your own
- going to and reviewing concerts
- learning to play an instrument together
- going to art fairs
- drawing or taking photographs together
- playing checkers, chess, or Scrabble
- gardening, landscaping
- rebuilding cars, going to races
- shopping for clothes, antiques, used books, or collectibles
- building bookshelves or furniture for someone's room
- taking a cooking class and experimenting with family dinners

want to do than to make time for those we see as a chore or a waste.

To find activities that will motivate you and your teen to spend time together, try starting with your son's or daughter's interests. For Joe White, that meant shooting baskets for hundreds of hours with his son Brady. It meant catching thousands of son Cooper's football passes, going on countless morning jogs with daughter Courtney, and helping daughter Jamie practice gymnastics—even installing her own balance beam in the family play room.

■ ■ ■

## *Davenport vs. Disneyland: A Memory My Parents Made*

My parents filled their crowns in heaven on this one. When I was growing up, they would bring family decisions before my brothers and me. We would all gather around the dining room table and discuss issues pertinent to the family's resources—"money talks," we called them.

One summer Sunday afternoon, my parents offered us an unusual choice. My mother had been saving for years to buy a new couch for the family room, but the sermon at church that day was giving her second thoughts. She decided we should have a money talk about it.

There had been rumors of a possible family vacation to Disneyland someday, but so far no official word had been given. When the options—sofa or theme park—were presented, there were a few shocked moments of silence while my brothers looked around. Before Mom knew what had happened, it was over. That particular money talk turned into a noisy celebration.

Because of that afternoon, all the members of our family have fond memories to share about that vacation. We talk about them when we get together at my parents' house, sitting on the old couch, laughing, our backsides scraping the living room floor. Mom always looks at the vacation pictures hung above the sofa and laughs right along with us.

When it's a choice between buying a "household necessity" or buying an experience you and your teen will remember for a lifetime, think of the foolishness of my mother: She let us decide.

—Mick Silva

RELATIONSHIP

For Gordon, another dad, it meant driving his astronomy-minded son to the top of a mountain to see Lick Observatory in California. For you, it might mean attending a writers' workshop with your daughter or searching flea markets with your son for a rare comic book or trading card. To help you spend larger blocks of time together, try cultivating some mutual passions, too.

As you invest time in your teen, try to focus on making memories that will last you through the inevitable clashes of adolescence. One family will always remember seeing America by car, hopping from one campground to the next, discovering new places and subcultures. Another family will never forget its tradi-

■ ■ ■

## Car-versations: Making the Most of Transportation Time

As a taxi driver/parent of a teen, you probably log plenty of car time. How can you turn those minutes into teachable moments? Here are some ideas.

1. If you're ferrying a group of your teen's friends, listen. Let the conversation flow around you as if you weren't paying attention. If something comes up that could harm someone, step in and direct the conversation toward a point you'd like to make. For example, the group might be giggling about pulling a practical joke on an unpopular classmate. You can ask how the kids would feel if someone did that to them. This might lead to a discussion on valuing the differences between people instead of ridiculing them, and to the fact that God loves each of us equally.

2. If you're listening to the car radio, discuss what you hear. Let's say the news tells of a professional football player who's been arrested for drunk driving. You can start a conversation by asking something like "How do you feel when someone you respect makes a mistake?"

3. Talk about what you see as you drive. For instance, you're looking for a parking space and spot a frustrated mother outside the grocery store, screaming at her child. Ask your teen, "What would you do in a situation like that? How could it be handled better?"

—Lissa Johnson

tion of dining out once a week, where the lack of distractions like TV and telephone encouraged conversation between parents and teens.

Whatever you do when you spend time together, let it be the common ground that allows you access to spiritually mentor your teen.

### Jewel 6: Use "Little" Times Between "Big" Events

Hard to find big blocks of time with your teen? Try taking advantage of the small spaces between larger events. Here are some suggestions:

- Talk while cleaning up after dinner.
- Meet at a coffee shop after school.
- Share a getaway breakfast before school.
- Meet at or near school for lunch.
- Play a game (board or video) after homework.
- Walk somewhere instead of driving.
- Chat while waiting for dinner to cook.
- Wash the car together before a big date.
- Talk during TV commercials.
- Share your thoughts on the way to church (or the way back).

### Jewel 7: Make Your Teen Your Hobby

Whether it's golf, stamp collecting, or something else, a hobby can consume a lot of hours that could be applied to a teen. Some parents have chosen to make their sons and daughters their hobbies; that is, they've made the teens a major focus of their free time and recreation.

This approach doesn't always mean giving up your current hobby. Suzie, for example, found a way to blend her favorite pastime (shopping) with her daughter's (pop culture). They hit the antique and secondhand stores every Saturday, searching for nostalgic collectibles like Cabbage Patch dolls and Wonder Woman lunch boxes. "It's an absolute miracle," Suzie says. "It opens [my daughter] up to talking about things. I can't imagine if I hadn't found it."

RELATIONSHIP

**RELATIONSHIP**

Suzie feels fortunate that her daughter's hobby is one in which Suzie can be involved. The more time they spend together, the more Suzie finds that her daughter has become her real hobby.

Making your teen your hobby may mean cutting back on, or even temporarily giving up, your regular pastimes. But here's a question to think about: If golf and stamp collecting aren't shared interests that you can enjoy *with* your teen, might there be time enough for those hobbies when your son or daughter has left the nest?

**Jewel 8: Take Advantage of Unplanned Opportunities**

Youth speaker Josh McDowell tells how one day he sat with his kids in a public place that had been vandalized by offensive graffiti. Instead of trying to shield them from the profanity and quickly ushering them to more neutral territory, he pointed it out

## Teens' "Ways in Which a Parent Was Spiritually Influential," Part 4

- "My dad and I would read Scripture, usually Proverbs, before I went to school in junior high. This kept me floating during a period when I was lukewarm in my Christian life."

- "During high school, Dad and I would often eat breakfast together at our kitchen table, and we'd sometimes talk about spiritual questions I had. My favorite part, which encouraged me most, was when we ended that time in prayer. It really prepared me for the day."

- "My mom and I had long conversations in her room at night before bed. These 'debriefing' conversations not only allowed me to share my heart and struggles with her, but they also allowed her to give me guidance and the assurance that she was always there to encourage as I tried to be a godly teen. The culmination of these times—the laughter, tears, and times of conflict—created an impenetrable bond between us."

- "When I made wrong choices, my mother would sit down with me and discuss the situation and conclude with how Jesus would handle the situation. I didn't always appreciate this time!"

- "In middle school, my parents were separated for a while. My mom encouraged my brother and sister and me to memorize a passage to help us through that time. Jeremiah 29:11-14 is still my favorite passage."

to them. He answered their questions about the "colorful" language and helped them identify the artist's distorted values.

Josh hadn't planned to deliver an object lesson that day. But when the opportunity presented itself, he took full advantage of it.

You can do the same with those teachable moments. This is what Deuteronomy 6 means when it says you're to teach your children "when you sit at home and when you walk along the road, when you lie down and when you get up" (verse 7). Such moments are easy to miss, however, unless you're looking for them.

Even life's little disasters can provide chances to connect. Hannah recalls what happened when she was 15. "I tried to sneak the family car out of the garage late at night. I planned to have it back before anyone noticed, and I guess I was thinking too far ahead or something. I went to back out, but it didn't go backward. It went forward instead, right through the wall of my sister's bedroom. Luckily, she was away at college. But I just shut off the car and started crying. My dad came out and saw me, but if he was angry, he didn't show it. He made sure I was all right and helped me get the car back in the garage. Then, over the next few months, he rebuilt the wall and we actually repainted the room together."

Hannah's dad made that time count. His response left her with a lasting image of her father's love and patience that she'll never forget.

## No Time Like the Present

In *What Kids Wish Parents Knew about Parenting,* Joe White wrote: "When the final song is playing, when the remaining grains of sand are so few in a loved one's hourglass of time . . . our life's priorities distill to purest value. And the certainty hits: You never spend enough time with your family."[6]

Yes, there will be days when you'll be sure you couldn't get any busier—and then you will. But no matter how complicated life gets, the simple truth is that making time for your teen is a decision you won't regret.

# CHAPTER 10

# Appreciating Your Teen's Uniqueness

Corey (not his real name), a teenager in Los Angeles, was one of a kind.

He didn't belong in the popular crowd. In fact, he seemed odd even to his family. His personality and sense of humor were quirky, and he cared nothing about hair or clothing styles. His casual way of looking at time and space made people crazy.

On the positive side, he had a strength of conviction and character. He could look people in the eye and debate ideas. Those who knew him knew he was a good person—but where in the world would he fit?

The summer before his junior year of high school, Corey went to Central America on a short-term mission trip. Even though he was failing Spanish in school, he fell in love with the region and the language. When he returned to the States, he began getting A's in Spanish.

> God has given your teen a unique personality, maybe even one that's hard for you to appreciate.

Next, he enrolled in a university that connected Latin and American cultures. He took his required classes in Spanish instead of English. Finally he returned to Latin America for a year-long exchange program.

It was there that his sister visited him. She was astonished to see that the personality traits that seemed so at odds with Americans fit perfectly in the Latin culture. The people loved him. Now *she* felt awkward and unsure, while her brother moved with a grace she'd never seen before.

Corey became a missionary to Central America and Brazil. God had obviously prepared this boy's personality to suit *His* plans.

## Your Teen's Personality

God has given your teen a unique personality, too—maybe even one that's hard for you to appreciate. Some parents react to such a situation by trying to re-form their kids' temperaments, and they're baffled when the result is frustration and fighting.

As Dr. James Dobson wrote in *Solid Answers*:

> You can teach new attitudes and modify some behavioral patterns, but you will not be able to redesign the basic personality with which your child was born. Some characteristics are genetically programmed, and they will always be there. For example, some kids appear to be born to lead, and others seem to be made to follow. . . .
>
> Some parents worry about an easygoing, passive child—especially if he's a boy. Followers in this society are sometimes less respected than aggressive leaders and may be seen as wimpy and spineless. And yet, the beauty of the human personality is seen in its marvelous uniqueness and complexity. There is a place for the wonderful variety of temperaments that find expression in children. After all, if two people are identical in every regard, it's obvious that one of them is unnecessary.
>
> My advice to you is to accept, appreciate and cultivate the personality with which your . . . child is born. He does not need to fit a preconceived mold. That youngster is, thankfully, one of a kind.[1]

Successful parents discover that their role is to encourage their teens in the strengths God has given them and to help them cope with their weaknesses. They understand that their teens' personalities are not cosmic mistakes.

To help your teen make the most of his uniqueness, it's important to understand his personality. With your adolescent in mind, try taking the following test—adapted from *The Two Trails* by John Trent and Judy Love.[2] Under each type, circle the words and phrases that apply to your teen.

**TYPE "L"**

| | |
|---|---|
| Takes charge | Bold |
| Determined | Purposeful |
| Assertive | Decision maker |
| Firm | Leader |
| Enterprising | Goal-driven |
| Competitive | Self-reliant |
| Enjoys challenges | Adventurous |

**TYPE "O"**

| | |
|---|---|
| Takes risks | Fun-loving |
| Visionary | Likes variety |
| Motivator | Enjoys change |
| Energetic | Creative |
| Very verbal | Group-oriented |
| Promoter | Mixes easily |
| Avoids details | Optimistic |

**TYPE "G"**

| | |
|---|---|
| Loyal | Adaptable |
| Nondemanding | Sympathetic |
| Even keel | Thoughtful |
| Avoids conflict | Nurturing |
| Enjoys routine | Patient |
| Dislikes change | Tolerant |
| Deep relationships | Good listener |

**TYPE "B"**

| | |
|---|---|
| Deliberate | Discerning |
| Controlled | Detailed |

RELATIONSHIP

| | |
|---|---|
| Reserved | Analytical |
| Predictable | Inquisitive |
| Practical | Precise |
| Orderly | Persistent |
| Factual | Scheduled |

Now, under which types(s) did you circle the most words and phrases? Those indicate your teen's dominant personality type(s). The letters stand for Lion, Beaver, Otter, and Golden Retriever.

This whimsical system is just one way of categorizing personalities, of course. But it can be a useful one. As John Trent explains in the *Focus on the Family Parents' Guide to the Spiritual Growth of Children*, here are descriptions of these four temperaments:

*Lions (High "L" People)*
Lions are take-charge, assertive, go-for-it people. . . .
They like leading and being in charge, even of you. . . .
You rarely have to motivate Lions—just point them in a direction. . . .
When a Lion's strengths are pushed out of balance, they become too strong or assertive and insensitive in their words or actions. They can become so intent on a project that they communicate that the project is more important than the people involved. But when a Lion's strengths are balanced with loving sensitivity, they make wonderful leaders, great friends, and some of the best parents.

*Otters (High "O" People)*
. . . Otters love life and especially people. They're tremendous networkers. . . .
Otters usually aren't into details. In school, they often start their papers the night before (why hurry?). . . .
Like the Lions, their strengths can be pushed to an extreme. Their tendency to be late or to put off doing routine things needs to be balanced with responsibility and an understanding of the pressure their lateness puts on others. With some added structure, their sensitivity

can be a tremendous asset, especially when they serve as a spiritual leader in a home or ministry.

*Golden Retrievers (High "G" People)*
Sensitive and caring, Golden Retrievers have difficulty saying no. They're compassionate, wonderful team players, and are very loyal and loving. They care about *individuals* and want everyone to feel included. They're adaptable and willing to go with the flow. While the Lion often challenges the status quo and suffers the consequences, Golden Retrievers watch others make mistakes and avoid them (thus avoiding the pain). . . .

When they're older, Golden Retrievers can be called on to "put out fires" and make those around them feel loved and accepted. But these children can have their feelings easily hurt (they're not weak, just sensitive).

*Beavers (High "B" People)*
. . . Beavers are detailed and organized. They do things "right." They tend to start, *and complete,* a few projects each year. . . .

Beavers have a way of mentally filing things so they can always find them. This inner filing system includes details and experiences. For example, they remember what you said precisely a year ago—and what you were wearing at the time.

They're very good at analyzing and taking things apart. But when their strengths are pushed to an extreme, they can be so good at it that they take people apart as well. There is no critic like a Beaver—and that includes how they view themselves. They set high standards and can be very hard on themselves if they don't reach those goals. Overall, however, Beavers are wonderful to have on a family or work team. They follow through, are predictable, and make lasting contributions.[3]

To help all the members of your family understand and appreciate one another's uniqueness, you might try taking a personality

RELATIONSHIP

inventory like the one above together. It can be fun as well as revealing. Another popular inventory is the Myers-Briggs Type Indicator (MBTI). A mini-test based on the MBTI can be found in the book *Please Understand Me* by David Keirsey and Marilyn Bates.

## Guys and Gals are Different

Your teen's gender is part of her uniqueness, too.

For years, some wanted us to believe gender differences were strictly a result of upbringing. Now scientific studies are proving there are fundamental differences between males and females.

Take the brain, for example:

- Men have more white matter, women more gray matter.
- Women have a larger corpus callosum, the bundle of fibers that runs down the center of the brain and enables the two hemispheres to communicate.
- Men's brains are larger.
- When given the same task, men and women use different parts of the brain to accomplish it.
- The primary center of aggression in the brain, the amygdala, is larger in males than in females.
- Females are "wired" to respond in internal ways, males in external.
- The female brain produces more serotonin, a chemical that helps calm the nervous system.
- One recent study at the Indiana University School of Medicine discovered that men use only half their brains when listening; women use both sides of their brains. This may show that men and women process language differently.

> *Scientific studies are proving there are fundamental differences between males and females.*

Then there's the huge difference testosterone makes. Andrew Sullivan reported in the *New York Times Magazine* that "an average woman has 40 to 60 nanograms of testosterone in a deciliter of blood plasma. An average man has 300 to 1000, and a teenage boy can range up to 1300 or so." Three times in his life, a man experiences a flood of testosterone—"in the womb several weeks after conception, during the first few months after birth and at puberty."[4] Is it any wonder that adolescent boys struggle with excessive aggression, energy, and sex drive, all of which are fueled by testosterone?

Parenting specialist John Rosemond wrote, "Boys are more active, more physical, more aggressive, have shorter attention spans. Girls will work out conflict emotionally, boys aggressively." Teen boys are likely to be stressed by the events of their lives—a game, school performance, or family move. Girls, in contrast, are more likely to feel stress as a result of problems in relationships.

Boys and girls are *very* different. The wise parent keeps this in mind when dealing with a son's or daughter's concerns, missteps, and expressions of spiritual commitment.

## Treat Your Teen Uniquely

Not only are the genders different, but each child is also different from his or her siblings. This is especially important to remember when we discipline our teens.

Carla, 17, has displayed a budding talent for writing. Unfortunately, the last thing she wrote was her mother's signature on a credit card charge slip. Keeping Carla's uniqueness in mind, Mom assigns the girl to write an essay entitled "Why Forging a Signature Is Illegal, and What the Consequences Could Be in the Future."

Carla's brother Nicholas, 14, has no interest in writing. He's a living, breathing action figure, always on the move. Last night, during an argument with his father, Nicholas angrily threw a dinner plate in the sink, and the plate broke. Dad assigns his task-oriented teen to wash dishes carefully for a week in order to earn money to replace the plate.

Choosing consequences for your teen according to his personality is far more effective than choosing *your* favorite consequence for every misbehavior. This requires that you know your teen's strengths and weaknesses almost as well as you know your own.

"But my kid keeps changing!" you may say. How true! Many teens try on new personalities as if they were changing clothes, wanting to find out who they really are. One shy girl at a youth conference volunteered to stand in front of the crowd. Her reason? To "branch out" and "be someone different." Keeping up with these transformations can be daunting, but we need to let our teens decide for themselves which identities fit them best.

Remembering your teen's uniqueness is important when encouraging her, too. Kathy, 15, prefers a written note; Doug, 13, likes to hear praise in person. Tamara, 16, responds best to a gift certificate for clothing or music; Bennett, 14, likes to be taken to a movie. Fifteen-year-old Shanielle, on the other hand, feels most encouraged when Mom or Dad comes alongside to help with a chore on a day when she's feeling tired or lonely.

Treating your teen as an individual, whether you're disciplining or encouraging, shows respect, strengthens self-confidence, and communicates caring.

## Strengths in the Making: Finding Positives in Your Teen's Personality

It's easy to see a teen's most striking personality traits in a negative light. But even negative traits in milder doses can become positives. Help your teen to turn down the volume on those troublesome traits and you may be surprised to discover strengths. Here are some examples.

| *Tone Down This Weakness . . .* | *. . . And Discover This Strength* |
|---|---|
| Critical | Analytical |
| Insincere | Appreciative |
| Domineering | Assertive |
| Overtalkative | Communicative |
| Worrying | Concerned |
| Self-sufficient | Confident |
| "Know-it-all" | Counseling |
| Reckless | Courageous |
| Nosey | Curious |
| Stubborn | Determined |
| Weak-willed | Diplomatic, Tactful |
| Rigid | Effective |

## Coaching Your Teen's Personality Type

When it comes to spiritual mentoring, one size doesn't fit all. As you encourage your teen's relationship with God, you'll want to do so in a way that works *with* his or her personality rather than *against* it.

To see how that might look, let's use the Lion, Otter, Golden Retriever, and Beaver types as examples. Adapted from the *Focus on the Family Parents' Guide to the Spiritual Growth of Children*, here are some tips on how to approach each type when acting as a spiritual coach:

1. *Lions (assertive leaders).* Emphasize God's purpose for the world and their lives. They want to know why and how it all works. Let them lead, have a say in how things are done, and help develop the program and they'll be committed to it.

RELATIONSHIP

| | |
|---|---|
| Flattering | Encouraging |
| Flowery | Expressive |
| Overly lenient | Forgiving |
| Wasteful | Generous |
| Daydreaming | Imaginative |
| Uncommunicative | Listening |
| Idolizing | Loyal |
| Judgmental | Moral |
| Overdependent | Obedient |
| Indecisive | Open-minded |
| Unrealistic | Optimistic |
| Perfectionistic | Orderly |
| Oversensitive | Sensitive |
| Undisciplined | Spontaneous |
| Dull | Stable |
| Harsh | Straightforward |
| Stingy | Thrifty |
| Fainthearted | Tolerant |

Encourage them to study Bible accounts of leaders like Moses and David—a Lion's heroes. Give their faith a purpose; they need to understand the goal and have something to strive for. Get them involved in helping, leading, and teaching others, including siblings.

2. *Otters (the social animals)*. Emphasize relationship with God and others; that's what interests them. To them, life is all about people. Vary Otters' spiritual training, and include plenty of fun; if something becomes routine, they'll lose interest. They need to learn discipline, but that's easier when it's enjoyable. Encourage them to read about the most "human" Bible characters, like Peter. Make sure you plug Otters into a lively youth group.

3. *Golden Retrievers (sensitive, caring team players)*. Emphasize God's personal love and care for them and the world. Love, acceptance, and individual care are the keys to their hearts. When acting as a mentor, build on your relationship with them. When you're exploring spiritual things together, they'll feel safe and take part eagerly. They need the context of personal bonds. Encourage them

■ ■ ■

## *Just the Way You Are: How a Mom Accepted (and Helped) a Daughter*

When I was a teenager, my mom told me I would never be organized. It wasn't said in anger, frustration, or with intent to ridicule. It was a statement of fact gleaned from many years of watching me, trying to help me, and seeing how difficult this task was for me.

Mom said I would never be a natural organizer. But she also said, "If you work extra hard at it, you can become organized enough to do all right." Her recognition of this weakness and her subsequent comment helped me to see the problem—and to focus on working hard at becoming better organized.

I'm still not very organized (just ask anyone who works with me). But I'm far better at it than I used to be. I've learned to put photographs into albums immediately, to create notebooks for projects and files for papers. (The only problem with filing is that I often forget what I filed something under.) My mother's gentle observation and encouragement helped tremendously.

—Lissa Johnson

to study accounts of God or human beings taking care of others—the Good Samaritan, Jesus healing people, Paul's missions to help others know Christ, and so on. Help Golden Retrievers form the right kinds of friendships. Lead them in praying and caring for others; let them assist in the church nursery, for instance, or in visiting shut-ins.

4. *Beavers (organized, methodical analysts).* Emphasize truth and right. Be consistent and predictable; they like to know what's coming and when. This provides safety and security. Encourage them to study Bible passages where principles are foremost and right and wrong are contrasted (the Sermon on the Mount, Paul's epistles, and so forth). Build on their certainty that there are right and wrong ways to do things. Help them make sense of their faith, finding specific answers to their questions. Explore apologetics, the reasons and "proofs" for beliefs and doctrines.

## Let Your Teen Be Himself

David grew up in a solid Christian home. His parents took him to church and youth group every week. They taught him the importance of following Jesus, loving God, and doing what's right.

David had artistic talent. His brother Paul was a great athlete. Instead of encouraging David in art, the boys' father ridiculed David for not excelling in sports. Even David's straight A's

---

### Teens' "Things I Wish My Parents Had Done Differently," Part 4

- ■ "I wish we'd had times when the family came together to discuss what God had taught us through our time spent with Him. I also wish we had prayed together as a family, praying individually for one another."
- ■ "I wish they had lived as Christians, prayed with me at meals and at night, and encouraged me in my faith."
- ■ "I wish we had invested more time as a family in prayer and in the Word."
- ■ "It would have been great if they had prayed with me and discussed their faith more openly."
- ■ "I'd like for them to have been more intentional."

brought no words of approval from Dad. It seemed being a rugged, athletic male was the only thing that would please Dad, and David couldn't do that.

When David left home, he went to a prestigious art school. Instead of following his parents' faith, however, he abandoned it. He became immersed in a homosexual lifestyle. In that world he found the acceptance and applause he could never get from his father.

Why did David's father reject his son? Perhaps the man had a narrow view of what a "real" male is. Or maybe he wanted to live vicariously through the sports careers of his sons. Either way, he lost the right to be a spiritual mentor to David.

The good news is that David's story doesn't have to be played out in your family.

Consider the story of a father we'll call Will.

Will loved sports. He'd loved them for as long as he could remember. After Will married, he dreamed of the son he would have. He dreamed about how he and his son would go to all kinds of games; Dad would coach his son's teams and cheer the boy on; they'd play catch and go golfing together.

Finally the hoped-for son, Mark, appeared. But Mark wasn't interested in sports. He liked books, movies, music, and art.

Will was disappointed, but he didn't want to push Mark into sports. Will and his wife, Gina, read

> *No teen is wired exactly the same way as Mom or Dad.*

books on parenting and talked about what to do. They decided to encourage Mark in his own interests and participate in building the unique person God intended Mark to be.

So Will and Gina went to the movies with Mark. They got him art supplies and books. When Mark bought his own guitar, they got him sheet music and instructional videos. When Mark became discouraged with his guitar playing, they said, "You'll get better. You're already better than the last time you played for us."

Today Mark is soaring. He has won awards for his acting. He's planning a career in art. His relationship with his parents is terrific.

It's only natural for us to want our teens to enjoy the experiences we enjoyed as adolescents. But no teen is wired exactly the same way as Mom or Dad. God has unique plans for your teen. Let your teen grow into all God wants him or her to be.

## Understanding Your Teen's Gifts

What is your teenager good at? The arts? Athletics? Academics? Being a leader? Mechanics? Debate? Thinking? Sewing? Cooking? Serving? Languages? Friendliness? Politics? Tenderness?

To gauge your adolescent's abilities, watch him. What comes easily to him? What makes him smile and brings a light to his eyes? What activities does he go back to year in and year out?

Ask your teen what abilities she sees in herself. Teachers, friends, and youth leaders may be able to add to the list.

To discover spiritual gifts (hospitality, evangelism, service, and so on), try studying Bible passages like 1 Corinthians 12 with your teen. Does your teen recognize herself in these passages? What has she tried successfully in the church youth group? What would she like to try?

Another option is to use a spiritual gifts inventory. Most of these tests are geared toward church volunteering; your church may offer such an inventory as part of its program. If not, visit a Christian bookstore for recommendations.

RELATIONSHIP

■ ■ ■

## *Teens Think Short Term*

Notice that the dominant crises [for teens] are immediate and short term. That's the way teenagers think and live, more than ever before. They are not overly concerned about things that may be significant problems eons from now—such as health and career decisions and opportunities. Also, recognize that teenagers do not tend to think about underlying causes as much as they wish to confront the outgrowths of those causes. For example, morality and values are a frontline issue for just 1 out of every 20 kids. Faith decisions and choices are of pressing concern to 1 out of every 25 teens.

—George Barna in *Generation Next*[5]

**RELATIONSHIP**

## Your Teen's Unique Future

"If you could design a specific way to serve God and knew you wouldn't fail, what would you do?"

Doug Fields, youth pastor, asks that of his students. What a great question! Try asking it of your teen, along with queries like these:

- "What really drives you?"
- "What's the most fun you've ever had helping someone else?"
- "What dreams do you think God has given you?"
- "What can you do that most people can't?"

## Teens' "Ways in Which a Parent Was Spiritually Influential," Part 5

- "We did not have anything we did consistently, but we had very open lines of communication."
- "My pops would take me to Denny's before school once a week. This lasted about three weeks, and then I realized I was much too cool to hang with Daddio. Now I regret this."
- "After my freshman year of college, I decided that I wanted to take some time off from school. Of course, my parents didn't agree, but instead of simply telling me what to do, they encouraged me to seek God's will in the situation and supported me in whatever decision I came to."
- "There were no ducks that morning. We sat cold and shivering in the duck blind. After a night of fierce debate, we didn't feel like saying much. Dad is the wisest man I know, but at that time I was less than impressed. I felt like Dad had no clue what I was feeling. When he broke the silence, I braced myself for lecture number 101. He proceeded to explain exactly how I felt. He shared a similar experience he had when growing up. He told me he loved me and that it was his job as a parent to offer guidance in my life. When all was said and done, I felt a total peace. I knew I was loved and was reassured that he had my best interest at heart. He understood me yet still held on to what he thought was best. His excellent parenting directed me straight into God's will."

- "What ability would you most like to develop?"
- "If God hired you for a summer job, what would you hope it would be?"

Talking over questions like these can help you understand and nurture your teen's uniqueness. As you do, your adolescent will begin to see that God cares about him as an individual and wants him to be the best he can be. (For more ideas on helping your teen pursue God-honoring dreams, see chapter 16, "Helping Your Teen Dream Productive Dreams.")

When that happens, life becomes an exciting journey to the future. And you, as a caring parent, become a welcome part of that journey.

RELATIONSHIP

# CHAPTER 11

# Giving Grace

Joe White sat peering at the screen, watching videotapes of his son Brady playing high school basketball. Joe planned to give Brady the edited result—a "highlights of basketball" video—as a graduation present.

As Joe viewed the scenes, however, he noticed something: This had been a tough year in basketball for Brady.

Still, that didn't prevent Joe from coming up with a good-looking tape. He simply fast-forwarded through the times when Brady had tossed the ball away or missed a shot, and he kept the successful three-pointers, passes, and drives. By ignoring the mistakes, Joe filled the tape with moments Brady would want to remember. The final product looked like an NBA all-star highlight film!

In the middle of this editing session, it was as if the Lord spoke quietly to Joe: "You know what, Joe? As your Daddy, that's the way I view your life. As I edit the videotape of your life, watching you struggle from day to day, I know you're going to throw the ball away. I know you're going to make bad shots. But my highlight video of you is of all the good shots you made. It's all the things you did that were profitable or left fruit on the tree of life. When you get to heaven and we pull out the video, that's the tape I'm going to show you. And your assignment as a daddy is to be that kind of an editor for your children. When they make mistakes, deal with them and then edit those out, tossing them in the trash can forever."

Forgetting your teen's mistakes is one of the greatest gifts you can give him. As parents, we sit in an "editing room" every day, deciding what to keep and what to toss. We can choose to make "highlights" tapes or "bloopers" tapes.

Yes, there are times when we need to say something to our teens about their errors. There are times when disciplinary action is required. Once we've taken those steps, however, it's time to edit the day's tape and put the embarrassing footage in the trash can. When we talk with our sons and daughters at the end of the week, and certainly at the end of the year, all we should show is the highlight tape.

God has done the same for us. In Romans 7, Paul discussed the dilemma we all face in our spiritual lives: The more we try, the more we seem to fail. But Romans 8:1-2 says, "There is now no

> *Forgetting your teen's mistakes is one of the greatest gifts you can give him.*

condemnation for those who are in Christ Jesus, because through Christ Jesus the law of the Spirit of life set me free from the law of sin and death." In other words, our video-tapes have been edited.

We parents need to be mirrors reflecting back to our kids the unconditional love we get from God. The most accelerating fuel we can put in our teens' lives is a mixture of unconditional love, unconditional regard, and unconditional acceptance. Kids who have that fuel are motivated—excited about going to youth group, excited about serving, excited about Bible study, and excited about leading godly lives.

They're excited about grace.

## Giving Our Teens What They Don't Deserve

The concept of grace is one Christians experience each day of their lives, whether they realize it or not. It's the audacious but biblical idea that we can have a personal relationship with a holy, eternal God that requires no work on our part, only accepting for ourselves the work of Jesus Christ. Even though our wrongdoing should result in lethal punishment, we are offered forgiveness and life—a second chance to go out there and get it right.

This outrageous gift of grace is not to be hoarded but is to be extended in our relationships. In Matthew 18:23-35, Jesus told the parable of a servant who was forgiven a great debt by a king. The debt was so huge that the servant couldn't have paid it off in a lifetime of hard work. Yet that servant roughly collared another man who owed him a very small debt, demanded to be paid immediately, and threw the man into debtor's prison. When the king found out about the forgiven servant's actions, punishment was swift and decisive.

Because God's mercy has been great toward us, our mercy can be great toward our teens.

Some parents don't mind extending grace to friends or even strangers but find it hard to give grace to their sons and daughters. Perhaps these parents are forgetting how much they needed grace when *they* were teenagers.

Remember what it was like? Chances are that you had good intentions yet made plenty of mistakes. "Stupid! Stupid!" may have been your inner theme song. Others may have joined in, but you probably sang it most often yourself. You needed grace and forgiveness. You needed someone to say that even though what you did was wrong or misguided, you were still loved and worthy. You needed to hear that mistakes would not be tied to you for the rest of your life, dragging you down and holding you back.

Your teen needs huge doses of grace and forgiveness, too, even if she doesn't always seem to deserve it. After all, God loved us before we loved Him (see Romans 5:8; 1 John 4:19).

## Spiritual Growth and Failure

We wouldn't need grace without failure, and failure is a part of every life. Thomas Edison failed many times in his attempts to make the lightbulb work, laboring more than two years and testing 1,600 materials before he found the right filament. He logged 40,000 pages of notes—for *one* lightbulb.

In a relationship with God, there is also plenty of failure.

■ ■ ■

## *Kodachrome:*
## *A Picture of Parental Grace*

**RELATIONSHIP**

A monstrous crime was committed against me when I was in junior high: My friend Steve Anderson knocked over my telescope and put a dent in the end of it.

It was an accident, and the telescope still worked—but that didn't lessen my fury. "You owe me $60!" I yelled at Steve, recalling the original purchase price.

Hearing the commotion, my parents rushed into my room. To my consternation, they told Steve he didn't have to pay. I vowed never to forgive or forget this catastrophe.

Not long after that, however, I had to look again at the incident in a different light.

It happened when I developed a roll of slide film for my parents. We had just returned from a vacation in San Francisco—a rare treat for a small-town pastor's family that had little money for such luxuries. Our Instamatic cameras had been loaded with one roll of Kodachrome each, just enough to capture memories of the roller-coaster streets, the Golden Gate Bridge, and the brightly colored fish at the city aquarium.

I considered myself an expert at film developing, even though I'd processed only black-and-white rolls so far. A friend had just bought a kit for developing slides, and he said I could use it in my darkroom for free.

At my request, my parents agreed to let me develop both of their rolls of film. No doubt they knew I would never allow harm to come to the only record of their once-in-a-lifetime trip. They knew that I—unlike Steve Anderson—understood the value of others' prized possessions.

I did everything the instructions said to do. But when I finished the final step, opened the developing tank, and gently lifted out the reel that held my parents' film, my breathing stopped.

There were no pictures. Even the numbers on the border of the film had disappeared. I held in my hand two wet strips of clear plastic, the clearest plastic I had ever seen.

Looking in the tank, I saw black sludge settling to the bottom. Nothing more was left of Mom and Dad's photographs.

The finality of it closed on me like the door of a bank vault. The pictures were irreplaceable, and I'd destroyed them. It was the kind of thoughtless act one might expect from . . . Steve Anderson.

With trembling hand, I grabbed the instructions and reread them. There at the bottom, in fine print, was a list of the film types this kit would develop. Ektachrome was there but not Kodachrome.

I'd used the wrong kit.

I wanted to stay in that darkroom forever, but eventually I had to come out. I trudged into the living room. Avoiding my parents' eyes, I tried to explain what had happened.

There was a disappointed "Oh." And then, softly, "That's okay."

Then came the sentencing: Like Steve Anderson, I was free to go.

I waited for the rest—a lecture about how important those pictures had been or a warning or at least a long sigh and a shaking of heads. It never came.

It was as if the whole thing had never happened—as if my parents had put my awful mistake as far from them as the east is from the west.

More than 30 years have passed since the Kodachrome incident. I'm still waiting for my parents to bring it up, but I guess they never will. As for Steve Anderson, I hope he forgave and forgot the way I yelled at him.

I still have some of the slides I took on that vacation. I sent them *out* to be developed.

But my most important memories of those days were ones that Kodachrome couldn't capture. Next time I forget how important it is to forgive my own kids, I'd better pull those mental pictures out and look them over once again.

—John Duckworth

RELATIONSHIP

There will be times in every teen's life when, no matter how greatly she desires to do one thing, she does something else instead.

Take, for example, the struggle many teens face concerning sexual urges. As Dr. James Dobson wrote in *Solid Answers*, between 95 and 98 percent of adolescent boys have engaged in masturbation—"and the rest have been known to lie." A smaller but still significant percentage of girls have also engaged in this activity. Many teens do this in spite of their belief that the act is wrong, and guilt is the frequent result of this failure to abide by their convictions. Dr. Dobson explained:

That guilt has the potential to do considerable psychological and spiritual damage. Boys and girls who labor under divine condemnation can gradually become convinced that even God couldn't love them. They promise a thousand times with great sincerity never again to commit this despicable act. Then a week or two passes, or perhaps several months. Eventually, the hormonal pressure accumulates until nearly every waking moment reverberates with sexual desire. Finally, in a moment (and I do mean a *moment*) of weakness, it happens again. What then, dear friend? Tell me what a young person says to God after he or she has just broken the one thousand first solemn promise to Him? I am convinced that some teenagers have thrown over their faith because of their inability to please God at this point of masturbation.[1]

Failure in an area like this can scuttle a teenager's efforts to maintain a close relationship with God. What can a spiritual mentor do to help a teen cope with such failure? Extend grace, as Dr. Dobson advised.

I would suggest that parents talk to their twelve- or thirteen-year-old boys, especially, in the same general way my mother and father discussed this subject with me. We were riding in the car, and my dad said, "Jim, when I was a boy, I worried so much about masturbation. It really became a scary thing for me because I thought God was condemning me for what I couldn't help. So I'm telling you now that I hope you don't feel the need to engage in this act when you reach the teen years, but if you do, you shouldn't be too concerned about it. I don't believe it has much to do with your relationship with God."

What a kind thing my father did for me that night in the car. He was a very conservative minister who never compromised his standards of morality to the day of his death. He stood like a rock for biblical principles and commandments. Yet he cared enough about me to lift from my shoulders the burden of guilt that nearly destroyed some of my friends in the church. This kind of "reasonable" faith taught to me by my parents is one of the primary reasons I never felt it necessary to rebel against parental authority or defy God.[2]

This is not to say that masturbation should never be a cause for concern. Dr. Dobson wrote that it may have harmful implications when it involves oppressive guilt, extreme obsession, or pornography, or when it becomes a substitute for healthy sexual relations in marriage. But as with other struggles our teens experience, it is best approached with grace in mind. Grace makes it possible for spiritual growth to continue despite failure.

## Modeling How to Handle Failure

When your teen sees you dealing with your own failures, can she tell that grace is part of the equation?

Bette is a mom who berates herself audibly and at great length when she makes a mistake. Her guilt is palpable when she confesses at family devotions, "I'm just terrible at remembering to pray during the day. I'm sure God isn't very happy with me."

Jerry, on the other hand, is a dad who tries to hide his mistakes. He fools no one, but he believes his facade of perfection will inspire his teenage son to reach for "a high standard."

Though the approaches of Bette and Jerry are different, they share something in common: Their children, watching their examples, will learn little or nothing about grace.

## Teens' "Traits of Great Parents," Part 4

- "Loving parents who put aside their desires to nurture and minister to their teen. Parents who are open and honest with their child."
- "Involved, vocal, set an example, understanding, compassionate."
- "(1) Genuine inside and out. (2) Loving concern is always evident. (3) Loyalty to teen. (4) Model Jesus."
- "Honest, fun, compassionate."
- "More than a friend; needs to be a *parent* first."

Bette's openness about her shortcomings could be an asset—if she didn't attach a load of guilt to her failures. To model a more hopeful response to failure, she needs to remind herself of God's love and forgiveness.

So does Jerry. Admitting weakness can be frightening if we assume that parents must give the impression of being flawless. As Charles Stanley wrote in *How to Keep Your Kids on Your Team*, "When parents try to hide their mistakes from their kids, they are usually trying to protect the image they feel responsible to portray—the perfect parents who have their act completely together and who can handle anything at any time."[3]

> *When your teen sees you dealing with your own failures, can she tell that grace is part of the equation?*

But parents fail. If we take the risk of admitting that secret (which is actually no secret at all to our kids), our failures can

**RELATIONSHIP**

## Teens' Advice to Parents About Nurturing Spiritual Growth, Part 5

■ "Teaching the importance of forgiveness is invaluable. Kids are deeply affected by the tremendous cruelty the human race is capable of during their first year of school. Teach them how to guard themselves against criticism, and give them wisdom on how they can learn to change their initial anger in the face of rejection to pity or seeing things from a perspective that the other person does not understand."

■ "Do not hope that your kids will make correlations on their own between your love and actions and God's love and Jesus' sacrifice. Be intentional; make sure your kids don't miss the message of salvation and grace because you assumed they could make the connection on their own."

■ "Be available to your teens. Listen to them and don't *always* 'lecture' them. Encourage them (not naggingly) to get involved in your family church and youth group. Have family times of fun and teaching moments, such as a family Bible study."

■ "Get your teens in an active, alive youth group with leaders who truly desire to disciple the kids and see them live for Jesus. And practice what you preach."

■ "Listen, listen, listen. Be consistent with discipline, and watch your own example."

become times to show our teens that even though we're imperfect, God still loves us. And He loves them, too.

Even the apostle Paul, who did many things right, made mistakes. But he admitted that fact and kept moving ahead, growing as he went. He said, "Not that I have already obtained all this, or have already been made perfect, but I press on to take hold of that for which Christ Jesus took hold of me" (Philippians 3:12).

## Saying "I'm Sorry"

Another way to extend grace to your teen is to say you're sorry when you've hurt him or the relationship. Some parents seem to believe that saying "I'm sorry" is a sign of weakness. Instead, it's a sign of strong character.

Sarah wasn't fond of her father. She treated him with respect but didn't *feel* respect for him. She felt he viewed himself as perfect—as one who never needed to apologize. One day, when her sister Susan said something rude and disrespectful to him, their father slapped Susan on the face. Stunned, both girls moved to a bedroom to quietly nurse their fear and anger.

Soon, however, their father knocked on the door. He poked his head in and said, "Susan, what I did was very wrong. I'm very sorry, and I won't do that again. I hope you will forgive me."

At that moment, both Susan and Sarah gained new respect for their father. As a result, Susan began to work harder at controlling her words and attitude. And the parent-teen relationship was soon marked by greater grace.

Charles Stanley wrote, "If you want to keep your kids on your team, you need to let them know you understand; you understand their weaknesses, struggles and failures; you understand because you have a few yourself. Admit your errors, own up to your mistakes, share your weaknesses and you will have taken another positive step toward keeping your children on your team."[4]

## Be a Great Forgiver

Imagine a father who keeps track of his children's wrongs in a notebook. Every day or two, he reminds them of their failures.

This is his duty as a dad, he says; after all, he's just telling the truth.

His children live in fear and hopelessness. They see no way to get past the wrongs they've done, no matter how much good they do in the future. They think, *Why bother trying?*

That father doesn't sound like God, does he?

God's relationship with us is characterized by forgiveness. So should be our relationships with our teens. Forgiveness cuts the chains of sin and guilt and releases us to find freedom and new direction.

In his role as director of Kanakuk Kamps, Joe White has seen many teens who desperately needed forgiveness. He tells the story of one in particular:

> Rob was a very unusual camper. I'm not sure how he got to Kanakuk, since most of our kids are from very godly homes. Yet Rob came to camp saying he wanted to "kill the director."
>
> When I met him, I discovered Rob was born to a 14-year-old mother and a 15-year-old father who were killed in an accident when he was eight years old. His rage and anger translated into numerous fights and encounters with the law. He was probably the angriest young man I've ever met. He'd been in a teen lockup facility for four years and involved in fights there. His hands were scarred from those fights.
>
> As soon as he got off the bus, we asked to see his luggage (as we do with all kids) to make sure that there was nothing unsafe inside. He lashed out at me, wanting to take me out, as he had been doing with others for so many years.
>
> Ironically, tattooed across Rob's back in two-inch letters was the word *forgiven*. Yet Rob knew nothing about forgiveness. His home environment was filled with rage.
>
> Over the course of the next two weeks, I had the privilege of showing Rob unconditional love. Even though he tried to beat me up the first night of camp, I returned the anger with love and warmth and uncondi-

tional regard, which is my privilege as the "father" of these campers.

Two weeks went by, and one night I observed this boy—who had never really seen freedom as a teenager—watch and truly experience the sunset. As I walked by after the sun had set, Rob came to me with tears streaming down his face. He threw his arms around me, hugged me, and wept on my shoulder for five minutes. I quietly held him.

He looked at the scars on his hands and said, "I can't believe I've been this horrible to people my whole life, unnecessarily hitting people. Coach, I saw a beautiful painting in the sky tonight, and I knew that the painting had to have a painter."

I said, "Rob, you know what's better than that?"

"What?"

"To know that painter as a personal Friend."

Rob, who always had the last word, said, "You know what's better than that?"

I asked, "What?"

"To take that personal Friend into your heart and take Him home with you."

And so Rob gave his heart to Jesus.

That word *forgiven*, the word tattooed across his back, had become reality in his life for the first time. Rob found forgiveness. And he felt forgiven. The strength that forgiveness gave him enabled him to go back to his gang to pay off his $753 drug debt—and turn his back on the lifestyle and gang he'd been heavily involved in.

The forgiven teen can find the strength to strive for secondary virginity, to turn away from violence, or to make a parent proud again.

Forgiveness is not excusing a teen's wrong behavior. It isn't saying, "Oh, it's okay that you smashed my car while you were reckless. Have a nice day." It isn't saying, "It's okay for

> *Forgiveness jump-starts new beginnings.*

you to scream obscenities at me. Just let it all out." Instead, forgiveness admits the seriousness of the wrong but ceases to desire vengeance for it, because Jesus already paid the eternal price for all our wrongs with His death.

The forgiven teen may have to work to pay for the car repair after reckless driving, or to earn back your trust after telling a lie. But forgiveness says, "I love you anyway, and I will not hold this against you. I won't bring this up time and again. The incident will be put to rest."

When we forgive our teens, we show them grace. And we offer what God wants to give them for the rest of their lives—one chance after another to keep growing closer to Him despite their mistakes.

# CHAPTER 12

# Demonstrating Commitment in Your Marriage

Imagine that your teenager invites you to peruse a scrapbook full of photographs, cards and letters, awards, newspaper clippings, and journal pages. Contained in this album are all the mementos, keepsakes, and remembrances that constitute his childhood memories. You come upon a page with the heading "Mom and Dad's Marriage," and you can't help but stop to take a closer look. *Oh, boy. This should be interesting!*

What do you expect to see there? What perceptions of your marriage might your teen have? Would you find photos of you and your spouse laughing, hugging, and enjoying each other? Would you discover notes and journal pages describing how "Mom and Dad really seem to love each other"? Or would the pasted-on snapshots and mementos signify something less than ideal—a marriage that's contentious, cold, dreary, or depressing?

Although your child may or may not be compiling an actual scrapbook, she is undoubtedly accumulating an abundance of experiences and recollections about family life, including your marriage. Every day, as your teen watches her parents talk, laugh, argue, debate, hug, and kiss, she gathers more material for the family album. And all these disparate images and impressions will someday form a complete picture of your marriage that she will carry into adulthood.

Listen as two college students speak in starkly contrasting terms about their parents' marriages:

*Andrew from Vermont:*
My sisters and I had no doubt that Mom and Dad loved each other. Not only that, they just flat-out *liked* each other! They were always hugging and giving shoulder rubs. They would laugh and tell stories and talk for hours about everything. Many times, I walked into their room and interrupted them praying or reading together. Of course they weren't perfect—they argued sometimes. But they always worked it out and didn't hold grudges.

There were times when I was in high school that I thought they were *so* corny and embarrassing. But now I realize how lucky I was to grow up with parents who had a good, fun, stable marriage. If I'm fortunate enough to get married one day, I want to have a relationship like my folks have.

*Corrine from Nebraska:*
My parents rarely, if ever, showed affection for each other. I can't remember them saying "I love you" or "I'm so glad we're together" or anything like that. Everything was businesslike and boring. There certainly wasn't much warmth or touchy-feely stuff. I even felt sometimes on holidays and family vacations that my parents were going through the motions—you know, trying to do the "happy family" routine, even through their hearts weren't in it.

When I got to be about 13, I started wondering if they were staying together just for me and my older brother. Sure enough, a few months after I graduated from high school, they separated, and then finally divorced the following year.

My own feelings about marriage? I just don't know. Seems awfully risky these days, with so many people getting divorced and who knows how many more staying in miserable relationships. I honestly can't see myself getting married—it's just not worth it.

There's no question that kids of all ages are—for better or worse—profoundly shaped by their parents' relationship. We could spend pages outlining the dozens of research studies showing the detrimental effects of divorce on children. In fact, few people would dispute that kids suffer enormous emotional damage when they are forced to endure the breakup of their parents' marriage.

> *There's no question that kids of all ages are—for better or worse—profoundly shaped by their parents' relationship.*

But the issue here extends far beyond the effects of divorce. As critical as it is for children to grow up in an intact home, it's also vital for them to see a marriage that is loving, supportive, devoted, and tender. As psychiatrist Ross Campbell says:

> The first responsibility of parents is to provide a loving and happy home. And the most important relationship in the home is the marriage bond, which takes primacy over the parent-child relationship. The security of a teenager and the quality of the parent-child bonding are largely dependent on the quality of the marital bonding. You can see how important it is to assure the best possible relationship between husband and wife, since this is the basis for seriously attempting to relate to a teenager in a more positive way.[1]

Parents who stay together for the kids may be giving their children a gift by not subjecting them to the hardships of divorce. But parents who nurture their marriage, striving to keep it strong and robust, give their sons and daughters a far more valuable gift: a safe, positive, nurturing environment in which to develop and mature into adulthood. And that's just the beginning.

## A Few Good Reasons to Keep Your Marriage Strong and Healthy

God intends a husband and wife to enjoy a lifelong marriage that is deeply meaningful and continually growing. That's the number-one reason you and your spouse should strive for a solid, committed, healthy marriage. But as we've said, the effect your marriage has on your child provides even more motivation to pursue a great relationship. Let's look at three of the foremost ways your teenager will be influenced by your marriage:

*1. Marriage is often where our Christian commitment is demonstrated most clearly.* You may have heard the well-worn phrase "The best sermon I'll ever preach is the way I love my spouse." There's a lot of truth in that adage (some sayings become well worn because they contain so much wisdom!). The faith training you give your teen will be reinforced and reaffirmed when it is lived out in the context of your marriage. And naturally the opposite is also true: Your preaching and teaching about Christian values will mean little if they're not displayed in the relationship your son or daughter sees up close and personal every day—your marriage.

Writer Mark Galli said, "It's harder to live out your faith after you're married, especially as you try to live out your faith *together*. But it's one of the hard ways that lead to abundant life."[2] At least part of the abundant life Galli referred to comes from knowing that, by maintaining a godly marriage, you're demonstrating for your teen what the Christian faith is all about.

> *The faith training you give your teen will be reinforced and reaffirmed when it is lived out in the context of your marriage.*

The fact is, some people might be able to put on a plastic smile and play the perfect Christian for Sunday worship service or when church friends come over for dinner. But the ongoing, persistent, day-in-and-day-out quality of marriage has a way of bringing to light our real, genuine, deep-down beliefs. Marriage is where our faith is played out and put to the test. Stated another way, it's hard to fake your faith at home for very long.

Suppose your wife comes home and confesses that she backed your brand-new, still-shiny-and-spotless car into a light pole and crunched the fender and trunk. Ugh! Your dreamed-about car, the one you'll be making payments on for the next four years! How you respond speaks volumes about your innermost perspective on grace and forgiveness. Will you hug her and say, "Of course I'm disappointed, dear, but it's all right. The main thing is that you weren't hurt. Besides, I know you feel bad about it, and I know it was an accident"? Or will you chide her: "That's great! Why can't you be more careful? You're always doing dumb things like that!"

What if your husband has been unemployed for six months, and he's lost all motivation to look for work? He scans the Sunday classifieds, but that's about it. To make matters worse, your savings account has been sucked dry, and you're sinking further into debt just to pay the mortgage and buy groceries. Can you live by your convictions to support, encourage, and respect this man? Or will you give in to the temptation to disparage and deprecate him ("You're getting lazier all the time. If you would have worked a little harder, you wouldn't have gotten laid off in the first place")?

Oh, how the challenges of married life put our faith to the test. And just to ratchet up the significance of your response in situations like these, you can bet your teenager is soaking it all in.

*2. You're modeling what a godly marriage should (or shouldn't) be.* For better or worse, the attitudes, behaviors, and beliefs you and your spouse demonstrate about marriage will be emulated by your child. How do kids learn that husbands and wives should honor each other? By observing the way Mom and Dad respect and regard each other. How do kids learn constructive or destructive ways of handling conflict? By watching how their parents manage disagreements.

Think of it this way: The 18 years your child lives at home is, among other things, an extended, comprehensive, experiential course in how to be married. The curriculum covers how to treat one's spouse, how to communicate, how to make God the center of a relationship, what roles husbands and wives play in the home, and a thousand other factors that make marriage what it is. All of this is more caught than taught, but it is clearly and forcefully learned nonetheless. As psychologists John and Linda Friel say:

> Most of what we learn while we are growing up is below the conscious level. We just pick it up by being immersed

RELATIONSHIP

**RELATIONSHIP**

in the family. This means that we all learn the lessons of our own particular families. Perhaps Mother always made your school lunches for you, and Father always gave you extra spending money "on the side." If so, these things would just seem normal to us. That is how our lessons are learned. Sometimes we all need to learn additional lessons. For example, some people will need to learn how to nurture their marriages, while others have learned this all through childhood by simply being in the family and being around Mom and Dad's marriage.[3]

Consciously or subconsciously, your kids are learning how to "do" marriage by taking dozens of daily mental notations on how

## How We Try to Model a Good Marriage

The following parents of teens offer suggestions for modeling a strong, healthy relationship (and all are quick to point out that they don't have *perfect* marriages):

- Caryl Altmeyer, Spokane, Washington: "When Phil and I get into arguments, we try to let our kids see us resolve them. This is tough! I especially have had to learn to work through conflicts rather than just sweep them under the rug and stay angry for days. But I want my four kids to understand that conflicts are a natural part of marriage and there are constructive ways to deal with them."

- Al Janssen, Colorado Springs, Colorado: "My wife and I hug and kiss in front of our three kids all the time. They always give us a hard time and act embarrassed, but they love it. We're not affectionate just to put on a show for the kids, but we do want them to see that a happy marriage has lots of affection and tenderness."

- Bob Verhoven, Tulsa, Oklahoma: "Encouragement is a big part of our marriage. Mary and I try hard not be negative with each other or put down each other's opinions and ideas. We want to make our home positive and cheerful—a place where we say yes a lot more than no."

- Christy Smith, Spokane, Washington: "My husband, Ed, and I became Christians in our early thirties—after we'd been married 11 years. So we had some unhealthy patterns that needed to be corrected. I had to learn to let Ed be the leader of the family, and sometimes that's still not easy for me. Our children have seen us work on this area of our marriage, and I think it's good for them you and your spouse relate to each other. You may not have signed up to become a marriage instructor, but that's exactly what you are.

*3. You set the example for how to treat your spouse.* If you have reached the stage where your children are teens or preteens, you've probably learned that kids play "follow the leader" when it comes to responding to their parents. In other words, how *you* speak and act toward your mate is very likely the way your child will speak and act toward your mate.

If you talk to your wife in a sarcastic, cynical tone, you just might hear your son or daughter say, "What a stupid thing to do, Mom! That was totally lame." If you are demanding and bossy with your husband, your teen will probably follow suit: "Don't be a tightwad, Dad. I need 20 bucks." Thankfully, the flip side of this imitation situation is also true—if you are kind, gentle, affectionate, and respectful toward your spouse, there's an excellent chance your teen will be the same.

It's impossible to overstate the importance of how parents represent, interpret, and translate each other for their kids. Positive, upbeat, constructive relating between parent and teen begins with the standard set by Mom and Dad. Kids learn how to be humble servants by watching Dad humbly serve Mom. They develop a joyfully submissive heart by watching Mom joyfully submit to Dad.

## Hallmarks of a Healthy, Christ-Centered Marriage

What are the ingredients of a godly marriage? The Bible doesn't give us an itemized, 10-point checklist for evaluating the quality of marriage. However, Scripture is clear that God values certain characteristics in all relationships, especially marriage. Let's look at four of these components, which are mentioned consistently in God's Word:

### Servant Leadership

"Wives, submit to your husbands as to the Lord. . . . Husbands, love your wives, just as Christ loved the church" (Ephesians 5:22, 25).

The biblical admonition for wives to submit to their husbands and for husbands to love their wives must be important because it is repeated several times (see also Colossians 3:18-19 and 1 Peter 3:1-7).

RELATIONSHIP

In fact, Ephesians 5 contains a detailed tutorial on how spouses ought to behave toward one another. From this passage and others, it's clear that God intends for husbands to be the head, that is, the leader, of the family. But it's also clear that He wants husbands to demonstrate servant leadership as Christ did. That term—servant leadership—is a fancy way of saying, "Show love through service." For men in particular, this means that they should demonstrate that they are leaders in their households by serving their wives.

*Any husband who is living out Paul's instructions in Ephesians 5 could never treat his wife as a second-class citizen or with chauvinistic disregard for her feelings.*

Men and women are to submit to each other and to serve each other's needs. In marriage, there is to be mutual submission where a man denies himself in order to love his wife as Christ loved the church. He is still the leader, but he submits his life to his mate. Any husband who is living out Paul's instructions in Ephesians 5 could never treat his wife as a second-class citizen or with chauvinistic disregard for her feelings. In fact, just the opposite would be true.

Jonathan Wilkins of Atlanta tells about how his two boys picked up on his attitude of servant leadership. His wife, Danielle, worked full-time outside the home, in addition to handling many of the household chores. She would arrive home from work exhausted, with aching feet and tight shoulders. Nevertheless, she always cooked a nice dinner for Jonathan and the boys. Most nights, the men of the family would head off to the living room after dinner to play games, watch a sporting event on TV, or talk about the day's happenings. All the while, Danielle would be in the kitchen, washing the dishes, putting pots and pans away, and wiping the countertops.

"When my oldest son, Evan, was about 14," Jonathan said, "it just hit me—Danielle has worked all day, come home to cook us dinner, and then cleaned up the kitchen afterward. Every night. That just wasn't fair. She never complained—she was happy I could spend time with the boys after dinner. But I knew I had to change that situation."

So without saying anything to his sons, Jonathan began ushering his wife out of the kitchen after dinner each night, and he would tackle the cleanup duties.

After a couple nights of this new arrangement, Evan came into the kitchen while his dad was scouring a casserole dish and said, "Dad, whatcha doin'? The Braves are on TV tonight."

"Doing the dishes, son," Jonathan replied. "I'll be done in a few minutes."

The next night, Evan again came into the kitchen and this time asked, "Why do you do the dishes now, Dad? You didn't used to."

"I know, son," Jonathan said. "And I feel bad about that. You see, your mom works all day, then comes home and does a lot of work here. I just wanted to give her a break and show her we're in this together."

The following night, Evan, with his little brother in tow, came into the kitchen and said, "Dad, can we help? We want to give Mom a break, too."

What's more amazing is that this attitude of service began to extend beyond after-dinner chores. Jonathan said the boys became aware of how much their mom did for them, and they began pitching in more.

"I didn't intend my nightly kitchen cleanup to be a lesson in servanthood for my boys," Jonathan said. "I was just trying to help Danielle and show her I love her in that small way. But it just goes to show you—kids notice these things, probably more than most of us parents think they do. They notice, and a lot of times they follow our example."

## Grace

"Let your conversation be always full of grace" (Colossians 4:6).

In the last chapter, we talked about the importance of demonstrating grace to your teenager, and we told the story of the dad who spliced together a videotape showing all his son's outstanding moments on the basketball court while erasing all the mistakes. This guideline for giving grace—highlighting the good moments, deleting the bad—is just as important in the way you treat your spouse. Train yourself to remember and celebrate all your husband's accomplishments and achievements—and choose

■ ■ ■

## A Legacy of Love and Commitment

My mom and dad have been married for 58 years at this time. These two lovebirds have survived and thrived through the Depression, World War II, and a whole lot of husband-wife disagreements that typify most married couples trying to cope with the ups and downs of raising kids, putting meals on the table, and paying the mortgage through good times and bad, for better or worse.

Whether it was richer or poorer, my dad has always loved my mom and treated her like the fantastic lady she really is. Almost every day, Dad still writes Mom a love letter and leaves it by the sink for her to enjoy with her first cup of morning coffee. My mom meets my dad at the door each evening as he comes home from work, to help him unlace his shoes before they share an evening meal and romance. Dad is 83 years old and Mom is . . . well, "39 and holding."

Their almost six decades of dedication together have taught me some precious lessons about being a dad. The most irreplaceable gift I can give my kids is to love my wife, serve her, and meet her needs for security and affection.

Jesus said, "By this all men will know that you are my disciples, if you love one another" (John 13:35). The best way to secure my kids' own relationship with Christ is to give His love, mercy, and grace to the one who walked down the aisle in that breathtaking wedding gown a quarter of a century ago.

—Joe White

to forget his blunders and bungles. Concentrate on your wife's strengths and overlook her weaknesses.

In the midst of life's constant hustle and bustle, stress and strain, everyone blows it sometimes. We get grouchy, lose our temper, make insensitive comments, and do stupid things. How do you like your spouse to respond when you falter and fail? And how do you react when your partner messes up? Counselor Norm Wakefield hit the bull's-eye when he said, "Grace is the powerful ingredient that will bind a man and woman together when their imperfection pulls them apart."[4]

If you and your mate are consistently gracious with each other, congratulations! You've mastered one of the most challenging aspects of a Christian marriage. If, on the other hand, your relationship is weighed down by resentment and rancor, score-keeping and finger-pointing, resolve to make a fresh start. Ask God to help you grow in this area—to make your home a place of acceptance, understanding, and kindness.

**Encouragement**
"Encourage one another daily, as long as it is called Today" (Hebrews 3:13).

Is the communication in your home inspiring and uplifting or disheartening and deflating? Are you the kind of person who says to your mate, "That's a great idea . . . I like the way you do that . . . You're terrific"? Or are your words tinged with sarcasm and

**RELATIONSHIP**

## Teens' "Things I Wish My Parents Had Done Differently," Part 5

- "Growing up, I always felt like I had this 'good girl' image to uphold. My parents, I felt, loved me both for my performance and for who I was. So I hid a lot of things and didn't let people know who I really was."
- "I wish my parents had been a little more aware of how important times spent with my mentor and youth group were. Mom sometimes resented all the time I spent there, but it was very instrumental in developing me spiritually. Also, they needed to understand that my walk with the Lord would develop differently from theirs and that's okay."
- "I wish they had stayed married and that my father had been a spiritual leader and better example."
- "I would have liked for them to pray with me and discuss spiritual issues, how I was growing, what was I learning, and what things in my life needed to be changed so that I would be more a servant of Christ. I wish, too, that both of them had done personal Bible studies and set an example of how to seek Christ."
- "I wish my father had been more involved in my life. I also wish he would have lived the way he told me to live. I found it hard to listen to his guidance because he would sometimes live differently."

cynicism: "That'll never work . . . I hate it when you do that . . . You're so lazy"? If your speech is more sour than sweet, it may be time to work on correcting the imbalance.

Joe White and his wife, Debbie-Jo, live next door to author and speaker Gary Smalley and his wife, Norma, in Branson, Missouri. The four of them, along with another couple, Jim and Suzette Brawner, regularly have lunch together, and their conversations sometimes turn to what makes a great marriage and how to keep relationships sharp. At one lunchtime gathering, Gary brought six bags full of red kidney beans and white navy beans, which he handed out to each person around the table.

"I'd like to have a little contest," Gary announced. "For the next month, we're going to see who is the most encouraging marriage partner."

Then he explained that each person had been given an equal number of red and white beans. Every time one of the spouses made an encouraging, uplifting, or complimentary comment, he or she would be given a white bean. And when a spouse said something critical, disparaging, or derogatory, he or she would receive a red bean.

Gary finished by saying, "When we get together for lunch next month, we'll spill the beans—we'll spread them out on the table and see who among us is the number-one encourager."

> "The first great gift we can bestow on others is a good example."
> —Thomas Morell[5]

Turns out Gary had read a study by psychologist John Gottman and his colleagues that showed that couples who give five times as many positive comments as negative ones have a 94 percent chance of enjoying a happy marriage. He decided to put the research findings to the test in real-life situations.

Joe thought, *I may not be the world's best husband, but I am competitive. I'm going to beat Smalley on this one!*

As Joe went home, he dedicated himself to becoming a "white bean husband." Polite, appreciative, giving flowers and hugs—you name it, he did it. The white beans were flowing. When he would feel critical or negative toward Debbie-Jo, he would bite his tongue because he didn't want her producing a red bean at the next couples' gathering.

RELATIONSHIP

No one will say who took home the prize from that next meeting, but all six spouses agreed that their homes had been much more pleasant places in the last month. The experience was so positive that they've all stayed in the "white bean business" ever since, and all three marriages are vastly better off because of it.

Joe sums up the experiment this way: "Keeping a running total makes you acutely aware of every little comment. When you've got a tangible, visible reminder, it makes you hold your tongue when you want to make a jab, and it makes you look for all the positives you can point out. I'm sure that if spouses carried bags of beans with them all the time, we'd see a dramatic increase in marital satisfaction."

> *Unity means working toward consensus and choosing to set aside differences for the sake of harmony.*

So how about you and your spouse? If the two of you turned into "bean counters" for a month, who would have more red beans and who would have more white ones? More to the point, if your red-to-white ratio is tilted in the wrong direction, take this as a challenge to increase encouragement and decrease discouragement. After all, your teenager is listening in.

### Unity

"May the God who gives endurance and encouragement give you a spirit of unity among yourselves as you follow Christ Jesus" (Romans 15:5).

The root of the word *unity* is *unit*, which one dictionary defines as "a collection of parts assembled for a common function or purpose." Come to think of it, that's not a bad definition for marriage. For married couples, unity means turning two "I's" into one "we." It means meshing and merging two people's emotional, physical, and spiritual lives so they become one.

Naturally, being unified does not mean you and your spouse agree on everything. After all, you're still unique individuals with your own preferences and predilections. Unity means working toward consensus, pursuing compatibility and agreement, and choosing to set aside differences for the sake of harmony.

Spouses who are unified bring strength to the task of parenting.

**RELATIONSHIP**

**RELATIONSHIP**

Most children are adept at spotting and exploiting any dissension in their parents' perspectives (ever heard the argument "But Mom said I didn't have to"?). That's why parents should try to speak with one voice: "Dad and I firmly believe that . . ." or "Your mother and I talked this over, and we think . . ."

Another important aspect of unity within marriage is developing a common vision with your spouse for things like how and when to nurture and discipline children, what limits you'll set for your child's activities and behaviors, what qualities you want to instill in your son or daughter, and how you serve God together as a family. When you and your mate decide *together* all the issues involved in raising a teenager, you establish a consistent, stable environment for growing up.

## What Teens Admire About Their Parents' Marriages

■ Mike from Colorado: "The attribute my parents etched into my heart is commitment. They've been through many hard times, but through them all, they remained committed to each other and to Christ."

■ Bridgette from North Carolina: "My parents would talk to each other all the time. Our family would go to church together and then discuss the lessons we learned on the way home. After lunch, when my sister and I would go to our rooms, we could hear my parents talking all afternoon. They were great communicators."

■ Sara from Oregon: "My dad always encouraged and loved my mother, and she in turn respected and openly admired him. They demonstrated their love and commitment in everyday living."

■ Steve from California: "My parents always put each other above us kids. They believed that even though they had a God-given responsibility to raise children, they were also held accountable for keeping their marriage strong. My sister and I were never neglected, but we knew that Mom put Dad first, and vice versa (after God, of course)."

■ Bridgett from Ohio: "Every night that my dad was away from home, he would call my mom to talk and say he loved her. He would also call throughout the day just to see how she was doing. And when he came home, Mom would hand over the reins of running the household, even though I knew this was a struggle for her sometimes."

## Keep Great Memories Alive

We started this chapter by posing the hypothetical situation involving your teenager's scrapbook. So now ask yourself: *Are we creating memories that reinforce the four marriage qualities mentioned above—servant leadership, grace, encouragement, unity—and other characteristics we want to model? Are we giving our child a positive picture of what marriage can be? Are we ensuring that our home is a place our child will look back upon fondly?* If you are, terrific! Keep it up! If you're not, take heart: There's still time. As long as your child is under your roof, you have opportunities every day to build great memories. Let the words of pastor Chuck Swindoll sink in:

> The beautiful music of living is composed, practiced, and perfected in the harmony of the home: The freedom to laugh long and loud, the encouragement to participate in creative activities, the spontaneity of relaxed relationships that plant memories and deepen our roots in the rich, rare soil of authentic happiness. . . . We're missing it—God's best—if the fun memories are eclipsed by the fierce ones. The world outside the family circle is dark enough. When the light goes out *within* the circle, how great is the darkness!

Chuck summed up his thoughts on family memory making with this compelling statement:

> I'd much rather my brood remember me as the dad who tossed their mother fully clothed into the swimming pool—and lived to tell the story—than the preacher who frowned too much, yelled too loud, talked too long, and died too young.[6]

That's the kind of goal all parents can aim for! Make your home a place of fun and celebration. Etch images in your children's minds and hearts that demonstrate what a happy, committed, godly marriage is all about. Show your kids a marriage filled with love, respect, and admiration. Let them see you and your spouse hug and kiss and tango across the living room floor. Celebrate your

**RELATIONSHIP**

**RELATIONSHIP**

wedding anniversary in grand style. Enlist your kids in preparing a fancy dinner for your spouse—for no particular reason. Plan a surprise birthday party for your husband six months before his actual date of birth (it's sure to catch him off guard!). Set aside whole days for nothing but fun and frivolity.

Your child's mental and emotional scrapbook—the one containing indelible images of family and married life—is being assembled *right now*. Grab hold of every opportunity to show your teen that a marriage centered on God is (while not problem-free) enjoyable, fulfilling, and deeply meaningful.

# CHAPTER 13

# Overcoming Conflicts

- While your car is being serviced, you borrow the one your 17-year-old son usually drives. As you start it, the radio nearly blows you out the door with its volume. But even more disturbing are the few words of the song you can actually decipher—mostly profanity filled with hatred and violence.
- One morning over breakfast, your 13-year-old daughter tells you about the body piercings her friends have recently received. You attempt to lose yourself in the newspaper until she drops the bomb: "So I'm gonna get my belly button pierced."
- Your 15-year-old son asks, "Can I go to Tom's Friday night? He's having some of the guys from church over for a video night." Before you agree, you ask what they're going to see. His answer: "*Lethal Death and Destruction*, a cool action flick that most of the guys have already seen. The effects are incredible!"
- Your 16-year-old daughter is heading out the door for school wearing a skimpy tank top and jeans with holes nearly everywhere. When you question her about her appearance, she says, "Daddy, you are so old-fashioned! Everybody wears stuff like this, and I love it because it is so comfortable. See ya!"

Whether you have faced situations like these or not, you will inevitably find yourself in conflict with your teen at various stages of adolescence. Your child views this time as an opportunity for increasing independence, while Mom and Dad watch their authority ebbing away. Personal preferences create some of the points of disagreement, while others stem from moral and safety issues. Fashion and fads may provide battlegrounds in some families, and life-and-death decisions (like drug and alcohol abuse) may invade others.

As parents, we must make choices between carrying responsibility for the welfare of our children and allowing that responsibility to rest on our increasingly mature young people. The lenient parent who establishes no guidelines and allows the teen to do whatever she wants runs the risk of exposing the teen to physical danger and losing respect in the eyes of the teen.

> *When a teen is given no opportunity to make his own choices, he may not have the logic or realization of consequences to act wisely.*

Susan, now in her thirties, recalls that her mother allowed her free rein through her teen years. She says, "I think I wanted her to tell me no, and I'd do more and more outrageous things to get her to act. But she never did. I had to hit rock bottom, as if I'd fallen off a cliff. It's taken me a long time, over 10 years, to forgive her."

On the other hand, rigid, overbearing parenting can also produce young adults who either rebel out of frustration or do not have enough experience and discernment to make wise decisions on their own when they arrive at maturity. When a teen is given no opportunity to make his own choices, he may not have the logic or realization of consequences to act wisely.

Raymond, recently graduated from college, grew up in such a home. "My parents loved me very much," he says, "but because they had been pretty wild in high school and college, they went the opposite way. My brothers and I had a strict curfew and few chances to socialize or to make our own decisions. When I went away to school, even though it was a Christian college, I was blown away by the freedom. I made some bad choices both in activities and in the company I kept. I regret some of the things I did, but fortunately I have learned from them. I've even talked my mom and dad into loosening up on my younger brothers so they'd be able to bounce those choices off [my parents] before they left home."

For parents like Raymond's who realize they may have been too strict, however, loosening those rules without an explanation can cause confusion for the teens. As Chuck Swindoll wrote, "If the standard the rule is based on is a good one, keep it. But lessen or change the associated rule. Pray for wisdom in making the rules more flexible. Try to stress the fact that you want to maintain the administration of the home, but that you're ready to do it under a new philosophy. If you are open and honest and willing to take responsibility, the teenager will probably be excited about the change."[1]

Conflicts and differences of opinion can help teens and parents to see opposing points of view without creating a bleeding wound in the relationship. The key is to develop a balanced, respectful manner of discussion before differences arise. Scripture illustrates this balance through two easily remembered verses: "Honor your father and your mother," and "Fathers [or parents], do not provoke your children to anger" (Exodus 20:12; Ephesians 6:4, NASB).

Parental integrity is vital in building a relationship that can withstand conflicts. Teens are no longer at the stage where nearly anything Mom or Dad does must be right—just because they *are* Mom and Dad. No, teens have arrived at the maturity level where they evaluate the actions and words of others, including their own parents. If your talk doesn't match your walk, your teens are liable to question motives and point out inconsistencies. As Joe White says, "You have a strong tool for developing good decision-making skills if you continue to nurture a strong relationship with your children. As a result, they're going to tend eventually to imitate you. If your choices are poor, their choices will be poor. If you rationalize in your own life, they will tend to rationalize as well. But if they see you making wise choices, the chances are better that they will make wise ones as well."

## How to Avoid Conversational Roadblocks

What does balanced, respectful discussion look like? Let's begin by considering what it *doesn't* look like. The type of language and the tone used can stop meaningful discussion in its tracks. Here are eight examples of how *not* to communicate with your teen routinely:

1. *Direct orders.* ("You have to do it this way; I don't care how your friends do it.") These reduce the teen to an enlisted man hearing the commands of a superior officer. Orders cut off communication and tell him his needs and opinions are not important.
2. *Threats.* ("If you do that one more time . . .") Threatening statements produce fear and uneasiness. They also create the temptation for the teen to see whether the warning will be carried out, which can result in rebellion.
3. *Preachiness.* ("Christians shouldn't do that sort of thing.") While a preachy assertion may be true, the reasoning should be explained instead of simply giving a religious-sounding, guilt-inducing bromide.
4. *Blame and criticism.* ("How'd you ever get a crazy idea like that?") Personally critical messages create feelings

## Fighting Fair

Gary and Greg Smalley are communication experts, and they're also a father-and-son team who have ridden the rapids and survived in their own relationship. They suggest that ground rules be set before issues of conflict actually arise, so that both sides know the boundaries. Of course, that doesn't mean the rules will be followed perfectly in the heat of battle, but at least an effort can be made to set a proper tone. Here are the Smalleys' rules for fighting fair:

■ *Listen for understanding.* Make sure that both sides are truly paying attention to what is being said instead of simply preparing a rebuttal. Listening is the heart of effective communication.
■ *Avoid yelling, verbal threats, or abuse.* After all, what can really be accomplished when emotions flare and voices get out of control?
■ *Maintain an honoring, respectful, and loving atmosphere.* The relationship between the parent and child will last far longer than the thrill of victory or the agony of defeat in this particular battle.

of inadequacy and inferiority rather than lay a groundwork for meaningful discussion.

5. *Name-calling.* ("You're acting like a spoiled brat.") Instead of talking about behavior, this action puts the teen in a category. When a person feels misunderstood or stereotyped, he tends to either quit trying to communicate or to respond with anger.

6. *Analyzing.* ("Here's the way I see your problem.") Analysis is a communication stopper if it's not requested. If a negative analysis hits the mark, the person feels exposed and angry; if it misses, she feels hostile and embarrassed. Often the teen simply wants the issue to be heard, not to be solved.

7. *Unfounded reassurance.* ("Things will be better tomorrow.") Blithely saying that everything will turn out all right may communicate that you don't want to accept the teen's feelings, or it may communicate the message "I really don't care enough to help you deal with this now."

RELATIONSHIP

- *Use open communication.* Clearly communicate your feelings as well as the "evidence" you have compiled to win your case.
- *Don't bring in past "garbage."* One father indicated that his daughter became "historical" whenever they argued. When he was questioned whether he actually meant "hysterical," he said, "No, she remembers everything I've ever done wrong in full historical detail."
- *Keep the focus off the person's character.* You are discussing an opinion or a behavior. If you allow the argument to move into areas of virtue, you are less likely to come to any sort of compromise.
- *Avoid accusatory language,* like "You never . . ." and "You always . . . ." Both are untrue and far too vague.
- *No violence or name-calling.* Discussions that fall to this level are not worthy to be called discussions, and reconciliation is much more difficult afterward.
- *Make sure only one person talks at a time.* This really returns to the first point. A person who is talking has little energy or attention left to listen.[2]

8. *Sarcasm.* ("Yeah, sure. Quit kidding around. You're fine, aren't you?") If she is made fun of, chances are good that the communication channel will shut down.[3]

See chapter eight for more about how to communicate effectively with your teens.

## Control Versus Independence

So, who is really in charge during a child's teen years? Are you still running the show, or is your adolescent having the chance to spread his wings? The answer is—both. Even though you retain the responsibility and the authority for the household, you must balance that control with the need to prepare your teen to assume his own adult responsibilities. The most effective way to do this is by gradually increasing the opportunities to make decisions.

Think about the raising of your teens as a type of pilot training. Young fliers don't simply hop into a cockpit, roar down a runway, and take off into the clouds. Before and during the first flights, hours and hours of practice occur under the watchful gaze of a trained, experienced professional. If an inexperienced pilot confronts a difficult situation on his own, without appropriate training, disasters can happen (and probably will). However, if the trainer is present, chances are good that the damage will be minimized or avoided altogether.

> *When a teen opens up to share a problem or concern, she wants to be taken seriously.*

The teen years represent those training times while you're still available to take over the controls if the plane malfunctions. Some of those training situations involve risk, and feelings between the rookie and the trainer can become strained. You need to show a special sensitivity, recognizing just when to step in to reduce the risk or save the day. Stepping in too soon can solve the problem, but it may keep your young person from working out a solution on her own. The goal is to get that young pilot to the point of being able to solo, and that won't happen without the opportunity to test her wings.

**RELATIONSHIP**

Realize that many of the issues that create conflict are truly areas of personal opinion, not significant moral disputes. Later in this chapter we'll focus on choosing your battles, and the specific topics included here touch on the most common conflicts. Throughout these discussions, remember Dr. James Dobson's overriding advice: "The objective of parenting through the teen years is to keep your kids on your team. Don't throw away your friendship over behavior that has no great moral significance. There will be plenty of real issues that require you to stand like a rock. Save your big guns for crucial confrontations."[4]

Don't view resolving a particular conflict as the end of the battle, either. The conflict-causing issue—disrespect, breaking curfew, or whatever—may only be a symptom of a deeper concern. Keep asking questions gently to probe for the real problem. Once you've identified it, you can take appropriate action.

Now let's look at some of the specific common areas of parent-teen conflict.

## Areas of Conflict

### Music

The world of popular music has been a primary source of conflict between parents and teens at least since today's parents were teens. From the days of Elvis and the Beatles (and probably back into the Swing Era as well), dads have been grumbling about the inappropriateness of music, and moms have been wringing their hands about what their kids are listening to. However, even though you may have faced challenges on these issues with your own parents, contemporary music creates even greater concerns.

To better understand the depths of indecency, sexuality, and violence to which today's popular music has fallen, please read chapter 20 on media discernment. It will convince you, if you have any doubts now, of your need to set guidelines for what your children listen to. And how do you set those guidelines?

First, by finding out about your teen's music. It will do you no good to express disapproval if you are going on the basis of what others say. Listening to a CD (as painful as that may be) or having your teen read you the lyrics out loud will give you a level of credibility beyond the "Well, I hear it's just terrible" stage. If your teen is not willing to listen with you or to let you read the lyrics, chances are good that he knows it won't meet with your approval. But ask to see the CD, sit down, and listen with him anyway.

Holly's dad, Jim, took this advice. He reported, "By actually sitting in front of the stereo and listening carefully, I was forced to pay attention instead of just thinking about the noise she was listening to. A couple of the songs pleasantly surprised me by what they were communicating, but then there was one that became a definite 'no-go.' The best part was that we talked about the songs person to person, which led to a conversation about other things going on at her school. Because I listened, I gained the right to have an opinion in her mind."

Holly had a similar response. "I thought Dad was kidding when he suggested a date to listen to 'my' music. It made me nervous at first, but he pointed out a couple things that I hadn't realized about the music—particularly about how women were presented. It really wasn't respectful at all in a couple of the songs, so I agreed to not listen to those. On the other hand, he really liked a couple and asked me to play them while we were eating dinner. Go figure! I think Mom was shocked."

Remember, the goal is not to make good decisions on our

## Teens' "Traits of Great Parents," Part 5

- "Being honest and consistent. The spiritual lessons my parents taught me were also lived out in their lives. There was no double standard, no 'Here's what we do when God's around, but this is how we really act.' "
- "They listen, they pray before they give an answer, they're honest, they're willing to admit they made a mistake, they're forgiving, they're helpful, they care, *they are loving!*"
- "Discerning; good communicator; healthy relationship prior to teen years."
- "Loving involvement in child's life: trusting; caring; understanding; forgiving."
- "They are good listeners, compassionate, affectionate, strong in their love for the teen (they must be able to say no and lovingly but firmly enforce the rules. Tough love must win out!). Not too caught up in their own lives that they have no time to spend with the teen, and they must love each other unconditionally."

teens' behalf; rather, it is to instill discernment and a recognition of consequences so they will make wise decisions on their own. In our media-saturated society, we can't keep our children in a protected greenhouse even if we ban particular music from our homes. They may not hear it there, but a friend's house or car radio—even a computer—can become a channel for listening. If a teen doesn't have the wisdom to make good decisions, she is at the mercy of what she hears.

While you may be able to head off some of the problems with this kind of preemptive strike, what do you do if your teen still decides to make choices about music contrary to what you think is best? He may say, "I know you don't like it, but I do, and I'm going to keep listening to it. I don't even listen to the words, but the beat rocks!" With most teens, taking a hard line and forbidding particular music may result in a rebellious spirit and a tendency to sneak around the restrictions.

Jim, a Texas dad, learned this the hard way when he made a big deal out of destroying a group of CDs. "I hated some of the music my daughter was listening to, so I took some of them out in the backyard and whacked them with a hammer. Sure, I was overreacting, but I thought I was making a point. Once the tears stopped, we had a long talk about what was appropriate, and I thought she understood. But she was playing a game. Within two days, she had her friends make cassette copies of every single one of those CDs. I didn't know about it for quite a while, but what I'd done had forced her to deceive me."

Musical tastes run according to popular trends, so the best advice may be to just be patient. Instead of arguing with your teen, observe him. Be aware of mood swings, because the negativity of some music can lead a teen toward depression, while the anger in other songs can lead to violence. Know your child and promote openness, even about music you don't approve of, because that opportunity for meaningful discussion can come at any time. You might want to suggest some type of compromise. For example, for every half hour of listening to "his" music (the stuff you don't like but isn't totally unacceptable), you can ask him to listen to Christian contemporary music (or even something secular that has redeeming qualities) for a half hour.

RELATIONSHIP

The key here is keeping the lines of communication open on both ends so that your teen feels your willingness to be involved in his world and to understand what he's encountering. If he feels that, then some of the potential conflicts can actually be avoided, or at least the effects can be lessened.

No, we're not suggesting you will become a fan of Guts R Us or whatever the current hot rock group is. But at least your teen won't think you haven't listened to any contemporary music since the Carpenters and the Lettermen. And by the way, this listening suggestion can also come into play with contemporary Christian music artists. One dad went to a Newsboys concert with his teens (during the band's aluminum foil period) and said, "While I couldn't really hear anything for a couple days afterward, the enthusiasm of the crowd even during the songs that were more worshipful was pretty inspiring. They weren't worshipping the group but the same God the band was praising."

Before leaving the musical arena, here's another suggestion. Sit down and talk with your teen about the music of your era versus the music of today. Music has a

> *Music has a powerful effect on people's lives and our society.*

powerful effect on people's lives and our society. What did the songs from the Stones, the Doors, and Jefferson Airplane really say to your generation? What political and social movements correspond? How did the antiwar violence of the 1960s and 1970s affect the world in which you grew up? How is the racial and political violence of today reflected in the music, and how much of it is a reflection of the music? In the wake of the feminist movement, how can today's music still be so degrading toward women?

Again, for more advice on helping your teen make good choices in regard to the media, see chapter 20.

### Television and Movies

Like music choices, television and movie selections provide plenty of opportunity for conversation and mutual decision making. You need to recognize once again that your role, particularly as the teen matures, is not to just dictate choices to your child but to help him develop discernment in making his own choices. And both of you need to remember that rating systems, whether for movies or on television, are only intended to be guidelines and advisories. As a parent, you still need to provide the guidance.

But suppose your teen sees attending R-rated movies as a rite of passage related to his seventeenth birthday. "I've followed your rules all my life, even when most of my friends haven't," he tells you. "Now that I'm 17, I'm even legal, so what's the big deal? A lot of the shows on TV are worse than that movie, so I'm going to go with my friends—and you can't stop me." The problem is that he's right. Even if you can stop him on that occasion, you can't keep him from going at some other time. And besides, regardless of the rating, the movie will eventually be available through video rental and sale.

As parents, we can only provide a certain amount of protection. Is stopping your teen from viewing this movie worth endangering your relationship with your teen? No. So perhaps the compromise approach can work here, too. Before she watches a movie that would cross your line, you can ask her to read a review from a trusted review source like *Plugged In* and talk it through with you. At least that way you will know that she's aware of the material she will encounter. You might also have your teen give you a review after she sees a film. That way, she'll pay closer attention to what she's viewing. One caution: Don't overreact if the review honestly confirms your worst fears about the movie. If you do, you will close that discussion way too quickly and inspire your teen to gloss over the truth the next time.

Things like foul language, sexual innuendo, and suggestiveness may not cause a film to receive a restrictive rating, but they may still have a dramatic influence on your young person's mind. Work toward developing a relationship in which the use of such things in a movie can be discussed openly and honestly. By doing so, you can keep communication channels open. You'll know what your teen is seeing and how she's responding to it, and you'll be able to talk about the pros and cons, the benefits and costs, of various choices.

Even if you could dictate the movies your teen attends in theaters, with the advent and expansion of the VCR/DVD and cable

TV, you don't have the same control over what your teen sees either in your own home or the homes of friends. Therefore, Mom and Dad, sit down and talk with your child about what is and isn't appropriate to see. Joe White tells parents, "The standard we have chosen in our home is P & P. I don't pay attention to the rating system because even PG movies can have one of the P's (pornography or profanity). For me, if there's pornography or profanity in a movie, it's out. And my kids know that's my standard in TV, magazines, movies, or anything else."

Always remember, too, that young people carefully watch what their parents do and compare the parents' actions with their words. You lose a lot of influence if your own viewing habits contradict what you expect of your teen. Don't give him the opportunity to accuse you of living by the hypocritical double standard of "Do what I say, not what I do."

Movies and television also can provide opportunities to communicate about issues related to the media. Like music, these artistic works carry ideas in a medium that subtly captures minds. When your teen wants to see a movie, at the very least you should do some research through reviews of trusted publications or Web sites, ones that you know reflect your outlook. Another approach is to preview the movie before allowing your child to see it.

Yet a third manner of video and television review is to sit down together to watch. Doing it as a family (or as a parent and teen) will give you the chance to discuss issues raised in the film and provide a more mature interpretation of what is being presented. As the *Focus on the Family Complete Book of Baby and Child Care* states,

> Whatever you and your teenager see, talk about tone and content. Is this film or program selling a viewpoint, and if so, what is it? If something struck you as offensive, why? Was there a positive message involved? Before he's living on his own, he's going to need to learn discernment. Otherwise, while you may succeed in keeping every scrap of offensive material off his mental radar screen while he's in high school, he's eventually going to be exposed to it later on—but without your preparation or guidance.[5]

For more advice on helping your teen make good media choices, see chapter 20.

### Earrings, Piercings, and Tattoos

While poking holes in parts of the body other than the ear may seem strange to most adults in our culture, the reality is that fashion doesn't always follow common sense. Dr. Allen Johnson of the Auburn Family Institute takes a practical approach to talking with teens about piercing.

> First of all, recognize that body piercings are fads—and fads die out. Most hippies of the sixties now wear suits to their jobs. Calmly discuss the medical risks of the proce-dures. Navel piercing can take a year to heal, because that area is prone to infection and easily irritated by clothes. Tongues swell tremendously when first pierced and always remain tender. Improperly placed piercing, even in the cartilage of the ear, can damage nerves and cause disfigurement. Suggest temporary solutions such as faux piercings with magnetic studs.[6]

Earrings for guys may fit into the personal preference cate-gory rather than being a conflict worth battling over. They're becoming so common throughout the fashion world, both adult and teen, that some parents may choose to take their stand on other issues. However, even if you're willing to let your son wear an earring, if you make it clear that your motivation is his best interest, you can have a good discussion. Why did he want to have his ear pierced? What does he think other people will think about his fashion statement? How is he going to feel about his decision two or five or ten years from now?

One mom with two daughters and a son said, "They did some things just to shock, rebel, and do something that did not have [the parent's] approval. Thus, when my son wanted to pierce his nose—something that grossed me out—I responded with, 'How boring. Everyone else is doing that.' His grandparents gave him a similar reaction. The result? No pierced nose. Now, I'm not saying that this would work in every situation, but with all my kids, I

RELATIONSHIP

explained that I wanted to be sure they were doing it because *they* wanted it done, not because everyone else was doing it."

Another increasingly popular trend among teens, tattooing, can also create conflict between you and your teen. Some tattoos may be hidden or tiny, while others may appear in a highly visible location. But in either case, many parents will express concern over the practice. How should parents respond to this new fashion statement?

> *As difficult as it may be, try to get your youngster to see things from a long-range view.*

As difficult as it may be, try to get your youngster to see things from a long-range view. Ask how she thinks her future husband would feel about the flower near her belly button. What would your son's future wife think about that heart on his shoulder (especially if it contains someone else's initials)? Talk with your daughter about what will happen 50 years down the road when her grandchildren ask why Grandma has that little butterfly by her ankle. Encourage your children to weigh the cost of eventual embarrassment.

Safety concerns also creep into this discussion when teens choose to have piercings done by unauthorized people or in unsterile settings. If you know that's what your teen is planning, you can legitimately say no out of concern for her health. If your young person wants to get her ear pierced and you agree, encourage her to have it done by a professional who knows what she's doing.

Tattoos also involve medical risk, including increased possibilities of contracting hepatitis B, HIV, or tetanus from the needles and dyes. Dr. Allen Johnson suggests, "Take your teen on a field trip to a tattoo parlor. Often these are dirty places and will disgust most teens. Explain that the process hurts in the first place, but if someone wants to reverse the process later, the laser surgery necessary can be even more painful and costly. The skin does not return to its previous appearance, and some colors (like red) are often impossible to remove."[7]

Sometimes a parent does have to draw a line. As long as your teen is living in your home and receiving your support, don't feel guilty when you're compelled to say, "Enough is enough. We're not going to do that."

RELATIONSHIP

**RELATIONSHIP**

## Clothing and Hairstyles

Battles over clothing can take place on two different fronts: the sloppy or the indecent on one hand, and the designer-label demand on the other. Clothing wars need not be destructive conflicts, however, if the same guidelines we've been advocating prevail: effective communication and use of the situation to build awareness. As with music, movies, and earrings, clothing choices are influenced by the society around us. What we need to help our teens realize, however, is that our clothes also speak to the society around us.

Fashions change rapidly (a look into our closets will reveal just how rapidly). At the time of this writing, styles popular with teens range from supersophisticated to grunge to preppy to casual. So how do you guide your teen toward proper and appropriate clothing styles?

Common sense and clear communication are the keys once again. At times the hole-filled jeans may drive us crazy, but come back to the main question: Is it worth arguing over? One mom stated, "Our rule was that as long as the clothing was not immodest, indecent, or vulgar, it was their choice. The clothes didn't have to match (although one daughter would rather die than wear mismatched clothing). But the call on immodesty came down to Mom, not to them. They could wear ripped, ugly, smelly clothes if they wanted, but I found peer pressure was a great factor in them keeping their clothes clean."

Sit down with your teen and discuss what clothes say to others. If you wear a shirt that has the name of a particular band or product (beer, for example) on it, will people think you are endorsing it? If you're heading to a job interview, how should you dress differently compared to going to a football game? What do you think when you see a guy wearing his pants way too low, or when you see a girl dressed in a provocative or revealing outfit? What are those who dress all in black with outlandish makeup—the goth group—trying to communicate through their clothing? The clincher—an important question for any of us, but particularly for teens—is "What do you want people to think about you?"

A father or an older brother can be a tremendous help to a teen girl if he respectfully and honestly helps her understand how guys look at girls. A Florida dad named Peter said, "I value my role as a clothing checker for my daughter. As a male, I can indicate to her how boys would respond to what she's wearing. We have a special relationship, and she knows how I value her. For the most part, if I tell her I think something is too revealing, she respects that, even though she may disagree."

One parent, Joe White, draws the modesty line like this: "I would fight over any clothing styles that would be too revealing or skintight. And I would hold out against boys' showing their underwear as guys do now. At the same time, certain clothing styles may not be very tasteful in my opinion, but I would probably only encourage against them instead of prohibiting them. The question to ask yourself about a style is, does it create lust or is it just an issue of personal taste?"

The other big area of concern with teens' clothing is the "need" many feel to have name-brand clothing. Label watchers can run a family's clothing budget into serious trouble in a hurry. Becky Foster Still, writer and mother, cautions,

> Look at your own lifestyle. Think about the messages getting through to your children about the relative importance of image and consumption. Help your children understand the principle of limited resources. Many parents have solved clothing disputes by setting definite amounts they'll pay for wardrobe items, with any additional costs having to come from the youngster's own earnings. Use balance. Be firm but understanding. Educate yourself on what the kids are wearing at school and be fair in setting limits.[8]

Other parents establish what they think is a reasonable clothing allowance and then push their teen to make his own decisions. This involves a little more risk, but it also can show him an added bit of trust and build a greater sense of value, hopefully encouraging him to think from a longer-range view than simply what seems desirable at the moment. Dr. Mary Manz Simon wrote, "Sometimes your teen might try to push his new freedom further than you are willing to go (a South Park T-shirt, for example). Sit down and talk. Listen to why your child likes it. State why the item offends you, then mediate a solution. You might decide your son can wear the shirt but only for working around the house."

Dr. Simon went on to write, "Whether the issue is hairstyle, jewelry or clothing, fighting over personal preferences usually isn't worth damaging the relationship. Ask yourself, 'Can I live with it?' If your answer is yes, but you still find it difficult to put up with, just do what our teens do: When you're walking down the street together, pretend you don't know them."[9]

Hairstyles can seem tremendously important at certain stages of our lives, but in the grand scheme of life, how critical are they? A generation ago, the issue was shoulder-length hair on boys. Today's debate may occur over a proposed shave job. Fashions change, but the question remains: What is the young person communicating or trying to? That question can serve as the foundation for a meaningful conversation, just as in discussing clothing.

"When my son initially came home having tinted the top of his head," one father said, "I have to admit I was a little startled and began to call him 'Golden Boy' (or 'Margarine Head,' in my less sensitive moments). But as I grew used to it, I realized it wasn't a point worth arguing over, just a phase he was going through."

A mom said, "Who really cares if their hair is shaved funny or dyed a pretty color that you only see on rainbows? I'd rather have my kid come home with hair that makes me cringe than to rebel through the use of drugs. The rule I've had in our house is that I will pay for a standard haircut, but anything else comes out of their own pockets."

**Curfews**

As young people grow older, and particularly as they begin to have social lives independent of the family, the curfew issue can also create conflict. As with most of the topics in this chapter, smooth sailing is more likely if there's clear communication and honesty between parent and teen. When discussing a curfew, help your teen to see the big picture, to consider such issues as how busy his weekly schedule is, how challenging it is to get him up in the morning, what his plans are for the following day, and who is doing the driving.

Curfew timing can serve as a real learning opportunity in negotiation, particularly as your youngster proves responsible in keeping the curfew. It can also provide the chance to teach delayed gratification or the concept that being faithful in a small way can lead to more freedom. Help your teen to understand that curfews are not simply a way for you to control him. They are related to safety, communication, and overall balance of schedule. If you and your daughter can't agree on a reasonable curfew for a particular situation, you may want to accept her suggestion once with the understanding that your decision will stand the next time.

One family developed a rolling pattern based on the age of the children. The mom said, "In ninth grade, the curfew was 11:00 P.M.

## Teens' Advice to Parents About Nurturing Spiritual Growth, Part 6

- "Parents need to listen to what their teen has to say. They want to be guided, but they first want you to hear them out."
- "Keep it constant but gentle, not 'in your face.' More like a very soft, light rain that lasts for hours rather than a monsoon after a convicting church service. Don't ever pass up an opportunity to nudge your teen in the right direction. And don't patronize them. Sure, they are not adults yet, but they aren't kids, either."
- "Pray! I know I am where I am today because my parents were faithful in praying for me. Also, set a good example by having a daily quiet time. Family devotions and a nightly family prayer are also extremely helpful."
- "Talk! Engage them in discussion after church. Talk about cultural issues and current events and their relation to their faith. Send them to summer camps; send them to the Summit Ministries program!"
- "Pray with them; keep your children accountable; encourage them to be involved with their youth group; read the Word with them; take special 'dates' with them to talk with and encourage them spiritually; practice what you preach."
- "You must be involved in every aspect of their lives. Listen to them! Although their problems may not seem like life-or-death situations to you, your child's life depends on their solutions (or so they think)! Hug them often and say, 'I love you.' They need to hear it. Spend both quality and quantity time with them."

> *Remind your teen of your expectations well in advance so you don't get backed into a corner as he's heading out the door with his friends.*

as long as there was no school the next day. The time advanced a half hour each successive year. There were some special-event curfews that varied from that, but there was always a curfew of some kind. Weeknights or Sundays when school followed the next morning, the curfew was 10:00 P.M. for one night, but if there were multiple nights out in a week, it may have been moved forward to 9:00 or 9:30, depending on the circumstances."

While general guidelines can provide valuable consistency for a teen, curfews should adjust depending on the circumstances. Timelines for dates may differ from outings with friends of the same sex, and group activities (like get-togethers under supervision, such as church youth group events) may vary yet again. If your teen can justify a proposed curfew and it's reasonable, let him own the decision. And remind him of your expectations well in advance so you don't get backed into a corner as he's heading out the door with his friends.

What happens if curfew is violated? The appropriate response should be based on the circumstances and on the teen's attitude. We all lose track of time once in a while, so you might respond to a first offense with a serious talk. But if additional misses occur, or if your teen deliberately chooses to disobey, does not communicate that he will be late, or shows little remorse, you should react more firmly. Perhaps his driving privileges should be suspended temporarily. Certainly the next proposed outing should have an earlier curfew than normal. While parents need to be flexible if extenuating circumstances occur, they still need to show that consequences result. Did the teen make an effort to call? Was the missed curfew the result of being irresponsible or losing track of time? Was a ride missed someplace along the line? Were any other options available for the teen to make it home on time?

One Colorado father recalled an incident with his teen son. "He drove nearly an hour away with some friends to go to an amusement park, and they expected to be home around 11:00. We got a call around 10:30 indicating they had stopped to eat and

RELATIONSHIP

wouldn't make it on time. An hour later, he called again. 'Dad,' he said, 'we're just leaving now. The waitress was so-o-o-o slow, and it took forever to get our food. I'm really sorry.' By this time, my concern was fatigue for the drive, especially after a long day of having fun. He assured me that the girls he was with would keep talking enough to keep him awake.

"By the time he dropped the others off at their cars, he didn't get home until after 1:00. But what made the 'broken' curfew palatable was the fact that he kept us informed. We were still pretty uptight by the time he came through the door, but he certainly didn't need any added punishment on our end. Getting up the next morning for church was tough enough already."

As with so many of these areas of conflicts, parents need to keep in mind that curfews are not ends in themselves but are simply part of the overall parenting package. What's the purpose of curfews? So that parents know the whereabouts of their teens and can monitor and help them develop their time-management skills. Some teens have a tendency to run and run, entertaining themselves into exhaustion. When parents establish curfews, they need to remind the teen that it's in her own best interest.

Depending on your family's financial situation, you may want to consider getting your teen a cell phone. There are two reasons for this: first, so she can keep you informed of her whereabouts or changes of plans, and second, so she can call for help in an emergency.

### Drugs and Alcohol

Parent-teen conflict arises in many areas because of differences in personal preference. In some cases, however, life-and-death issues are at stake. Drug and alcohol abuse kills thousands of young people each year, including many from Christian homes. High school hallways and activities provide temptation to become involved, even if it's only on a recreational level. Many teens confront their parents with the familiar arguments that their friends are doing it and that their usage is not really dangerous as long as they're careful. How can parents deal with this threat to their children's well-being?

As with so many of these issues, dealing with drugs and alcohol will be far easier if you've built a good relationship, with clear and honest communication, before the temptations arise. Talk to your children about the effects of drugs and alcohol and about the loss of control experienced by those who use them. Ask why they think young people are tempted to participate in drinking and drug usage. Encourage them to communicate with you when they're confronted with the possibility of using drugs or drinking alcohol.

Family traditions vary widely, particularly in the area of drinking. In some families, drinking beer in moderation or wine with a meal may be acceptable for those of legal age, while others may choose to abstain from alcohol entirely. In either case, Scripture clearly speaks out about avoiding drunkenness. And whatever your family rules, you must remember how important your example is for your teen. If he sees you drinking when you've said he shouldn't, or abusing alcohol by drinking to excess, he has little incentive to follow more-restrictive guidelines you might choose to set on him. Remember that morals are more "caught" than taught.

Above all, be aware. Don't assume that, because your teen attends a Christian school or is home-schooled, he will not be tempted by such activity. Pay attention to changes of behavior, and don't hesitate to be involved in decisions for her welfare. Observe the friends she associates with (see the section on peer influence below). Radio psychologist Dr. Laura Schlessinger says, "Parents are to respect their children's nest and 'stuff.' However, when a parent has reason to believe there might be a problem— sex, drugs, criminality, for example—it is their obligation to use whatever means necessary to help and protect their child. Children who are 'off track' don't generally talk openly to their parents out of guilt, shame, emotional problems or foolishness."[10]

Talk with your teen about why people drink or use drugs. Often the reason is to gain acceptance with a particular group of friends or to experience a sense of detachment from a difficult situation. Be bold in answering your son's "Everybody's doing it" with clear evidence that some are definitely not. And if your daughter says, "It's not really dangerous if you're careful," remind her of the thousands of teens who die in accidents caused by drunk driving each year.

Drug usage distorts your perception, lowers your general

barriers against inappropriate behavior, and causes you to act in ways you would not even consider if you weren't under the influence. Is that the picture of freedom that drug proponents present? Of course not. The abuse of increasingly popular designer drugs like ecstasy (alleged to be nonaddictive) can also lead to brain damage, memory problems, and heart or kidney failure. This is the straight truth that you need to communicate with your teen.

If your child does become involved in drug or alcohol abuse, you need to demonstrate the type of tough love that can draw him out of the pattern without destroying the relationship. Depending on the severity of the situation, intervention or treatment may be necessary. Trust has been broken, but unconditional love and forgiveness can go a long way if the teen is willing to turn from the destructive lifestyle. If he does, he needs a supportive environment to help him stand strong against the temptations of returning to it.

Tracy, now in his thirties, knew his parents loved him, but he also knew they didn't seem concerned with what he was doing during his teen years. "Dad was working a bunch, and Mom got a job to help start a college fund," he recalled. "I realize now that I was just hungry for somebody to pay attention to me, so I started hanging out with the loadies. I smoked a little pot and tried a couple other things, but drinking was what got me in trouble. I hid it pretty well until the night I decided to drive home from a party and put my car into a fire hydrant. Talk about waking up in a cold shower!

"I was terrified about how Dad would respond," Tracy continued. "Because of some anger issues, I wouldn't have been surprised if he had kicked me out of the house. But the accident was a wake-up call for him, too. He set firm restrictions on me and made me pay for all the damage to the car, but he and I also started to talk a lot more. He went with me to Teen-Anon (the only dad there the first night) and changed his whole work schedule. I know it sounds pretty trite, but I can honestly say my getting drunk and wrecking my car was the best thing that ever happened to my relationship with my dad, because of the way he handled it."

RELATIONSHIP

## Boyfriends and Girlfriends

As your teen begins to develop a new social life, another potential area of conflict arises: boyfriends and girlfriends. For those families

■ ■ ■

## *The Talk*

My kids had gotten this far without serious problems, so maybe they'd listened more than I thought. But we were in a new setting in Colorado Springs, and I couldn't make assumptions about the standards of new friends. It was time to take drastic action, especially with the boys lining up to ask Holly out. Thus, I started a routine known as The Talk.

The Talk consists of having Holly's would-be date answer pleasantly asked questions such as "How long have you lived in this area?" "What do your folks do?" and "Do you have brothers and sisters?" Within a few minutes, the questions advance to "What are you planning to study in college?" "What church does your family attend?" and "Do you have time to be very active in your church youth group?"

The first young man answered the opening questions politely but kept glancing toward the stairway, wondering when Holly would be ready.

I smiled. "It's okay. She'll be downstairs when this is over."

I settled comfortably into the sofa corner. '"Even though we met a couple of weeks ago, I didn't know anything about you before we began this chat," I said. "Right now you think this is ridiculous, but I guarantee you that in about 25 years, when a guy asks your future daughter out, you'll think of me and say, 'That ol' lady was right!' "

I let that thought sink in. Then I continued. "I know you two are just going out as friends, but I've lived long enough to know how quickly situations can change. So remember this, treat Holly the way you hope some other guy is treating your future wife."

His eyes widened at that thought. I knew I'd hit my target.

Since my first "Talk," word's gotten around school. Now when a new guy hints he'd like to ask Holly out, the others warn him about The Talk.

Only one young man has refused to meet with me. Holly told him not to call her again. "It's like my mom says, 'You don't have to like it; you just have to do it,' " she said.

—Sandra Picklesimer Aldrich in *Raising Them Right*[11]

who see dating as an option (as opposed to those who favor a courtship model), you want your child to date people who will provide a positive, encouraging relationship, but your opinion of desirable qualities may differ from your teen's. Some teens seek boyfriend/girlfriend relationships at an earlier age than others, but wise parents encourage group outings instead of one-on-one dating, particularly in the early teen years. Group activities enable young people to build a foundation of solid friendship before mutual interest in romantic involvement develops.

Establish guidelines well before the question of dating even arises in your family. Some parents set a particular age or grade as a prerequisite; others may tie the opportunity to a specific event. Because teens' matu-

> *Pay attention, communicate, be involved, and don't overreact.*

rity levels vary so widely, determining when one is ready to date defies a "This is the proper moment," one-size-fits-all rule. Talk it through as parents and teen after you (the parents) have agreed to stay with a unified approach.

If a special dating relationship does develop, the same guidelines hold as in other potential conflict arenas: Pay attention, communicate, be involved, and don't overreact. Notice how much time your daughter is spending with her boyfriend and the type of activities she describes to you. Are there many group events, or do they do most activities by themselves? Does she describe him as respectful toward her and consistent in the way he treats her whether they are alone or with other people? Without intruding into her life, your awareness can tell you a great deal about their relationship.

Talk with your teen about clearly defined expectations and boundaries before, during, and between dating relationships. Discuss the concept of setting limits in any dating situation at the beginning. Within this discussion with your teen (not with his girlfriend), you can establish some specific guidelines, such as avoiding situations in which they're alone together behind closed doors. By having this conversation before a relationship begins, you empower your teen to hold fast to boundaries and to show respect for his date by communicating them early. It is always easier to set limits ahead of time than to withdraw from inappropriate activities once those lines have been crossed.

Provide time for your teen to tell you what qualities she appreciates about members of the opposite sex and what she enjoys about being with them. While spontaneity is a key component of many teens' lives, establish communication channels for her to use when plans change, particularly regarding curfew issues and transportation.

Peer influence will be discussed in the next section, but with dating relationships, you have an even greater responsibility to

— ■ ■ ■ —

## Peer Pressure Can Be Positive

One afternoon after school, a sophomore lad slipped into Christi Ham's classroom.

Visibly distraught, the boy stood near the door. Mrs. Ham, a religion teacher at Pacelli High in Columbus, asked the student to sit down and compose himself.

"I can't stand it," he said in a choked voice, as the teacher patted his shoulder. "I can't fight the pressure anymore."

Gently, Mrs. Ham asked what was bothering him. Was he having trouble with his girlfriend? Was it the pressure to party and drink?

"No," the boy replied. "It's all the pressure *not* to drink."

In a flash, Mrs. Ham understood. Because of a peer counseling group on campus called Teen Advisers, drinking was no longer cool at Pacelli.... The sophomore, who liked to down beer at weekend parties, was tired of hearing his classmates tell him to abstain from alcohol.

The Pacelli Teen Advisers—and similar groups around the country—have turned peer pressure into a positive force. The message not to drink or do drugs is coming from the students themselves—not parents and school officials, a concept that makes the Teen Advisers so interesting.

—Mike Yorkey in *Raising Them Right*[12]

RELATIONSHIP

get to know the person your child is dating. A reasonably protective nature may cause some disagreements. A California father named David said, "Like many dads, I make it a point to meet any young men who want to go out with my daughter. I try not to be threatening, but I see it as an opportunity to let the boys know just how valuable she is to our family. I see this meeting as a chance to tell him that I am entrusting a treasure to him—temporarily—and that he needs to keep that trust in mind at all times."

You may have a greater tendency to show this level of concern for daughters than for sons, but parents of boys should also make the effort to get to know the girls their sons are dating. By seeing your family as a unit, your son's girlfriend will better understand where he is coming from.

Finally, avoid the temptation to overreact and yank in the leash. As Jack Crabtree wrote in *How to Get Your Teenager to Talk to You*, "Beware of provoking a desperate action. Resist giving ultimatums or making unbending statements. Always leave room for possible change of heart or mind."[13] Putting your daughter in an "us versus him" situation rarely leads to the desired end. She is forced to choose between two relationships that she values, and the final cost could be either a broken relationship with you, if she pursues the boyfriend, or bitter resentment toward you, if she honors your wishes.

Erin's story illustrates these consequences. "I was dating a guy that my parents really didn't like. They told me to break it off, but I was so stubborn that I continued to see him secretly. As much as I hate to admit it, they were right about Steve, and he finally hurt me when I found out he was dating one of my best friends. Maybe if Mom and Dad hadn't been quite so forceful, I would have come to the realization sooner. But the way they handled it pushed me to do something I still regret. The saving grace of the whole situation is that when I eventually came to them in tears, they didn't make me feel guilty for going behind their backs. And they didn't ever say, 'We told you so.' We're still rebuilding our relationship, but they took me back with open arms—like the father of the prodigal son. The trust was broken, but we all learned a lesson."

**Peer Influence**

As teens grow through the adolescent years, peer influence tends to increase and parental influence tends to recede. Although you may regret this loss of authority, it's a natural progression. After all, we are social creatures who seek acceptance from those in our peer groups. However, it is critically important for young people to develop confidence and security in themselves through their relationship with their parents. This self-confidence can lessen the influence of their peers to some extent and provide the strength to stand against the crowd when necessary.

You can reduce some of the conflicts over negative peer influence by one simple method: Get to know your teen's friends, and let them get to know you. Stay involved in your youngster's life. Allow your house to become the gathering place for your teen and her group of friends. Without pushing your teen into particular friendships, you can have a clearer idea about the young people with whom she's associating. Remember that peer pressure is not solely a negative influence; many teens' lives and decisions are improved through solid, encouraging friends.

However, some teens will gravitate toward peers who affect them negatively and draw them into making bad decisions. These choices can revolve around many of the conflict points in this chapter or a variety of other situations. So, what can you do if you see your teen involved with negative associations?

Wei-lin, a recent U.C.L.A. graduate, gives insight into how his parents handled his situation in high school. "Because I was new in the country [from Taiwan]," he said, "I wanted to distance myself as far as I could from the old ways, and that included my parents. I developed friendships with the rebels on campus. Initially my mother and father tried to forbid me from going out, but that just made me madder and more determined to break free. Then they started to get smart—they scheduled more family events with the expectation that I would attend. They sweetened the invitation by saying I could bring one or two friends.

"At first I thought I could shock them by inviting the rowdiest kids I knew," he continued. "We sat over in the corner and made fun of all my relatives. But before too long, I began to get embarrassed. I could tell that my parents' feelings were hurt, but they didn't say anything. I was pretty stubborn, so it took a few of these events for me to realize who really cared about me. I didn't want to give up my 'liberal' friends, but they started to get on my nerves because I understood that when they mocked my family, they were really making fun of me, too. Eventually I eased my way out of that group and found some friends whose backgrounds matched mine more closely."

Like musical tastes and clothing styles, friendships and the influence of particular peers also go through cycles. Overreacting to specific associations, unless they are directly tied to harmful activities, can result in pushing your teen in the undesired direction all the more. Encourage your child to consider what qualities she looks for in a friend and how well various individuals demonstrate those qualities. In time, your daughter may come to the realization that the relationship you share with her is far more valuable than a passing friendship with a young person whose values contradict how she was raised.

## Choosing Your Battles Carefully

When it comes to conflict-causing issues, how do parents decide which beaches are worth dying on? Through a great deal of prayer, conversation between husband and wife, and communication with your teen and with other parents. But perhaps it begins with the realization that every decision, every potential dispute, does not have to become a World War III. Actually, the ideal first step toward successful

> *Adolescents become increasingly savvy about situations where Mom and Dad are divided.*

parenting of teens comes long before they even reach adolescence, as you develop close relationships with them and communicate an unconditional love. With consistency, love, and discipline, the younger child can enter the turbulent teen years with a sense of trust. This trust can then serve as a foundation for meaningful discussions as the teen matures.

But some parents of teens will realize that, for whatever reason, they have not built such a foundation with their children. If that's your situation, it is still not too late. If you've been busy building a career and have neglected building a family, take a careful look at your day planner and make some adjustments. Lock in times with your teens, get to know them on a deeper level, and seek to understand what they are experiencing. Spend time praying for them and with them, stressing your commitment to them in times of conflict and in times of peace.

"A house divided against itself cannot stand," said Abraham Lincoln (quoting Jesus), and while he was talking about a country, the same holds true for your home. Both parents need to be in agreement before and throughout a confrontation or conflict with your teen. Adolescents become increasingly savvy about situations where Mom and Dad are divided. When conflict occurs, both parents need to put their heads together and present a united front.

Melissa, a mom from Illinois, said, "We quickly saw the need to change 'Go ask your father' to 'Have you talked to your father, and what did he say?' Without that question, there was always the possibility of our daughter getting two different answers and accepting the one she wanted to hear." While you may have differing opinions in the midst of the conflicts, settle those differences away from the teen and develop a resolution together. This approach is better for your relationship with each other and presents a more confident and comforting environment for your teen, too.

Expect that times will occur when your teen will not like you. For parents whose children have been fairly compliant through childhood, these feelings may arise far more often than ever before. You are the parent; she is a wannabe adult who may be struggling with desires for independence. In your own mind and in your communication with your teen, keep stressing your desire to retain and build your relationship, not allowing differences of opinion to create significant cracks that can last long after the dispute itself is forgotten.

Dr. James Dobson described the parenting approach he and his wife adopted as their son and daughter became teens: "The philosophy we applied with our teenagers can be called 'loosen and tighten.' By this I mean we tried to loosen our grip on everything that had no lasting significance and tighten down on everything that did. We said yes whenever we possibly could to give support to the occasional no. And, most importantly, we tried never to get too far away from our kids emotionally."[14]

Every family has to choose its own issues that are worth fighting over, and these issues may even vary among different children from the same household. Obviously, drug and alcohol abuse always qualifies because of the life-and-death nature of the situation. And negative peer influence can destroy far more valuable relationships, like those in your family. Some conflict areas can create significant spiritual and emotional struggles, particularly if your teen becomes involved in pornography. For some, movie choices may be battlegrounds; others may want to draw a line in the sand over music selection. But remember that discernment is the ultimate goal in dealing with these issues. As parents, we can't and shouldn't make every decision for our children throughout their lives, so we must use these situations to help them develop critical-thinking skills and awareness enough to make wise choices on their own.

Many parental desires are based on the impression of what others will think of us or of our families. Let's put others' opinions behind us and focus on the needs and best interests of our teens.

Whether you are just starting to face the conflicts that come with adolescence or are in the homestretch, keep your perspective. Some of the daily battles will be won and some lost, but even the victories are only momentary. Focus your eyes on the goal: a loving, supportive, encouraging relationship with your teen when he or she arrives at young adulthood. No individual triumph is worth the loss of that ultimate prize.

# PART 3

...

# Discipling
# by Intent

*Discipling your teen doesn't require you to be a perfect Christian. It can and should be a natural, caring, and even fun experience. But you will need to be intentional about it.*

# CHAPTER 14

# Making a Timeless Investment

How should you disciple your teenager? It's simple! All you have to do is follow these three easy steps: (1) Be a perfect Christian role model, never making a mistake. (2) Teach your child every verse in the Bible and every truth he or she might ever need to know. (3) Flap your arms and fly to the moon.

Okay, so those first two are a little more difficult than the third. But you didn't think this was going to be a picnic, did you? Anything as somber-sounding as "intentional discipling" has to be hard and unpleasant, doesn't it?

Fortunately, helping your teen to become an authentic follower of Jesus Christ doesn't require your perfection. It doesn't have to be a form of torture, either. In fact, if the process feels like a straitjacket, a knife fight, or a migraine, there's something wrong. Being a spiritual mentor to your teenager can and should be a natural, caring, even *fun* experience that benefits both you and your child—for eternity.

## Consider the Return

Leading your teen toward spiritual maturity isn't always a breeze. Nor is it painless. But consider the potential return on your investment:

**DISCIPLING**

■ It's your son's wedding day. You and he are waiting in a little room off the sanctuary, the rich bass of the church organ filtering through the wall. Your throat is already tight with emotion, and you wonder whether you can make it to your pew without visible tears. You reach over to adjust the black velvet bow tie of your son's tuxedo, and he smiles a crooked smile.

"Thanks, Dad," he whispers.

Trying to look casual, you shrug. "Hey, what are fathers for?"

Your son clears his throat. "No, I mean thanks . . . for everything. You taught me stuff that . . . helped Tracie and me make it to this day without feeling sorry, you know? You showed me how to have a Christian home. I just hope I can do as well as you and Mom did."

You want to say "You'll do fine," because you know he will. But for the moment, all you can do is blink and keep readjusting that tie.

■ Your daughter E-mails you from college: "Mom, I had this super-intense conversation in world religions class. The professor was ragging on 'fundamentalists' and made it sound like Christians were ready to blow up anybody who didn't accept 'their narrow way.'

"I remembered that video about absolute truth that

## Teens' Advice to Parents About Nurturing Spiritual Growth, Part 7

■ "Be involved. Talk with your kids about God, and pray with each child specifically about his or her concerns."

■ "Talk about it! Be sensitive to what they are struggling with, and don't discount it. Relate your experiences as a young person. Verbally and practically, create a 'safe' environment."

■ "Take time to pray with your teens. My mom would pray with me as we drove to school. This shows that the parent truly cares about what is going on in her teen's life. Encourage them to get involved in Christian groups, and find Christian music you watched with me last year, and how you said that the 'one way' thing came from God, not us. You said something about how He had the right to decide how people could reach Him, kind of like the phone company can decide which number you have to dial to reach somebody. I asked the professor whether he'd considered that.

"I don't think I convinced him of anything, but afterward this girl came up to me and said she was glad to know there was another believer around, because her faith was getting pretty shaky. I think we're going to get together next week to pray and just talk. Cool, huh?"

"Cool," you E-mail her back. "Totally."

■ You're playing with your first grandchild, bouncing that bubbly two-year-old girl on your knee. She's giggling, and so are you. There's nothing you'd rather do for the rest of your life.

Suddenly your son approaches and gently lifts the girl into his arms. "Sorry, Grandma," he tells you. "Time for Kayla's devotions."

"Devotions? Isn't she a little young? And we were having such a good time—"

Kayla grins and claps her hands. "Je-sus love me," she sings, "da Bible temme so."

**DISCIPLING**

they enjoy. Music really is powerful in affecting an individual, so be sure to plug them in to the good music!"

■ "Have a *relationship* with your teen, and talk openly and often about your faith."

■ "Spend time in God's Word with them. Pray with them and for them. Open doors of communication. Explain that God does not wait on the edge of His seat for us to make mistakes so He can judge us. He loves us and wants us to walk in His grace."

■ ■ ■

## *Thanks, Mom and Dad: Two Teens Remember*

*Katie:*

Not until college did I clearly recognize what makes our family unique, what sets me apart. The common component in the lives of my parents (as well as my extended family of grandparents, aunts, uncles, and cousins) is a deep, genuine understanding of the love of God displayed in His Son—Jesus Christ.

Many of my friends come from Christian homes, yet few of them have been "discipled" by their parents. Daddy and Mommy sacrificed twenty-plus years of their energy and dreams to demonstrate the life of Christ to me. . . . If I could describe the way my parents displayed a passion for Jesus (beyond leading me to a knowledge of this grace), it would be found in the "little things" of every day. My parents lived like Christ in a *radical* way each day before my very eyes. The Bible was our source of knowledge and strength. We memorized verses as children. We read stories from it every night. We sang praise songs on car trips. We openly shared our hearts. We prayed together as a family. We went overseas on missions trips. We were disciplined for disobedience because God disciplines those He loves. The life of Christ was lived out daily in practical ways to us as children, adolescents, and adults. By catching a glimpse of their passion for our Savior, my life will never be the same.

*Jonathan:*

When I was six years old, Dad led me in the sinner's prayer of repentance, and I asked Jesus into my heart. Mom tucked me in bed every night of my life until I moved to college. My parents prayed with me and for me every day. I would open up my lunch to find an encouraging note. I would come home from school to find my room in order with an uplifting verse on my bed. They disciplined me in love, and they cried with me through the pain and failures of my life. They took me on special trips, accompanied me to church, and always encouraged me to pursue Christ with more passion.

However, apart from my salvation, none of these acts of love would have impacted my life for Jesus had they not already abandoned themselves to God. Their determined purpose, long before I came on the scene, was to know Jesus Christ. When I woke up early to spend time with God (as Dad taught me to do when he discipled me), Dad was already in his study, doing the same. When I came home from school in the afternoon, Mom's Bible was open on the dinner table, along with her journal, prayer lists, and Scripture memory box. My parents, imperfect as they were, not only modeled Christ and nurtured me in a moral, loving Christian home, they themselves also pursued Jesus Christ with undying passion, which became the life-giving, grace-abounding, transforming power of our family.

—From *Ignite the Fire*, by Barry and Carol St. Clair[1]

Your son chuckles. "Don't worry, Mom. You'll get to play later. But some things are important. It's the way I was raised . . . remember?"

You remember, all right. You watch in wonder as the baton of faith you passed just a few years ago is passed on yet again. And there's nothing you'd rather do for the rest of your life.

Chastity. A certain faith. A Christian home. And those are just a few possible benefits in *this* life.

DISCIPLING

## Teens' "Traits of Great Parents," Part 6

- "Loving, involved, nonjudgmental, caring , concerned, spiritual leaders."
- "Encouraging, open to questions, provide explanations; serious, maintain authority; love their spouse."
- "An important trait in a great parent is open communication. No topic is off-limits. My mom exemplified this wonderfully! Another great trait is being an involved parent. My parents supported me 100 percent. They made an effort to come to all my games and concerts."
- "Easygoing, open, good communicators."
- "Confident, committed, follow the biblical definition of love—patient, kind, and so on. More concerned about the heart of the child than about church involvement and ministry involvement."

Imagine that you're in heaven, having spent a few decades basking in the perfect presence of God Himself, when you hear a familiar voice behind you. You turn, the gold street smooth beneath your feet, and recognize a face. It's changed somehow, as yours has, becoming all it was meant to be. It's your teenager, grown up, striding through the north gate, approaching you with a joy that could only come from knowing that everything will be all right now—and forever.

How will it feel?

More than anything else, don't you want to find out?

# CHAPTER 15

# Creating an "Eager Learner" Attitude

You may be ready, even eager, to help your teen grow spiritually. But you're not the only part of the equation. Your teen must be ready, too.

Steven is a case in point. He prayed to receive Christ in early elementary school, and his parents made sure he was in church every Sunday. They taught him to pray at bedtime and meals; they bought him Bibles; they had family devotions whenever they could. They did their best to let Steven know that they loved him, to teach him right from wrong, and to follow Christ consistently themselves.

But Steven had problems. He struggled in school. He made some less-than-desirable friends. When adolescence hit, he tried marijuana. Soon he was a regular user. Later he began to drink, and he eventually became an alcoholic.

Steven's parents were devastated. No matter how much they tried to "water" their son, he seemed unable or unwilling to grow spiritually.

Steven wasn't ready.

Like many teenagers, Steven found himself in the grip of habits and hurts that kept him from making spiritual progress. Thankfully, through God's grace and the help of wise counselors as well as his persistent parents, Steven has begun to get his life back on track as an adult.

He bears the scars of those turbulent years, however. His parents do, too, no doubt wondering what they could have done to prevent the "waste" of Steven's adolescence.

Your son or daughter may not be burdened by problems like Steven's, but it doesn't take dramatic conflicts and addictions to keep a teen from being an eager spiritual learner. Sometimes seemingly small, unresolved issues can stall the discipling process.

The good news is that those issues aren't a mystery. Experienced youth mentors have identified seven factors that make the difference between the ready and the resistant. A teen is motivated to grow when he or she (1) feels your unconditional love, (2) sees you visibly demonstrate grace, (3) experiences the right kind of discipline, (4) is helped to dream, (5) sees results from personal accomplishments, (6) sees personal achievements celebrated, and (7) gets help in unloading psychological baggage.

How can you make sure these factors are present in your teen's life? Let's take a look.

## Showing Unconditional Love

"Of *course* I love my child unconditionally!" most parents might say. "There are no strings attached. I love him (or her) no matter what he (or she) does."

But here's the million-dollar question: Does your child *understand* that your love will always be there, no matter what?

As one writer observed with great insight, when it comes to self-image, the subconscious reality for each of us is that "I'm not who *I* think I am; I'm not who *you* think I am; I am who I think you think I am." And teens, with their fragile egos, are more dependent than most on the opinions of others for their sense of self-worth. So, again, is your teenager truly convinced of your unconditional love?

> *Teens, with their fragile egos, are more dependent than most on the opinions of others for their sense of self-worth.*

**DISCIPLING**

Robert's parents thought they had made him feel secure in their love. Since Robert was little, his dad had told him "I love you" every night at bedtime. Mom had supplied plenty of hugs and kisses. Robert turned out to be a straight-A student, never in trouble at school.

Until today. This afternoon, Robert cheated on a test. His teacher caught him peeking at a classmate's paper and copying an answer.

"Why would you *do* that?" the teacher asked, disappointed. "Even without that answer you would have gotten a good grade. You don't have to get a perfect score."

"Yes, I do," the boy said in a small voice. "My mom wants me to get 100 percent."

Told of this, Robert's mother was stunned. *How did he get that idea?* she thought. Then she remembered. For the last few months, she'd been collecting Robert's spotless papers in a special stack at home, praising him for each new one he brought home. She'd never meant to communicate the idea that only perfect grades would win her approval, much less her love. But Robert had made the connection, faulty or not.

In a world where people are valued not for their God-given worth but for their chiseled jawlines and computer savvy, it's easy for kids to get the wrong idea. If they don't measure up, they don't earn love—or at least not enough of it.

When spiritual growth is what's being measured, the problem is no less real. *If I try to memorize a chapter of the Bible and can't do it, my parents will be disappointed. If I admit that I have doubts about God, my parents will be mad. If I don't tell all my friends about Jesus, my parents will think I'm a bad person.*

The result: Kids don't attempt the Scripture memory program for fear of failure, and this becomes a pattern that follows them into adulthood. They keep their doubts a secret, and their unanswered questions become time bombs that explode when they get to college. Or they strain to be Billy Graham, even if their gifts lie elsewhere, and eventually burn out.

As Ross Campbell wrote in *How to Really Love Your Teenager*, "If I love them only when they meet my requirements or expectations, they will feel incompetent. They will believe it is fruitless to

**DISCIPLING**

do their best because it is never enough. Insecurity, anxiety, and low self-esteem will plague them. There will be constant hindrances in their emotional and behavioral growth."[1]

Uncertainty about your unconditional love makes it tough for your child to try new things spiritually, to be honest about imperfection, and to keep expectations reasonable. How can you make sure your teen really knows you love him or her—with no fine print?

Here are some suggestions:

1. *Say it, even if it seems obvious.* No matter how many times you've told your teen "I love you," keep it up. He may not respond, except to roll his eyes skyward, mumble an impatient "Yeah, yeah," or even look queasy, as though you've offered a sandwich filled with squirming worms.

Many adolescents, beginning to think of love in terms of the opposite sex, flinch at "love talk" from their parents. But the fact is that each teenager is mentally asking the same question over and over: "Do you love me?" Make sure you answer it clearly and often—in conversation, E-mail, letters, cards, and phone calls.

2. *Don't stop with words.* Cliff is a dad who has told his two sons many times that he loves them. But he knows that, for his boys, "proof" of love means spending time together, even going out of his way to do so when necessary. For one son, that means taking time to play basketball in the driveway; for the other, it means learning to draw together on the computer. Lately, Cliff has tried spending 90 minutes of one-on-one time each weekend with each son, letting the boys choose the activities. The boys clearly relish the time together—and Cliff does, too.

Remember, too, that if the relationship is good, teens never outgrow the desire for physical expressions of affection—a hug, a kiss, a pat on the back, a shoulder rub, and so on. They may not want you to do much of this in front of their friends and other peers, but like all human beings, they still crave loving, appropriate touch. Being the major supplier of that need is one of your highest privileges as a parent.

3. *Don't save love for special occasions.* Purposely or not, some parents withhold expressing love until their children "earn" it. An

underachieving teen might get only frowns until the report card improves; another might hear praise only when all the right notes are hit at the piano recital. The parent may think, *I'm improving my child's behavior by rewarding only the behavior I want to see.* But the teen hears, *I love you only when you meet my standards.*

You can make it abundantly clear that your love has no strings attached by expressing it when it's "undeserved." Try praising your teen when he's *lost* the 50-yard dash, or when she's done nothing at all. Penalize disobedience with lost privileges or a fine, but enclose the sentence in a card that contains a loving, worth-affirming message.

*4. Keep your teen's emotional tank full.* Ross Campbell observes that every teenager has an emotional "tank," a set of needs that must be met through love, understanding, and discipline. A teen with a full tank displays more positive feelings and greater readiness to try new things. "Only if the emotional tank is full," Campbell wrote, "can a teenager be expected to be his best and do his best."[2]

The challenge is to make it easy for your teen to keep coming back to you for emotional gasoline. If conflict has raised a wall between the two of you, your child may patronize other "service stations"—peers, Web chat rooms, even cults—in search of a full tank. Showing unconditional love, the kind that persists despite a teen's outbursts of anger and stretches of sullen silence, posts a permanent Yes, We're Open sign.

*5. Hate the sin but love the sinner.* Let's face it: Teenagers can be exasperating. They can be rebellious, insulting, lazy, stubborn, and obnoxious—just like adults. If we don't distinguish between the person and the behavior, we can easily end up expressing love only during those times when kids are at their best. If it's hard to remember this when your teen has pierced another body part or deposited another layer of pizza crusts and CDs on the floor of her room, keep this verse in mind: "God demonstrates his own love for us in this: While we were still sinners, Christ died for us" (Romans 5:8).

*6. Learn to accept yourself, too.* Cathy is a mom who never gives herself a break. Whether it's a misspelled word in an office memo or forgetting to bring enough cotton balls for Vacation Bible

DISCIPLING

■ ■ ■

## *Braking Away:*
## *One Dad's Grace Under Fire*

Scott, our oldest son, had his learner's permit. He played on a basketball team that practiced across the city. Three afternoons a week I sat on the passenger's side as he drove back and forth in the Atlanta traffic to practice. One principle of driving that he had not yet conquered was the proper use of the brakes. When the brake lights lit up on the car in front, instead of applying his brakes, he would accelerate. We had spoken of this several times. I would explain, "Scott, one day you will not stop in time, and you will hit a car."

One afternoon after practice we were cruising along. Suddenly the brake lights of several cars came on, but this time they stopped more quickly. Scott slammed on the brakes—hard. Tires squealed. The smell of burning rubber filled the air. I grabbed the dash and prayed out loud, "O Lord, help us." God answered that prayer. We missed the car in front of us by half an inch or less.

I looked over at Scott. His hands were shaking, and his face was white as a sheet. He mumbled with a trembling voice, "Dad, I think you'd better drive." We switched places. On the way home we stopped to get a burger and gather our wits. We talked it over. As we walked out of the restaurant, I headed toward the driver's side of the car. Then I stopped dead in my tracks. "Scott," I said, "here, you drive." I tossed him the keys.

That, ladies and gentlemen, was the grace of God in action! My natural response was, "Choke the boy!" Furthermore, I would never have thought of tossing those keys on my own. It spoke volumes about how I had grown in this area, because grace is rarely ever my first response. I could have easily defaulted to extrinsic motivation by applying fear, guilt, and performance to this situation. "Scott, you could have killed us, and if you had, it would have been your fault. You are a terrible driver. If you don't improve, I won't ever be able to let you drive again." Instead, I was intrinsically motivated—I was led by the Spirit to toss him those keys. My response was the difference between a negative and positive learning experience. And we gained the added benefit of becoming closer as father and son.

—Barry St. Clair in *Ignite the Fire*[3]

DISCIPLING

School crafts, she beats herself up for every misstep. Is it any wonder that she has only scowls and stern warnings for her daughters when they fall short? Cathy needs to understand that even if her own parents turned on the "love faucet" only when she did things perfectly, God loves her in spite of her mistakes. The pattern to follow is His, not the one she recalls from childhood.

## Demonstrating Visible Grace

When George W. Bush ran for the Republican presidential nomination in 2000, two kinds of rumors swirled around his campaign: that he had committed youthful indiscretions and that he had since undergone a life-changing conversion to Christianity. Facing the Republican National Convention to accept his party's nomination, he seemed to confirm both stories when he declared, "I believe in grace . . . because I have seen it."

Teenagers need to see grace, too.

Grace is an undeserved gift, the prime example of which is God's gift of salvation to us. The story of the prodigal son (Luke 15:11-32) offers a good model of grace, especially for parents of teens.

Philip Yancey, in his book *What's So Amazing About Grace?* updated that story:

> A young girl grows up on a cherry orchard just above
> Traverse City, Michigan. Her parents, a bit old-fashioned,
> tend to overreact to her nose ring, the music she listens
> to, and the length of her skirts. They ground her a few
> times, and she seethes inside. "I hate you!" she screams
> at her father when he knocks on the door of her room
> after an argument, and that night she acts on a plan she
> has mentally rehearsed scores of times. She runs away.

In Yancey's tale, the girl boards a bus for Detroit, where she falls under the influence of a pimp. She becomes a prostitute and a drug addict. Eventually she's used up, and the pimp throws her out. Sick, cold, and starving, she longs to go home. Three tries at calling her parents connect only with their answering machine,

DISCIPLING

and on the final attempt she leaves a message: "Dad, Mom, it's me. I was wondering about maybe coming home. I'm catching a bus up your way, and it'll get there about midnight tomorrow. If you're not there, well, I guess I'll just stay on the bus until it hits Canada."

Yancey picks up the story:

> When the bus finally rolls into the station, its air brakes hissing in protest, the driver announces in a crackly voice over the microphone, "Fifteen minutes, folks. That's all we have here." Fifteen minutes to decide her life. She checks herself in a compact mirror, smoothes her hair, and licks the lipstick off her teeth. She looks at the tobacco stains on her fingertips and wonders if her parents will notice. If they're there.
>
> She walks into the terminal not knowing what to expect. Not one of the thousand scenes that have played out in her mind prepares her for what she sees. There, in the concrete-walls-and-plastic-chairs bus terminal in Traverse City, Michigan, stands a group of 40 brothers and sisters and great-aunts and uncles and cousins and a grandmother and great-grandmother to boot. They're all wearing goofy party hats and blowing noise-makers, and taped across the entire wall of the terminal is a computer-generated banner that reads "Welcome home!"
>
> Out of the crowd of well-wishers breaks her dad. She stares out through the tears quivering in her eyes like hot mercury and begins the memorized speech, "Dad, I'm sorry. I know . . ."
>
> He interrupts her. "Hush, child. We've got no time for that. No time for apologies. You'll be late for the party. A banquet's waiting for you at home."[4]

Like the father in that story, the parent who extends God's grace to a teen opens up a world of possibilities. By setting aside the past, that mom or dad permits a future. Grace creates a clean slate, a fresh page on which the next chapter of a teenager's spiritual journey can be written.

A home without grace, on the other hand, stifles spiritual growth. Picture 16-year-old Max, whose father has a photographic memory for every sin Max has ever committed. Max's dad never misses a chance to bring up these "ongoing problems" as exhibits A through Z in what seems to Max like an endless criminal trial.

> **The parent who extends God's grace to a teen opens up a world of possibilities.**

If Max is wrestling with a secret sin that he needs to get beyond in order to grow, is he likely to confess it to Dad? Will Max even be *interested* in growing in order to resemble his "spiritual," quick-to-condemn father?

In his book *Feeling Guilty, Finding Grace,* Larry Weeden described a girl whose spiritual growth is at a standstill:

> Tiffany is a teenage girl who attends a public high school. In this day and age, that means she's constantly bombarded with foul language. Her friends and other classmates use profanity routinely in casual conversation, not seeming to give it a second thought. Even some teachers think nothing of sprinkling their lectures with obscenities.
>
> Now the habit is rubbing off on Tiffany. She finds herself, against her wishes, swearing with her friends from time to time.
>
> As soon as the words are out of her mouth, she always feels convicted and guilty. She knows there's a Bible verse she's violating that says we should only speak words that build others up. When she uses the Lord's name, she realizes, she's breaking one of the Ten Commandments.
>
> Every time this happens, Tiffany tries to pray for forgiveness. Yet she feels uncomfortable about it, because she has done it so many times before and keeps on doing it. *Surely God is getting fed up with me now,* she figures. And more and more, she feels far from God. Compared to just a year ago, she's reading her Bible less, praying less, and feeling less desire to go to church and youth group.[5]

**DISCIPLING**

What will happen next to Tiffany? That may depend on whether she finds grace at home. Choose your own ending to her story:

**Ending 1:**
One evening after supper, Tiffany confides in her mother as the two of them are clearing the table. "Mom," the girl says hesitantly, "Do you ever find yourself using . . . well, swearwords?"

Her mother stiffens. "No," she says, rinsing a dish in the sink. "You know we don't believe in using words like that."

Sighing, Tiffany nods. "Yeah, I know." She pauses. "Do you think someone who uses those words can really be a Christian?"

Mom raises her eyebrows as she puts a handful of forks in the dishwasher. "I suppose it's possible," she says. "But I'd have to wonder, wouldn't you?" Mom straightens up, her eyes narrowing. "Who are we talking about here?" she asks.

Tiffany gulps. "Nobody," she says. "Just kids at school."

The dish clearing continues, but the conversation is over.

Tiffany doesn't raise the subject again. In the coming months, she thinks frequently of her mother's words: "I'd have to wonder, wouldn't you?" More and more she wonders—and begins to conclude that she's not a "real" Christian and probably never will be. The gap she feels between herself and God continues to widen.

**Ending 2:**
When Tiffany confides in her mother, Mom smiles ruefully. "Sometimes I *feel* like using those words," she admits. "But I try not to."

"But did you ever?"

Mom sighs. "I probably have a few times. I'm not proud of it. I'm sure I asked God to forgive me."

"And did He?"

"I'm sure He did."

Tiffany looks down at the plate in her hands. "How many times will He forgive you for the same thing?"

Tiffany glances up and sees her mother gazing at her with a mixture of puzzlement and compassion. "I'm 47, and I haven't reached the limit yet," Mom says. "And neither have you."

**DISCIPLING**

Smiling shyly, Tiffany busies herself with collecting cups from the table. She isn't ready to talk more yet, but two nights later she opens up to Mom about the language problem. Mom doesn't have a quick answer, but the two of them agree to pray about it and to start working together on a solution. For the first time in a year, Tiffany feels hopeful about her relationship with God.

Grace usually makes the giver and the receiver feel better. But for those of us who want to guide our teens, it does far more. It clears the way for spiritual growth. As Chuck Colson wrote:

> When God gets a grip on our lives, nothing is left untouched. That's what makes His grace dangerous. It unsettles our preconceived ideas, uproots our ingrained habits, redirects our deepest desires. When we give ourselves to God, He becomes our security—but He is never "safe." He is determined to make us the very best we can be, and He will never let us rest comfortably in our weaknesses and sins. He works ceaselessly to remake us into the image and character of Christ.[6]

As parents, we can aim for the same goal with our teens—but not without grace.

**DISCIPLING**

## Disciplining Effectively

Maybe you've noticed: When it comes to discipline, tactics you used to use—time-outs, spankings, counting to three in a voice meant to sound like the "great and powerful Wizard of Oz"— don't cut it now that your child is a teenager.

Still, the right kind of discipline is as important to your teen as it was to your two-year-old. No matter what the age of the child, the basics of discipline are the same: setting limits for the child's good, making them clear, and applying appropriate penalties when the limits are willfully and defiantly crossed. Your goal is to transfer power and independence in an orderly way from parent to child—a process that reaches its climax during the teen years.

**The Discipline-Spirituality Connection**

You'll find helpful resources on the how-tos of discipline listed at the end of this book. For now, you may be wondering, *What does the way I discipline my teenager have to do with his or her spiritual growth?*

Here are four answers:

*1. The way you discipline can shape the way your teen thinks and feels about God.* As Dr. James Dobson wrote in *Raising Them Right*:

> God has given us the assignment of representing Him during the formative years of parenting. That's why it is so critically important for us to acquaint our kids with God's two predominant natures: His unfathomable love and His justice. If we love our children but permit them to treat us disrespectfully and with disdain, we have distorted their understanding of the Father.
>
> On the other hand, if we are rigid disciplinarians who show no love, we have tipped the scales in the other direction. What we teach our children about the Lord is a function, to some degree, of how we model love and discipline in our relationship with them.[7]

Janna grew up under the harsh discipline of a perfectionist mom. "Even at six years of age, I was required to have nothing wrong with my appearance or surroundings," Janna recalls. "She constantly yelled at me, like you yell at a dog." By the time Janna was a teenager, she was furious at God, "blaming Him for everything."[8]

> *The way you discipline can shape the way your teen thinks and feels about God.*

Contrast that with the experience of Courtney, whose father has worked hard to balance love and justice in his discipline. Today she declares, "I am so blessed to have my dad. He puts so much time and love into us. I can see Jesus shining through him. Really!"[9]

*2. A teen who is allowed to defy parents probably will reject God's authority as well.* Dr. Dobson summed it up in *Raising Them Right*:

One of the characteristics of those who acquire power very

early is a prevailing attitude of disrespect for authority. It extends to teachers, ministers, policemen, judges, and even to God Himself. Such an individual has never yielded to parental leadership at home. Why should he submit himself to anyone else?[10]

3. *Kids without boundaries often fall into activities that distract them from following Jesus.* Tim Smith, in his book *Life Skills for Girls*, told the story of Jenny, a high school freshman who responded to a gospel presentation at the end of a concert. Jenny became active in the church youth group—but not for long. She was allowed to

■ ■ ■

## Car Keys:
## A Small but Mighty Discipline Tool

**DISCIPLING**

When one of my girls turned 15 and a half, she was in the middle of an attitude year. Her words to her mom were often not seasoned with grace. Her disrespect was annoying.

On the night before she was to get her driver's permit, she came to me with a happy proclamation: "Hey, Dad, guess what? Tomorrow I turn 15 and a half, and I get my driver's permit. What do you think about that?"

"Well," I replied carefully, "I don't think much of it."

"What? Why not?" she protested.

I went on soberly, "Thirty days from tonight, you *might* get your permit, *if* your attitude in the home improves immensely. This year you've forgotten how to treat your mom with grace. As far as I'm concerned, until you remember the sweet girl you once were, you'll never get your driver's permit."

The next month was one of the sweetest months around my house that I can remember. It has not been perfect since, but amid all the failures due any budding adolescent, that daughter has determined to value her mom and watch her attitude when addressing her. Thirty days later (not 29), she received her driver's permit with great appreciation.

Car keys are like golden handcuffs. They can be used to a parent's fullest advantage.

—Joe White

go to two parties every weekend, where she drank at least three beers a night. She was also permitted to date Todd, a senior who introduced her to tequila and marijuana. Eventually, Jenny stopped going to the youth group, saying she wanted nothing to do with her "old, immature friends from church."[11]

4. *The goal of discipline is to help kids develop self-discipline, a quality vital to discipleship.* Without self-discipline, kids will find it hard

■ ■ ■

## Discipline 101: Give Your Teen Boundaries

A 17-year-old girl in the throes of rebellion screams to her parents, "Where are my boundaries?"

Discipline was rare and inconsistent when she was a child. If a school administrator or caring friend criticized her, her parents ran to her defense. Though her parents disagreed with her judgment, she began to go out with boys when she was barely 14. She was going steady at 15; again her parents protested but looked the other way. She got her own car for her 16th birthday even though she broke her midnight curfew repeatedly.

Now she's gone to bed with several boys. She drinks compulsively. She's no stranger to drugs.

She, like all kids, preaches one message to her parents' increasingly deafened ears: "I know your boundaries. What I want to find out is, how serious are you about them?"

God created people with definite boundaries that He was dead serious about. Kids long for rules. They cry out for parents who will enforce those rules with fairness, firmness, and forthrightness. Their cries can be heard in the keg parties, the bedrooms, and the dance clubs.

If you're struggling with your child's behavior, pick up Dr. James Dobson's book *The New Dare to Discipline* as my wife and I did years ago—and inhale the wisdom.

"I know your boundaries, but are you serious about them?"

Do your kids know yours? Do they know what the consequences are if they push down the fence?

—Joe White

to start or stick with quiet times, Bible memorization, or anything else. There's a reason these things are called "spiritual disciplines," after all. They take time and effort. They take saying no to other pursuits.

Ed and Susan discovered the connection between discipline and self-discipline when their kids were in elementary school. "No Nintendo till your homework is done!" these parents found themselves saying frequently in the early grades. Then it was, "It's *your* responsibility to remind me to sign your agenda for the teacher." Slowly but surely, the kids learned to resist the lure of the Mario Bros. until they'd finished their assignments, and to manage their time. Discipline became internalized, and persistence became a skill the kids could apply to prayer, Bible study, and service to others.

**Tips for Discipline**
Here are four ways to practice the kind of discipline that helps a teen become an eager spiritual learner:

*1. Show mercy as well as firmness.* Once in a while, when meting out punishment, try suffering the penalty along with your teen—or even in your teen's place. Ground yourself along with your child. Match a monetary fine he must pay. You can't do this every time, of course, but even a few such incidents will show your teen compassion—and reflect the way God's Son paid the ultimate penalty for us.

*2. Don't relinquish your parental authority too soon.* Give your teen as much freedom as he or she is ready to handle, but continue to penalize defiance. Letting rebellion slide encourages disrespect for you and other authority figures, including God.

*3. Limit time-wasting activities as well as banning dangerous ones.* Allow plenty of room for fun. But if hours of video games, mall cruising, and phone calls are crowding out any possibility of Bible reading or youth group projects, work with your teen to keep fluff from taking over her life. Consider setting aside a Sabbathlike "rest period" of 30 minutes a day, for example, and using that time to talk or read with your teen about spiritual concerns.

*4. Think long-term.* When you're hurried, it's easy to be satisfied with the kind of discipline that simply exerts external control—

issuing threats that temporarily silence bickering between brothers, for instance. If you want to help your teen develop self-discipline, however, you'll need to switch the "control center" to your teenager's heart. Talk through the attitudes that lead to unwanted behavior. Suggest ways in which your teen might defuse a conflict (counting to 10, seeing the other person's point of view) without your intervention. Try to spot your adolescent using self-control—and when it happens, praise him.

> *Try to spot your adolescent using self-control—and when it happens, praise him.*

## Seeing the Possibilities

"Imagination," said Albert Einstein, "is more important than knowledge."

That's debatable. But it's clear that imagination *is* crucial to your teen's eagerness to grow spiritually.

Why? Because the child who sees only what *is* can't envision what *could be*. The teen who knows only the current state of the world can't dream of ways to change it. The young person who understands only that he isn't perfect can't grasp the concept that God isn't finished with him yet.

Like many teens, Marcia leads a life that discourages dreaming. Her day is packed with nose-to-the-grindstone classes and homework, followed by a mind-numbing after-school job in which she endlessly repeats the phrase "Would you like fries with that?" When she has free time, she chats with friends about the trivia of who's wearing what and dating whom. Or she sits in front of the TV, which bombards her with images telling her the best she can hope for is a good hair day and a chance to be a game show contestant.

Marcia needs to have her sights lifted. She needs to know that the world is bigger than study hall, the fast-food restaurant, and the cineplex. She needs help to imagine her future, a place with many doors that lead to a thousand different options. She needs to be assured that things can be different.

Ron is a man who was helped to dream about spiritual things.

DISCIPLING

After making a personal commitment to Christ during his teen years, he was interested in a conventional church staff position. But all that changed one day when he was in college. A visiting speaker fired Ron's imagination with vivid stories of hunger and oppression among the world's poor.

Soon Ron found himself seeking advice from a faculty member at the school. The man became a mentor, encouraging Ron to think outside the box, to discover unique ways in which God might be calling him to serve the needy. To the consternation of his family, Ron abandoned his plans for professional ministry and moved to a poverty-stricken, crime-ridden part of his city, where

■ ■ ■

## The Vision Thing:
## Seven Ways to Help Your Teen Become a World Changer

**DISCIPLING**

1. Invite people who are pursuing God's vision into your home. Ask them questions about what God is doing around them.
2. Put as much effort into involving your children in ministering to others as you do into getting them to play sports or the piano. Have a family project to expose your children to a suffering world—feed the homeless, sponsor a child, visit a juvenile jail, host international students, or take a mission trip.
3. Even if you have to change churches, involve your family in a body of believers where the worship is alive, the Bible is talked about warmly, people tell what Jesus is doing, and the youth program is geared to ministry, not entertainment. Support the church by driving, cooking, praying, or whatever is needed.
4. Take your children to camps, conferences, and mission trips where they can deepen their understanding of God's vision for them.
5. Pray for the Lord to bring along other adults who will take an interest in your children and support you in discipling them.
6. Decide on a ministry activity that you can do with your children weekly.
7. Take a training course with your children in how to share your faith, and then do it together.

—From *Ignite the Fire* by Barry and Carol St. Clair[12]

he worked odd jobs and did whatever he could to help the residents in Jesus' name.

Twenty years later, Ron is still an unconventional servant. He has followed his dream and God's calling from inner-city Denver to Central America, from Egypt to Israel to India to Poland, supporting himself and learning new languages and helping to change the world one life at a time. His parents still worry about him, but he has won their respect. They know Ron has accomplished things for God's kingdom that he never could have done as a "professional," thanks to the mentor who helped him imagine what might be.

How can you help your teen see exciting possibilities in his or her spiritual future? Here are a few ideas:

1. *Encourage exploration.* One of the chief tasks of adolescence is identity formation—figuring out who you are. Many kids try on personalities, lifestyles, and hobbies as if they were changing shirts, searching for the person they want to become. As much as possible, let kids try their hands at various activities. Don't expect every interest to turn into a career, and don't worry if that childhood passion for baseball or flute lessons fades away. From time to time, ask your teen, "What activities do you like the most these days? Can you think of any ways to serve God through them?" Your encouragement will affirm your teen's value as well as help him understand his God-given uniqueness.

2. *Welcome a desire to help others.* When teens lift their eyes from daily concerns and notice the needs of people around them, many are spurred to think of ways to help. As the authors of the *Focus on the Family Complete Book of Baby and Child Care* put it:

> Altruism often peaks during the teen years, and [teens] may find considerable satisfaction in helping others solve problems and in volunteering to serve in worthy causes. Teenagers can be surprisingly empathetic to the suffering of others, and they may go to great lengths of energy and time to lend someone a helping hand. You will obviously want to encourage selfless and sacrificial behavior—at times you may find your own conscience stirred by your adolescent's willingness to love the unlovely.[13]

One dad found this to be true while visiting San Francisco with his teenage daughter. There they saw a homeless woman rummaging through a garbage can for food. When the daughter reached for her purse in order to help the woman, the father warned, "Don't you *dare* give her any money! You don't know what she might do with it."

The daughter said nothing. That evening the two of them ate pizza in a restaurant. When the father reached for one of two remaining slices, the girl asked, "Are you sure you need that, Dad?"

"Of course I don't *need* it," he said. "I *want* it."

Gently, the daughter pointed out that there was probably at least one person outside the restaurant at that moment, picking through the Dumpster, who *did* need that pizza. The two of them went outside, where they found a homeless person to whom they gave the food. The father was ashamed of his own callousness—and proud of his daughter's compassion.

3. *Supply examples.* Bill can still remember the guests who streamed through his house when he was growing up—missionaries, church deacons, Christian musicians, Sunday school teachers. As he watched and listened to these role models, Bill wondered, *What would it be like to be a missionary? What kind of deacon would I make? Should I teach?*

The more examples Bill saw, the more options there seemed open to him. Simply spending time around adults who serve God in a variety of ways can get kids thinking about their own goals, too.

For further tips on helping your teen dream productive dreams, see chapter 16 in this book.

## Seeing Results from Personal Accomplishments

Charlie Brown, of *Peanuts* comic strip fame, was an expert loser. He failed gloriously and repeatedly—at love, on the baseball diamond, and in battles with his nervous stomach in the middle of the night.

But Charlie was perhaps best known for failing to kick a football. Every fall the cynical Lucy would entice him into trying to boot a pigskin she balanced on the ground. And every time she

DISCIPLING

would snatch it away at the last moment. Charlie's ensuing crash was humiliating—and entirely predictable.

Why did he keep trying? In real life we need successes, not failures, to keep us going. Teens are no exception. The guy who asks 12 friends to a Christian concert and gets 12 turndowns isn't likely to ask number 13. The girl who raises $100 toward a new youth group van, only to see the campaign canceled due to lack of interest, won't be eager to sign up for the next car wash.

Kids need to see that their efforts make a difference. They need success experiences, starting with small and "unspiritual" ones like these:

- *I worked hard to clean my room, and now it looks really neat.*
- *I studied for that test, and I got a good grade.*
- *I practiced the piano every day, and now I can play the theme from my favorite TV show.*

The same principle applies to more spiritual pursuits:

- *I prayed that God would help me make friends, and He did.*
- *I gave money for hunger relief, and I got a letter back from a little boy who was helped.*
- *I told a girl at school about Jesus, and she listened without laughing at me.*

You can't insulate your teen from failure, but you can increase the chances that his effort will yield positive results. Here's how:

1. *Make sure he is prepared.* Karl's parents wanted him to discover the value of bringing God's love to nursing home residents. On their next visit to such a facility, they brought Karl along. Not knowing what to expect, Karl was freaked out by the smells, the sights and sounds of babbling and trembling old people, and a blind man who kept grabbing Karl, squeezing his arms, and asking whether he was a football player. It would be years before Karl was willing to visit a nursing home again.

You may also need to prepare your teen by giving her a dose of street smarts. The authors of the *Focus on the Family Complete Book of Baby and Child Care* advise:

You should model practical concern for the needs of others and at the same time offer guidance as to the parameters of your teen's involvement. For example, your daughter might want to rescue a friend from an abusive family situation by inviting her to stay at your home. Perhaps you are able to offer a safe haven—certainly an honorable and meaningful action—but you will also need to walk your daughter through some of the realities and details that may not have occurred to her in the rush to help. If you have a particularly generous and tender-hearted teen at home, you will have to pass along a little street wisdom to help prevent her charitable instincts from being soured by encounters with users and abusers who might take advantage of her.[14]

2. *Aim for realistic goals.* Every New Year's Eve, Sherrie would resolve to read her Bible each morning. Every year, by February 1, she'd miss a day or two and give up. When she finally dropped the "each morning" requirement, she was able to relax. When she fell behind in her reading, she simply started again, picking up where she'd left off. What seemed at first to be a failure became a success, and it encouraged her to keep reading regularly.

3. *Explain that results aren't always visible, predictable, or instantaneous.* What if your teen prays that a sick relative will get well, and the person dies? What if an attempt to tell a friend about Christ is rebuffed?

Like the rest of us, your teen needs to learn that prayers may be answered with "yes," "no," or "wait" (or "yes" and "trust Me")—and that sharing faith means risking rejection. Help your child understand that God's definition of success may not be the same as ours and that He operates on His own timetable. Things will ultimately work together for good (see Romans 8:28), but the fact is that, in the meantime, life's little mysteries can be frustrating (see John 16:33).

4. *When a project goes wrong, talk about it.* Amy was asked to write a play for church. She worked hard and stayed up late to meet the deadline. Unfortunately, a disagreement between the drama director and the worship leader led to dropping the skit.

■ ■ ■

## *Hoop Dreams:*
## *Unloading Baggage at Bedtime*

My older boy, Brady, as a junior in high school, had developed quite a basketball game. He was starting for a very good team.

But somehow the pressure got to him. Playing basketball in high school had become a huge dream and passion of his, and he'd worked thousands of hours to get where he was. But the situation with his coaches and with his own sensitive heart and meek spirit broke him.

By God's grace, I had developed the habit since he was tiny of lying next to him at bedtime. Now, even though he was six-foot-three, taller and a lot bigger than me, it wasn't awkward for me to be lying on his pillow when he came to bed. Night after night, for four months, we'd cry together. Almost every day he'd come home broken, scared, and confused. His world had caved in. But I was able to give him the gift of warmth, because his head would be on my shoulder and his tears would be on my chest.

I gave him the gift of empathy, sharing with him times when I had fallen apart in football games and performed poorly. I gave him the gift of unconditional regard, letting him know that I loved him every time he shot a brick, every time he passed the ball out of bounds, and every time the coach screamed at him.

I let him know he was my hero. I kept reminding him of qualities in his life that I loved and respected that were far more valuable than basketball. I would ask him the "What's wrong?" and "How are you feeling?" questions.

One night he came in after a game. He said, "Dad, I'm so tired of building character. I don't want to build any more character in my life." There were times when we could laugh at it. Slowly, as the year went along, Brady's heart began to heal.

That boy and I became bonded as friends for life. It happened with two big ears, a soft shoulder, and some gently asked questions to help peel off the baggage—in his case, the baggage of depression and despair.

Before my eyes, I saw the Lord heal that boy. His basketball season didn't end up spectacular, but his heart ended up healed. Today he's a man noted as one that anybody can come and talk to, that anyone can share a problem with, that anyone can get wisdom from to heal their brokenness.

—Joe White

No one ever explained to Amy what had happened; all she knew was that her work had been in vain. Next time she was asked to write a skit, her answer was no—an outcome that could have been avoided with an honest conversation.

5. *Follow up.* When possible, help your teen find out how his effort made a difference. Ask for a report on the fund-raising walk, the evangelistic campaign, the gift packages sent to the Third World country. Not every accomplishment will have measurable results, but those that do will be a special encouragement to your teen.

Nothing succeeds like success, Charlie Brown notwithstanding. You can help your teen connect with that football—and have a reason to try again.

## Celebrating Achievements

"You did it!" cried Dick and Carolyn in unison when their three-year-old son, Jason, finally used the potty by himself for the first time.

"Great job!" they said with a smile when Jason, age eight, performed in a handbell concert at school.

During the next few years, Dick and Carolyn will have plenty of opportunities to celebrate Jason's achievements as a teenager. They'll take him out to dinner when he gets his driver's license. They'll hug him after he crosses the stage at graduation.

But how will they mark his spiritual progress?

Parents who show appreciation for their child's accomplishments are

> *Parents who show appreciation for their child's accomplishments are setting the stage for bigger and better things.*

setting the stage for bigger and better things. That's true for significant moments in a child's spiritual growth, too. The teen whose God-honoring achievements are celebrated sees that growth is valued by others and becomes a more eager spiritual learner.

In *Life Skills for Guys*, Tim Smith told of Robin Spurlock, a woman whose family found a way to celebrate her spiritual progress. "For my sixteenth and eighteenth birthdays," she said, "my family and significant others wrote letters affirming the growth they had seen in my life. They noted the growth of my character and evidence of spiritual growth. They reflected on the past and anticipated a favorable future."

Armed with positive reinforcement like that, Robin went on to serve in Christian camping and youth ministry. Smith concluded, "These are the kind of memories parents want to be building. . . . We want [kids] launching into adulthood with confidence and the support of wise mentors. We want them making wise choices that will favor them with a positive future."[15]

In addition to writing letters on birthdays, how can you recognize and reward your teen's spiritual progress? The possibilities are endless; here are just 10 ideas to get you started.

1. If you've been asking your teen to change a particular behavior (griping about going to church, for example), thank him when he does.

2. Ask your teen's opinion about a spiritual matter into which she has recently shown insight. If she has demonstrated discernment in choosing her music or TV shows, for instance, ask her to critique a song or program you like.

3. When your teen gets serious about Bible study, ask him to lead the family in a discussion of a passage he's found meaningful.

## Teens' "Ways in Which a Parent Was Spiritually Influential," Part 6

- "We had devotions as a family. My dad would read from the *Character Sketch* book, which tells stories about animals and how they display different qualities we all should emulate. Also, my dad and mom were always open and willing to have deep spiritual conversation with me—they wanted to know what God was teaching me."
- "My dad rotated among children, taking them out for breakfast Saturday morning. We would talk about what was going on in our lives. We would also all talk after Sunday lunch about our spiritual lives and where we were at."
- "(1) My father took me to a father/daughter camp in California for a week. Our time together was special, and our relationship was strengthened. We also both grew spiritually during this time and helped to keep each other accountable.

4. If your teen has helped lead someone to become a Christian, throw a "new birth day" party for the fledgling believer, your teen, and anyone else who played a part in the event.

5. When you spot your teen acting as a servant to someone else, volunteer to be her servant for an hour.

6. When your child expresses a deeper understanding of a spiritual concept, buy him a teen study Bible or devotional book and say, "I think you're ready for this now."

7. Tell other adults—within earshot of your teen—about one of her God-honoring accomplishments. To make sure your teen will be pleased rather than embarrassed, make sure the achievement was a public one (for example, defending her faith in class) and not a private one (for example, overcoming a bad habit).

8. If your teen has started praying more consistently, confide some of your own concerns, and ask him to pray for those, too.

9. When your teen risks rejection by resisting negative peer pressure, have all the members of the family stand by her by writing messages on a card, making affirming comments at the dinner table, or having a group hug.

10. Remember that pizza is a good idea for practically any occasion.

**DISCIPLING**

"(2) My family had family devotions together, which allowed us to grow spiritually as a family."

■ "From the time I was in fourth or fifth grade until I was in high school, Dad and I would get up at 6:00 and read to each other from a book called *Character Sketches*, which took a character trait and showed how it was present in the life of an animal and a biblical character. These special times taught me how important a daily time with the Lord is. I will always treasure them because they belonged to only Dad and me—no one else. I had his undivided attention."

■ "In eighth grade, I was really struggling with knowing that God was knocking at the door of my heart, but I didn't know what to do with that. Mom took me in her bedroom and led me in a prayer asking Christ to come into my life."

## Unloading Psychological Baggage

Nothing puts the brakes on a teen's spiritual growth quite like dragging around the baggage of guilt, shame, fear, and indecision. If 17-year-old Andy feels ashamed because he's addicted to Internet porn, no one will be able to convince him that spending more face-to-face time with God is a good idea. If 14-year-old Charmaine is afraid to go to school because three students have threatened her, sharing her faith with classmates will be the last thing on her mind.

Psychological baggage isn't always that heavy, of course. Day-to-day problems—worries about a test, troubles with a boyfriend or girlfriend—can weigh kids down, too. The perceptive parent learns to help the teen unload that baggage regularly, before the accumulation becomes unmanageable.

### Asking the Right Questions

How can you help your teen get rid of emotional burdens? It doesn't take a degree in psychology. You can start by learning to ask three key questions, as veteran youth worker and speaker J. David Stone has pointed out:

1. *What's wrong?* This is the intellectual question. It gives your teen permission to take off the first layer of baggage. After asking it, simply sit back and listen.

2. *How do you feel?* This is the emotional question. Again, listen closely to the answer. If your child says, "I feel sad," follow up by asking what the sadness is like. If your child says, "I feel confused," ask, "What are you confused about?" Resist the urge to issue a verdict on your teen's feelings or to leap in with a solution at this point.

3. *What are you doing?* This question is behavioral. If your child doesn't know how to answer it, go back to question one. Say something like "You told me X is wrong; what are you doing about that?"

The first time you ask those three questions, the answers may not be long. Be patient. Try saying, "Could I ask you those questions again? This time, maybe you could put your answer in a little different way to help me understand."

If your teen isn't ready to talk, trying to force him to open up will be futile. Postpone the discussion, perhaps asking, "When would be a better time during the next couple of days to talk about this?"

When the hour comes, you may need to go through the three questions several times. Chances are that the layers of sadness and despair around the core problem will slowly be removed as you listen patiently. It's like looking for the surprise in a box of Cracker Jacks; the questions take out the popcorn and peanuts, and eventually you get to the prize.

### Creating the Right Atmosphere

You won't find the prize, of course, simply by repeating the three questions as if they were magic words. They help *under the right conditions*. Your tone of voice, your relationship with your teen, and other factors create those conditions. According to Dr. Jim Oraker of Young Life, here are four keys to creating an atmosphere for this kind of conversation:

1. *Warmth.* This is a shoulder to cry on and a steady, caring eye. It's facial expressions and body language that show you want to be close to your child when he or she is talking with you.

2. *Empathy.* This means identifying with and caring about what your teen is saying.

3. *Unconditional regard.* The parent who has this quality is thinking, *There but for the grace of God go I. And I care for you as much as, or more than, I did before you told me what's going wrong in your life.*

4. *Congruency.* When things are congruent, they fit together. Here, congruency means practicing what you preach—following in your own life the same advice you're giving your son or daughter.[16]

When you ask the three questions with warmth, empathy, unconditional regard, and congruency, you may be amazed at how willing your teen is to open up—and to come to you the next time she has more baggage to unload.

### Bringing the Conversation to a Close

To bring closure to your conversation, try asking, "What do you need to do to get what you want?" If you've worked through the

**DISCIPLING**

three questions, it's likely that your teen will already have some ideas. If not, you can offer advice. Either way, pray with your child, and help him come up with a plan of action.

When that happens, you're clearing the path to spiritual progress. Unloading psychological baggage enables your child to return to a learning mode. That's when she's ready to grow again.

DISCIPLING

# CHAPTER 16

# Helping Your Teen Dream Productive Dreams

Since he was six years old, Chris has been fascinated by flight. Every airplane heading over his house has drawn his eyes up to watch it soar. Jeff and Keli, Chris's parents, heard him say (like many children), "I want to be a pilot when I grow up," and they assumed his childish interest would be superseded by the desire to be a fireman or a ballplayer. But Chris's love of flight continued, rarely wavering. When he was in high school, his parents arranged for him to visit a small airport and even bought him some flying lessons. Today, he is still pursuing aviation and aviation mechanics, with the eventual goal of applying his skills on the mission field.

Your job as a parent often seems anchored in the here and now, in the day-to-day decisions of raising a teen. You are committed to the long haul, but how can you help your teen look down the road and develop a dream to serve God? Top-ranking corporations achieve success by developing and pursuing a focused vision statement. General targets may be adjusted through the years, but the overriding goal is constantly before the employees, from the president and CEO to those at the bottom of the organizational ladder. What are we here for? What do we want to do in relationship to our customers? Whom do we seek to serve, and in what manner?

In the same way, we want our teens to develop and pursue a vision statement—to know the answer to Chuck Colson's question, "How now shall we live?" A recent survey asked teenagers the things they most wanted in their lives when they reached adulthood. Along with the expected results of good physical health and close personal friendships, more than 80 percent of the teens indicated that they wanted to have a clear purpose for living.[1] But a vision, a dream, rarely arrives fully developed in a teen's mind. You can take specific steps, however, to help your teen build that desire and pursue a passion that God has placed within him.

First, remember that a dream goes far beyond career planning. Parents tend to push a child toward a particular occupation, and the child may eventually achieve some recognition within that career. However, financial and professional success do not necessarily equate with satisfaction or the achievement of a purposeful life. Certainly, a dream for serving God will probably include an eventual vocation, but a career may be just a portion of the vision your teen develops and pursues with your help. Actually, the vision is more a tuning in to God's calling in the teen's life—an understanding of where God has gifted him or her and of the opportunity to use the blending of knowledge, skills, spiritual gifts, and interests in sensing and pursuing a passion.

## Understanding Your Teen's Gifts and Talents

What gifts and talents does your child possess? He may have demonstrated some obvious ones early in life: Aptitude for music, athletics, communication, and art often show up in early elementary school. But you may not recognize other abilities until later—such skills as the art of dealing with other people (both peers and adults), a gift for working with children, a desire to help others or to make them feel comfortable in awkward situations, organizational or administrative expertise, or the ability to motivate others to do something they don't necessarily want to do (and to feel a sense of achievement once those tasks are accomplished).

Besides inborn talents and interests, there is the wide variety of gifts given by the Holy Spirit to God's people for the building up of the church (see Romans 12:6-8; 1 Corinthians 12:27-31). They include not only preaching and teaching (normally more visible gifts) but also service and hospitality.

Look at a typical church youth group. If the youth pastor is intentional about building leadership in the students he serves, you may see some who are coordinating worship times and songfests, others who have prepared items for the bake sale, and some who are keeping their eyes peeled during the get-acquainted time to spot newcomers and make them feel welcome. While none of these interests may translate into eventual career placement, all can give direction about what taps the teen's interest tank and what inspires him or her.

> **Be actively on the lookout for your teen's gifts and interests in daily life.**

As a parent, you can help your child discover his spiritual gifts by getting him a spiritual gifts test from your pastor or a Christian bookstore and helping him complete it. Also, be actively on the lookout for your teen's gifts and interests in daily life. Watch for that glimmer, that spark of excitement, when she's telling about her time at school. Does she reveal a caring, compassionate heart toward another girl in her class, the one who was heartbroken in the hallway? Perhaps, with your help, a counseling ministry could be on the horizon. Does he evidence enthusiasm when he's describing a student body activity and how he helped to get the committee over a hurdle? Maybe one day, with your encouragement, he'll solve problems for a ministry or other organization in a management or administrative role.

Is your daughter fascinated by current events? You might want to help her explore opportunities in print journalism, broadcasting, or politics. If your son shows an interest in working with his hands, he may have a future in mechanical engineering or cabinetmaking. Ask questions, listen to his conversations, and observe his attitude and reactions.

At the same time, don't just sit around and wait for something to grab your teen's fancy. Make a deliberate effort to expose her to different fields; on their own, teens tend to focus on their current activities and so may not initiate exploration into new interests.

DISCIPLING

Summer and part-time jobs can also open teens' eyes to new directions—both to introduce interests they may want to explore further and to identify careers they definitely want to avoid.

One father recalled, "One summer I worked as a groundsman at a school because I wanted to work outdoors. I was miserable because of the early hours, the smog (this was in California), the hard work, and the dirt. That summer convinced me of what I *didn't* want to do. Last summer, when my daughter was looking for a job, she worked at a preschool. She has always loved working with kids, and that experience confirmed her direction to pursue her dream of teaching."

Most high schools have inventories of skills and abilities available for their students to take. With the assistance of community organizations, some schools also sponsor career days. Some bring in speakers, while others give students the chance to "shadow" a community member. Encourage your teen to participate in such programs so she can see what's involved in an occupation of interest to her. Be realistic about her skills and abilities, and don't assume that just because she displays talent in a particular area she is interested in developing it as a career.

Megan showed a lot of promise as a child actress. "But although I had some lead roles in plays when I was younger," she said, "I didn't really enjoy the attention and the pressure after a

DISCIPLING

## Teens' "Traits of Great Parents," Part 7

- "They are involved with their teens. They go to their teens' activities. They have a ready ear to listen."
- "Active, involved, caring, spontaneous, firm, disciplined, loving, affectionate, open, servant-hearted, loving, touchy, and compassionate."
- "Prayer warrior, disciplinarian, fun! Open, honest, living faith, loving to spouse, affectionate."
- "Strong Christian convictions, Christian nurturing, faith in God and knowing He is in control, living example of Christ's love, loving each other (as Christ loves the church)."
- "Communication in love, discipline in love, leadership in love, to gain the respect of your child by the love you have for him or her."

while. My mom didn't push me, even though I think she would have liked to see me continue to perform. Instead I got involved in more behind-the-scenes stuff, painting backdrops and working on the sound board. Now that I'm a young adult, my occupation doesn't have anything to do with drama, but whenever my church is putting on a production, the director knows she can count on me to help out any way I can."

## Provide an Environment for Progress

Once you have started to help your teen recognize areas of interest and gifting, explore the options available to turn those talents into ways to serve and to develop and pursue dreams. You can rarely predict which experiences will most inspire your teen, so provide plenty of opportunities for those sparks to be struck. Also encourage him to associate with other adults who have set goals and accomplished them.

Amy, a college student, recalled, "My parents were active in our little church while my sister and I were little. It seemed like we were always having missionaries stay at our house, folks who came to speak at church. When we were young, they'd usually take the guests out to dinner and get a baby-sitter for us. But on one visit, the missionary said he'd rather just eat at home with the family if that was all right. I will never forget that evening. He told us about the opportunities he'd had to help people and to learn their language."

That conversation sparked an interest in Amy's mind for eventual mission service. "When I was in junior high," she continued, "my family went on a short-term mission project in Mexico. We were on a construction team, and we worked so hard building a house for a family who had been living in basically a cardboard shack. I don't know how much good I actually was to the team, but I saw the tears in that lady's eyes when she realized she was going to have a real home for the first time. I became sold out for overseas missions that day.

"We talked about it on our way home from Mexico," Amy said, "and I told Mom and Dad what I wanted to do. They didn't shoot me down or tell me I was just a kid. Instead, they decided to give me whatever experiences they could to either confirm or redirect my dream. In high school, our youth group did a mission trip to Cincinnati, and then I had the chance to go on a mission trip to Costa Rica with girls from all over the country. We did evangelistic work based on a drama, and seeing little kids and families make decisions to follow Christ convinced me that I wanted to keep pursuing those goals."

Amy is now pursuing her dream in college, preparing for ministry on an overseas mission field. Although her parents don't look forward to having their daughter on the other side of the world (at least potentially), Amy's mother said, "We saw that flame start burning on the Mexico trip, and because

> *Provide a home where dreams can be dreamed without a fear of mockery.*

she is a deliberate young lady, we knew we had two choices. We could either stand in her way and get run over, or we could do what we could to help her achieve her dreams. There is no question in our minds that we made the right decision."

Parents, provide a home, like Amy's, where dreams can be dreamed without a fear of mockery.

Joe White tells about his son Brady, who in fourth grade dreamed of one day being a starter on his high school basketball team: "Here was a kid who had been laughed off the soccer field since he was about eight years old because he was a slow developer. So I agreed to get under the basket at night when I came home from work, and Brady was always waiting for me. In the next five years after he shared his dream, I probably caught about 100,000 of Brady's shots. He never made the NBA, but we built a great friendship."

Brady's dream was a short-term and personal goal, not a life-long vision for serving God. But working toward that goal gave him the confidence to pursue more significant and longer-range dreams. In his teen years, Brady developed a passion for leading youth in worship. "Brady recently produced his first CD," Joe said, "and helping him pursue a goal like that is so much more satisfying than basketball, because it has eternal significance in helping teens know about and praise God."

You can likewise give your teen a launching pad for his dreams. Certainly those dreams and those passions may change, and it is important not to allow your child to be crushed by unrealistic expectations. But think of the heroes of history who had dreams and pursued them despite the odds against them. Helen Keller overcame blindness and deafness to become a world-famous speaker. Glenn Cunningham's legs were badly burned when he was a child, yet he became a world-champion miler. Abraham Lincoln overcame poverty through self-education and is regarded as perhaps the greatest president of the United States. Do not squelch the dream and cause your child to lose hope.

Look outside your family to discover other adults who can help to provide that spark and additional knowledge of what's involved. One young man named Rob, with the encouragement of his parents, connected with his high school teacher. "While I was in college, with so many options open to me, I sat down and decided to go into education with my parents' blessing," Rob said. "After I became a teacher, Mr. J. and I talked about what had drawn me into teaching, and I told him, 'Those Friday afternoons when I could see what a difference a caring teacher could make.' If Mom and Dad had not allowed me to build that rapport with my teacher, I would have probably missed out on a calling that has continued to inspire me and to give me a ministry to the next generation."

Suzanne wanted to be a writer when she was an early teen. Her parents encouraged her to pursue that dream, so she wrote a letter to the editor of a magazine for teen girls, asking, "What do I need to do to work for a magazine like yours someday?" The editor responded, encouraging her to keep writing on a regular basis, to explore work on the school newspaper or yearbook, and to hang on to that dream.

Today Suzanne reports, "I took that advice to heart. I knew it might be a long shot to land a job with that magazine. I took each of the steps that editor suggested. I was home-schooled, so the school newspaper wasn't an option for me. But what my mom did was to allow me to devote an entire year of English to producing a magazine for home-schooled teens. That experience, as she critiqued my writing and encouraged me to pursue stories for the magazine,

**DISCIPLING**

played an integral part in the development of my journalistic skills. Instead of sticking to a strict curriculum, she supported me by letting me study the type of writing I was interested in." And shortly after graduation, Suzanne became an assistant editor with the same publishing house that produces that magazine for teen girls.

## Provide Encouragement of Progress

Once the environment is established, the pursuit of the dream and the parental role have only begun. Times will come when your teen wants to give up; the road to the dream just seems too hard. That's where you can step in and give the booster shot, the motivation to keep on going. The legendary college basketball coach John Wooden used to say, "When the going gets tough, the tough get going." And as a loving parent, you may sometimes need to be that "get going" type of coach for your child.

Yvonne was a gifted musician whose parents recognized her talent when she was young. "She was one of those rare children," her mother recalled, "who actually enjoyed practicing. The major problem was that she was so hard on herself. Her dad is a perfectionist, too, and I had to tell him to just stay out of the house while she was rehearsing because she would become so self-conscious. We got her a good teacher and just tried to be a support for her all the way through her high school years.

"I will never forget the first performance of the youth symphony," she continued, "when Yvonne played a solo. These were young kids who tried their best, but some of the notes were downright painful. As we walked out afterward, Yvonne was upset because of the group performance, even though she had done her solo flawlessly. She said, 'I bet you'll never want to come to another performance of mine.' We assured her that day that at least one of us would be at every performance, and we kept that promise all the way to her exquisite cello solo at her high school baccalaureate.

"Was it convenient? No. Did we enjoy sitting through those never-ending music festivals with so many different schools performing? Definitely not. But we knew that Yvonne was going to be playing and that she would try to catch our eyes just before the performance began. That made it all worthwhile."

Yvonne was a multitalented student who chose to follow a direction other than music in college. But she said, "The way that my mom and dad supported me in my music gave me the confidence to pursue other goals. What Mom didn't mention was their constant prayer support, too. Before every performance, they would pray with me—not for my own success but that the Lord would be glorified. Whether I played poorly or well, whether the orchestra shone or stunk it up, they would be there with encouragement. As much as I loved music, I felt that a career in that field would have benefited me more than others. I loved playing and performing, but I also found myself overly concerned with what others thought of me as a result.

"I wanted to focus on service to others and had always loved science and children. Instead of music, I changed direction toward medicine, with an emphasis in pediatrics. Although I think my dad was disappointed that I didn't pursue music vocationally, my parents assured me of their support in this new venture. Even with the long grind of preparation ahead of me, I knew they would be in my corner, doing whatever they could to help me along."

Yvonne completed her medical training but didn't leave her love of music behind. She helped her church begin an orchestra, in which she plays the cello. In addition, she says, "Once my husband and I had our son, I cut back on my medical practice. I started offering music lessons to some of my former patients, including a couple of kids with special needs. I love blending my two great loves to help children."

In an interview with Christian music artist Michael W. Smith and his son Ryan, the proud father illustrated his encouragement. Ryan's real passions, besides playing the guitar (including accompanying his dad on stage), are writing and film production. Ryan told *Breakaway* magazine, "I'd love to work in the film industry as a writer and a director. It would be great to tie in music somewhere, but if the film stuff doesn't happen, I still want to write."

Michael said, "My dream for Ryan is to start a small, independent film company. Judging from the stuff he shoots with the

**DISCIPLING**

■ ■ ■

## For the Sake of the Call

Janelle was only six, but the Lord touched her heart as she watched a movie about Hudson Taylor, a missionary to China. Tears streamed down her face as she cried, "God wants me to be a missionary, Mom!"

Something inside told me her calling was real. So I encouraged her all I could, from having a globe and map of the world visible in our home to helping her learn about missions. In her Christian school, she was introduced to several foreign languages and met missionary kids, and at home I supplemented her experiences with books, music, and multicultural meals.

Because our church had a missions vision, international flags hung in the sanctuary, and services often highlighted missionary speakers. Our family watched movies set in various international settings, prayed for the world, and housed visiting missionaries.

As the years passed, Janelle's global vision never wavered. When she was 12, the Association of Christian Schools International (ACSI) held a national contest, and Janelle was chosen to be the ACSI ambassador to Russia. So with an association official, we traveled to Moscow, where she spoke in Russian schools and cultural centers.

Putting her into the Lord's hands on international trips was not easy. But the following year, I let go, and Janelle spent a month as a camp counselor in Russia, near the Black Sea. The next year, she went to work with the Masai in Kenya, and when she was 16, she ministered in Thailand. At age 17, she worked in Ghana, West Africa.

Each trip took endless hours of planning, hard work, and fund-raising, but it was all worth it. Sacrifice was a constant reality as we committed to each trip, yet I reasoned, *What sacrifice is too great to have my child know and fulfill the call of God?*

Because I was a single mother, our finances were inflexible, so 15-year-old Janelle opened a Christian dance studio to raise mission trip money. I managed the studio—and her—on top of working full-time, going to university half-time, and renting rooms in our home. But the emotional, psychological, and spiritual lessons I learned as I gave her to God and helped her fulfill her call far outweighed the physical and financial challenges.

When she got malaria and nearly died in Ghana, however, I felt like Abraham offering my Isaac on the altar. For three days the missionaries called me, assuring me she was still alive, and in those three days I experienced God in a way that deepened my faith and trust in Him as He held my daughter's life in His hands on the other side of the world.

Janelle pulled through, but it was six months before she was really well. Yes, the battle with malaria scared both of us. Yet it didn't snuff out Janelle's passion for the world. So she and I traveled to Europe for a graduation trip.

Janelle is now studying international politics and communication in college, and she plans to be a diplomatic missionary. She will soon travel to several countries in the European Union with her school to experience the intricacies of foreign diplomacy. For the sake of God's call on her life, I continue to carry the priority of helping Janelle prepare for ministry and experience all God has for her.

—Susan Goodwin Graham

disc camera, I know he'll be making films one day. I believe this is how guys like Ryan and I can impact the culture for God. This is a dream of ours. And when God gives you a dream—look out!"[2]

## Ask Questions to Clarify and Refine the Dream

As your teen matures, ask both the penetrating and the potent questions to keep the dream alive. Help him to keep a long-range view when he makes choices by asking, "What would this decision contribute to what you want to do? What difference will it make in your life 10 years from now if you take that path? How do you think you can serve people by pursuing that dream? Do you see this direction as something you want to do as a career or as a sideline?"

But asking the questions is only one step. Listening carefully to the answers (and searching between the lines) can help you know the best ways to encourage your teen. Allow her to be vulnerable, to be honest with you even at the risk of sounding foolish. Don't "lead the witness" by asking the questions in such a way that she will feel she's disappointing you if she answers in a way you would not expect.

One author described her own life this way: "Can you help

DISCIPLING

your teen pull out her dream? Make an environment so safe that she can share the scary thing she really wants to do but feels is impossible. I wanted to be a writer, but I never told anyone and shoved the dream aside for something I thought would be more acceptable and practical. I don't think I ever gave my parents a clue that I wanted to write. They could not encourage something they did not know about."

At the same time, give your teen the opportunity to alter course. Dreams can change, and you don't want your teen to become frustrated in an expected role simply because it was his dream at one point in the past.

Throughout high school, a young man named Todd expressed an interest in film and audio production. He purchased a video camera and experimented with some success. But when he entered college, long hours in a studio helped him realize that was no longer his dream. "I realized I was much more of a person who wanted to relate with people instead of doing my own thing in a studio," he said. "I enjoyed being outdoors and active, so I changed my major to physical education and recreation. My mom and dad didn't make me feel guilty because I'd shifted gears. In fact, my dad is a former teacher, so I think he was shocked to think I might become a teacher, too."

### Their Dream, Not Yours

Stage mothers and Little League fathers share a common curse: They try to live their lives through their children, and even

## Teens' Advice to Parents About Nurturing Spiritual Growth, Part 8

- "My parents held back their faith so as not to push us. Yet I would have really appreciated a better understanding of their faith, and I would have loved for them to have taught me more. I feel I really came to a full understanding of Christ on my own. That was hard."
- "Start early and develop a special time to meet and talk. Parents need to continually try to improve as parents and spiritual leaders, to be involved. Parents must intentionally make time for spiritual development."
- "Fathers, please lead your household in God's will. This is crucial to your

though the children may become successful in the world's eyes, rarely do they achieve real happiness. As Joe White tells parents, "Don't make the mistake of living vicariously through your children. Type-A parents, be careful. Goal-driven parents, be careful. Allow the child to grow at the rate the child wants to grow. Your child may be a third-team player. Help him enjoy being a third-team player. Help him enjoy being an encouragement to the team. Whenever you or I get involved in an adolescent's dreams, don't own the dream. If you do, the kid will begin to hate the dream and will go a different direction—as far from you as he can get."

Teens long for independence and revel in what they want to do. Each one has individual goals and dreams. Resist the temptation to make your teen feel that he must pursue a particular path because you want him to. The burden of accomplishing his own goals becomes far heavier if he is carrying the load of others' expectations as well.

"I knew that my father wanted me to take over his business," a young adult named Roberto said. "But I was bound and determined to go my own way. His expectations felt like a combination between a harness and a leash. I needed to be independent for a while. Amazingly, while I was out there trying to blaze my own trail, the Lord kept showing me all the meaningful ministry my dad was doing in a 'secular' business.

"About three years later, I humbly came to my father and asked if I could come alongside him in the agency. If he'd forced me to do it right out of school, I would have been resentful, but

**DISCIPLING**

marriage, your family, your children, and yourself. Do not be afraid to lovingly discipline your children. Pray for and with your children faithfully and unashamed. Make sure that discussions on spiritual matters and God are not an uncommon occurrence in your home."

■ "Christian parents need to learn to give their kids to God. It will save a lot of yelling. Parents like to be sheltering. This just hurts the kids, makes them want to be bad."

■ "In order to have a *relationship*, you must make it your goal to *relate*."

> *Resist the temptation to make your teen feel that he must pursue a particular path because you want him to.*

the fact that I came to my own decision made it much more palatable. Now we are not only father and son but also partners in a business that reaches out to people in need."

Remember that the dreams discussed in this chapter are not limited to vocations and careers. What a person does to earn a living is only one portion of his calling and of who he is. Emily had the lifelong dream of becoming a doctor specializing in obstetrics and gynecology, but midway through med school, her family ran out of money. She headed in another career direction but retained her strong pro-life stand. She now spends six hours per week volunteering at a crisis pregnancy center. Her medical knowledge allows her to explain the medical implications of various options to clients she counsels there.

What parents want to develop in their children is a sense of faithfulness, of satisfaction in following God's purpose in their lives. Joe White reminds parents, "Passions that aren't under the umbrella of God's nurturing, disciple making, and spiritual growth are heading for tragedy. If what goes on in the home is not directed toward knowing, loving, and following God, these passions will turn into kids sitting at the end of a swimming pool with a trophy in their hand, crying because the trophy means nothing to them. I've seen kids with NFL contracts rip up the contract because that was all they had. The parent who puts God and the Word into the home can allow earthly passions to turn into heavenly accomplishments for the child."

What do you want for your teen? What do you want him to accomplish as an adult? By recognizing his talents and abilities, his natural bent, you can help him to find a truly successful place in this world, a calling that honors the God he serves and gives him great satisfaction. Stay involved in his life, and ask him the questions that can keep him on track toward his goal. Undergird his dream with your prayers, and give him advice as he asks for it. May you be rewarded by seeing his satisfaction and accomplishment in fulfilling God's true purpose—honoring Him with the talents and abilities He has bestowed and being faithful to His call.

**DISCIPLING**

# CHAPTER 17

# Ensuring Your Child Is a Christian

Marilyn was five when she prayed the "sinner's prayer" at church. Later, she couldn't remember why she decided to do it; all she knew was that her mother hugged her afterward and said it was a "great moment" in Marilyn's life.

Not long after that, Marilyn's parents divorced. Marilyn was raised under the watchful eyes of her mother and maternal grandparents, who forbade her to view or listen to anything other than Christian TV and radio. She attended the small Christian school sponsored by her church. She went to church camp in the summers, where she felt pressured to do the "right" things in order to prove she was a true believer. She didn't study the Bible much on her own, but she became a top performer on the church's Bible quiz team.

Marilyn hated her life. She hated it when her mother called her a "teenager for Christ."

When the time came to go to college, it was Marilyn's chance to escape. She chose a school that didn't teach the doctrines of her childhood. She stopped going to church. Her professors encouraged her to think for herself. At last she had found the freedom she'd craved.

Before long, Marilyn's rejection of Christianity was complete. For a while, she felt twinges of guilt and fear that she might go to hell. But eventually those feelings went away, too.

■ ■ ■

## *The Gospel in a Nutshell*

Does your teen know the basics of how and why God sent His Son, Jesus, to die for him or her? Knowing the facts of Jesus' life, death, and resurrection is vital. But understanding why these things matter to your teen personally is even more important. As needed, you might want to make the following points in your own words.

- Everyone has sinned.
- The penalty for sin is death.
- Jesus never sinned and so didn't deserve death.
- Jesus willingly paid the death penalty for everyone else.
- Because of that, all who accept Jesus' death as payment for their sins can be forgiven and have a wonderful relationship with God that lasts forever.

Some helpful verses to discuss with your teen include the following:

- "All have sinned and fall short of the glory of God" (Romans 3:23).
- "The wages of sin is death" (Romans 6:23).
- "Without the shedding of blood there is no forgiveness" (Hebrews 9:22).
- "God so loved the world that he gave his one and only Son, that whoever believes in him shall not perish but have eternal life" (John 3:16).
- "The gift of God is eternal life in Christ Jesus our Lord" (Romans 6:23).
- "If you confess with your mouth, 'Jesus is Lord,' and believe in your heart that God raised him from the dead, you will be saved. For it is with your heart that you believe and are justified, and it is with your mouth that you confess and are saved" (Romans 10:9-10).
- See also Romans 3:21-26, Colossians 2:13-15, and Hebrews 9:23-28.

—Adapted from *Parents' Guide to the
Spiritual Growth of Children*[1]

**DISCIPLING**

Today Marilyn counts herself among those who have "walked away" from "fundamentalism." She says she will spend the rest of her life working toward being herself, something she was denied during her growing-up years.[2]

Marilyn's "faith" clearly was not her own. The "mentors" in her life pressed her to act the way they thought a believer should, but her conformity was strictly external. No wonder she walked away from the church.

As a caring Christian parent, you don't want Marilyn's story to be the story of your family. You want your teen to follow Christ willingly, wholeheartedly. You want your adolescent's faith to be real and lifelong.

Discipleship begins with a personal choice to follow Jesus. As Marilyn's story shows, you can't make that choice for your teen. But you can help him understand the importance of having a vital, growing relationship with God instead of simply trying to get your teen to "act like a Christian."

## Making Sure the Relationship Has Begun

Is your teen a Christian?

Researcher George Barna, in his book *Generation Next*, noted that the answer to that question might not be as simple as it seems:

> Not surprisingly, most teenagers call themselves Christian. Nationwide, almost 9 out of 10 adults (86 percent) use the term "Christian" to describe their spiritual preference. Like their parents, however, they use this term without assigning moral or ethical content to it; in fact, they pretty much use the word by default. After all, what else would they call themselves?
>
> The bankruptcy of the term itself is demonstrated by how few teenagers ascribe true value to the substance behind the label. Less than half of all teenagers (42 percent) claim that the Christian faith is very important in their lives today.[3]

So let's define our terms. For purposes of this book, let's say that a Christian is one who has decided to receive God's gift of eternal life by placing his or her trust in Jesus Christ as Savior and who wants to follow Him.

How can you tell whether your teen has made it to that point? After all, Marilyn's family thought she was "a teenager for Christ" because she'd "gone forward" long ago and seemed to say and do many of the "right" things. Inside, though, she felt resentment, not loyalty, toward God.

## Indications of Faith

There are no formulas for assessing the spiritual state of another person, even when that person is your child. But here are some suggestions for getting a more accurate read on the teen who claims to be a Christian:

1. *Look for fruit.* "I am the true vine, and my Father is the gardener," Jesus said. "He cuts off every branch in me that bears no fruit, while every branch that does bear fruit he prunes so that it will be even more fruitful" (John 15:1-2). While we are not called to inspect the fruit of others, it should raise questions in our minds if a teenager displays *no* love for others, *no* willingness to obey God, and *no* interest in becoming more like Jesus (see 1 John 2:3-11).

2. *Ask for an update.* Some young children make "decisions for Christ" that consist mainly of repeating a prayer or walking down an aisle; these incidents may be forgotten by the time adolescence arrives. As in the parable of the sower (see Matthew 13:3-23), the cause of this "amnesia" may be traced to competing interests—or to a failure to put down spiritual roots due to a lack of nurture by caring adults. Ask your teen to tell you what Jesus means to her *now.* You might have her draw a map showing her spiritual journey to the present, or ask her to write an answer to the question "How does belonging to Jesus make a difference in your life today?"

> *Ask your teen to tell you what Jesus means to her now.*

3. *Check with peers.* Some teens lead Jekyll-and-Hyde lives, toeing the line at home and church but dumping Christian standards

at school and with friends. This may indicate a struggle with temptation or peer pressure, or it may indicate a desire to hide one's real self from parents and youth leaders. While spying on your teen might be unwise, getting to know his friends and teachers probably will yield hints of a double life if one exists. If it does, ask your teen to tell you which self is the real one.

## Ways to Encourage Belief

If your teen *has* made a decision for Christ and has a desire—even a small one—to follow Him, you have the foundation for discipleship. If not, you can encourage your teen to take that step.

How? Here are some ideas:

1. *Make sure your teen understands the basics.* If your teen knows little or nothing about God, Jesus, or the Bible, this would be a good time to fill in those gaps. Encourage her to read the Gospel of John and discuss it with you. Or see the sidebar "The Gospel in a Nutshell" for one way to communicate key points.

2. *Ask for a decision, but don't press.* When your teen appears to understand the basics of what Jesus has done for him, ask something simple like "Do you want to pray now to ask God to forgive you and to let you start a relationship with Him?" Using the word *now* makes it easier for your teen to pray on his own or for you to ask again later if necessary.

3. *Enlist the help of a youth leader.* If your teen isn't ready to make a commitment, she may be open to further exploration in a neutral setting away from your direct influence. Explain the situation to a leader in your church's youth ministry, and ask whether he or she can help provide opportunities for your teen to encounter the claims of Christ at a retreat, concert, camp, or youth group Bible study.

4. *Encourage friendships with Christian teens.* As the old saying goes, "Birds of a feather flock together." Or as the Bible puts it negatively, "Do not be misled: 'Bad company corrupts good character' " (1 Corinthians 15:33). In other words, the kids your teen chooses for friends and spends time with will fuel in him either a desire to get closer to God or a desire to move further away from Him. So know who his friends are, and encourage him to hang around with people who will bolster his appetite for the things of God.

DISCIPLING

5. *Pray*. The most important thing you can do to help your teen begin a relationship with God is to ask for His aid. Keep praying. And try to relax, leaving your teen's response with the God who has given your child the freedom to decide.

## Turning Beliefs into Convictions

Once your teen chooses to accept Christ as Savior, he faces a multitude of other forks in the road. If you tell him that premarital sex is off limits, for example, your teen can choose to ignore that belief, to adopt it in theory but not practice, or to internalize it as a personal conviction. The same is true of beliefs about God's nature, how to interpret the Bible, and what God wants of us.

In *Bound by Honor*, Gary and Greg Smalley tackled the issue of turning beliefs into convictions. Gary began by recalling an experience from his days as a youth worker:

> As a youth director in my twenties, I came to recognize an interesting phenomenon. I saw many parents who were "Rockys"—world-champion Christians—but whose teenagers struggled to step into the boxing ring of commitment. In other words, the kids who grew up in Christian homes did not seem to possess the same religious commitment as did kids who were raised by unbelievers and became Christians after the age of 12. Many of these teens from devout homes continually made compromises that resulted in a hollow faith. Even worse, when those adolescents grew up, they tried to pass down a compromised faith to their own children.[4]

What was the problem? Many of the kids who grew up in Christian homes had collected their parents' beliefs as one might collect shoe boxes full of baseball cards, but the beliefs had never become personal convictions.

Turning beliefs into convictions is not easy. Nor does it happen quickly. For some kids it never happens at all. As Gary Smalley wrote, "If you feel frustrated trying to get your teenager turned on to the Lord, take comfort in knowing that no one is perfect. Even King David—who had tremendous spiritual passion—could not pass down strong convictions to his son and grandson."[5]

Note that last sentence: David could not *pass down* his convictions. That's because convictions must grow from the inside out. As parents, we can instruct and encourage and guide and pray, but the process of developing convictions is largely an internal one. It happens when our teens struggle through their own questions, doubts, and trials.

We, as parents, can help our kids with that struggle. The Smalleys suggest seven ways to help teens turn their beliefs into convictions:

1. *Remember that the relationship always comes first.* The two biggest factors in building a healthy relationship, say the Smalleys, are honoring your teen regularly and helping to keep her anger level low. Remember the story of Marilyn, who walked away from Christianity after years of being pressured to "act like a Christian"? She seethed her way through adolescence; instead of recognizing and addressing her anger, the adults in her life simply gave her more reasons to be angry.

As the Smalleys wrote, "The more honor and the less anger [teens] feel, the greater the probability that they will want to make our values and faith their own. Of course, the more these two principles are violated, the greater the chance that they will reject our ways."[6]

2. *Sharpen your own convictions so you can be an effective model.* Children adopt our values during their early years—and question those values upon reaching adolescence. If our walk doesn't match our talk, we give our teens all the more reason to reject those values.

Referring to Jesus' teaching in Matthew 7:3-5, the Smalleys wrote, "As parents, we need to make sure we don't have a 'plank' in our eye before we try to remove 'dust' from our teenager's eye. Our everyday words and actions must match what we claim to believe."[7] The Smalleys also suggest writing down your key convictions in areas like integrity, money, and church, to clarify them for yourself and ensure that you're passing on the intended message.

3. *Once you're modeling your convictions, provide formal instruction.* The focus of formal instruction is to help kids develop beliefs, which can deepen into convictions.

■ ■ ■

## What Should You Expect? How Teens Develop Faith

There is a sense of unity and wholeness about adolescent development; faith development is part of that whole. Note how each of the following areas influences the development of a teenager's faith:

*Mental development.* Most senior highs think like adults. They lack experience and mature judgment, but in terms of the *process* of thinking, there is no qualitative difference. The older teenager's level of intellectual development has reached the point at which sophisticated thought processes can be handled. Jean Piaget, authority on the development of the intellect, labeled this stage as that of *formal operations*.

Able to think abstractly, the teenager can develop a faith that is consistent with the increasing complexities of life. Such thinking is necessary to consider, understand, and talk about concepts regarding God, man, and the universe. High school students have the mental capacity to develop their own philosophy of life.

*Emotional development.* The major emotional task of the adolescent is to develop a sense of self—a "feel" for who one is apart from one's parents. The process is characterized by a movement away from parents and a movement toward the peer group. Physical distance comes first (spending time in one's own room; preferring to be with friends rather than family), but emotional separation must follow. Progress toward emotional independence is indicated as adolescents relate more and more to their parents in an adult-to-adult manner and less and less as child to parent. Dependence upon parents decreases, and dependence upon one's own resources increases.

It takes time, however, to answer the question, "Who am I?" This task is difficult and complicated. If the process were complete, teenagers would be able to define and maintain their faith in a more personal way. The fact that it isn't finished makes it necessary to seek a faith that conforms to the beliefs of valued people around them. The high schooler simply doesn't have a strong enough identity to construct an "original" faith.

*Social development.* Adolescence is a time of great socialization. As the

**DISCIPLING**

significance of peer relationships increases, the teenager's need to be accepted becomes dominant. As one freshman boy told me just two weeks into the school year, "Well, I think I have high school figured out. You just act like you know what you're doing, and look like everyone else."

The conformist nature of an adolescent's faith is consistent with this social need to be accepted and approved by one's peer group. The teenager's faith, therefore, looks pretty much like everyone else's faith. What we have is a kind of "group" faith. None of this is to suggest that the faith of a senior high student isn't real or sincere. It's just that a teenager's *expression* of faith is consistent with the overriding need to conform.

*Physical development.* The way in which physical and spiritual growth interact is significant. Most teenagers reach physical and sexual maturity during high school. This means that some teens will be experiencing growth spurts, others will be developing secondary sex characteristics, many will be experimenting sexually, and others will suddenly look physically mature.

Due to these changes and obvious differences among adolescents, teenagers are typically self-conscious about their physical appearance. It is obvious to them that they have adult bodies, but they are often unsure of what to do with them as they relate to their peers. Their general uncertainty about physical appearance and sexuality easily feeds into their need to look and behave so that they are not singled out as different or weird. Their expression of faith becomes safer when it looks like that of their peers.

*Moral development.* Moral development occurs in stages as well. Younger high school students are typically motivated toward good behavior because they believe it helps others and may gain others' approval. Older high school students, however, demonstrate good behavior because they are beginning to believe in the importance of law and order, and are developing a renewed respect for authority.

To sum up: Adolescent faith development is heavily influenced by the teenager's need to gain the approval of peers and the respect of "worthy" authorities.

—Dr. William Rowley, marriage, family, and child therapist,
in *Pacesetter: Rites of Passage* (David C. Cook Publishing Co., 1987)[8]

DISCIPLING

*Formal* doesn't have to mean stiff. Here it means being intentional and verbal, spending time with your teen and watching for teachable moments that provide opportunities for you to have a natural conversation about spiritual things.

4. *After providing formal instruction, allow teens to find their own answers.* Gary Smalley told this story about his son:

> Greg had asked one day why the Bible didn't mention anything about "petting" with girls. "The Bible talks about not having intercourse," he said. "What about all the other stuff?" What a great conviction-building question! But instead of encouraging him to look up several scriptures on his own or read a Josh McDowell book, I explained what I thought was the correct answer. And because Greg didn't have to wrestle with the issue, he developed a passive stance toward petting and experienced difficulties with it when he got into college.
>
> We're not saying, of course, that Greg's struggle with sexual temptation was all because I gave him an easy answer to his question years before. He was still responsible for his own choices. But we do encourage parents to refrain from trying to give their teens all the answers.[9]

Within boundaries determined by their demonstrated maturity, and with resources provided by you if needed, allow teens to explore conviction-building questions like the following:

- What do I really believe about the Bible?
- How much money should I spend on myself?
- What's my position on attending R-rated movies?
- What should I do if my friends are negatively influencing me?

5. *Provide encouragement during times of belief questioning.* Teens who question their beliefs usually end up going in one of three ways: (1) walking completely away from the faith; (2) staying dependent on their parents' beliefs; or (3) developing independent beliefs based on all or part of their parents' values.[10]

As parents who would like to see our kids exercise the third option, we need to encourage them during this potentially scary process. We can do that by telling them we're proud that they're wrestling honestly with their questions. Rather than panicking and becoming defensive or preachy, we can empathize with the confusion and frustration our teens feel.

6. *Monitor teens during the belief-questioning process.* If 14-year-old Maya's doubts about the Bible lead her to skip classes at her Christian school, should you applaud her independence? If 16-year-old Alan's search spurs him to join a cult, should you just wave good-bye and say, "I hope you find what you're looking for"? No. Kids need limits as well as freedoms.

To show why, the Smalleys told the story of watching a father who was trying to get his young son to jump off a diving board into his arms. The father said, "Don't worry, son, I'll be right here to catch you. You can do it. Don't be afraid." It took the boy a few minutes to gather his courage, and just before he jumped, the father was distracted and so failed to catch him. *Smack!* The boy did a painful belly flop into the pool—and was screaming when he surfaced.[11]

In the same way, teens who are questioning their beliefs need the freedom to jump off the diving board of life, but they also need someone to catch them. Family rules and limits can provide that kind of security.

The Smalleys suggest adding an article to the "family constitution" that reads, "We agree to give each teenager the opportunity to

**DISCIPLING**

## Teens' "Things I Wish My Parents Had Done Differently," Part 6

- "Emphasized personal devotions more."
- "More home spiritual development, such as family devotions, family night, and one-on-one talks."
- "Share personal stories of spiritual conflict within their lives."
- "I wish that my parents would have just asked us openly what we thought about what was happening around us so that they could explain how God was working."
- "Make spiritual training more of an everyday thing, rather than a huge lump every few months."

develop his or her own beliefs and convictions. We will allow the questioning of our family values. However, if we feel that harm will result from the questioning process, we will intervene and provide a boundary."[12] (For more about family constitutions, see "Encourage Your Child to Write a Personal Constitution of Core Values" in chapter 26.)

> Teens who are questioning their beliefs need the freedom to jump off the diving board of life, but they also need someone to catch them.

7. *Remember that conviction building is a process, not a quick fix.* Should you expect your teenager to have all his convictions set in cement by age 20? No—and not by age 30 or 40, either! Building convictions is a lifelong process. It can be painful, too—full of poor choices that take a child far from the straight and narrow, plus trials that provoke hard questions. But as the Smalleys observed, "God has forever to mold their character. . . . The *beauty* of detours is that they're the very things that can produce a strong faith. . . . We can take refuge in God's promise that when our teens' convictions have been 'refined,' they will be 'more precious than gold' (1 Peter 1:6-7)."[13]

## Turning Experiences into Growth Steps

Can trouble really refine your teen's faith? Consider the experiences of these young people, recounted in Joe White's book *Over the Edge and Back*:

■ Angie has struggled with a learning disability all her life. When she had to be held back in school, her parents moved to a smaller town to make it easier for her. Even with hard work, though, she's barely made it from one grade to the next. Nevertheless, as a high school junior, she said, "I used to wonder why the Lord would allow me to have this problem, but now I know. He allowed it for a reason: so I could tell my story and maybe help others through their problems, too. I know now that if you put your faith in the Lord, He will come through for you in your time of need." She even quotes Isaiah 54:10:

" 'Though the mountains be shaken and the hills be removed, yet my unfailing love for you will not be shaken nor my covenant of peace be removed,' says the LORD, who has compassion on you."[14]

■ Sandi was only 14 when her father, an alcoholic, died from the ravages of drinking. Just two months later, her 18-year-old brother, David, riding with a drunken driver, was killed instantly when the car went off the road and smashed into a guardrail that split the vehicle in half.

Did Sandi grieve? Of course. She said later that she cried unceasingly, that the experience was awful. But she also said this: "Through it all, I learned the value of prayer a lot more. I'll never take prayer for granted again. . . . The Lord is really my best friend. He's been through it all with me. Through it all I had hope. No matter how much I give Him, no matter how bad, He handles it."[15]

■ April was born addicted to cocaine and was left to fend for herself by a coke-addicted mother and stepfather. She was raped at age four, and soon afterward she had to start taking care of her brother. At age five she was selling the drug herself.

After her mother married a third husband, April's second stepfather died. Following the funeral, April freebased cocaine and dreamed that she was in hell. She was seven years old.

At age 13, however, April accepted Jesus as her Savior. A year later, she was able to say, "In some ways I'm glad of my past experience. I've learned from it. Now with the help of God, I can teach people and tell them about my life. I plan to keep going forward and to make something of my life. But I can't do it without the power of Jesus Christ, our blessed Lord."[16]

■ Joel, a student living at home with his parents, had been in and out of therapy for depression. When he had a violent manic episode, his parents were forced to make an agonizing decision. They had him committed to a mental hospital, where he was attacked by other patients and struck one of the mental health workers. Dragged to a five-by-ten-foot seclusion room, Joel stared through the Plexiglas window in the door and screamed, "Let me out! Somebody, please let me out!"

Eventually Joel was diagnosed with bipolar disorder and treated with medication. What was his attitude toward those, including his parents, who had made him endure the seeming indignity of being committed? Here's what he wrote just nine months after being released from the hospital:

> Even though my pride was totally stripped away when I was forced by court order to go to a mental hospital, I can say that my personal bout with manic depression has been the most valuable experience in my . . . life. I believe the only way I can say this with total confidence is because Jesus is my Lord.
>
> Like anyone else who believes in God and has endured hardship, I questioned why He would let me have this condition. I was angry at God during my depressed times, and verbally abusive of my dad also. But when I began to get well, and as I slowly accepted this hereditary illness, . . . God brought a gentle restoration of my relationship with Him as well as with my dad.[17]

The stories of Angie, Sandi, April, and Joel show that even the darkest tunnels of a teen's life can lead to a more vital relationship with God. Their paths could have taken a much different turn, though, if caring Christian adults hadn't helped transform suffering into strength.

In *Bound by Honor*, Gary and Greg Smalley suggest helping teens "treasure hunt" their trials. Treasure hunting is finding ways to turn pain into progress. It's turning the sourest of life's lemons into lemonade.

> *Even the darkest tunnels of a teen's life can lead to a more vital relationship with God.*

Treasure hunting *doesn't* mean neglecting a suffering son or daughter, deliberately seeking painful experiences, or short-circuiting a teen's

■ ■ ■

## A Win-Win Situation: Learning from Good Times, Too

It's said that the general of the winning army doesn't learn nearly as much as the general of the army that loses. So it is with adolescence. My children probably had more losing battles than victories when they were teenagers, so God kept them pretty humble. I'd had plenty of failures, too, so it was easy to empathize with them.

There are so many losing battles in adolescence, in fact, that it's wonderful that there *are* some winning ones. Those times give us a chance to cheer our kids, to see them encouraged.

Wins can also be an opportunity to make spiritual strides. Here are three ways to use victories for spiritual profit:

1. *Don't take the joy away.* In your zeal to teach something through the incident, be careful not to throw cold water on your teen's elation. Avoid saying things like "Now, don't get a big head." Celebrate!
2. *Help your teen process the win.* Talk about it. Ask, "Do you think God showed you something about your strengths in this? About how He might use you in the future?" For example, whether the victory was in debate or music or sports, your teen's gift of leadership or service might have come into play.
3. *Give God the glory.* Temper the win with a bit of guidance, a gentle reminder. You might ask, "Why do you think God allowed you to win?"

—Joe White

grieving process. "Several days, weeks, or even years may go by before a person is ready to hear the message that God can bring good out of hardship," the Smalleys wrote. "We must allow enough time to grieve painful and discomforting experiences; it's the first step toward healing."[18]

How will you know when your teen is ready to treasure hunt? By asking! Gary Smalley wrote:

When my . . . kids seemed ready, one way I brought up the subject was to say, "Are you satisfied with what you're experiencing out of the trial you've been through?"

**DISCIPLING**

■ ■ ■

## *At Death's Door:*
## *How One Teen Grew through Crisis*

Scott had a sore throat and fever, but that wasn't enough to keep him from playing in his high school basketball tournament that weekend. On Sunday night his fever shot up. Then early in the morning, we heard him crying out for us. Hurrying downstairs, we found him violently ill. As we rushed to get him to the hospital, he collapsed on the way by the door. An already bad day only got worse. The doctors put him on a respirator. They diagnosed him with a staph infection, which resulted in double pneumonia. Scott asked me pointedly, "Dad, can I die?"

That night I asked some men from our church to come to the hospital to pray for Scott. We gathered around his bed. My athletic son, who only two days before played basketball, lay comatose in the bed with needles stuck in his body, each one leading to a bank of machines behind his bed. It was eerie. Five men dressed in yellow hospital gowns and masks gathered around my son and prayed, following the instructions of James 5:14-16. The Lord impressed on us specifically what to pray:

■ That the Lord would dramatically change Scott's physical condition overnight so the hospital personnel could see God's hand at work.
■ That God would reveal Himself to Scott in his subconscious mind.

I slept fitfully that night. The next morning the nurse greeted me with these words: "The difference in Scott's lungs between last night and this morning is like night and day. It's a miracle!"

When I went into his room, Scott wrote on a tablet (he couldn't talk because of the tube):

The other day the news reports said that the number of *deaths* from the flu and pneumonia had reached the point of epidemic proportions. When I found out about double pneumonia, it threw me for a loop. Lately my Christian walk had not been growing but was at a standstill. Last night the Lord changed my view of Him, the world, and myself. He put His vibrant Spirit wholeheartedly back into me. I woke up today praising the Lord just to be alive. I am exalting Him. Every time the nurses woke me up to do testing, they said I had a great big smile on my face. I woke up singing, "This is the day the Lord has made . . ."

Then Scott wrote in large letters: "PRAISE THE LORD!"

Yet it wasn't over. Although God had performed a miracle to save his life that night, Scott spent eighteen days in the hospital. His weight dropped from 155 pounds to 127 pounds. Ten days later, after he spent his sixteenth birthday in the hospital, I walked into his room, and he broke down and cried:

Dad, bear with me. I just need to pour my heart out to the Lord. Lord, I'm so frustrated. I'm sick of everybody telling me how sick I am. I want to get up and get out of here now. But, Lord, You are the Author and Finisher of my faith. You are in charge of my life. You can do anything You want. You can make me well in five minutes or five years. I want You to know that I trust You whatever.

We held each other and cried. Then through the tears he began to sing:

My God is an awesome God.
He reigns from heaven above . . .

That was the most harrowing experience of our parenting years. Even now when we talk about it, tears flow. Yet from that Scott discovered his destiny. Since then he has pursued God wholeheartedly. Out of it has come the strong calling to medicine—a pediatrician, no less!

—Barry St. Clair in *Ignite the Fire*[19]

If they hadn't talked about the trial yet, they'd almost always say, "No, I'm not. I'm miserable and unhappy."

At that point I asked, "Would you like to spend some time this week 'unwrapping' the treasure you've received?" I'd usually give them a hug and a reassuring smile.

If the answer was yes (and nine times out of ten it was), that's when I would start to help them find the good in their troubled times. If the answer was no, I didn't

**DISCIPLING**

■ ■ ■

## *Stained-Glass Windows: Helping Kids Put the Pieces Together*

The fine art of making Romans 8:28 a reality in the life of your teen is a huge challenge—but a wonderful one. Every young person will go through pain and brokenness, especially in today's tragic world. Every young person needs to know that all those things *do* work together for good when God gets His hands on them.

How can you turn your teen's traumas into opportunities for spiritual growth? I've found it helpful to use a word picture with my kids, that of stained-glass windows.

As I've told my children, God is in the business of building stained-glass windows. None of his "paintings" are on canvas. They're all made of thousands of broken pieces, skillfully picked up and dusted off and soldered together into magnificent murals. The broken pieces are made of our hurts and hard times. With my kids I've used examples of my own hurts, and theirs, to show how God is slowly making stained-glass windows of our lives.

Employing this word picture with your teen is not an overnight experience. It takes lots of asking the "What's wrong?" and "How do you feel?" and "What are you doing about it?" questions, not to mention hours of warmth and empathy and unconditional regard. You need to build up a bank account of together time and tender moments in order to make the word picture meaningful.

Once you've done that, and once the moment comes when your child's heart breaks (when the girlfriend writes the "Dear John" letter, for instance), you can use the word picture. You can sit down with your teen and say, "God makes stained-glass windows. Let's look at yours."

When my daughter Jamie was younger, she was cut from the gymnastics team. Later, she found my lap, and we rocked and talked. After half an hour, her tears dried and she bounded off. That night I tucked her into bed, prayed with her, and worked on memorizing a Bible verse. As I walked out of the room, I heard a little voice in the darkness.

"Daddy?" Jamie said.

"What, Peanut?"

"Thanks for tying my heart back together again."

I walked back to her bed. "What did you say?"

**DISCIPLING**

"I just said thanks for tying my heart back together tonight."

"What do you mean by that?" I asked.

"Well, when I came in tonight, my heart was broken. And you tied it back together again."

God does that for us, but He does even more. He makes something beautiful from our brokenness. With time and patience, you can help with that process in the life of your teenager.

—Joe White

---

panic. I just came back another day and softly but persistently presented another opportunity.[20]

To help your teen treasure hunt a trial, give her a sheet of paper and a pencil. Have your teen list the following:

1. *"Several things I like about myself . . ."* This helps to counteract the damage that some trials—failing a choir audition, losing a girlfriend or boyfriend, being sexually abused—can do to your son or daughter's self-esteem. If your teen has a hard time coming up with ideas, suggest a few to get the process started.
2. *"A description of the trial I've been through . . ."* Revisiting trauma can be difficult, but it can also help uncover facts and feelings of which the sufferer was unaware.
3. *"The people I can turn to for help as I treasure hunt . . ."* You'll hope to find yourself on this list, of course. You may also find friends, relatives, coaches, youth workers, and counselors. If needed, remind your teen that God wants to help, too.
4. *"All the possible benefits I can think of from this trial . . ."* Your teen may need help with this one. Here are some examples you might want to cite:

■ A boy who was devastated at being cut from the football team might realize later that he'd defined himself only in terms of athletic ability, and now he knows that he has other interests and gifts. Or he recognizes that he'd been sacrificing too much in order to play. Or he realizes that

**DISCIPLING**

he'd been looking at nonathletes as losers, and now he appreciates people of all kinds.

- A girl who lost a friend to AIDS might gain the ability to comfort others who lost loved ones. Or she might have a new desire to help other victims of the disease.
- A boy who flunked his driver's license test might learn to be more patient as he waits to try again. Or he might learn to exercise more self-control as he concentrates harder. Or he might begin to enjoy the beauty of God's creation as he walks to school instead of driving.

If your teen is open to the idea, talk through the list when it's finished. Pray together about it. Follow up in a week or so with questions like "Have you thought of anything to add to that list? Is anything good starting to come out of that experience? Have you learned any lessons I might benefit from?"

It's also important to watch how your teen, after a trial, is handling anger. It's natural to be angry when things go wrong, but *staying* angry can block spiritual growth. To help your child release resentment, follow the steps summarized in "Unloading Psychological Baggage" (p. 262). If anger or depression persist, consult a counselor or pastor for extra assistance.

Remember the story of Joel, the young man who was committed to a mental hospital? When he analyzed the experience later, his insights showed that treasure hunting is worth the effort:

> I strongly believe that the prayers of my pastor, parents, college professors, and many friends sped up the healing process. I am so thankful that God in His wisdom allowed me to endure such a trial, that I might feel first-hand the healing power of His love. I am especially thankful to God for teaching me the importance of letting others help me when I am in need, instead of being too proud to receive the love of concerned friends and family. And now the peace of God, times of testing, and brotherly love are more than interesting topics discussed at a Bible study. For I have personally experienced them all.[21]

Joel discovered that growth can be a painful process. As parents, we may wish we could shield our teens from life's slings and arrows, but we can't. Fortunately, when we help our young people make the most of trials, they can develop the kind of faith that's real, personal, and lasting.

DISCIPLING

# CHAPTER 18

# Guiding Your Teen Toward Faith-Affirming Friendships

## *by Jim Weidmann*

A friend of mine and her husband are currently living through the nightmare all parents of teenagers fear. Both of their children have openly rebelled against the values they were taught, due in each case to the influence of a close friend.

Their 16-year-old son, well on his way to becoming an Eagle Scout, was the first to turn away when he became friends with a girl from a dysfunctional, non-Christian home. She told him that his parents were mean and overprotective and were preventing his independence. He became convinced that this girl and her single mom understood him much better than his parents did, so he moved in with them! His older sister was appalled at what she saw her brother doing and how it was hurting their family. After several months and much prayer and counseling, he returned home.

Less than a year later, that same sister became involved with a young man who convinced her they were in love and should live together. She abandoned her plans to attend a Christian college and moved into an apartment with the man. Her heart was obviously blind to the similarity between what she was doing now and what she had so recently been critical of in her brother's life.

Recently I had dinner with a father who told me that after raising two daughters successfully (that is, the daughters stayed close to their parents and to the Lord), he had his son following the same path. However, this father said he hadn't consciously tried to know his son's friends, since his daughters had done so well in the same school. To make a long story short, his son and a buddy got into the drug scene. The father said he lost his relationship with his son during those years.

Now contrast those negative experiences with this one: Another friend's son was active in soccer. At the start of a practice, as the team was standing around talking, the conversation went downhill quickly with foul language and dirty jokes. This young man made a comment suggesting that he didn't need to hear that kind of talk and excused himself. As he walked away, he heard footsteps behind him. Another team member had joined him, saying he agreed with him. The second boy had just needed the strong influence of another to encourage him to walk away.

> *Friends can help keep our children on the path of righteousness or lead them down a path of destruction.*

Friends can help keep our children on the path of righteousness or lead them down a path of destruction. As the Bible says, "Bad company corrupts good character" (1 Corinthians 15:33).

Half of all teenagers today admit that their friends influence

**DISCIPLING**

## Teens' "Ways in Which a Parent Was Spiritually Influential," Part 7

- "We had regular family prayer."
- " I went to a Catholic high school for two years, which was 30 minutes from home and near my dad's office. I still think back to all the days my dad and I rode together to work and school. We had some great talks about religion and theology. I had many questions because I did not grow up in a Catholic home like all my friends at school. I learned a new culture and figured out my beliefs in the process. Dad was more than willing to express his ideas and philosophies."
- "My family ate dinner together every night, and often my father would ask

them "a lot." Yet a whopping three-fourths still point to parents as their biggest influence.[1] So it's not too late for us to get involved by helping our teens learn how to choose friends.

## In the Know

Realizing the power of such relationships, my wife, Janet, and I actively try to know our children's friends. We talk to our teens about who they "hang" with at school, church youth group, and sports events. We seek to understand the hot topics they're discussing. And we're very old-fashioned: We want to know where they're going, who they're going to be with, and what time they'll be home. If they miss curfew, they know they will be grounded.

I tell them I also reserve the right to show up at any place they tell me they're going. This could be a sporting event, a party, or a friend's house. I don't do that out of a lack of trust but as a loving parent who knows there are situations in a teen's life that aren't always what they seem to be. Your teen can be expecting a simple gathering with friends for a movie but have it turn out to be a beer bust in a house where no adults are present.

My teens and I sometimes differ over what needs to be considered in their plans: "Are the parents going to be home? Who else will be there? When is the party going to end? How will you get home?" Some parents don't share your values and will actually buy alcohol and drugs for their kids. My intent is to be a

DISCIPLING

my brother and me what God was doing in our lives, how our prayer life was, or how our relationship with God was. It was very awkward to talk to my parents about this, because I wasn't living for Jesus very well at that time."

■ "My mom was continually, and still is, involved in guiding me in my dating life. She would always tell me she was praying for my relationships, and she always made an effort to know my 'significant other.' That meant a lot and showed me that she was interested in my life not only then, but also that she was interested in my future happiness."

safety net for my children and to provide as many ways out of any bad situation as possible.

I remember when I was in high school and went to a party after a football game. I told my dad where the party was and that the parents would be home. They were there, all right, and they bought the keg! They believed this was okay since they were there to supervise the drinking. They weren't thinking about the drive home or the other parents' values.

My dad sensed something wasn't right, and he came to the party unannounced. He wanted to meet and talk with the parents. I was in the basement when someone told me my dad was upstairs. Immediately I got rid of the beer, went upstairs, and faced my dad as though nothing were wrong. I really didn't want him going to the basement! He simply told me it was time to go home.

I left with my dad. I wasn't upset, because I knew that what I had been doing was wrong. If I had told him he had embarrassed me and that I felt he didn't trust me, he would have said I was right. I had just proved I couldn't be trusted by choosing to go against our house rules. If there had been no alcohol at the party, he would have simply visited with the parents and not bothered me. As it was, he had made a strong statement to my friends, their parents, and me: He would exercise his right as my father to show up when and if he felt something was amiss. His primary goal was to protect me because he loved me.

## The Yoke's on Us

The Bible tells believers not to become intimate friends with non-Christians. The apostle Paul wrote: "Do not be yoked together with unbelievers. For what do righteousness and wickedness have in common? Or what fellowship can light have with darkness? What harmony is there between Christ and Belial? What does a believer have in common with an unbeliever?" (2 Corinthians 6:14-15).

Because our hearts are not one in spirit, we would be focusing on God while our friends would be focusing on the things of this world. Sin is still attractive to our old nature, and nonbelievers can persuade us to compromise our commitment, beliefs, and integrity.

This is not to say we should isolate ourselves completely from non-Christian friends. We are to share the Gospel with them as we go and make disciples of all nations (see Matthew 28:18-20). As Francis of Assisi said, we are to share the gospel always and use words when necessary.

So it is with non-Christians who become our friends. We are to live in such a way that they ask why we have a joy or peace that passes all understanding. Then we're to tell them the Good News. This is known as friendship evangelism. However, these are not intimate friendships or boyfriend-girlfriend relationships.

When our children become teens, we lose much of the control over their lives that we once had. However, we can influence their choice of activities, encouraging them to become active in things that provide a positive environment, such as a sports team, youth group, or hobby club.

In high school, I was a member of the football team. From this team I gained my identity. As beneficial as this sort of affiliation can be, however, you still need to be on the alert. Sports, too, can be a seedbed for immorality.

When my son went out for the football team, I wanted to know who he was spending time with. If he were going to hang around other Christians on the squad and maybe get involved in leading prayers before games, he could influence the culture instead of being shaped by it. But after two months, he reported that he had no Christian friends and wasn't getting any playing time, so I encouraged him to walk away. We decided that he could get greater satisfaction and self-esteem out of lifting weights with one of his Christian friends.

*Church youth groups can be a good source of friends, yet you also have to watch them closely.*

Church youth groups can be a good source of friends, yet you also have to watch them closely. Parents with troubled teens, wanting them to experience the positive, send their children there as well. I'm appalled when I hear what my daughter tells me about the kids who attend her youth group. So, remain conscientious and talk with your teens about the kids they're associating with

DISCIPLING

and what's being taught. Find out if they're understanding and applying the lessons. If not, you may want to encourage them to try another youth group. Observe their friends; what youth group do they attend? To have your child stay in a group just to be at the same location with you can have a negative impact. You may even need to change churches to keep your family together.

What if your older teens are ready to date but don't know any Christian kids they're interested in?

In that case, wait. God is clear that we are to separate ourselves from the world while living in the world, particularly in dating. We need to encourage our children to participate in activities with other Christians. This could be in church youth groups, on a mission trip, while attending teen Christian camps, or by joining Christian clubs at school.

My son Jacob, 16, attends a public high school. He tells me it's pretty obvious who is a Christian and who's not, and he chooses his close friends accordingly. We're having him pick out a youth group to participate in on weekends. We told him that we'd like him to attend the Sunday school class at our church to see if it's engaging and spiritually challenging. But if it's not, he's free to attend another church's youth group with one of his Christian acquaintances. The idea is not to exasperate him with church attendance but to have him participate weekly in developing Christian relationships.

What should you do when your teen is already in a relationship with a non-Christian and showing signs of bad behavior?

Your best resource is prayer. Pray that your child will see the foolishness of his friend's ways. Point out any unacceptable behavior that occurs when your teen is with the other person. Use it as a warning, noting that your child is being influenced and not doing the influencing. Add that if the behavior doesn't change, you will change the situation by limiting or fully restricting their relationship.

Some friends of ours took their son out of one school and put him in another, completely cutting off all communication between their son and a bad influence. Their son is improving in his grades and now has a Christian girlfriend. The family is not out of the woods, but things are a lot better than they were a year ago.

Once, my son was being influenced by a friend to move into the punk scene. His music sounded more and more angry. His dress was becoming more and more symbolic of the culture. I pointed out that he was beginning to billboard the punk culture and not Christianity. We talked about how he was to imitate Christ (see Ephesians 5:1-2) and how he thought the music and dress honored God. He told me it was just fun. I took the position that it attracted the wrong type of kids and evoked the wrong emotions. I explained that I am accountable to God for how my house serves the Lord and that I was not asking him to agree with me, just respect and obey me.

We agreed that he wouldn't listen to any music with bad language, sexual immorality, or anger (see Colossians 3:5-10). And he was not allowed to wear clothes that could be viewed as promoting a hostile culture. As an example of respect for our agreement, he continued to wear a chrome bike-chain necklace but hung a cross on it.

Another time, one of my sons encountered a Mormon girl. We really liked her, and she was a good friend for him at the time. However, we had a clear understanding that he would not date her, because the Mormons' Jesus is not the Jesus of the Bible. We talked at length about why God tells us not to be unequally yoked in our beliefs. It turned out to be a great teaching opportunity and established a basis of understanding for all future relationships. She could come over and kick around with him at our house, but they were not to get into any situation where intimate conversation could take their relationship to a deeper level. The relationship stayed at the friendship level and never went deeper, and eventually they drifted completely apart.

Janet Parshall, host of the *Renewing the Heart* and *Janet Parshall's America* radio programs, told me about her family's approach to schooling their children. They agreed that the teens could attend the local public high school as long as they were standing and growing in their faith. At the end of each semester, they would discuss whether they were influencing the culture or being influenced by it. A big part of this evaluation centered on who they were hanging around with and what they were doing in their free time.

**DISCIPLING**

## Teach Your Children Well

Telling your children to become friends with fellow Christians is one thing; helping them *find* those friends is another. We need to teach them how to identify other followers of Jesus. (Many people claim to be Christians simply because they go to church or were raised in Christian homes.) In high school, the chance to be friends with the most popular kids is always tempting.

In John 15:1-4, Jesus gave us the parable of the vine, branches, and gardener:

> I am the true vine, and my Father is the gardener. He cuts off every branch in me that bears no fruit, while every branch that does bear fruit he prunes so that it will be even more fruitful. You are already clean because of the word I have spoken to you. Remain in me, and I will remain in you. No branch can bear fruit by itself; it must remain in the vine. Neither can you bear fruit unless you remain in me.

His point was that those branches still connected to the vine will produce fruit because they get nourishment from the vine. Those who stay close to God will produce fruit, displaying qualities of strong Christian character. Just as you can identify a tree by its fruit, so you can identify a Christian by his intentions, words, and deeds.

The rule in our house is that you can date a person only once to determine if he is a believer. The person will reveal herself by her words and actions. I encourage my children to ask a date what church she attends and how often, whether she is part of a youth group, and so on. Character can be revealed by the type of movies a person goes to, the music he listens to, the magazines he reads, the friends that seem to hang around him, the language he uses, and the sort of relationship the teen has with his parents (is there respect or not?).

If the parties that a potential friend wants to attend include smoking, drinking, or drugs, you begin to know his own desires. If a friend wants to do things that Jesus would not do, you have to ask yourself whether she is truly a friend. True friends encourage us and hold us accountable to what Jesus would do in each situation.

## What a Friend Is

The secret to having a godly friend is to be one. We need to teach our children what it means to be a friend.

Building a friendship requires us to spend time in the other person's presence. The friend truly becomes a priority in our lives, and we become one in his. We will be called upon sacrificially to put his desires above ours. Therefore, we must come to understand his desires, needs, weaknesses, and interests. Friendships are like saving money in a bank. If you only make withdrawals, at some point the bank will have nothing left to give. We need to love a friend as we love ourselves. As we learn to give to him, he in turn will give back to us.

Friends are vulnerable and accountable to each other. With our best friends, we can reveal our innermost thoughts and desires with no fear of judgment. It has been said that a true friend is someone who knows so much about you that he could destroy you, but he doesn't! This idea builds on Proverbs 27:17: "As iron sharpens iron, so one man sharpens another." As you expose your weaknesses and faults to another Christian, the dark enticement of temptation and sin is uncovered in the light of Christian love.

> *The secret to having a godly friend is to be one.*

Friends are of the same mind. Jonathan and David are the biblical model for God-honoring friendships. These two shared from the heart their faith, perspectives, and passions. Friends need to have the same set of priorities and values or their desires and motivations will be different. The concept of not serving two masters (see Matthew 6:24) applies to an intimate friendship.

Friends are good listeners. Teens want to be listened to and paid attention to. This is one of the reasons why they spend so much time talking on the phone or instant messaging on the computer. Encourage your son or daughter to be a good listener. My

**DISCIPLING**

wife is an expert in this area. On our third date, she had me confessing everything. She will tell you that a good listener is someone who hears. A good friend takes in your words and thoughts, feeling your pain and sharing your joy.

## The Role of Prayer

A godly relationship is one that involves and honors God. We need to teach our children to pray for their friends. The principle of "You do not have, because you do not ask God" (James 4:2) definitely applies here. I pray almost daily that godly friends will surround my children.

Talk with your children about what an ideal friend for them would be like. What kind of character qualities, tastes, and interests should they look for? Then encourage them to pray for someone with those qualities, and promise that you will pray as well. This is also a great opportunity to pray for their future spouses.

It has been interesting to see how God has answered my prayers for my kids' friends. My older son is on the national youth speaking tour and doesn't have much time for friends because he travels extensively. He's also taking college courses by correspondence and so doesn't have contact with his college classmates. So God brought a great girl from a strong Christian home into his life. They are both committed to their relationship and to keeping it honoring to God. Both have made a pledge of virginity until marriage.

His younger brother travels with him and speaks as well. Though he has few Christian friends in school, God gave him a girlfriend who lives in another state. He met her on a speaking trip and developed a relationship with her over the Internet and phone. They get to see each other every three months or so. The distance is great enough to keep the sexual pressure under control and let them learn how to become best friends. This girl is perfect for my son at this time. She is a strong Christian and a developing musician. Her passion is to become a worship leader and serve God with her music. Both of these kids have made a pledge of purity as well.

There are no guarantees that our children won't rebel like

those of my friends. However, our teens will have a greater chance of walking the path of righteousness if their friends are positive rather than negative influences. As parents, we can be intentional about teaching and guiding our teenagers into positive, God-honoring relationships.

*Jim Weidmann is the executive director of the Heritage Builders ministry, vice chairman of the National Day of Prayer Task Force, and a general editor for this project.*

DISCIPLING

# CHAPTER 19

# Instilling a Christian Worldview

## *by Andy Braner*

I walked into the classroom and picked out a seat in the front row. I had just finished registering for my freshman classes and was adjusting to the creaky wooden desk when the teacher of my first college class walked in. He was a short man with bright gray hair. His goatee was darker, obviously a fashion accessory to his profession.

I remember my heart beating in apprehension because of all the horror stories I'd heard from college graduates—having to read five chapters a night and getting a pop quiz the next day, or having one test count for my entire semester grade. Nevertheless, I was here and ready to learn.

The professor stepped up to the podium and asked his first question of the semester: "How do you know the sky is blue?"

The class laughed. One of my fellow students raised his hand and began scientifically to discuss water molecules and their reflection of sunlight.

The professor quickly retorted, "How do you know that the sky isn't really green and that society has conditioned us to call it blue?"

The student fell silent.

I didn't realize it at first, but this professor had an agenda. The next few questions haunted me for four years at college. Within one hour, he had deconstructed the entire view of the world that my parents had instilled in me over the preceding 18 years. He challenged the facts of my youth and began replacing them with his own postmodern interpretation of life. Although the questions seemed trivial, they began to change the way I looked at every class in the coming semesters.

"How do you know you're alive?"

"How do you know you're not dreaming?"

"How do you know you're not a butterfly dreaming that you are a human being sitting in this class today?"

With every question, the laughter became more uneasy. My fellow students and I were unable to respond because we couldn't grasp the implications of these new ideas and didn't have a comprehensive, integrated worldview from which to judge the professor's words. Seeing an opportunity, he strategically dismantled the boundaries of truth in our lives. If we couldn't understand the fundamental facts of our existence, how could we possibly say that absolute truth existed at all? If we couldn't stand on solid fact, where would we find answers to the important questions:

"How do you know God really created the world?"

"How do you know the Bible is true?"

"How do you know that Christianity is a valid religion, and the only way to God, when the majority of the world seeks other truths and other ways?"

"How do you know there is a God at all?"

## A Home with a View

A few years ago, I flew to Philadelphia for a youth conference. After I disembarked from the plane, I walked downstairs to the rental car desk. I signed out a car and asked the salesman for a map of the city. He assured me that a map had been placed in the visor above the driver's seat. I thought no more about it until later, when I got lost on the outskirts of the city. I reached up and found a map of New York City instead of Philadelphia. Fear ran through my body. How in the world was I going to find my way through an unfamiliar city without a map?

When your kids realize that life is a maze of roads and intersections, and that they have choices to make every day, they will try to find a good map to help point the way. Such a map is called a worldview, and everybody has one. A worldview provides answers to life's most basic questions, such as "Who am I?" and "Why am I here?" Your teens have many worldviews to choose from today, but only one offers true answers and good direction.

> **Your teens have many worldviews to choose from today, but only one offers true answers and good direction.**

God alone has supplied us with an accurate map of reality, and that map is the Bible. Though it doesn't tell us how to solve a differential equation or offer a cure for schizophrenia, it does give us a framework for viewing all of life, whether math or medicine, history or economics, politics or science. It tells us how the world came to be, who is behind it, what happened to cause so much misery, and what God has done to intervene in history on our behalf. Nothing in life can really be understood apart from its place in God's big picture. In Christ, we are told, "*all* things hold together" (Colossians 1:17, emphasis added).

This suggests that every Christian should be trying to view all of life in the light of what Christ has done, as portrayed in the Bible. The apostle Paul even spoke of taking "captive *every* thought to make it obedient to Christ" (2 Corinthians 10:5, emphasis added).

Jesus said the first commandment is to "love the Lord your God with all your heart and with all your soul and with all your *mind*" (Matthew 22:37, emphasis added). So many teachers and preachers have taught that being a Christian means loving God with all your heart. We know that inviting Jesus into your heart means inviting Him to be the Lord of your life.

Other people emphasize the need to love God with all your soul. You should pray for hours upon hours. You can listen to God speak to your soul and move where He leads you. You can even offer up your life to ministry in the deepest parts of Africa if God calls you there.

**DISCIPLING**

Few teachers, however, invite Christians to *think* about their faith, to love God with their minds, and to analyze everything else by using the biblical worldview as their starting point.

## Why Does It Matter?

What happens if you fail to develop a solid Christian worldview yourself? What will befall your teen if you don't work diligently to pass on such an understanding of the world?

Think back to my experience in Philadelphia. It's obvious—isn't it?—that if you try to use the wrong map, you're lost. And lost people tend to end up in dangerous neighborhoods.

Paul wrote, "See to it that no one takes you captive through hollow and deceptive philosophy, which depends on human tradition and the basic principles of this world rather than on Christ" (Colossians 2:8). He was telling the Colossians to use a "Christ map" so they could navigate the world safely in the light of their faith. Without such a map, we often aren't even aware that we're lost. Imagining that all is well, we pick the wrong route and end up far off the path to God.

Any failure to take seriously the greatest commandment is not only disobeying God but also putting ourselves in a vulnerable position. We live in a world where spiritual warfare is an unseen but potent reality. When your mind goes unprotected by a comprehensive, biblical perspective, you are a sitting duck for misleading ideas that could cost you your life. At the very least, you'll end up thinking and living like those around you who are without God instead of like followers of Jesus Christ. The same goes for your teens.

Aware of it or not, we become confused and unable to make sense of life. Whatever map we latch on to doesn't seem to match what we see. Every book, magazine, schoolroom, and TV show becomes a minefield of lies and errors. For example, God tells us in the Bible that sex is a pleasure reserved for wives and their husbands. But our media and our culture shout that anything is permissible between any two (or more) consenting individuals.

As Christian parents, we spend years consciously or subconsciously drawing our kids' attention to our views of God, life, and truth. Loving parents would never keep these things from their children. Even so, scores of Christian students wander aimlessly through the halls of secular universities today, paying thousands of dollars to have professors convert them to other views.

Take evolution as an example. If your student has not been exposed to this worldview, he or she will be soon. E. O. Wilson, an evolutionary entomologist and sociobiologist, said, "As were many persons from Alabama, I was a born-again Christian. When I was fifteen, I entered the Southern Baptist church with great fervor and interest in the fundamentalist religion; I left at seventeen when I got to the University of Alabama and heard about evolution theory."[1]

> *Seventy-five percent of all children raised in Christian homes who attend public schools will reject the Christian faith by their first year of college.*

Wilson understood that, if he believed in naturalistic evolution, God was no longer part of the equation. Further, he saw that if Adam hadn't been created by God, then Adam couldn't have "sinned." If Adam didn't sin, then mankind is basically good. If mankind is basically good, there is no reason for Jesus to have died on the cross. If Jesus didn't die on the cross for our sins and rise from the grave on the third day, Christianity is a false and worthless religion.

It took two years to pull E. O. Wilson out of the church and into a humanistic mindset. Did you know that 75 percent of all children raised in Christian homes who attend public schools will reject the Christian faith by their first year of college?[2] This is happening because our kids are not entering those classrooms with a firm grip on the Christian worldview.

## Truth or Consequences

The damage is not confined to individuals, either. False ideas have destroyed whole nations and races.

One of my mentors lectured at a political science class in Boulder, Colorado, where 250 students were learning the judicial history of the United States. They were new thinkers in the

**DISCIPLING**

making. Their minds were sharp, and they were beginning to formulate their opinions on courts, laws, attorneys, and the issues that are worth fighting for. Certainly they were ready for the question my friend posed: "Can any of you in this class tell me that Adolf Hitler was morally wrong by doing what he did in World War II?"

To his astonishment, not one hand went up.

He continued, "Are there any Jews in this classroom?"

One young woman in the front row raised her hand.

He walked over to her and said, "In effect, you are telling me that a man who killed 6 million Jewish people in one of the largest genocides in history isn't morally wrong. Are you saying you cannot find fault with a man who hung his own men by piano wire and watched them squirm while the wire slowly cut their throats? Are you telling me that a man who ordered vivisection on infants to learn how to effectively kill the human body is not morally wrong?"

She looked up at him with confidence and said, "In my opinion, what he did was wrong, but I will not stand and make a moral judgment on him."

Moral judgments in our society have become the hallmark of bad character. If someone decides to stand up for what's right, he is immediately ostracized from society and treated as if he were the cause of all the hate in the world.

## Teens' "Things I Wish My Parents Had Done Differently," Part 7

- "I would have liked my dad to have taken a more dominant role in my spiritual development."
- "I wish they had read the Bible and taught me more about it. I needed an adult to teach me."
- "I wish we had continued to do morning devotions as a family. Also, I wish we would have talked more specifically about our spiritual growth during family evening meals."
- "They did the best job they could, because they knew that if they had pushed at all, I would have rebelled. But I wish they would have encouraged me more to be different because I was a Christian instead of just fitting in with the crowd."

Yet we must stand up and identify right from wrong. Where there is no standard, there will be mass destruction from within. Ideas like those of Hitler have consequences. Six million Jews lost their lives. Several hundred thousand Allied soldiers were killed in battle. Untold numbers of civilians died.

The consequences of wrong ideas in your children's lives can be no less disastrous. This is the source of nearly every evil affecting our teens today, including promiscuity and abortion, drugs and other addictions, aimlessness, despair, and suicide. Without a clear vision of the world as God made it, we are all doomed.

## A Checklist to Get Started

Where to begin? Here are four worldview questions you can ask your teenager right now that will help you grasp what kind of teachings he has been assimilating.

1. *What is God?* The answer to this question is remarkably basic but immeasurably profound. Whatever your teen decides she is going to believe about this question will dictate much of the passion in her life. Here are a few related questions:
   a. *Is there a God?*
   b. *Is God personal or impersonal?*
   c. *Are there many gods?*

2. *What is man?*
   a. *Why do you wake up in the morning?*
   b. *What are your long-term goals in life?*
   c. *Is mankind an evolutionary step to another being?*
   d. *Was mankind created to worship God?*

3. *What is your ultimate purpose in life?*
   a. *Is your purpose in life to experience the most pleasure you can at all times?*
   b. *Is your purpose in life to understand how the mind and body work together to overcome trials and struggles?*
   c. *Is your purpose to know and serve the God of the Bible?*
   d. *Is your purpose to be rich, powerful, or famous?*

4. *Where do you find truth?*
   a. *Is truth a relative explanation of events?*
   b. *Is truth found in yourself?*
   c. *Is truth found in the Bible?*
   d. *Is truth found in any other religious work as well?*

## The Christian Worldview

Once you've had those initial conversations to determine where your teen is, the fun really begins. We will soon offer some practical ways you can influence your child to think more biblically. But first let's review several fundamental truths, or cornerstones, of a Christian worldview.

### God Is a Personal Being

The first point to make is that God is a personal being. Naturalistic thinkers deny the existence of God altogether and tell you plainly that there is no God. New Age philosophies tell you that you are your own god, and that it's your responsibility to awaken your godhood. The Christian worldview is unique: It tells us God is a real supernatural being who desires a personal relationship with man.

Jesus spoke of God as our Father: "Your Father knows what you need before you ask him" (Matthew 6:8). He conveyed the idea that God is not only an authority but also a compassionate being willing to provide for the needs of His people. How much greater can our relationship with God be if we understand that He is personal?

God wants us to spend time with Him, crying out for help, worshiping His greatness, praising His authority and magnificence, and thanking Him for everything He does in our lives. The Creator of the universe wants to be a part of our lives. After all, that's the reason "God so loved the world that he gave his one and only Son, that whoever believes in him shall not perish but have eternal life" (John 3:16).

> *When you teach kids that God is personal, it removes their blurred notion of a distant God.*

When you teach kids that God is personal, it begins to open their eyes and removes their blurred notion of a distant God. If God is personal, they can pray to Him. They can count on Him. They can have faith that He has a plan. They begin to understand that God has their best interests in mind. Ideas like "I have to take care of myself in this world" start to disappear.

### The Breath of God Formed the World
The Bible says plainly, "In the beginning God created the heavens and the earth" (Genesis 1:1). It is most important to know what followed:

> Then God said, "Let us make man in our image, in our likeness, and let them rule over the fish of the sea and the birds of the air, over the livestock, over all the earth, and over all the creatures that move along the ground." So God created man in his own image, in the image of God he created him; male and female he created them. (Genesis 1:26-27)

If God created man in His own image, then He created you and your kids, too. This is a great time to help your teenagers contemplate the creation of all things, especially humanity. If God created people, how should we deal with the issue of euthanasia? Should we intentionally kill people who no longer give anything back to society? How should we view Alzheimer's, AIDS, or any other terminal illness? As your children grasp the concept of God's creation, they will begin to clean their spiritual lenses and see issues in a new and exciting way.

If we as a society cease to believe in God's creation, then the degree to which an individual serves the common good will determine whether he or she is allowed to live in society or is forced to die by society.

The public school will not teach your teens that God created the world. So take responsibility for their education at home and explain to them why it's crucial to recognize that God created the world with His own breath.

DISCIPLING

**Human Nature Aspires to Perfection**

People are attracted to what is perfect. But often the world defines perfection in an unbiblical way—the perfect body, the perfect vacation, the perfect job, and so on. If your teen thinks material possessions will make his life perfect, then the latest car, the biggest house, and the most expensive toys will be his pursuit.

The Christian, however, should take on the attitude of Paul:

> Not that I have . . . already been made perfect, but I press on to take hold of that for which Christ Jesus took hold of me. Brothers, I do not consider myself yet to have taken hold of it. But one thing I do: Forgetting what is behind and straining toward what is ahead, I press on toward the goal to win the prize for which God has called me heavenward in Christ Jesus. (Philippians 3:12-14)

The Christian pursues Christlikeness, which is as perfect as you can be.

How would your kids' lives change if they truly desired to be as perfect as Christ? What kind of movies would they watch? What would be their view of material possessions? What kind of music would they listen to? When your teenager understands that perfection is found in Christ, and that God's power in us "is made perfect in [our] weakness" (2 Corinthians 12:9), failure becomes an easier pill to swallow. As long as they believe that they are "pressing on" toward perfection in Christ, the pitfalls in the road of life are just helping them reach that perfection.

**Absolute Truth Is Found in God**

Many people today say that ultimate truth is a figment of our imagination. The Christian worldview, on the other hand, says there is absolute, objective truth, and its source is God. First John 1:5-6 declares, "This is the message we have heard from him and declare to you: God is light; in him there is no darkness at all. If we claim to have fellowship with him yet walk in the darkness, we lie and do not live by the truth."

John helps us understand that there is no ambiguity in God. He is light. He is truth. Some statements about Him are correct;

others are false. Moreover, He has created a real world where some actions are clearly right and others are definitely wrong.

The key to finding absolute truth in God is learning how to walk in His light and see the world through His eyes. Your children can discover how to do this even in the darkness of an educational system that labels them as unintelligent or intolerant for having believed in Christianity.

### Jesus Christ Is the Son of God

I have never heard God speak from the clouds. I've never seen His handwriting on the wall or had an angel tell me, "Peace be with you. I have a message from God." So the easiest way for me to get to know God is to study His character throughout the Bible. He is most evident in His Son, Jesus.

Some people call Jesus a good teacher. Some call Him a prophet. Some say He is the best example of a man who incorporated His own godhood in daily life. I call Him the Son of God. C. S. Lewis pointed out that if you study what Jesus actually said, you have to conclude that He was either the Son of God or a lunatic. Not a good teacher. Not a prophet. Not a New Age figure. Just a madman or the very Son of God.

> *If you study what Jesus actually said, you have to conclude that He was either the Son of God or a lunatic.*

In John 8:12, Jesus said, "I am the light of the world. Whoever follows me will never walk in darkness, but will have the light of life." How many people who walk around your neighborhood claiming to be the light of the world have all their marbles?

Jesus made it even clearer to His critics when He said, "I and the Father are one." That statement was enough for them; they tried to stone Him for claiming to be God Himself (see John 10:30-33).

### Evil Is a Result of Man's Sin

The apostle Paul wrote, "Sin entered the world through one man, and death through sin, and in this way death came to all men, because all sinned" (Romans 5:12).

It is important for your teens to understand that sin is a result of man's early rebellion against God. Sin was then passed from

**DISCIPLING**

generation to generation, so that the world is full of sinful people. Romans 3:23 says, "All have sinned and fall short of the glory of God." All people—Jews, Gentiles, Israelis, Americans, Sudanese, Chinese, Iranians, Brazilians, and all other races and nationalities—try to be masters of their own lives and end up behaving in ways that disgust God.

When your kids begin to grasp the worldwide problem of sin, it will help them understand issues like homosexuality. Today, our society calls homosexual relationships an "alternative lifestyle." That sounds much more appealing than "sin." The idea behind this lifestyle is that, if men or women feel sexually attracted to others of the same sex, they are entitled to live accordingly. Our society justifies this practice by saying we have evolved into a more diverse and accepting people.

But the Bible addresses homosexuality like this:

> Do you not know that the wicked will not inherit the
> kingdom of God? Do not be deceived: Neither the sexu-
> ally immoral nor idolaters nor adulterers nor male prosti-
> tutes nor homosexual offenders nor thieves nor the
> greedy nor drunkards nor slanderers nor swindlers will
> inherit the kingdom of God. (1 Corinthians 6:9-10)

Paul listed many "alternative lifestyles" in those verses, but the majority of society has yet to condone adultery or theft. What if my idea of an "alternative lifestyle" is to be a robber? Are you going to let me come over to your house and take your money? Can I be justified in holding up a bank downtown and not going to jail? When will society evolve into accepting drunkenness as an "alternative lifestyle"?

When your teenagers grasp the consequences of sin in their lives, they will be able to appreciate the forgiveness God has offered them.

**Jesus Came to Die on Account of Our Sin and Reconcile Us to God**
We're told that "since death came through a man, the resurrection of the dead comes also through a man" (1 Corinthians 15:21). That man is Jesus.

The cross is the center of the Christian faith. Jesus in all His glory decided to come down to earth to pay the penalty of sin with His own life. He reconciled us to Himself and called us to help others find Him as well.

Our culture often labels Christianity as a religion that fosters hate. Christians should, however, be people who reach out to the community not to hate but to love. Jesus didn't hate anything in the world except sin. He didn't hate people, just their sinful actions.

Help your kids to understand that we are to help the pregnant teenage girl, not ostracize her. We need to bring the drunkard to the Water of Life, not send him back to death at the local bar. We should lovingly present the consequences of sin to the homosexual, not mock his lifestyle or physically attack him. Jesus loved sinners of all kinds so much that He died for them.

## Passing It On

Needless to say, passing on a Christian worldview is not as simple as sitting your teens down for a series of lectures or family devotions. That may or may not be an option in your home; just be aware that boring your kids will hurt rather than help your cause.

A far better approach is found in Deuteronomy 11:18-21:

> Fix these words of mine in your hearts and minds; tie
> them as symbols on your hands and bind them on your
> foreheads. Teach them to your children, talking about
> them when you sit at home and when you walk along
> the road, when you lie down and when you get up. Write
> them on the doorframes of your houses and on your
> gates, so that your days and the days of your children
> may be many in the land that the LORD swore to give
> your forefathers, as many as the days that the heavens
> are above the earth.

Every casual dinner conversation, every movie or TV show you watch together, every drive to the store or hike in nature is rife with opportunities to discuss some aspect of the Christian worldview. After all, what your kids need from you is not just a

DISCIPLING

clear understanding of biblical truth, but also practice in detecting and responding to the world's lies. Even a video that promotes evil, when viewed discerningly, can make us all want to stand more firmly than ever for God's values.

That is not to say we should freely indulge in whatever entertainment our culture offers. Heaven forbid! But more and more, as your children learn to love God, they will be less attracted to the music or other influences that promote un-Christian values or perspectives. Try to get their enthusiastic agreement on what TV programs your family won't watch. Ask them pointed questions to help them judge for themselves the latest CD being raved about at school.

> *What your kids need from you is not just a clear understanding of biblical truth, but also practice in detecting and responding to the world's lies.*

Speaking of school, your choice of educational options for your children is critical. Some Christian schools will help your kids view all of life in the light of Scripture. Others may simply add a religious component to the curriculum but fail to approach, say, math or economics from a Christian worldview.

Perhaps home schooling, even in your kids' teen years, will prove to be a better route for you. Public education can work, too, as long as you stay actively involved in monitoring what your teens are being taught and helping them adopt a biblical perspective.

Whatever direction you decide on, the responsibility lies with you. No Christian school or Sunday school can ever replace what your kids fail to learn at home.

Feel inadequate? The Lord will be there to help you. Plus, there are many resources available, as you will see in appendix B.

## Summary

Many times in our day-to-day lives, we run right over the fact that Christ is the true Savior. Sometimes we take for granted the meaning of supernatural grace. However, as we reacquaint ourselves with the basics of the Christian worldview and teach it to our kids, life tends to take on a new meaning. Be sure to make it a priority to reinforce the Christian worldview with your teenagers. With it, they will walk with God, avoid dangerous detours, and reach their destination just fine.

*Andy Braner is a director at Kanakuk Kamps in Branson, Missouri, where he regularly teaches Christian worldview to young teens. He earned his bachelor's degree at Baylor University.*

**DISCIPLING**

# CHAPTER 20

# Teaching Your Teen Media Discernment

## by Bob Waliszewski and Bob Smithouser

Not long ago I (Waliszewski) met my wife and our two children for lunch at a nearby restaurant. Seated catercorner to us was a mother and her teenage sons. I couldn't help but notice that one of the guys had on a T-shirt emblazoned with the name of a perverse and violent rock band in big letters across the front.

When the teens took off, leaving mom to cover the bill, I went over to her and calmly said, "Do you mind if I ask you a question?" She didn't. "I was wondering how you handle the fact that one of your sons sports the shirt of a band whose lead singer fantasizes on one of his CDs about brutally torturing his mother."

As her jaw dropped, she replied, "I had no idea."

Like this woman, many parents have no idea what's really happening in their teenagers' entertainment world. After all, many of our young people have their own television sets in their rooms, don headphones when they're in our vehicles, and head to the local cineplex with a simple "See you later."

> Many parents have no idea what's really happening in their teenagers' entertainment world.

■ ■ ■

## Creature Feature:
## A Tale of Two Lizards

Teens need to understand why discernment matters. They need to see how the messages carried within movies, television, and music fortify one of two forces engaged in spiritual conflict. Telling them the following story may help.

A few years ago, I satisfied an unfulfilled childhood urge by adopting a pair of baby iguanas. Liberty and Justice were about the same age and size when they arrived at their new home. Like any good father of two, I did my best to treat them equally. They scampered around the same 55-gallon aquarium, drank from the same water dish, and soaked in warmth from the same hot rock and heat lamp. A Vita-lite shone on both. In short, my leathery pals shared an identical environment. There was just one noticeable difference in their lifestyles: diet.

While Liberty consumed fruit, vegetables, and various forms of protein, Justice was a picky eater with a meager appetite. Consequently, Liberty grew bigger and stronger—a richly colored, muscular animal. But lacking proper nutrition, Justice became more lethargic. She got thinner and assumed a paler shade of green.

From that point on, if Liberty wanted to bask on the hot rock, he commandeered it. If he chose to drink, Justice had to get out of his way. It was only a matter of time before Justice's poor diet, aggravated by Liberty's bullying, led to her death. This left just one healthy iguana to rule the aquarium.

This illustrates the inner conflict facing all of us as Christians. Within each of us dwell two natures: the flesh and the Spirit (John 3:6; Galatians 5:16-17; Ephesians 2:1-3). They share the same environment, body, and senses.

Like reptilian roommates, these two natures become territorial, even adversarial. Each wants to rule the "aquarium" of our hearts and minds. The one that "eats" best will be the one that thrives.

But keep in mind that the dietary preferences of the Spirit and flesh are quite different. The Spirit is nourished by Bible study, prayer, Christian fellowship, and serving others. The flesh has an appetite for junk food: movie scenes of a sexual nature; violent video games; television programs filled with profanity, perversity, and graphic violence; songs celebrating rebellion, drug use, casual sex, or skewed theology.

**DISCIPLING**

Like all believers, your teen has both natures at war within, fighting for control. As one prospers and grows to dominance, the other withers.

Imagine a pair of twin teen Christian guys—same school, home, youth group, and friends. One avoids all entertainment of a sexually perverse nature. The other dabbles in Internet porn, enjoys sexually suggestive music, and regularly goes to movies the reviewers call "teen sex comedies." Which young man is more likely to see his spiritual nature grow strong?

Which hungry nature is your teen feeding? Which will dominate the "aquarium" of her heart and mind? In the daily battle between flesh and Spirit, it's winner take all.

—Bob Smithouser

But for Christian parents committed to passing the faith baton to their children, and then safeguarding that heritage, having no idea when it comes to the world of media is not an option these days.

After spending most of the past decade immersed in the world of pop culture, we'd like to offer some tips on guiding your teen to be literate, discerning, and self-controlled when it comes to entertainment.

## A Brave New World

Today's media preoccupation with sex, violence, and profanity would have been unthinkable in the minds of entertainment's pioneers. Even if computer-generated graphics, advanced special effects, and digitized audio had been available to carry the messages so explicitly, public sentiment would not have embraced music that glamorizes rape, murder, and drugs, nor much of what passes for entertainment at the local movie theater. Nor would MTV, the Playboy Channel, Showtime, and even a lot of major network programming have made the grade.

Approximately 40 years ago, Federal Communications Commission chairman, Newton N. Minow, described American TV as a "vast wasteland." Three decades later, his concerns regarding TV were quite different. "In 1961, I worried that my children would not benefit much from television, but in 1991 I worry that my children will actually be harmed by it," he explained.[1]

As parents who put a high premium on instilling our faith,

DISCIPLING

values, and character in our young people, we should share
Minow's concern about the media. That's what Larry from Michi-
gan sadly discovered a bit too late. Accompanying a stack of his
teen's CDs (all except one labeled with an Explicit Lyrics sticker),
Larry sent us a letter that told of their estranged relationship and
underscored the emotional struggles of dealing with a prodigal
son. Larry offered this overview: "My son is hooked on this degrading, offensive music. After 14 years of Christian schooling, church,
and Sunday school, he is rejecting Jesus and Christianity." With his
closing words, this father pleaded, "Please get the word out to parents before their children fall for this God-insulting music."

How can you ensure that Larry's story doesn't become your
own? The first step is to understand your teen's current media
diet.

## Entering the Brave New World

In many homes today, an adolescent's entertainment has a figura-
tive Keep Out sign above the entrance. If that sounds like your
home, it's time to take a tour. You can enter this normally alien
pop culture domain via heart-to-heart conversation. Your main
goal at this point is to discover what your teen likes and why.

What you find out—not just your teen's preferences but also
the reasons for those preferences—may astound you. We've
found that many of the churched young people who contact us
base what they choose to watch and listen to on various shaky
foundations. Instead of rooting decisions in biblical principles,
they evaluate entertainment product by perceived value. *Will I
most likely enjoy it? Is it popular? Is the buzz surrounding it positive?
Do my friends say they liked it (or think they probably will)?*

For many teens, guarding the heart is a low (or nonexistent)
priority. Consider these thoughts from Alicia in Maine, whose letter critical of our opinion is representative of many churched
teens on troublesome entertainment:

> I am not a sick pervert because I enjoy [problematic]
> music. . . . [You say] "the album also promotes dangerous
> acts of sex and violence"? So? What doesn't these days?

Everywhere you turn, you see it. Television, movies, music, magazines, even video games. . . . And what is so abnormal about liking gory horror films? I bet every nine out of 10 people enjoy them.

Notice that Alicia doesn't appeal to a scriptural passage that she thinks would bring clarity to her disagreement with us. She makes her argument solely on prevalence and popular opinion.

Perhaps you have an "Alicia" in your home. You know that any attempt to "meddle" will be messy. Is this a battle you should skip?

No. For your teen's sake, don't avoid the issue. Be compassionate, but come fully armored and prepared for the long haul.

## "But It Doesn't Affect Me!"

Maybe you doubt that "mere entertainment" could have such an impact on your teen. Chances are that your teen doubts it, too. But consider the following:

- Statistics show that entertainment ranks as one of most teens' top priorities. Students spend 900 hours per year in school but nearly 1,500 hours in front of a TV set.[2] The average teenager listens to 10,500 hours of popular music between the 7th and 12th grades—about the same amount of time spent in the classroom from first grade to graduation.[3] Four out of five teenagers say they've seen a movie during the previous month, with the average teen watching two or three films during that period.[4]

- Christian teens are no exception. Pollster George Barna discovered that a larger percentage of Christian teenagers (42 percent) had watched MTV "in the past week" than non-Christian teens (33 percent).[5] And according to Alan Weed, president of the Christian music organization Interlinc, "Christian kids listen to four hours of music a day—most of it mainstream—not Christian. That means a serious kid who goes to two services a week, has a personal quiet time and invests time with a mentor still spends more time getting messages from the secular world than he does with spiritual things."[6]

> *The song lyrics and movie scenes you may have grown up with would seem quaint today.*

- The song lyrics and movie scenes you may have grown up with would seem quaint today. And of course, the video games and Internet Web sites that are so popular today weren't even around in your youth. As one media journalist put it: "The current crop of radio hits makes the once-controversial Madonna now seem as innocent as Mary Poppins."[7] One recent album from a Grammy-nominated rapper, for example, featured the artist boasting about sodomizing his own mother.

- Tunes get stuck in our heads. Lyrics rattle around in there, too, and some of them may be rather disturbing when we stop to think about them. As for the visual media, most of us can recall images we wish we could erase from our minds—things we've seen in movies, in magazines, or on TV.

- Media can help create an emotional state. After a rough day at the office reviewing a disturbing metal CD, the last thing I (Waliszewski) want playing in my car stereo system is something loud and bass-heavy. Typically I'll locate a station that airs praise and worship, which refresh my spirit. As a runner, however, I wouldn't want that station broadcast over the PA system before a big race. I want to hear something like the theme from *Rocky* before the starting gun. In light of the relationship between entertainment and emotions, it's reasonable to ask whether negative media messages can negatively influence kids, especially when they're feeling rejected, betrayed, hurt, or lonely.

- Violent media content can shape behavior. In one of the most definitive statements yet on violence in American culture, four national health associations in July 2000 issued a joint statement linking the violence in television, music, video games, and movies to increasing violence among children. "Its effects are measurable and long-lasting. Moreover, prolonged viewing of media violence can lead to emotional desensitization toward violence in real life," explained the American Medical Association, the American Psychological Association, the American Academy of Pediatrics, and the American Academy of Child and Adolescent Psychiatry. "The conclusion of the public health community, based on over 30 years of research, is that viewing entertainment violence can lead to increases in aggressive attitudes, values and behaviors in children."[8]

■ The advertising industry knows that media have influence. That's why the intelligent people who run large corporations plunk down $3 million for a mere 30-second commercial during the Super Bowl. They bet their business on our propensity to recall and respond to their jingle, skit, or montage.

Of course, the cause-and-effect process is not as simple as monkey see, monkey do. Rather, the media first affect our moods, attitudes, and emotions. Then these, in turn, influence our actions. Dr. Richard G. Pellegrino, an M.D. and Ph.D. in neurology and neuroscience who has worked with the brain for 25 years, says nothing he does can affect a person's state of mind as powerfully as can one simple song.[9]

## Philosophical Hurdles

In addition to the argument that "It doesn't affect me," you may encounter a few philosophical obstacles when you discuss media with your teen. Some of these may be based on confusion—confusing truth with reality, tolerance with love, and false spirituality with the real thing. Here are suggestions for clearing those hurdles.

### Truth vs. Reality

Of the hundreds of letters we receive from churched teens about media issues, the most disturbing ones reveal confusion in this area. If we object to an album that romanticizes sin, we're told to lighten up because the artist is singing about "real life." When we say a movie is over the top because it glamorizes violence, we get, "What doesn't these days?"

Many adolescents judge entertainment's appropriateness on

DISCIPLING

■ ■ ■

## "But It's Just One Little Scene!"
## One Way to Reply

Once when I spoke at a church on media discernment, a young man came up afterward and challenged me about a movie I had mentioned as an example of what is popular yet out of bounds. He argued that, despite nudity and a fairly explicit sex scene, the movie was worthwhile because of its superb special effects and the overall story line.

While not disagreeing that the effects and plot were both well crafted, I asked the teen something like this: "But have you ever battled lustful thoughts because of the nudity and sex you viewed?"

It was clear that my question had hit home. The young man hung his head and soon walked away.

How a media product affects a person's thoughts, will, and emotions is the critical issue. Why make guarding our hearts tougher by ingesting entertainment that titillates, arouses passion, and applauds sexual behaviors that God sees as damaging? Next time your teen sounds like that young man who spoke to me, you might try asking a similar question.

—Bob Waliszewski

the changing reality of the world around them, *not* on the unchanging truth of God's Word.

When we questioned some of the themes running through popular music, a girl named Sarah wrote, "Music and spiritual beliefs are two different things. Sex, drugs, alcohol—those things are all found in more places than in music. It is reality." She didn't try to refute our evidence; she simply deemed it irrelevant.

A guy named Matt objected to our disdain over obscenities and the glorification of alcohol in pop tunes. "In case you haven't noticed, there's a real world out there," he chided. "A little profanity and alcohol won't send you to hell in a handbasket." Maybe not, but compromise in the realm of entertainment is often symptomatic of a heart prone to waffle in other areas as well.

Every form of depravity is "real." Does that mean it's acceptable as entertainment? Of course not!

So how can we help teens learn where to draw the line? Only

DISCIPLING

through the eternal truth of God's Word. To make sound entertainment choices, teens must first understand the difference between eternal truth and finite reality. Studying the Bible together on this subject (John 10:10; Romans 12:2; 2 Timothy 3:1-9; 4:3-4; 3 John 4) would be a great place to begin.

**Tolerance vs. Love**
Respecting others and embracing the multiplicity of humankind is, at its root, a virtue. But that virtue can become a liability for teens who are unable to distinguish between diversity and perversity.

When we suggested that a concert featuring an openly gay band singing pro-homosexual lyrics isn't appropriate for Christian teens, we figured it wouldn't generate much controversy. We were wrong.

A girl named Becky scolded, "There is nothing wrong with opening with a gay band. It's great that they are open about their sexual preference. Being gay does not make them different in a bad way, or bad people. . . . I think we need to keep an open mind and respect others' preferences and style and even learn a little from them."

A girl named Vickey stated, "I am really upset about your comment on homosexuality. You make it sound like it's a horrible thing. I thought that if you believed in Christ, you were supposed to love your neighbor and not judge people."

Students of Scripture realize that the same Jesus who said, "Do not judge, or you too will be judged" (Matthew 7:1) also commanded, "Stop judging by mere appearances, and make a right judgment" (John 7:24). In order to make a

> *Speaking the truth in love—now that's real caring.*

"right judgment," believers must judge. This can seem confusing because there are two meanings of *judge*. One means to condemn; the other means to evaluate.

While we are forbidden to condemn (that's God's job), we are required to evaluate. Somehow many teens have picked up the idea that loving people means never evaluating or criticizing their actions.

Speaking the truth in love—now that's real caring. It's how

Christ dealt with the woman caught in adultery (John 8:1-11). He forgave her and told her to leave her life of sin. Likewise, you can help your teen learn to reach out in love to everyone and not take an apathetic approach to sin.

### Real vs. False Spirituality

"I'm totally into [a certain gangsta rapper]," wrote a teenager in a recent letter sent our way. "I listen to him a lot. I know his lyrics aren't very 'good,' but I can't help it. At the end of every CD he does a prayer and sings a song about God. Does that make it okay?"

A lot of young people are confused when artists demonstrate a form of godliness while the entertainment they produce doesn't measure up spiritually. When an on-screen hero is seen with hymnal in hand at church in one scene and in bed with his girlfriend the next, the spiritual dimension seems hollow. *But,* many kids might reason, *isn't it better than no church at all?*

It should be easy to see that freshwater and saltwater can't flow from the same spring (James 3:11). Yet the brackish combination that flows from movies, television, and pop music can, for many adolescents, seem pure enough. It's up to us to make sure we've ingrained this principle in our young people: "Out of the same mouth come praise and cursing. My brothers, this should not be" (James 3:10).

To help your teen sort through two-faced displays of reverence in the media, try pointing out scriptures in which God calls us to a holy life. Remind your teen that God isn't interested in our *looking* like Christians; He wants genuine, sold-out, radical, obedient faith. Even demons "believe" in God (James 2:19), but that's miles apart from submitting to Him.

## Where Do We Go from Here?

With some of the philosophical hurdles crossed, the question is "So, what can I do to help my kids make better lifelong choices in entertainment?"

The following suggestions are born out of years of interaction with the world of media—and with teens who consume those media daily. Feel free to adapt and apply these in your own home.

### Keep the Main Thing the Main Thing

One of the best Bible passages for direction on the road to media discernment is Colossians 2:8—"See to it that no one takes you captive through hollow and deceptive philosophy, which depends on human tradition and the basic principles of this world rather than on Christ." Every movie, TV show, and song offers a philosophy. Not all entertainment is "hollow and deceptive," but much of it is. Some teens—even Christian teens—willingly allow themselves to be taken "captive" by the world.

For these young people, teaching media discernment is getting the cart before the horse. What they need first is to give Jesus Christ the foremost priority in their lives.

### Know Your Kids' Entertainment

As already noted, it's important to enter the usually private haunt known as your teen's entertainment world. But how?

Begin by finding out what entertainment picks are spinning inside your teenager's head. With pen and paper and a listening ear, ask about your teen's five most favorite musicians. Then list the movies and TV shows your son or daughter says are the most exciting and engaging. Follow that up by asking about his top five Internet sites. Does she go into chat rooms? If so, which ones?

Refrain from jumping in and playing judge and jury at this point. Listen, listen, and listen some more. Remember, you're taking a poll. There will be a time to offer your views, but not during this exploratory stage.

This exercise can also offer a rare window into your teen's soul. Perhaps you'll find that your teen is mature beyond his or her years and has already established some good media habits. In that case, offer praise and encouragement. Most likely, you'll find a mix of good choices and instances of spiritual confusion or immaturity.

If you discover entertainment choices that concern you, schedule a follow-up time to discuss them. This will give you a chance to mull over how you're going to broach the subject (and give you time to pray). If you find that your teen is choosing very "dark" entertainment, take it as a warning sign that he or she may

**DISCIPLING**

■ ■ ■

## *Food for Thought: The Olympic Media Diet*

Here in Colorado Springs we have the privilege of hosting U.S. Olympic hopefuls at the U.S. Olympic Training Center. There I conducted an interview with Judy Nelson, nutrition coordinator with the center's sports medicine division. The more Judy described her relationship with aspiring Olympians, the more she unknowingly offered a prescription for parents who want to help young people develop a healthy media diet.

*1. Even good kids need coaching.* "You'd think that, being Olympic athletes, they'd eat what's good for them, but that's not always the case," Judy admitted. Just as a body driven by an Olympic dream can be seduced by a quarter pounder with cheese, so kids from solid Christian homes and dynamic youth groups will be tempted to entertain themselves with movies, TV, and music that are little more than media junk food. That's why parents need to guide even the most serious young Christians toward edifying choices.

*2. Avoid a hit-list mentality.* Judy has learned that delivering sermonettes about nutrition doesn't work. Instead of giving athletes a rigid list of dietary dos and don'ts, she earns their respect by addressing each on his or her own level. In the same way, a heavy-handed attempt at controlling teens' entertainment choices often breeds frustration. That's because presenting adolescents with a hit list of forbidden fare doesn't build critical-thinking skills or involve them in godly decision making. If you do have to say no to something, take the time to explain your decision in terms of previously agreed upon biblical principles (see the section "Set a Family Standard").

*3. Maintain a healthy relationship.* Judy mingles with the athletes, building a rapport that earns her the right to give advice. Too many parents believe they have a license to lecture youngsters simply because they've been around the track a few more times. A close, day-to-day relationship is vital to our effectiveness as counselors.

*4. Adapt diets to individuals.* Judy recognizes that an athlete's age has significant impact on his or her diet. So it is with popular media. What might be acceptable for a teen may not be suitable for an eight-year-old sibling. On the other hand, there are poisons that should not be consumed by anyone.

*5. Help kids "dine out" wisely.* "[The athletes] eat best when they're here at the training center," Judy said, "but if they're away at school or somewhere else, they can get into bad habits." Likewise, it may easy to monitor your teen's entertainment diet at home. But what happens when he or she goes to a friend's house or off to college? Only those who have internalized a biblically based discernment message will leave home equipped to run the marathon of a holy life.

    *6. Accept your own limitations.* Finally, Judy Nelson realizes that all she can do is offer prospective Olympians her wealth of dietary wisdom. She can't force-feed them. We parents hate to admit it, but we can't indefinitely control the media diets of the young people we love. After we've done our prayerful best to give them healthy guidelines, it's up to them to bring home the gold.

—Bob Smithouser

---

be harboring deep pain (see the sidebar "When Teens Like 'Dark' Entertainment"). Above all, be firm yet respectful, allowing open and free communication.

### Set a Family Standard

Once you've got a handle on your teen's entertainment preferences, it's time to work together on setting healthy, biblically based boundaries. Of course, there are no verses in the Bible that read, "Thou shalt not watch slasher films" or "Thou shalt not listen to music that glamorizes substance abuse." Instead, each family must decide together where to draw the line, using scriptural principles as a guide (see the sidebars "Good Questions" and "Read All About It"). Furthermore, factor in an understanding of each family member's maturity, critical thinking skills, and commitment to holiness. Don't forget fervent prayer.

Go to great lengths, if necessary, to find common ground with your teen on media standards. Keep leading him or her back to important Bible verses and asking what conclusions he or she draws from them.

Avoid jumping prematurely to the rule-making stage. That will not help you achieve your real goal, which is to help your teen become a discerning adult for the rest of his or her life. Only in dire cases should you resort to *shielding* your teens from mainstream entertainment rather than *discussing* standards with them.

Now articulate your family's decisions in writing. Develop a

**DISCIPLING**

"family constitution" dealing with entertainment habits in your home. Take your time. Ponder the specifics for several days and give the Lord a chance to speak to you all about the matter. It will help you work through those gray areas.

If you're parenting with a spouse, make sure the two of you agree on the "constitution" (after all, it will be up to both of you to enforce it). This can be a daunting task, especially if your spouse doesn't share your vision for discernment, or if you're a single parent whose child spends time with a permissive ex-spouse. In such cases, ask that your rules be respected, pray for everyone involved, and when necessary, seek out a pastor or counselor as a mediator.

If your teen is already a fan of questionable media, you face a special challenge. You can start operating under the new standard "from this day forward," but you—and preferably your teen—must determine how to deal with the garbage festering in his or her entertainment collection. Here are some possible scenarios:

■ After discovering the need for discernment, your teen may feel supernaturally convicted and voluntarily purge the junk from his CD and movie library as well as change his TV viewing habits.

## Can We Talk?
## Media Discussion Starters

Here are some questions that may help you engage your teen and crack open the door to media discernment:

■ What is it about this form of entertainment that attracts you? Why do you like this particular style (or genre or show) more than others?
■ Why do you listen or watch? (If it's simply because friends do, ask, "Why do your friends listen to or watch it?")
■ How does this form of entertainment make you feel?
■ Do the themes reflect reality? Do they reflect truth? If they reflect reality, do they also gloss over evil?
■ How do the messages conveyed compare with the values you've been taught here at home or in church?

- You can humbly accept responsibility for taking too long to set the boundaries and can agree to replace the offending media products with ones that meet the family standard. Since you're picking up the tab, you may even want to limit substitutes to edifying projects by popular Christian artists or to movies you've prescreened.
- A local pawnshop might pay two or three bucks apiece for the discs, videos, and video games you're anxious to get rid of. Since you probably don't want to put these products back into circulation, you might agree to purchase them from your child at the same rate and then break out the sledgehammer and the Hefty bag. (Hey, they're yours now; you can do anything you want with them!)
- If you have one or two out-of-bounds products still in nearly new condition, you can try returning them to the store that sold them. Some retailers will refund the purchase price—or offer store credit—to a parent who makes a return because of offensive content.

After you've established family standards and weeded out everything that flunks the test, you're ready to start fresh. Hold firm to the new guidelines. From now on, if your teen asks to purchase a

**DISCIPLING**

- Do you think these messages have any effect on how close you feel to your family, friends, or God? Why or why not?
- Would you feel comfortable if Jesus sat here listening to or watching this with you (see Matthew 28:20)? Do you think He'd be concerned, or would He enjoy this particular entertainment product?
- Does this entertainment reflect an opinion about God? What is it?
- What would happen if you imitated the lifestyles and choices of the characters in these songs or this program?
- What do you consider to be inappropriate entertainment? Where do you draw the line? Where does Scripture draw the line? Are they the same?
- How does it make you feel to know that, by purchasing a CD, going to a movie, or watching a TV show, you are supporting the ideas being promoted?

certain media product, you can say, "Sure, but when you bring it home, we'll review it together. If we can't agree that it meets the family standard, you'll have to get rid of it. You'll be out the money."

Rest assured: If your teen knows it's his money on the line, he'll be much more selective about which entertainers he invites home.

**Be Wary of Extremes**

Setting family entertainment standards requires work. For that reason, some parents opt for an all-or-nothing approach rather than teaching and reinforcing biblical principles on a case-by-case basis.

At one extreme, some moms and dads choose to lay down the law: no movies, no television, no secular music, period. While this approach may seem to simplify things, it may also breed rebellion if you haven't taken the time to convince your teen that it's reasonable. Young people bide their time, waiting for the day when they can sample the entertainment industry's forbidden fruit: "Just wait till I move out—I'll watch and listen to whatever I want." When they head off to college or career, this attitude often plays out in unwise choices.

Other parents go to the opposite extreme, adopting an anything-goes philosophy: no boundaries, everything is okay, do what you want. This permissive approach leads to "indecent exposure" as children wander, aimless and wide-eyed, through the culture's enticements.

> *Teaching discernment gives teens life skills they'll carry with them throughout adulthood.*

Neither of these extremes works for most families. One often creates rebels; the other fosters destructive attitudes. A discerning middle ground—one that tests entertainment against biblical standards—is the more reasonable and protective plan of action. Teaching discernment encourages balance, leads to critical thinking, bonds families, and gives teens life skills they'll carry with them throughout adulthood.

**Don't Judge on Style or Ratings**

Let's be blunt: Rating systems are unreliable. For motion pictures, a PG-13, PG, or even a G says almost nothing about whether a film will uplift the human spirit and avoid glamorizing evil. The same is true with television and video-game ratings.

Trusting a rating system is like buying a used car solely on the basis of a classified ad that boasts, "Great car." Who decided? Based on what criteria? Though it takes a little more research, it's worth your time and effort to go beyond the rating and find out about a show's content.

Likewise, musical styles can be deceptive. While "harder" genres can offer positive messages, some mellower musicians dump lyrical sewage on their fans. In this area, perhaps more than any other, we parents are tempted to make decisions based on personal preference. A better plan is to check out the message being conveyed, not the style or look of the messenger.

### Check Out the Ride Ahead of Time

Recently, my (Waliszewski's) daughter wanted to ride her horse, B. J. But this presented a problem. B. J. hadn't been ridden in a while and seemed to have too much pent-up energy.

Rather than tell Kelsey she couldn't go, I saddled up and took the reins first. I did so for one simple reason—to make sure it was safe. The same goes for entertainment. Consider checking out the "ride" before your kids hop on.

But who has the time to prescreen every movie, CD, and televised program? Fortunately, there are inexpensive (sometimes free), trustworthy media-review resources that can help. Not only do these identify the bad apples in the barrel but also they often uncover the good.

Our *Plugged In* magazine, for example, gives concise monthly reviews of what's hot in the media. You can also reach us online at www.pluggedinmag.com. In addition, we find www.previewonline.org to be a helpful site for movies and television. Another site, www.screenit.com, fails to judge movies by biblical standards but is nonetheless helpful if you want to find out in detail what a film contains in terms of sex, violence, or bad language.

When it comes to evaluating contemporary Christian music, your best resource may be the local Christian bookstore. The sales staff may be able to help you find positive music that suits your teen's tastes. Most youth pastors can help you navigate the contemporary Christian music world as well.

DISCIPLING

■ ■ ■

## *Founding Fathers (and Mothers): A Family Constitution*

Here's a sample form you can use as a guideline to compose your own standard of what's acceptable in your home. Although it avoids the specifics, you'll want to be as specific as you can in your own version so that family members understand (and agree to) the boundaries.

**Our Family Constitution for Acceptable Media**

As family members committed to the lordship of Jesus Christ and wanting to live out personal holiness as He commands, we pledge from this day forward to honor God in our media choices. Despite poor decisions that we may have made in the past, we desire to secure the blessings that come from obedience. Because we realize that certain types of entertainment are spiritually unhealthy, we ask the heavenly Father to guide us and strengthen us as we work to make good entertainment choices, empowered by the fruit of the Spirit (self-control—our part) and the ongoing work of the Holy Spirit (His part).

Knowing that God says, "Above all else, guard your heart" (Proverbs 4:23), we pledge to guard our hearts from harmful influences that work against our faith.

We agree to avoid all forms of entertainment (music, film, video, Internet, magazines, books, television, video games, and so on) that

_____.

In the rare event that one of us feels an exception to the above should be made, we pledge to bring this issue and the possible reasons for it to the family to discuss and evaluate, rather than make this decision in isolation.

*We understand that signing this family constitution has no bearing upon our salvation (which is 100 percent dependent upon our faith in Jesus Christ as our Savior and Lord) but is an outgrowth of our desire to please God and obey Him in every area of our lives.*

Family members sign below:

_____

_____

_____

Date _____

### Ask: WWJD?

Remember the WWJD? bracelets and other merchandise that were popular a few years ago? While the fad may have faded, the principle behind the What Would Jesus Do? products will never dim. If every Christian would ask this question before making an entertainment choice (not to mention every choice in life), it would eliminate most impure selections from our entertainment diets.

No doubt you've heard the saying "If you give a man a fish, you give him a meal. But if you *teach* him to fish, you feed him for a lifetime." By encouraging our teens to use the WWJD? principle in the area of media choices, we can teach them how to fish in this media-saturated culture no matter what's on the tube, screen, radio, or CD player.

It's never too late to start using this question. I (Waliszewski) have even seen it work with adults who weren't in the habit. At a social gathering a few years back, a Christian couple asked me to close my ears while they discussed with someone else an objectionable movie they'd recently viewed. Hoping not to sound holier-than-thou, I said something like "Don't worry about offending me—just worry about how Jesus would feel about it." Some time later, the husband told me my words had prompted his family to change its movie viewing habits.

### Model Wise Choices

One of the surest ways to derail your young person's media discernment is to act hypocritically. Nothing lasting can be accomplished if teaching discernment amounts to a parent saying, "No watching MTV in this house," while viewing *The Sopranos*.

Becoming increasingly discerning should be a lifetime endeavor for all of us. Do you struggle with your own choices? Do you, too, want to go to that R-rated thriller because everyone at the office has seen it?

Most of us can relate to that feeling at times. And it's okay to admit it to our children. But we must be careful not to teach a principle and then violate it ourselves. Parents who have been guilty of this find credibility hard to regain.

DISCIPLING

### Don't Lose Hope

I (Waliszewski) met Christ when I was 15. I was radically changed into that "new creation" promised in Scripture. But it wasn't until my early twenties that I cleaned up my act in the entertainment arena.

Many other areas of my life were transformed—some instantly. But this one I compartmentalized, believing that God didn't care much about it. Sermons on personal holiness didn't work. Neither did my own teachings on that subject, delivered in my role as a youth pastor. Somehow obedience and media didn't seem related.

Fortunately, God grabbed my attention. One day I was given a cassette tape on discernment that specifically addressed some of my favorite musicians—not in generalities, but using detailed examples and principles from God's Word. The speaker had done his homework, naming names and contrasting lyrics with what Jesus taught. After listening to this tape, I came away with a fresh perspective. The Holy Spirit began to work, revolutionizing my media habits. I destroyed hundreds of dollars' worth of albums (yeah, that was back in the days prior to CDs) and began replacing them with positive alternatives.

Perhaps you have a teen who just doesn't get it. Don't despair.

## Read All About It: More Passages to Ponder

For additional study, consider the following verses and topics:

### Avoiding Indecent Exposure
Exodus 20:1-21 • God's original top 10 list
Psalm 1 • Be careful whose counsel you accept
Psalm 11:4-7 • The dangers of loving violence
Psalm 101 • David's pledge of purity
Romans 12:9 • Hate what is evil
Ephesians 5:11 • Have nothing to do with darkness
Philippians 4:4-8 • Your heart's best defense
Colossians 2:8 • Watch out for deceivers
Colossians 3:1-10 • Trading junk for jewels
1 Thessalonians 5:21 • Test everything

Take it from a former hard case: There really is hope. It may be a matter of finding the right book or tape or CD that specifically addresses today's media (for example, try the book *Mind over Media* by Stan Campbell and Randy Southern [Tyndale, 2001] and the accompanying video of the same name). Or encourage your teen to attend a seminar on the subject at a church or youth conference. Note this message from a teenager who wrote to say how such a presentation changed his life:

> Here's living proof that Christians spreading God's Word [in this case, the message of godly media discernment] can make a difference in someone's life. I have just passed the one-year anniversary of the one event [a teen conference in which you guys addressed the topic of how God expects us to handle entertainment] that has permanently changed my life. . . . [Some time afterward], one by one we tossed our parental advisory CDs and others that were as bad into the [fire] barrel. Three hours and $1,300 worth of CDs later, six guys had burned the CDs clouding their life. A couple months later I was baptized along with my sister, and the fire of God is burning strong in my soul.
>
> —J. G.

**DISCIPLING**

1 Timothy 4:7-16 • A call to young Christians
2 Timothy 4:3-4 • Don't waffle on the truth

**Preparing a Defense**
Psalm 119:9-16 • Armed with God's resources
Matthew 6:19-24 • Protecting the eyes
Romans 12:1-2 • Don't be *con*formed; be *trans*formed
1 Corinthians 9:24-27 • Training to win
2 Corinthians 10:3-5 • Taking thoughts prisoner
Ephesians 6:10-18 • The full armor of God
1 Thessalonians 4:3-8 • Control your passions
1 Peter 1:13-16 • Follow the Commander
2 Peter 1:3-11 • Weapons of spiritual battle

After listening to a *Life on the Edge* radio broadcast addressing this subject, another teen wrote:

> Last year I was listening to all kinds of bad music, even music that I didn't particularly like in order to look cool. . . . I felt really guilty, like a betrayer, and I knew my relationship with Jesus Christ was going downhill. I threw away practically all my rock tapes and began to look into other types of music. . . . My relationship with the Lord is growing again and I want to hear everything I can that has to do with Jesus.
>
> —E. H.

### Hang Out with Wise Entertainers

One of my (Waliszewski's) favorite biblical chapters offering a media-related principle is Psalm 1. Even if you've read it before, read the first four verses again with entertainment in mind:

> Blessed is the man
> who does not walk in the counsel of the wicked
> or stand in the way of sinners
> or sit in the seat of mockers.
> But his delight is in the law of the LORD,
> and on his law he meditates day and night.
> He is like a tree planted by streams of water,
> which yields its fruit in season
> and whose leaf does not wither.
> Whatever he does prospers.
> Not so the wicked!
> They are like chaff
> that the wind blows away.

Today we can hang out with the sinner, the mocker, and the wicked without going near another human being. Each time we watch a movie, flip on the tube, or put on a headset to listen to tunes, we're hanging out with someone. Not all of those "someones" are problematic. But in today's media culture, a number qualify.

**DISCIPLING**

■ ■ ■

## *Good Questions: Scriptures to Talk About*

As you talk about media issues as a family, try reading and discussing the following passages. You might walk through them as part of a family devotional time, or you might tackle a passage each night at the dinner table.

*Passage:* Romans 12:2. *Question:* Does this form of entertainment conform to the "pattern of this world" or God's pattern?

*Passage:* Ephesians 5:11. *Question:* When would entertainment be part of what could be called "the fruitless deeds of darkness"?

*Passage:* Romans 12:9. *Question:* Is this entertainment selection glamorizing evil? If so, am I hating it (like I should) or merely tolerating it?

*Passage:* Proverbs 4:24. *Question:* This verse explains that it's important to guard our speech. How so? How does this verse apply to today's media?

*Passage:* Ecclesiastes 9:18. *Question:* Even if an entertainment choice is 98 percent good, how can one scene or stanza turn an entire project from something to embrace into something to avoid?

*Passage:* Ephesians 4:22. *Question:* While it's not always easy or popular, Christians are commanded to live life differently from everyone else. How so?

*Passage:* Proverbs 3:21. *Question:* Is it possible to preserve sound judgment and discernment and still be entertained? Explain.

*Passage:* Mark 9:43. *Question:* Evil behavior is often depicted by Hollywood and popular musicians as acceptable or preferable. But according to this verse, how important is it to God that we *diligently* seek not to sin?

*Passage:* Proverbs 24:1. *Question:* Substitute "entertainment" for "men" and reread the verse. What's the application here?

*Passage:* 1 Corinthians 10:6. *Question:* Read the verses preceding this one. What things occurred as examples? How does this underscore the importance of guarding our hearts?

*Passage:* Matthew 12:34-36. *Question:* These verses might be summed up in the words of the familiar saying "Garbage in, garbage out." What's the media application here?

*Passage:* Psalm 101:3. *Question:* At what point does this apply to television, the Internet, video games, and film viewing?

*Passage:* Philippians 4:8. *Question:* If we can't find entertainment as described in this verse, what are we to do?

**DISCIPLING**

■ ■ ■

## When Teens Like "Dark" Entertainment: Dealing with the Pain Factor

Why would a Christian teen crank up the volume on tunes that celebrate strangling a girlfriend, attacking a person with a chain saw, murdering a baby, committing suicide, smoking crack, or are otherwise hate-filled, hopeless, and angst-ridden? We've received a substantial number of letters and E-mails from kids who do just that. Here's an example:

> [Dark] music speaks to me. You should realize that the world is not fun and full of life, [but rather] full of hate, love, suicide and murder—and we as Christians cannot deny it. You need to look at music with an open mind and understand that not only I, but millions of depressed teens and kids, turn to music that understands us.

While other factors (rebellion, family dysfunction, rejection, peer pressure, a lack of hatred for evil) can lead a Christian young person to gravitate toward dark entertainment, our mail indicates that the most common denominator is what we refer to as the "pain factor." No one—teen or adult—wants to suffer, especially alone. For teens feeling that no one cares, a hate-spewing rock CD serves as a catharsis and a means of identifying with someone who appears able to relate.

Many teens dealing with pain can be helped by realizing that rejection, hurt, and distress are negative experiences they share in common with Jesus. The prophet Isaiah tells us that Jesus was "despised and rejected by men, a man of sorrows, and familiar with suffering" (Isaiah 53:3). If your teen knows only a Jesus who seems like an uncaring, untouchable being who can't be bothered by human problems, your challenge is to build a bridge to the truth. Point out that no one can empathize with suffering more deeply than the One who was whipped, beaten, mocked, spit on, crucified, and became sin for us (2 Corinthians 5:21). He is the only One who beckons, "Cast all your cares upon Me, for I care for you" (compare 1 Peter 5:7).

**DISCIPLING**

If your teen is suffering the kind of pain that makes dark entertainment seem like the only answer, talk with him or her about the sources of that pain. Consult a counselor if necessary. And be sure the discussion includes the introduction of the Jesus who wants to be a best friend and who can handle the difficulties of life. Faith in the real Jesus can transform pointlessness into authentic joy and purpose.

---

What are we to do, then, to be like a tree planted by streams of water? Besides getting into God's Word, we should evaluate those with whom we hang out—electronically or otherwise. That's a principle worth sharing with your teen.

### When You Can't Tune It Out, Try Teaching
No matter how careful you are about the messages you consume, there are still those inescapable situations when you're assaulted by something—an obscene bumper sticker, an unsavory T-shirt— that doesn't meet your family's standard. Usually those moments happen too quickly to avoid. What should you do?

A while back, my (Waliszewski's) family got away for a few days of snow skiing. After an afternoon of schussing, falling, and sunburning, we headed to a nearby pizza parlor. As our meal arrived, someone dropped a pocketful of quarters in the jukebox. The first song that blared through the establishment was one that would not be welcome in our home.

I looked across the table at my wife, Leesa, who rolled her eyes as if to say, "What's this trash we're stuck listening to?"

My instincts wanted to yell, "Okay, kids, grab the pizza and let's head to the car *right now!*" I resisted the urge. There had to be a better solution.

Indeed, there was. I turned the incident into a "teachable moment" by pointing out why the evening's dinner music failed to meet our family's standard.

I don't want you to think we have this down to a science. We don't. But we've begun using such moments to reinforce the principles of discernment we regularly talk about and model at home. And I know it's sinking in.

I was keenly reminded of that just a few weeks later. My daughter Kelsey and I were in the car together. I'd been channel

*DISCIPLING*

surfing and was tuned in to a country station. I'm usually good about changing the dial when I need to, but I got distracted. "Daddy," Kelsey asked, "is that a good song?" It wasn't. I turned the radio off, a bit embarrassed—but well pleased that Kelsey had recognized the problem on her own.

### Fight the Spiritual Battle

Helping our teens to have fun without being victimized by the wrong kinds of media messages doesn't just happen. It takes a fight to succeed. The words of Nehemiah are meaningful in this context: "Don't be afraid of them. Remember the Lord, who is great and awesome, and fight for your brothers, your sons and your daughters, your wives and your homes" (Nehemiah 4:14).

Whether we like it or not, we're in a battle—a spiritual fray for the hearts and minds of our young people. Fighting for this high ground is not optional; it's essential for their well-being and protection.

As in material-world warfare, we cannot approach spiritual skirmishes with a ho-hum attitude. As we train our young people to be discerning, we secure territory through the power of prayer and spiritual warfare. To think that the battle will be won solely on an "I can teach you" level is to significantly underestimate the enemy and the spiritual weapons (see Ephesians 6) we have at our disposal.

On the battlefield of media discernment, as with any struggle between righteousness and worldliness, we wage war first and foremost on our knees.

## Keep Treasure Hunting

Safeguarding our hearts, according to Proverbs, is something we are to strive for "above all else" (Proverbs 4:23). This takes determined effort—a family effort. It may be painful at first, but as we continue to embrace and apply God's standards and put our potential entertainment choices under its scrutiny, we will find media discernment becoming less of a struggle and more ingrained in our nature.

Fortunately, as we utilize our "metal detectors," we'll discover entertainment treasures as well. We'll uncover music with uplifting messages, movies that encourage the human spirit, television that challenges. But as with searching for diamonds, we'll often have to sift through lots of worthless dirt.

Still, for our teens' sake, media mining is well worth the effort.

*Bob Waliszewski is the manager of Focus on the Family's Youth Culture department. Bob Smithouser is the editor of Focus on the Family's magazine* Plugged In, *which reviews music, films, and TV shows aimed at the youth audience.*

DISCIPLING

# Learning to Let Go

"If you love something, set it free."

"Just as a butterfly must emerge from its cocoon, so our children must be released to reach adulthood."

Birds. Butterflies. We've all heard those analogies about letting go of children so they can mature, spiritually and otherwise. It all sounds so simple—until we actually have to *do* it!

Author Dean Merrill calls this part of parenting a "crazy, contradictory, push-pull job." It's summed up, he says, by the title of a Rich Wilkerson book: *Hold Me While You Let Me Go.* Dubbing that title "totally illogical," Merrill asks,

Well, which is it?

Every one of us knows that the task of raising kids entails controlling them, keeping the lid on, preventing harm, restraining goofiness, running the show, calling the shots. If we leave children unsupervised, they'll kill themselves within 20 minutes, we think.

That's the *Hold Me* part.

On the other hand, we don't want to do this forever; we want to launch our offspring, over an 18-year period, into responsible independence. We want to get them to the point where they are *self*-controlled, able to run their own show.

That's the *While You Let Me Go* part.[1]

Allowing adolescents to spread their wings is a delicate art indeed. No less an authority than Dr. James Dobson admits difficulty in this area:

> I understood the importance of turning loose before our kids were born. I wrote extensively on the subject when they were still young. I prepared a film series in which all the right principles were expressed. But when it came time to my hand and let the birds fly, I struggled mightily! I had loved the experience of fatherhood, and I was not ready to give it up.[2]

If a noted parenting expert has trouble letting go, is there hope for the rest of us?

## Getting Teens Ready to Leave the Nest

Much as we might like to cage or cocoon our kids to protect them from the world (or themselves), the day will come when they're on their own. The time-honored "As long as you live under my roof, you'll follow my rules" will be an empty threat. We know, deep down, that's the way it should be. But it's not an easy prospect to contemplate when we consider scenarios like these:

> *Allowing adolescents to spread their wings is a delicate art indeed.*

- Your son goes off to college, where his philosophy professor is a former preacher's kid who left the faith and now takes delight in convincing his students to do the same.
- Your daughter starts her first job, where she meets a charming, non-Christian guy who pressures her to ditch church and spend cozy weekends with him at his parents' beach cabin.

- Your son gets a roommate who keeps a marijuana stash in the closet and is only too happy to share.
- Your daughter rents an apartment with a young woman who is a very convincing spokesperson for her faith—which happens to be Buddhism.

Chances are that you won't be there to "straighten things out" when your newly liberated teen faces situations like these. Your son or daughter will have life-shaping choices to make—on his or her own.

How can you prepare your child for that not-too-distant future?

"The key is to transfer freedom and responsibility to her little by little from early childhood so she won't need your supervision when she is beyond it," wrote Dr. Dobson. He went on to tell this story:

> I learned this principle from my own mother, who made a calculated effort to teach me independence and responsibility. After laying a foundation during the younger years, she gave me a "final examination" when I was seventeen years old. Mom and Dad went on a two-week trip and left me at home with the family car and permission to have my buddies stay at the house. Wow! Fourteen slumber parties in a row! I couldn't believe it. We could have torn the place apart—but we didn't. We behaved rather responsibly.
>
> I always wondered why my mother took such a risk, and after I was grown, I asked her about it. She just smiled and said, "I knew in one year you would be leaving for college, where you would have complete freedom with no one watching over you. I wanted to expose you to that independence while you were still under my influence."[3]

Such a "final exam" may be a good idea. But what about testing *spiritual* readiness to leave the nest? Can we administer a "sanctified SAT" to see whether our teens qualify to go off on their own?

DISCIPLING

It's good to have guidelines for gauging the success of our spiritual mentoring (see chapter 27, "Measuring Success"). But the truth is that we can't hold our kids back to repeat adolescence, even if they don't seem entirely ready to graduate. What we *can* do is prepare them for spiritual commencement exercises while they're still under our influence. Here are three ways to go about it—three "prep points" that can get teens ready to spread their wings without going down in flames:

## Prep Point 1: Make Sure Your Teen Owns His Faith

The first step in preparing your teen for independent living is to make sure he owns his faith.

Appearing on a broadcast of the *Life on the Edge LIVE!* radio program for teens, a young woman named Casey had this to say:

> Picture yourself driving a car. . . . You're driving down the highway and you forgot to turn your lights on. But you can see because everyone else's lights are on and they're going the same way. But what would happen if everyone else left the picture? [You'd be] lost, too, because your lights aren't on. You've got to have that fire and that light inside of you from the Lord. It's got to be genuine and yours.

Does your teen have her "headlights" on? Or is she depending on others to show the way—others who may not be around when the going gets tough or who may be headed the wrong way?

Unfortunately, many Christian teens are leaving home with their headlights off. To begin with, they haven't internalized biblical truths that could guide them. Researcher George Barna found the following conditions among adolescents who profess to know Christ:

- Six out of 10 say there is no such thing as absolute truth.
- Nine out of 10 say that right and wrong depend on the individual and the situation—that is, they espouse moral relativism.

- One out of four deny the notion that acting in disobedience to God's laws brings about negative consequences.
- One-half believe that the main purpose of life is enjoyment and personal fulfillment.
- Almost half contend that sometimes lying is necessary.
- One out of three say that as long as something works, you can be sure that it is morally or ethically right.
- More than four out of 10 say that Satan is just a symbol of evil, not a living force.
- One out of three Christian teens contend that Jesus Christ committed sins while on earth.
- Three out of 10 say that all faiths teach the same lessons.
- About half of the Christian teens in America maintain that people can earn their way into heaven through good works or exemplary behavior.[4]

It's not surprising, then, that many teens aren't making good choices. Barna's research shows that it's hard to tell the difference between Christian and non-Christian young people when the rubber meets the road:

> Both segments were equally likely to volunteer their time to help the needy, to cheat on an exam, to steal posses-sions, to look through a pornographic magazine, to have had sexual intercourse, to have attempted suicide, and to spend time watching MTV during the week.
>
> Born-again teenagers were slightly less likely to have watched an X-rated or pornographic movie or to have used an illegal, nonprescription drug within the last three months. They were also more likely to have dis-cussed their religious beliefs with other kids their age and to have felt God's presence at some time in their lives. Overall, however, apart from their engagement in religious activity, most teenagers' lives do not seem to have been substantially altered by their faith views.[5]

The good news is that you, as a spiritual mentor to your teen, can buck this trend. By being intentional, you can pass along

**DISCIPLING**

biblical guidelines (see chapter 19, "Instilling a Christian World-view"). You can help your child make the connection between facts and action (for ideas, flip back to "Turning Beliefs into Convictions" on page 284).

But how will you know when your teen's "headlights" are switching on? Look for these five signs that your adolescent is beginning to own his faith:

1. He wants to discover more about God and what it means to belong to Him. The evidence: an interest in Bible reading, prayer, and asking questions.

*Caution*: This does not necessarily mean he does these things daily or with the rigor of a theologian.

2. She doesn't have to be nagged into being involved with other Christian teens.

*Caution*: This does not mean she has no complaints about church or youth group.

3. Given time, he can explain *in his own words* how he became a Christian and why he wants to live like one.

*Caution*: This is not the same as being able to repeat jargon like "I was saved." And if your teen's decision to receive Christ was made at a very early age, don't worry if he doesn't recall it. What matters are the ongoing decisions he's making to follow Him.

> *As parents, we need to distinguish between faith essentials and parental tastes.*

4. She shows an interest in what God might want as she plans for the future.

*Caution*: This does not mean she always knows what God's will is.

5. His views about how biblical principles should be applied sometimes differ from your own, or they are at least expressed in different ways.

*Caution*: This doesn't mean you're always arguing. It means your teen is starting to think independently about what it means to be a Christian.

That last point is a tough one. As parents, we need to distinguish between faith essentials and parental tastes, being sure to pass along the former and be flexible with the latter.

In *Ignite the Fire*, longtime youth worker Barry St. Clair told this story:

[A] dad called me one night. His anger made the phone rattle.

"John came home wearing an earring today," he said, seething.

"Is that a problem?" I asked.

"It's the worst thing he could have done, and I am kicking him out of the house," he replied in a loud voice.

"What's wrong with it?" I continued, knowing full well that it went against every fiber in his body. "Is it immoral, unethical, or illegal?" I asked.

"No, but it's not right!" His anger was still rising.

We talked through the issue. I tried to help him see that the earring was not the real issue, but *why* John wanted to wear it. He had a reason for it, and John's dad needed to discover it. I knew enough about the situation to understand that this dad had forced his views on his three boys for years in very demanding and unloving ways. It was the epitome of extrinsic motivation.

I explained to him, "God's grace is so much better. John needs to develop his own convictions through God's Word and the Holy Spirit, rather than your jamming them down his throat. This approach will motivate your son internally, causing him to want what God wants, and therefore what you want." This dad never got it, and he and his son are still estranged.[6]

Contrast that with the approach taken by Craig, a youth pastor. One day, after a Bible study on the teachings of Jesus, Craig was approached by Leon, a quiet 17-year-old from the group. Leon had been wrestling with Jesus' words about loving our enemies, and he had reached some conclusions. "I believe it's wrong for a Christian to kill," he said, "even if the government says to. I'm willing to die for my country, but not to kill for it."

Craig frowned but held his tongue. His personal conviction was that Christians could justifiably serve in the military and kill if ordered to do so. Most people in his church agreed. But he knew Leon was sincere; the boy had a habit of thinking for himself, usually after seriously considering what the Bible had to say.

Craig knew that Leon's conclusions about killing were based on the boy's reading of Scripture, not on defiance of it. Craig also knew that other believers had come to the same conclusions Leon had. So instead of berating Leon for taking the "wrong" position, Craig decided to keep the lines of communication open. "I may not agree with you," he finally told the young man, "but I believe you're sincere in your conviction."

Because Craig didn't insist on including military service in the list of faith essentials, his mentoring relationship with Leon was preserved. The two men maintained a friendship into adulthood, continuing to respect and challenge each other's convictions— and to appreciate the common ground they shared in Christ.

Christians sometimes disagree, of course, on where to draw the line between vital doctrines and matters of preference. Where should *you* draw that line with your teen? Here are five questions to ask yourself when you need to decide:

*1. Is my child's eternal destiny at stake here?* It's easy to forget, but the gospel boils down to a pretty simple statement: "Believe in the Lord Jesus, and you will be saved" (Acts 16:31).

*2. Am I upset because my teen is rejecting the Bible or because I feel rejected?* Is your child really discounting Scripture or just interpreting it in a way that differs from your own interpretation? Explain your position, but respect your teen's right to disagree— and try not to take it personally.

*3. Is this issue addressed in historic statements of what's essential in the Christian faith?* If not, it may be a matter of preference. For example, here is the Apostles' Creed:

> I believe in God, the Father almighty, creator of heaven and earth.
>
> I believe in Jesus Christ, His only Son, our Lord. He was conceived by the power of the Holy Spirit and born of the Virgin Mary. He suffered under Pontius Pilate, was crucified, died, and was buried. He descended into hell. On the third day He rose again. He ascended into heaven and is seated at the right hand of the Father. He will come again to judge the living and the dead.
>
> I believe in the Holy Spirit, the holy Christian

church, the communion of saints, the forgiveness of sins, the resurrection of the body, and the life everlasting.

*4. Is this worth risking our relationship?* Trying to force a teen to believe or behave can damage your ability to gain a hearing in the future. If the issue threatens a teen's safety, you might have to mark off boundaries and let the chips fall where they may. But if not, consider avoiding ultimatums in order to continue having a low-key, long-term influence.

*5. Do I need to leave this in God's hands?* When your teen seems headed in the wrong direction, anxiety and even panic are understandable. But sometimes it takes a hard knock to change a young person's mind, and administering those is best left to the One who does such things perfectly. Keep loving and praying for your teen. Like many adolescents, she may be tearing her faith apart in order to put it back together again in a form she can truly own.

## Prep Point 2: Give Kids Increasing Freedom to Make Choices

The second thing we can do to ready kids for independence is to let them make as many decisions as possible. It's great to help teens turn their beliefs into convictions, but we must go a step further and let them start *applying* those convictions, too.

That's what Andrew's parents did. One day their nervous son came to them, saying that social dancing would be the next subject in his P.E. class. Andrew's folks didn't dance. They had misgivings about the propriety of social dancing for Christians, but they also realized that others could reasonably disagree. They hadn't addressed the subject with Andrew yet, since it hadn't come up, though it was generally assumed in their church that Christians avoided the dance floor.

Now that the subject had to be addressed, they didn't panic. "It's up to you," they told their son. "You can learn to dance—or, if you personally feel it's wrong, we'll ask the school for permission to let you skip that part of the class."

As it turned out, Andrew chose to be excused from the dance lessons. But his parents would not have penalized him if he'd

■ ■ ■

## *Roots and Wings:*
## *Calculating the Risks of Freedom*

As Hodding Carter said, the two greatest gifts a parent can give a child are roots—and wings.

The parent who does a great job of providing roots can almost cancel the benefits of those roots by not giving the child wings. A young person who is confined or hovered over for too long can become a rebel or a grown-up invalid.

When my kids graduate from high school, I want them to be 100 percent free to do anything on earth that they want to do. That doesn't mean that if they do something irresponsible I won't step back in and correct them. But my goal is that, upon graduation, they'll have complete freedom. To give them that trust, I need to give them as many freedoms as they can succeed in during their adolescent years.

Whether the issue is making financial decisions, dating, or using the car or telephone, I have to calculate carefully the amount of freedom my kids can handle. Every day I have one visionary eye on what freedoms I can allow. It's like looking each day for something encouraging to say. When my child succeeds with one freedom, I know he or she is trustworthy in that area—and I can give a little more.

Sometimes, of course, kids fail with the freedoms we give them. For example, I increased the allowance of one of my children, adding the freedom to invest, to give to the church, to buy some things. As it turned out, the child wasn't ready for that freedom. So, for a period of months, that freedom was taken away. We worked through that for many hours each week, passing along financial planning skills and redeveloping appreciation for a dollar bill. Then the freedom returned.

Calculating "failure potential" has to be one of a good parent's greatest skills. It's pretty scary to allow your child to go into a situation where failure is likely. But he or she needs to experience failure sometimes, as long as the stakes aren't too high. For instance, there may be times when your teen wants to date a certain person, pierce an ear, or go to a certain movie. Your preference might be to say no. But by not fighting a losing battle, you may eventually win the war.

Here's an example. When my son was 16, he wanted to date a certain

*(DISCIPLING — vertical side tab)*

girl. I knew it wouldn't be a good relationship and that it probably wouldn't last long. But I also knew that she wasn't going to hurt him that badly. I knew his morals were in check, that he was firmly committed to virginity until marriage. So I didn't block him from dating this girl.

Sure enough, a couple of months later, the relationship went sour. We'd talk about it at bedtime, and at first my advice fell on pretty deaf ears. But when it was all over, he was able to say, "Yeah, everything you said kind of happened there. Sorry I was so hardheaded about that."

For both of us, it was a great learning and bonding experience. If I'd thought the girl would have taken away his virginity, I wouldn't have let him fail that badly. But I was able to give him the freedom to make that dating choice, even though it wasn't a good choice. Sometimes you've got to take a calculated risk.

(The end of that story, by the way, is worth telling. As my son and I discussed—in long, nightly visits—how he should handle the relationship, he gradually developed a friendship with the girl. And that friendship eventually led the girl to Christ. Today she's a shining light for God.)

According to some estimates, about 60 percent of Christian kids abandon their faith when they go to college and are completely on their own. Why? I think one reason is that many of them were raised in homes where freedom was not allowed to grow, to be trained, to flourish. As long as a child displays responsibility equal to the freedoms given, freedom is a good thing. When responsibility shuts down, the freedoms must shut down. When responsibility increases—whether it's displayed through good grades or a good attitude at home or making good choices—the freedoms should increase.

—Joe White

DISCIPLING

---

decided to participate. By letting him choose, they gave him the chance to exercise decision-making muscles he'd need to use for the rest of his life.

"But it's risky to let kids make choices," you might say. And you'd be right. Our teens will never truly grow up unless we take those risks, however. The key is to minimize the risks.

How? Dean Merrill recommends finding safe settings in which to use what he calls the "Two Magic Words of Parenting": "You decide." He wrote:

Not everything is a safe setting, of course. Not every decision can be handed over to a young person. You would never say "You decide" about whether to drop out of school, for example, or whether to drink.

But in hundreds of other matters, where in fact you can live with either option, parents can avoid tumultuous battles and teach responsibility for the future by handing over the power of choice. Granted, your adult wisdom says one option is better than the other, but neither one is disastrous. So why not let the child learn something along the way?

Merrill went on to recall the time when his ninth-grade twin daughters begged to attend a birthday party that wouldn't end until midnight. The problem was that the girls were supposed to leave the morning after the party for an important all-day music competition. Merrill was tempted to say no, but he wondered whether the girls might be able to understand what was at stake.

> "Okay," I announced the next morning at breakfast, "you can go to the party tonight. I'll even drive you and pick you up. But you might want to think about how hard you've worked the past three months to get ready for this competition. Do you want to jeopardize it? How late would you choose to stay?"
>
> "How late *can* we stay?" Rhonda asked, putting the onus back on me.
>
> "You tell me," I replied, refusing to take her bait. "If you were on your own, and I was out of the picture, when would you leave the party in order not to be dog-tired for Saturday?"
>
> They looked at each other. One girl said 9:30. The other said 10. Suddenly this wasn't a case of what Dad would allow, but rather what was in their own self-interest. Hmmm . . . then came the most amazing lines of all:
>
> "I don't think I want to go to the party."
>
> "I don't either."
>
> Problem solved—and no fight![7]

■ ■ ■

## *A Matter of Trust: Appealing to God's Spirit in Your Teen*

[Many] parents don't trust their children with God or God with their children, particularly in their teen years. Without trust, the only option is to establish a rule for every situation. How many rules will we need? We don't have enough paper to write them all down.

Yet through grace, we trust God with our children and our children with God. For example, let's say you believe in Christ, as does your eighth-grade son. In that case . . .

- Does the Holy Spirit live in you? (Yes.)
- Does the Holy Spirit live in your eighth-grader? (We could debate if eighth-graders have souls! Just kidding. Yes.)
- Then why do you play the role of Holy Spirit and tell your eighth-grader everything to do? What to wear? Who to have as friends? What to believe?

Before you think we've gotten weird, stick with us. If the Holy Spirit lives in you . . . and your child, can't the same Holy Spirit speak to both of you? "He's not mature enough to hear," you protest. Tell that to Joseph, Samuel, David, and other young men in the Old Testament. Because "God is no respecter of persons," why can't you trust God to work in your child's life, as you expect Him to work in yours?

Catch this point because it is the heart of intrinsic motivation. From early on you want your children to respond to God. How can they do that if you always tell them what to do? Can we relate to our children in a way that helps them discover for themselves what God wants them to do? This doesn't mean we don't discipline our children. . . . But it does mean that the focus of our discipline, rules, conversation, and all other ways we relate to our children is teaching them how to hear the voice of God, rather than just following our directives. If we trust the Holy Spirit who lives in their embryonic human spirit and appeal to Him, then over time and experience God will make them "strong in spirit" like John the Baptist—the person Jesus described as the greatest human who ever lived (Luke 7:28).

Our goal, therefore, is intrinsic motivation that causes our children to become "strong in spirit." Then they will possess the inner convictions to make the Spirit-led decisions in any moral, social, and spiritual climate.

—From *Ignite the Fire*, by Barry and Carol St. Clair[8]

DISCIPLING

Call it *empowerment* if you like. That's the $50 word for letting your kids make safe but significant choices. If we want our teens to make sound decisions when they're out of the nest, they need to hear us say "You decide" as often as possible while they're still under our wings.

### Prep Point 3: Give Kids Increasing Responsibility

The third way to prepare teens for independence is to hand them more responsibility. This means taking off the spiritual training wheels and letting kids pedal the straight and narrow for themselves, even if the ride is a bit wobbly.

Many of us tend to expect less of our children than they're capable of, especially when it comes to spiritual things. Rob, an eighth grader, is expected to practice the piano every day—but his parents wouldn't dream of asking him to commit to regular prayer or Bible reading. Candace, a high school junior, is a standout speech team member—but her folks assume that "giving her testimony" in church would be just too intimidating.

> *Many of us tend to expect less of our children than they're capable of, especially when it comes to spiritual things.*

Joe White, in *FaithTraining*, suggests that kids take on the following responsibilities at approximately the following ages:

*Age 12*—Regular youth group attendance
*Age 13.5*—Daily quiet times
*Age 14*—Small, peer-group Bible study
*Age 15*—Lifestyle witnessing to friends
*Age 17*—Intellectual preparation (apologetics, etc.) for college
*Age 18*—Summer missionary trip or serving/giving job.[9]

No two children are alike, of course; all mature at different rates. Some young people struggle with certain tasks because of personality, disability, or emotional trauma and should not be expected to achieve as others can.

DISCIPLING

A lot of us might be surprised, however, at what teenagers can do. Following the 1999 Columbine High School shootings in Colorado, many young people were galvanized into living their faith in a new way. At Sapulpa High School near Tulsa, Oklahoma, for instance, a group of Christian students delivered an impromptu evangelistic message in the lunchroom, after which five kids declared faith in Christ. Hundreds of student-led prayer groups sprang up throughout America, some aided by ministries like Revival Generation, which was founded by teenager Josh Weidmann.

Tom Gill, a student at Tulsa's Victory Bible Institute who worked for three years with the youth mission organization Teen Mania, told *World* magazine: "Teenagers have something no other part of the church body does. It's something like Timothy had— they aren't willing to believe there's something they can't do. Tell a teen he can't dye his hair green and he'll say, 'Yeah, right.' If there's a Christian teen seeking the heart of God, there's nothing that's going to stop him."[10]

### Areas of Teen Responsibility

Your teen may not be on the verge of founding a parachurch organization, but might she be ready to take on more spiritual responsibility? After all, it won't be long before she is *totally* responsible for everything from church attendance to stewardship. Why not start transferring accountability now, while you can still lend a guiding hand?

Here are five areas in which most teens can begin to take responsibility:

*1. Their relationship with God.* When children are young, some parents try to act as middle men in their little ones' link with the Lord. By adolescence, if not long before, kids need to understand that their connection with God is direct. Explain to your teen that God wants to relate to him in a one-of-a-kind way. Most teens can appreciate the idea that their relationship with God is private, not to be intruded upon by parents or anyone else. Taking responsibility for that one-to-one relationship includes keeping the lines open by confessing sin, learning more about what God is like, and growing sensitive to the Holy Spirit's direction.

DISCIPLING

■ ■ ■

## A Good Rap:
## Letting Teens Take the Lead

It must have been God's sense of humor that led Him to saddle me with a Sunday school class of four teenage boys. They were my dedicated physical therapists, stretching and pummeling me each week—destroying any illusion of control this longtime perfectionist might have harbored.

In the midst of this chaos, I went to a youth work seminar. There I heard that teens should be put in charge more often. "Student leadership," they called it.

*A terrible idea,* I thought.

But I couldn't stand being behind the times. So I decided to try a project, something small. Our class would study the Book of James and create a rap song about it. Maybe we could even perform it in church on a Sunday night—if it met my quality standards, of course.

The following week, we started studying James. I taught in the usual way, then read aloud two rap stanzas I'd written as a model. I asked the kids to write their verses during the week, then waited.

Seven days later, Joel brought a few lines and read them shyly. The meter was a little out of kilter, but the message was fine. Dan, on the other hand, had forgotten the assignment. Adam and Matt weren't even there.

I sighed. At this rate, it would take years to finish. I wanted to forget that wild let-them-do-it theory, but it was too late to back out.

Week after week, we kept studying and summarizing, and sometimes the kids would bring from home stanzas they'd scribbled on scraps of paper. At a glacial pace, something resembling a rap began to take shape.

When I asked our pastor's wife and worship planner if we might be allowed to perform the rap some Sunday night, she said yes—and rashly suggested that we do it on Sunday *morning* when the whole church would be there.

When I told the boys we were slated to perform, their eyes grew wide. They looked as if their only remaining choices were between the electric chair and lethal injection.

"No way!" declared Matt. Maybe he'd carry the boom box, he said, but that was it. The rest of us pressed on reluctantly.

Gathering all those slips of paper, I tapped their contents into my computer, resisting the urge to rewrite. Then we started practicing. Rhythms stumbled, words were mumbled, and inflections got stuck in monotone. The more we practiced, the worse it seemed to get.

*It would be so easy to fix,* I thought. *I'd only have to tell the kids how to say each word, each line, each verse.* But no, this project was supposed to be their own, thanks to those know-it-all youth experts.

Two weeks before Armageddon, Matt decided he wanted to join the group after all. It didn't help.

The big morning hit like a cold shower. We were all on the verge of nervous breakdowns. We waited in the hall next to the church platform—five pairs of lungs breathing shallowly, five pairs of eyes darting at the clock and the mirror, five pairs of sweaty hands fingering sunglasses and baseball caps and the fake dollar bills that were our props.

Suddenly it was time, and I led the Gang of Four onto the stage. This was it, the moment we'd been hurtling toward for three months.

The first turn at the mike was mine. Then came Joel, Dan, Adam, and Matt.

We rapped about hypocrisy and helping widows and orphans, faith and works, selfishness and bitterness, resisting the devil and praying for the sick. There were 17 stanzas in all, and we delivered them perfectly.

Well, not perfectly. Some of us were a bit hard to understand. Some of us seemed unaware that a tape was being played in the background, a tape that was in some way related to our presentation.

But none of that was of the slightest consequence. My guys had done it. My brilliant, exasperating foursome had studied some of the most pointed passages in God's Word and come up with their own way of expressing it. And now they were up here, rapping their hammering hearts out in front of the whole church. I listened, and a wave of pride swept over me—turning to humility by the time I thought about it.

We reached the last word of the last line, and applause exploded from one wall of the sanctuary to the other. It lingered loudly as we made our way off the platform and into the hall.

**DISCIPLING**

Breathless, I turned to look into the faces of those young men. There I saw the kind of light that comes only when you've struck the match yourself.

"That was awesome!" whispered one.

"Let's do it again!" hissed another.

"Let's take it on the road!" said a third.

I had a terrible time paying attention to the rest of the service. But maybe I'd already learned enough for one day.

—John Duckworth, adapted from
*Just for a Moment I Saw the Light*[11]

---

*2. Spiritual disciplines.* Prayer, Bible reading and memorization, giving to the Lord's work—all these are activities most teens can handle. Encourage your adolescent to set her own goals in these areas; then go over the goals together, offering advice if needed.

*3. Church involvement.* Some teens can't stand to miss a single youth group meeting, Bible study, or retreat. Others would rather be skinned alive than darken a church door. You may want to set a minimum requirement for church attendance, but give your teen options beyond that point. For instance, let him choose to attend Sunday school *or* a small discipleship group; allow her to pick youth choir *or* the church softball team. If your church's youth program isn't particularly strong and your teen wants to be part of the group a friend attends, let it happen. Kids who are forced to attend programs they loathe are prone to abandon church when they're on their own; kids who develop positive associations with church and a habit of regular, voluntary attendance are more likely to continue the practice.

*4. Living their faith.* When our children are small, we may try to help them resist temptation by hiding the cookie jar. We may try to minimize peer pressure by barring certain friendships. We may try to encourage gratitude by ordering kids to say "thank you" to Grandma and Grandpa on the phone. But we won't be able to do any of those things when our teens leave the nest. Adolescents need to know that saying no to wrong and yes to right is up to them. Our job is to make sure they have equipment for the former (like the whole armor of God described in Ephesians 6:10-18) and opportunities for the latter (like mission trips and service projects).

**DISCIPLING**

*5. Finding answers to their questions.* It feels good to be the fount of wisdom when our preteens come to us, wide-eyed and trusting, with their queries. In adolescence, however, those wide eyes tend to narrow considerably. Fortunately, teens need to practice answer-hunting anyway. Instead of playing oracle, point your child toward helpful books, pamphlets, and Web sites (see the resource list in appendix B). For example, a guy who's questioning the existence of absolute truth could find answers in a book like *My Truth, Your Truth, Whose Truth?* by Randy Petersen (Tyndale/Focus on the Family, 2000). A girl who's wondering which movies are acceptable might check out www.pluggedinmag.com on the Web.

### Tips for Encouraging Teen Responsibility

"All of that *sounds* good," you might say. "But how do I get my son or daughter to take on responsibility?" Here are four suggestions:

*1. Let God be the motivator.* As Tom Gill put it, "If there's a Christian teen seeking the heart of God, there's nothing that's going to stop him." If your teen *doesn't* care what God wants, you can't expect him to shoulder more responsibility. First work on helping him to own his faith.

*2. Offer the responsibility as a recognition of maturity.* Adolescents don't want more chores; they want to be recognized as grown up and to have the freedom they think comes with that status. Instead of presenting new responsibilities as a "to do" list, emphasize that your teen has earned the privilege of doing these things for herself—and the freedom to do them in her own way.

*3. Show how it's done.* It's unlikely that your teen will take on responsibilities you've neglected yourself. If necessary, work together on learning to pray, to study and memorize the Bible, to share your faith, and to deal with doubts.

*4. Let it be done imperfectly.* Once you've handed over a responsibility, resist the urge to grab it back. Your teen will make mistakes, but that's part of the learning process. If 16-year-old Allen wants to tithe 5 percent instead of 10, challenge him to think about his reasons in the light of Scripture, but don't divvy up his allowance for him. If 13-year-old Desiree quits reading a "boring" devotional book halfway through, help her find a better one instead of nagging her to finish the one she doesn't like.

**DISCIPLING**

■ ■ ■

## *Hola, Joey!*
## *A Transforming Mission Trip*

I will never forget how Mexico changed Joey. All I knew about him was that he was the tall, withdrawn kid who rarely came to our youth group. But when it came time to train for our Easter Mexico Mission, he came alive!

I was stunned. Normally, Joey was so timid, he would be afraid to lead out in silent prayer!

I gave him a ride home one Sunday after the training and ventured this question: "Joey, I need a strong guy to help with the set-up team. It is dirty work with a lot of sweat, frustration, and tension. You have to go down early and set up the camp. Your job is to have all of the problems fixed, so that when we get there with the rest of the team, everything works. Are you interested?"

"Yeah, count me in. Do you need help getting the equipment?"

I couldn't believe my ears. My biggest frustration with our annual trip had been obtaining and organizing the equipment. *What a relief to have someone offer to help!* "Sure. Do you have time?"

"What else would I do?"

"Don't you have homework or something else around here?" I gestured to his house as we sat parked in his driveway.

"Nope. My mom is never home. I don't do homework, and I really don't have that much to do around here."

Joey offered to organize the equipment. He even offered to get some new stuff on his own. "Leave it to me. It will be ready."

I had never left a responsibility this large in the hands of a 16 year old.

When we arrived in Mexico, our camp was perfect. Joey and his set-up team had done an excellent job. The generator was running. The tents were neatly pitched. We had plenty of light and water. Everything was in order. Even the set-up team looked relaxed and clean!

When we began work in our village, Joey instantly became a hero to the Mexican boys. He played volleyball and soccer with them. After lunch, he wrestled with them, gave them piggyback rides, teased them, and bought them sodas. He did all of this using the three words of Spanish he knew: *hola* (hello), *adios* (good-bye), and *andale* (run). Joey didn't need Spanish; he had learned the language of love.

At the end of the day, Joey would collapse in his lawn chair, looking completely drained. I have never seen anyone so tired and yet so alive at the same time. Mexico changed Joey.

What happened to Joey? What changed him so radically? Before Mexico, he had no real purpose to his life. No one really needed him to do anything. His mom was divorced and kept busy at work. Joey had no brothers or sisters. He would spend hours at home alone.

Joey came alive in Mexico because he discovered purpose in what he was doing. He realized that maybe for the first time in his life he was making a difference. For the first time in 16 years, he was doing something meaningful.

—Tim Smith, *Life Skills for Guys*[12]

---

## Sending Strong Kids to College

Brian's first night at college was an eye-opener.

Arriving on campus, he stared at the red-brick buildings and yellow-orange leaves of the oak trees. The place looked exactly as a college should, he thought—distinguished, stately. No doubt it would be a safe place for a guy who'd been raised in the church.

After all, the school had been founded by Christian missionaries a century before. It was still affiliated with a church denomination—not Brian's, but one that sounded okay. Brian knew that not every student would be a Christian, but he figured things would be less out of control than at the state universities.

After stowing his belongings in his dorm room, Brian ate at the commons. Glancing at the freshman orientation brochure he'd received in the mail, he noticed that a movie was about to be shown in the chapel. *Greetings*, it was called.

*Must be a welcome-to-the-college film*, he thought. Not having anything else to do, he headed across the darkening campus.

*Wow*, he thought when he stepped into the chapel. It was impressive—an auditorium, really. Big enough to hold the entire student body, it featured a stage at the front. The rich, purple curtains were parted, and Brian gazed between them at the focal point of the room: a massive pipe organ that spanned the entire wall. The gleaming metal pipes, arranged from stout bass to slender treble,

**DISCIPLING**

shot heavenward. As Brian sat down, it wasn't hard to imagine the organ thundering a rendition of "A Mighty Fortress Is Our God."

The crowd was small as the lights dimmed and a silvery screen descended from the ceiling. A projector in the balcony flickered to life, and the movie began.

> **When our teens go off to college, they're often entering a world where the old rules don't seem to apply.**

It soon became evident that *Greetings* was not a reference to welcoming new students. The film was a satire about the military draft. Brian watched with interest, but soon his interest turned to shock. His ears burned at the vulgar language. His eyes widened as the movie's first nude scene began.

He swallowed. He could still see glints of the organ pipes flanking the screen. *This is a chapel*, he thought, his head swimming. *What kind of college is this? What have I gotten myself into?*

During the months that followed, Brian would have many occasions to ask himself questions like that. There was the night his dorm sponsored its first "kegger," where underage students drank themselves into a stupor. And there was the morning his biology professor lauded a visiting abortionist as a hero. It wasn't long before Brian realized that, like Dorothy in *The Wizard of Oz*, he wasn't in Kansas anymore.

**DISCIPLING**

## Teens' "Things I Wish My Parents Had Done Differently," Part 8

■ "Summed up in one word—intentional. I wish they would have taught me the truth instead of taking me to church and just disciplining me when necessary. By my teenage years, I learned to stay out of trouble, not necessarily to do what was right."

■ "To be more intentional in practicing what they said they believed. They could also have listened to me more. If they had listened, I might talk with them more now."

■ "The most important thing my parents could have done (and could still do) would be to be real with their relationship and to lead by example. I would

Brian's story may send a few chills down our spines, but his experience is hardly unique. When our teens go off to college, they're often entering a world where the old rules don't seem to apply. Many Christian parents fear what might happen when college commences—and not without reason.

Take Janet, who was raised in a conservative church. She chafed at some of her parents' rules—no card playing, no movies except select Disney films. She was embarrassed by her mother's habit of evangelizing pedestrians by tossing cellophane-wrapped tracts out the windows of the family car.

But Janet truly believed the basics of the faith. When two girls in her youth group became pregnant out of wedlock, Janet was shocked. She determined to be "really good" and show the older folks that not all of her generation was going astray—that teenagers really could be good Christians.

When she went away to a Christian college, however, things began to fall apart. She'd never encountered subjects like psychology, sociology, and anthropology. Even though her professors tried to present those subjects through a biblical lens, she found the views of non-Christian pioneers in those fields to be more compelling. She started reading the novels of Ayn Rand, who believed religion was a mind-closing experience. That made sense to Janet, who felt that the church had kept her from learning about the wider world.

**DISCIPLING**

have loved to see them praying and studying the Word of God regularly. Knowing that their relationship with Christ was important to them would have helped me to see the need for an active relationship in my life."

- "I wish they had acted out their spirituality as I was growing up. Now I am seeing a humility and spiritual growth within my parents like never before, but when I was younger, I learned a lot by what they said, not so much by what they did."

- "Held me more accountable during my relationships with guys."

When Janet was a sophomore, a speaker with a reputation as a Christian intellectual came to chapel. His arguments against atheism were weak and hypocritical, she thought. As she left chapel that day, she had what she would later call an "unconversion experience." From that moment, religion made less and less sense to her.

It took a couple of years for her to drop her faith completely. Today, more than 20 years later, she considers herself an atheist.[13]

The cases of Brian and Janet raise a question for those of us whose teens are college-bound: How can we, as spiritual mentors, prepare our kids for what may well be the hostile environment of higher education?

## Making the Break

Using the transition from high school to college as an opportunity to leave the church is nothing new. Many adolescents seize graduation, a first job, or marriage as a chance to break with childhood, and religious activities are often the first to go. As researcher George Barna points out in *Generation Next*:

> The bad news is that many teenagers, having been exposed to and been participants in the teaching, worship, study, prayer, and other central activities of the Christian church, are already making their getaway plans. They have given the church a fair shot at convincing them to stay. Their exposure to the church in action, however, has led millions of them to choose to end their interaction with institutional Christianity once they have the freedom to do so.[14]

That was the case with Brian, whose initial shock over his secularized campus faded. He didn't join the keg party drinkers or the professor who stumped for abortion rights, but he did stop attending church. He didn't participate in student groups like Fellowship of Christian Athletes or Campus Crusade, either. The truth was that he'd been itching to get away from church for some time, having had to attend all his life without being especially enthused about it. Without a strong motivation, hunting for a church or forming new relationships in a student fellowship didn't seem worth the effort.

Do our college-bound teens have to turn out like Brian and Janet, rejecting to varying degrees the spiritual values and practices we've tried to pass on to them? Not at all. To find out how to encourage a more positive outcome, let's see how these teens could have been better prepared for collegiate challenges.

1. *Brian needed to know more in advance about college life.* The first in his family to attend college, he had only vague ideas about dorm living, study habits, and the temptations he might face. Had Brian or his parents arranged a conversation with a college student or graduate, preferably an alumnus of his chosen alma mater, he could have avoided the culture shock that made him feel isolated and intimidated.

2. *Brian and his parents needed to investigate his choice of schools more thoroughly.* They chose it primarily because financial aid was offered and because it was only 40 miles from home. After Brian started attending, they were surprised to discover that, despite the college's denominational ties, there were no regular chapel services, no chaplain on staff, and no enforcement of laws against drinking and drugs. Asking questions not addressed in the glossy college catalog might have led Brian and his parents to consider a different school.

3. *Brian needed more positive church experiences before he left the nest.* His lack of enthusiasm about the church made him a prime candidate to drop his involvement in it. Plugging into a vibrant congregation near the campus or joining a close-knit student fellowship might have nurtured him spiritually, socially, and emotionally. But previous church experience told him that "vibrant" and "close-knit" were words that didn't apply to Christian groups. Had his parents encouraged him in early adolescence to be honest about his dissatisfaction, and had they given him the freedom to try other youth programs, he might have made the effort to continue the connection at college.

4. *Janet needed earlier exposure to non-Christian worldviews.* She'd never heard of Freud's teachings, much less studied them. She hadn't been encouraged to think through the claims of other religions. She

DISCIPLING

knew her church disagreed with evolution, but she hadn't wrestled with the reasoning of evolutionists themselves. While her parents and youth leaders couldn't have covered every philosophical base, they could have honestly presented some opposing views and given Janet permission to consider them for herself while she was still there to ask questions.

5. *Janet needed someone to talk to about her struggles.* Once she began to doubt, she did so alone. There was no sympathetic ear, no one to reassure her that her feelings were normal. Perhaps she could have found such a mentor among her professors, but her parents and church had given her the impression that doubt was a dirty secret. It seemed that all her life she had been told what to do—and been told that she should not challenge those instructions. Had her parents and teachers welcomed queries instead of judging them, she might have felt comfortable enough to share her turmoil.

6. *Janet needed a defense that made sense.* When the visiting chapel speaker failed to "prove" Christianity to her satisfaction, Janet had no "proof" of her own to fall back on. Different people are convinced by different lines of reasoning; if Janet had heard a variety of pro-faith arguments while still in high school, she could have chosen those that resonated with her. Instead, she found a flaw in the speaker's approach and concluded that the problem was with Christianity itself.

As the story of Janet illustrates, teenagers *must* have a chance to challenge church teachings as thoroughly and as early as possible. George Barna explained why in *Generation Next*:

> We have noted that as teenagers age, they have a greater tendency to use their brains. The older they get, the less accepting they are of rules and imposed truths. . . .
>
> This is a generation that requires the ability to start its evaluation of Christianity by denying or rejecting its principles before entering into a sincere consideration of those truths. This group studies something not by reading and memorizing, but through debate and searching for examples of the principle in real life. Many of these teens never get that far in the process, because they feel

that those who profess to define Christianity are too closed-minded to allow for an honest debate and examination of the guts of Christianity.

The sense of many teens is that after the games and good times have ended, and the real discovery process is initiated, the defenders of the Christian faith take a "this is it, take it or leave it" attitude, prohibiting the necessary verbal jousting. Consequently, they contend that they are given insufficient latitude to subject the Christian faith to deep and intense scrutiny. Disallowing such a serious challenge is their clue that Christianity is not the meaty, resilient faith it had been cracked up to be. Sensing that the line has been drawn in the sand, they simply turn around and move in a different direction, seeking new spiritual horizons to examine.[15]

## Forming Faithful Freshmen

When kids are spiritually prepared for college, however, the picture is much brighter. Consider this recollection by Joe White:

No Disney movie . . . holds a candle to the excitement I felt the spring after Jamie's freshman year in college when that same little girl whose diapers have turned into blue jeans and whose "goo-goos" are now college English themes dove onto our king-sized bed and recounted with fulfillment the highlight of her week. God's grace had allowed her to lead her best friend back to a daily walk with Jesus Christ after a four-year detour! If that wasn't enough, I about fell over dead when I heard her on the phone counseling some notoriously wild football player toward his own pilgrimage with the Savior.

You bet we struggled through junior high.

We cried a million tears.

We shared the sting of corrective discipline.

We embraced the emptiness of chronic rejection.

But by God's grace, faith went to college the fall before. Faith left home and moved 600 miles to Texas.[16]

DISCIPLING

When Barry St. Clair's teens went to college, they, too, remained faithful. As reported in *Ignite the Fire,* son Scott went to Duke University, where he joined a fraternity with the express purpose of telling frat brothers about Jesus. For the next four years, Scott did just that, and several of his friends became Christians. Shortly before graduation, at a meeting of the fraternity, Scott's roommate stood and said, "One thing I have known about Scott is that he loved me. He is the only person I know who has stood for his religious convictions and has not compromised."

Barry's daughter Katie attended Furman University. During her sophomore and junior years, she lived in a freshman hall in order to share her faith with the girls. Some of those girls went on to lead discipleship groups of their own. Katie's brother Jonathan joined a fraternity at Furman in order to let the light of Jesus shine there, too.[17]

Your own college-bound teen's story will be unique. He will make choices over which you have no control and for which he will bear responsibility. But that story is likely to be more like Scott's and Katie's and Jonathan's, and less like Brian's and Janet's, if you get ready for college in the following ways:

*1. Let your teen know that your family is rooting for her.* Chris, a teenage caller to the *Life on the Edge LIVE!* radio show, had this exchange with cohost Joe White:

> *Joe:* How . . . do you keep your faith foremost in your life?
> *Chris:* Well, Joe, I'd have to say that my family is a really big part of that. They're behind me 100 percent in pretty much everything I do, including my walk with Christ. My whole family, we are all believers in Christ—and they help me immensely in my walk with Jesus Christ.

> *When giving your student a college send-off, remember to include pledges of spiritual support.*

Things can get lonely when you're a student. Knowing that family members are thinking of you and praying for you helps you feel less outnumbered. When giving your student a college send-off, remember to include pledges of spiritual support.

Communicate your family's continuing solidarity through E-mail, phone calls, and notes.

2. *Be the kind of parent your child can run to.* In the same *Life on the Edge LIVE!* conversation, caller Chris explained why he wanted to honor his Christian upbringing:

> Well, "obey your father and your mother." It's the most important thing that I can think of. . . . If you're not obeying your mother and your father, then who are you going to run to? I mean, you can run to God and you can get comfort from Him, but God is just going to tell you to run back to your parents and mend those open wounds. . . . [Our parents] have taken care of us. They love us. And I don't see why anybody would want to stray away from their parents. I love mine to death, and I would do anything for them.

3. *Prepare for the debate.* Your teen's faith will be challenged during the next few years—guaranteed. The challenges may be issued by an agnostic professor, a skeptical coworker, or the disappointment of a broken romance. Just as political candidates stage "dry runs" with stand-in opponents to get ready for debates, you can bring up tough questions in advance and seek answers together. See the "Christian Worldview" section of this book (chapter 19) and the resource list (appendix B) for further help.

4. *Make the church hunt as easy as possible.* Don't try to pick your teen's college-town church for her, but make the search simpler. Look together at Yellow Pages and newspaper church listings for the area. If possible, visit one or more congregations near the campus. Ask friends for recommendations. Encourage your teen to make a list of possibilities; call them and get campus-to-church directions. If she wants to try different denominations from the one(s) she grew up in, don't stand in the way. The important thing is that she finds a place to grow and be supported.

5. *Pray.* You'll probably be doing a lot of this when your teen is off on his own. You may as well start now!

When you're a Christian parent, sending your teen to college can be a scary proposition. Kids' spiritual journeys can take some

DISCIPLING

■ ■ ■

## Connections:
## Helping Kids Stay True at College

*J. Budziszewski, author of* How to Stay Christian in College *(NavPress, 1999), teaches government and philosophy at the University of Texas in Austin. This conversation he had with a doubting Christian student illustrates the importance of helping teens stay connected to the church—in their own way.*

"Let me make sure I understand you. You admit that you have no intellectual grounds for disbelief."

"Right."

"Absolutely none."

"None."

"But disbelief is creeping up on you anyway."

"Yes."

"As though a cloud of unbelief had simply drifted over you and begun to descend."

"Yes, that's just what it's like."

I realized that he was as puzzled as I was. No wonder he had been willing to seek out a perfect stranger. . . .

"Have you been made to feel ridiculous for being a Christian? I suppose you've noticed that it isn't 'politically correct.' "

"I know about that, but it hasn't affected me personally."

"No snide comments about Christianity from teachers or from friends? No sneers? Not even any raised eyebrows?"

"With the people I know, it just doesn't come up."

Belatedly, an indicator light had begun to flicker in my mind. "Why doesn't it?"

"It just—doesn't. It's not discussed."

"Do you have any friends you can talk over Christian things with?"

"Not really."

"Do you have a church where you worship regularly?"

"I used to, but I wasn't comfortable with the church I was brought up in, and I haven't kept it up."

"Why weren't you comfortable? Did you disagree with what you were taught? Did the people give you a hard time?"

"No, I agreed with everything taught there, and they were good Christian people. And I know I'm no better. But the worship was—well—too noisy somehow. I wanted to sit still and think about God. The worship made it hard to sense His holiness. Do you know what I mean?"

"Yes, I came to feel that way about the church of my childhood too. But there are lots of different kinds of churches. Some worship by 'making a joyful noise unto the Lord,' others by 'being still and knowing that He is God.' Have you tried looking around for another church?"

"No."

"Are you a part of any Christian student group here on campus?"

"No."

"Do you know any other Christians here at the university?"

"I don't think so. Or if they are Christian, they haven't said so."

The indicator light had stopped flickering and was shining steadily. "I think I may know the solution to the mystery."

"Do you mean why the cloud of unbelief is descending on me?"

"Yes. Tell me if this makes sense to you."

"Go ahead."

"I'm guessing that even though you didn't quite fit in at your old church, you and your family and your church were all pretty close."

"Oh, yes."

"So you saw the Christian life being enacted all around you."

"Sure."

"But here at the university, that's all gone, isn't it? You've lost your spiritual support network. I suspect that the reason why the Resurrection of Christ has come to seem unreal to you is that the Christian life had already come to be unreal for you."

"Is that so important? I try to live like a Christian."

"What do you think? Jesus gathered disciples, and He sent them out two by two. Paul founded churches, and said the Church is the Body of Christ. The author of Hebrews said 'Let us not give up meeting together, as some are in the habit of doing, but let us encourage one another.' "

He considered for a moment. "That makes sense."

"Sure it does. Even quiet people like you are social beings. God just made you to be social quietly. You have friends; well, you need spiritual friends, faith-partners."

"Where would I find them?"

"Join a student Christian fellowship to find Christians who are like you. And join a church to find Christians who aren't like you."

"Can you suggest any?"

"I've always wanted to write out a prescription," I said. On a slip I jotted the names of some healthy churches and student fellowships, being sure to include several "quiet" ones. Then I added the titles of a few good books, like Lewis's *Mere Christianity* and Stott's *Basic Christianity.* Finally I scribbled in the web address of an article on the Resurrection. Handing it over, I said, "If you *want* to get out from under the cloud of unbelief, I think this will help you."

He took it and shook my hand. "Thanks."

"Will you visit me later to tell me how your faith is doing?"

"Yes," he promised, and he was gone.

—From "Cloud of Unbelief" by J. Budziszewski[18]

unsettling turns within those ivied halls. But there's hope. Even Brian, who studiously avoided Christian fellowship for all four of his years at that secularized college, returned to church after graduating. He went on to a career in Christian ministry, much to the relief of his mom and dad.

But he still blushes when he sees one of those pipe organs.

# Finding Time to Train Your Teen

Do you grow impatient while waiting for the microwave to heat your leftovers? Do you mutter at the ATM to "hurry up" and dispense your cash? Do you fidget while your computer shoots an E-mail around the world? Do you look for ways to prepare Minute Rice more quickly?

If so, you've probably succumbed to our society's "need for speed." There's no doubt our culture is fixated on fastness, addicted to acceleration, hooked on haste. As physician and social analyst Richard Swenson pointed out:

> To understand how a society experiences time, you need only listen to the vocabulary of its members. As Americans, our sentences are peppered with words such as *time crunch, fast food, rush hour, frequent flyer, expressway, overnight delivery*, and *rapid transit*.
>
> What's more, the products and services we use attest to our addiction to hurry: We send packages by Federal Express, use a long-distance company called Sprint, manage our personal finances on Quicken, schedule our appointments using a Day Runner, diet with SlimFast, and swim in trunks made by Speedo.[1]

If you are one of those parents hurtling through hyperspace, going a mile a minute, hitting the highway full-throttle, we've got news for you: There are no shortcuts to mentoring God-loving and God-serving kids. It takes time—a steady, consistent, deliberate investment of your time. It takes long hours of sitting on your daughter's bed, listening as she tells you every detail of her day. It takes long hours at the café with your son, making small talk until he's ready to open up. What we said in chapter nine bears repeating: Kids of all ages spell love T-I-M-E.

> *There are no short-cuts to mentoring God-loving and God-serving kids.*

All this talk about time brings us to this bull's-eye issue: Just as building a great relationship with your teen requires a consistent investment of your time, so also your teen's spiritual development largely depends on your care, attention, involvement —and time. Sure, youth pastors, mentors, coaches, teachers, and camp counselors may contribute to your child's spiritual growth throughout the adolescent and pre-adult years. But there is simply no substitute for Mom and Dad as chief encouragers, supporters, advocates, motivators, and cheerleaders for your teen's spiritual life.

If you're feeling panicky, already mentally rearranging your calendar and Day-Timer, take heart: Nurturing your child's faith is one of the most important investments you'll make in your entire life—and it's an investment that will reap huge dividends.

### "Train Up Your Child in the Way He Should Go—in Just One Minute a Week!"

The above line is meant as a joke (you knew that, right?). After all, our society has become as enamored with quick fixes and easy solutions as it has with speed. Bookstore shelves are crammed with titles such as *Five Simple Ways to Revolutionize Your Life* and *The 30-Second-a-Day Prayer Warrior*. We see flyers posted on telephone poles that read "Lose 20 Pounds in 10 Days!" or "Earn $60,000 a Year Stuffing Envelopes in Your Spare Time."

Unfortunately, some parents let this easy-does-it, don't-break-a-sweat mind-set influence the spiritual training of their children.

They figure they're doing okay if they ask a question or two about "spiritual things" sometime during the week.

The scene: Family riding home from church on Sunday at noon. Dad turns down the radio (he checked the score—his team is winning) and says, "Well, Scott, what did ya think of Pastor Jim's sermon?"

Scott, who was daydreaming about that cute new girl in youth group, replies, "Huh? Oh, pretty good, I guess. I liked his story about the paratrooper who landed behind enemy lines and was captured as a POW and then escaped and freed the other prisoners. That was cool."

Dad: "Yeah, that was. And what do you think was the point of the sermon?"

Scott: "Uh, I'd say it was about being bold. Yeah, being bold for God."

Dad: "I think you got it, son. Way to go."

End of spiritual discussion for the week.

Parents who take a minimalist approach—asking a few perfunctory questions or offering a couple of "attaboys" for regular church attendance—shortchange their teens of rich opportunities to deepen their faith. To state this principle in positive terms, moms and dads who are intentional, who consciously spend time nourishing their child's spiritual life, *seize* valuable moments rather than letting them pass by.

Frankly, for some things in life, there are no quick and easy solutions. For all of us, growing in Christ is a long-term process. It takes diligence, discipline, and attentiveness over many years. We may sometimes experience a growth spurt—a big leap forward in our quest for Christlikeness—but most often the maturation process happens inch by inch, step by step.

This is why wise moms and dads allow plenty of time for cultivating, nourishing, and tending their children's spiritual development. Perhaps that's what the psalmist was getting at when he said, "Our sons in their youth will be like well-nurtured plants" (Psalm 144:12). Parents who are "spiritual nurturers" set aside ample time to talk, pray, and read with their teens. Time to participate in camps, conferences, and

*"All your sons will be taught by the LORD, and great will be your children's peace."*
—Isaiah 54:13

**DISCIPLING**

retreats. Time to get away from the hustle and bustle of daily life. Time to be together one on one and let iron sharpen iron (see Proverbs 27:17). As writer Marcelene Cox said, "Raising children is like baking bread: it has to be a slow process or you end up with an overdone crust and an underdone interior."[2]

## Redeem the Time

The Bible has much to say about time and how we can best use it. Dozens of scriptures zero in on this subject, and most highlight one of two aspects: the brevity of life or the admonition to use our allotted time wisely. Consider these passages:

*Shortness of life:*
- "Our days on earth are but a shadow" (Job 8:9).
- "Show me, O LORD, my life's end and the number of my days; let me know how fleeting is my life" (Psalm 39:4).
- "As for man, his days are like grass, he flourishes like a flower of the field; the wind blows over it and it is gone, and its place remembers it no more" (Psalm 103:15-16).
- "Man is like a breath; his days are like a fleeting shadow" (Psalm 144:4).
- "The living know that they will die" (Ecclesiastes 9:5).
- "You are a mist that appears for a little while and then vanishes" (James 4:14).

*Using time wisely:*
- "Teach us to number our days aright, that we may gain a heart of wisdom" (Psalm 90:12).
- "Do not work for food that spoils, but for food that endures to eternal life" (John 6:27).
- "Be very careful . . . how you live—not as unwise but as wise, making the most of every opportunity" (Ephesians 5:15-16; the literal translation of the last clause is "redeeming the time").

Do you find scriptures like these sobering? Challenging? Motivating? They should, in fact, prompt each of us to examine

> *It's all too easy to expend time on things that have little or no eternal value.*

our lives to discern whether we are investing our limited resources prudently. Our culture offers so many distractions and diversions that it's all too easy to expend time on things that have little or no eternal value.

The above passages may not have been written specifically for parents, but the principles woven throughout them can certainly be applied to moms and dads concerned about their children's spiritual maturity. In fact, if we could mix all those verses together and direct them toward parents, the paraphrase might be this: "Life is short—and your years of parental influence are *really* short—so take full advantage of every opportunity to help your teen grow into a man or woman of God."

## Seizing the Moment

Let's get practical. What does all this mean to parents who want to invest time wisely? Helping your teen develop spiritually does not mean you have to conduct hour-long family devotions each evening (your teen would probably balk anyway) or rouse your son or daughter from bed in the predawn hours to pray and meditate together (good luck!).

It does mean, however, that you ought to scrutinize your calendar. It means you should periodically reassess all the commitments and obligations that leave you unavailable for family time. It means you may have to make some tough decisions about job promotions, side projects, or "once in a lifetime" opportunities that would eat up more hours. It means you should evaluate whether you are "redeeming the time" and "making the most of every opportunity" with your teenager.

Let's look at two strategies parents can use for redeeming time with their teenagers.

### Daily Delay, Weekly Walkout, Annual Awakening

Joe White tells about a discussion with a friend of his named Royce, a busy man whose job involves shepherding some hundred small country churches. Royce has a jam-packed schedule,

DISCIPLING

■ ■ ■

## *And You Think You're Busy . . .*

Are you feeling pinched for time these days? Meet Pat and Camilla Cottrell, parents of 11 children, ages 2 to 22 (that's right—11 children). Pat is pastor of the 400-member Calvary Baptist Church of Huntington Beach, California, and he and Camilla home-school each of their kids (three are now in college). In addition, the kids are involved in many activities. Needless to say, Pat and Camilla are busy folks. So, how do they make time for their children? They offer these practical ideas:

*Tame the tube.* "We watch very little TV," Pat said. "With a busy, bustling household, time is precious—and TV is a time waster. So we just leave it off, and the kids, especially the older ones, don't ask to turn it on. Obviously, TV doesn't foster any interaction among those sitting in front of it. Our kids just prefer to spend time as a family, talking, goofing around, hanging out together."

*Use drive time strategically.* "Part of our kids' home-school education is learning to play an instrument, so most of them take lessons," Camilla said. "You can imagine that we spend lots of time in the car, and we make sure to use that time wisely. Often, that's individual time, when Pat and I drive one child to his or her lesson. So we focus on that child and try to ask questions that will help us connect: 'What's going on in your life? Are you feeling good about the things you're involved in? What's happening in your spiritual life?'"

*Listen when your kids want to talk, even if it's inconvenient.* "All of our older kids get revved up for conversation late at night," Pat said. "That's when they open up, so that's when we listen. Sometimes it's tough, because the alarm clock always goes off too early the next morning. But as parents of teens, we decided if that's when they'll talk to us, we'll be there."

*Establish a regular family time.* Four mornings a week, the entire Cottrell family has devotions together. Camilla explained, "We all gather around the kitchen table at seven o'clock and read through a Bible passage, talk about it, and then pray. It's informal and casual—sometimes we have great discussions, sometimes we don't. The important thing is for us to be together consistently as a family, focused on God's Word."

Pat believes that for all parents, especially the ones on tight schedules, being deliberate and thoughtful about time goes a long way. "I guess it all boils down to this: Be intentional about using time," he said. "One month rolls into the next, and the years pass so quickly. If you're not proactive about using your hours, they just slip by. With lost hours go many opportunities to build a relationship with your kids and help them grow spiritually."

---

but somehow he finds the time to maintain a great relationship with his wife. When he explained how he does it, Joe instantly recognized that this was also a terrific strategy for maintaining a great relationship with a teen.

Here is how Royce explained what he does: "Oh, it's simple. Once a day, I have a 'daily delay' with my wife. And once a week we have a 'weekly walkout.' And once a year we have an 'annual awakening.' "

Joe asked him to explain what all that meant.

Royce: "Well, at some point during every day, I get alone with my wife and just listen. We push the pause button on life. It might be for just 5 or 10 minutes. I use that time to totally focus on her life. I ask her to tell me what happened that day, how she's feeling, what we can pray about together."

Joe: "So, what about the weekly walkout?"

Royce: "That means once a week we get out of the house and spend an evening together. We go have dinner, maybe rent ourselves a nice motel. Just me and her. The kids don't get to come. This is time when we talk more in-depth and explore what happened during the week."

Joe: "I'm getting the picture. Go ahead and tell me about the annual awakening."

Royce: "As you might guess, that's when we get away for an extended period of time—a weekend or even a week. We do this once a year, making a vacation out of it, just the two of us. We get alone and love each other. For those few days, we concentrate on us and enjoying and appreciating what we have together."

The application to parenting is obvious. Making time for a daily delay, a weekly walkout, and an annual awakening with your teen would provide multiple opportunities for building the relationship

DISCIPLING

> *"How we spend our days is, of course, how we spend our lives."*[3]
> —*Annie Dillard*

and fostering her spiritual growth. It would also be a clear demonstration of how much you care for her—how high a priority she holds in your life.

Making such a consistent investment of time won't be easy. And on occasion, you won't be able to make the time for one reason or another. Of course—nobody's perfect. But putting forth the effort to spend even a little time one-on-one with your teen every day, and more-extended times once a week and once a year, can pay rich dividends both in your relationship together and in your child's relationship with God.

### "I Will Give Them a Godly Heritage"

Royce may be a busy man, but even he would admit he doesn't face the relentless time squeeze that Nadine Johnson does. Divorced nine years ago, Nadine struggles to raise her four kids (ages 7 to 17) while working full-time as a data entry clerk in her hometown of Bellingham, Washington. This is on top of normal life challenges such as broken-down cars, leaky plumbing, dentist appointments, and bills to pay. To add just a little more spice to her life, Nadine's kids are all involved in sports or other after-school endeavors. Nadine describes her household as "chaos just barely under control."

With this tornado of activity swirling under one roof, you might expect that Nadine's number-one objective would be survival—just getting those kids grown and on their own. And she admits that some days she thinks, *I just want this day to be over, so*

**DISCIPLING**

## Teens' Advice to Parents About Nurturing Spiritual Growth, Part 9

■ "Make sure you're developing consistently yourself first. Pray a lot for your teen. Hold accountability breakfasts or times during which you and your teen can be open and honest with each other and you can offer and receive spiritual guidance. Make sure your teen is involved in a good youth group, and volunteer to help out sometimes (if your teen isn't too embarrassed). Pray with your teen, do Bible studies together, and tie in spiritual principles to the mundane details of life."

■ "Live what you preach."

*I can collapse into bed and start over tomorrow.* But Nadine has higher aims for herself and her children than merely getting them through.

"A few years ago, I heard a sermon about raising godly children," she recalls. "It was challenging to me, because I realized I wasn't doing much in the spirituality department. I sort of figured my kids would pick up Christian teaching somewhere. But I remember the pastor saying something like 'Parents who don't fill up their children with God's teaching leave them with a void, and the world will gladly fill this void with destructive values.' Man, did that hit me. I wasn't filling my kids up with anything except frozen dinners and Tang."

Nadine admits that when she left that church service, she felt discouraged. She was trying as hard as possible; what more could she do? Most of all, she felt as if she wasn't being the best mom she could be to her children.

"Late that night, after the kids were in bed, I thought and meditated and prayed and read my Bible," she says. "Right then and there, I made a decision: I can't give my four children everything, but the one thing they will not do without is a spiritual foundation. I will give them a godly heritage."

The next night at dinner, she announced a new schedule. Every night, Monday through Friday, Nadine would spend 10 minutes sequestered with each child individually. This time would be spent praying together and talking things over. Then

**DISCIPLING**

- "Encourage camp and youth group attendance to get teens excited about being a Christian with others their age. The things they're learning must also be reflected at home. Ask your kids about what they're learning, and encourage their personal relationship with Christ by *your* example."
- "Be there, be involved, and listen."
- "Pray with your teens. Read the Bible together. Read missionary accounts together. Take them with you to church. Encourage them to build relationships with other Christian adults. Don't just say it—live it."

> *"It takes hard work and hard thinking to rear good people. The job is interesting, although the hours are bad, starting from the first day."*[4]
> —Marguerite Kelly and Elia Parsons, The Mother's Almanac

every Saturday, on a rotating basis, she would go out to breakfast or lunch with one of the kids. (No excuses, except in the case of dire emergency.) And one last thing: They would recommit to attending church together each Sunday morning. Nadine admits they had grown lax in their attendance, and she was determined to change that.

So, what did her children say to these new marching orders?

"At first, I got reactions you might expect: 'Oh, Mom, do we have to?' 'Every night? What'll we talk about?' 'What if my 10 minutes come during my favorite TV show?' But you know, the resistance lasted maybe two weeks. Once the kids saw I was serious, that I was going to follow through, they got into it. Sometimes one would yell down the hall, 'Mom, don't forget our prayer time in two minutes!' Another one would say, on Monday, 'So, where are we going to breakfast this Saturday?' And I try to use those precious few minutes to the fullest—getting right to the heart issues, the spiritual issues."

All of this priority shifting came at a high cost to Nadine. What little leisure time she had got further eaten away. The tasks she attended to during the time she now gives her kids have to be

## Teens' "Traits of Great Parents," Part 8

■ "Allowing their children to do a lot of talking, not being dictatorial, and actually considering what they think from their perspective. See that they have a right to an opinion and are allowed to be wrong about it. Invest enough confidence in them to see they may change their opinion, but they can be an individual who is growing up through wisdom and love. And make sure they have a mentor who bathes them with sincere encouragement."

■ "Unconditional love, consistent boundaries, and lots of prayer!"

■ "A listener, spends time with teen (quantity and quality; both matter), squeezed in somewhere else. With virtually no time for herself, most of her personal goals and desires were put on hold.

It has been two years since Nadine first implemented her plan, and she is understandably pleased with the results. "I gauge my effectiveness on two things: consistency and progress in my kids' walk with the Lord," she said. "I have been consistent, sticking to that original schedule all this time (with the exception of a couple weeks when I was going crazy from stress). More important, each of my children has grown spiritually. With four kids, of course, they grow at different rates and in different ways. But with each of them, I've seen steps forward, and that's all that matters to me."

## Making It Happen

Let's have a big round of applause for Nadine. She devised a plan to spend time nurturing her children's spiritual lives—a plan that was doable within their unique circumstances, a plan that would help them stay on course. She made a conscious, deliberate effort to encourage her children to grow in Christ, and she made it happen.

The bottom line is this: There are many ways you can use your time, including a lot of good and productive ways. But if encouraging your teen's spiritual growth is important to you, you can and will find time to invest in this vital process.

**DISCIPLING**

honestly answers questions and addresses situations and problems directly but also in love. An affectionate hugger and affirming toucher! Someone who verbally affirms and encourages as well as disciplines."

■ "A safe, supportive place to talk about what's going on, but not codependent. Willing to let their kids seek Jesus on their own terms, but giving solid foundation to spring from. Acceptance—unconditionally."

■ "Strong, consistent, compassionate, empathetic, unconditionally loving, understanding."

*"There are fathers waiting until other obligations are less demanding to become acquainted with their sons. . . . There are mothers who sincerely intend to be more attentive to their daughters. . . . When in the world are we going to begin to live as if we understood that this is life? This is our time, our day, and it is passing? What are we waiting for?"*[5]

—*Richard L. Evans*

DISCIPLING

# Moving Your Child from Selfish to Selfless

Okay, tell the truth. How many times in the past six months have you said any of the following to your teenager:

- "The world does not revolve around you."
- "Think of someone other than yourself for a change."
- "You are not the only person in this family."
- "Other people's wishes are important, too."
- "You can't always have it your way."

If you have not uttered one of these phrases (or something conveying the same sentiment), consider yourself both unusual and fortunate. After all, the teenage years bring out in kids what one psychologist calls an "acuteness of self," a heightened sense of I, me, and mine. If self-centeredness were a disease, most teens would be diagnosed with at least a mild case, and many would be classified as suffering from "chronic, inflamed egotism." (In extreme cases, quarantine may not be a bad option.)

As one mom said, "My 16-year-old seems to have delusions that the whole world is a theater in the round, and he alone is on stage. The spotlight is shining brightly on him, and everyone else is sitting in the shadows, hanging on his every word or gesture."

Another parent, a dad, said, "I'd always called my daughter my little 'princess.' It was my pet name for her, but I didn't think she'd ever believe she was actually royalty. When she turned 15, though, she started treating her mother and I, and her younger siblings, like her servants and subjects. Everything was 'Bring me this, give me that. I want, I need.' Once I asked if she'd like me to fan her with palm leaves and feed her grapes, and she got a look in her eye as if she was considering it. I said, 'Wait a second! That was a joke!' "

Writer Annie Dillard recalls being caught in the grip of self-centeredness during her own adolescence: "I couldn't remember how to forget myself. I didn't want to think about myself, to reckon myself in, to deal with myself every livelong minute on top of everything else—but swerve as I might, I couldn't avoid it. I was a boulder blocking my own path. I was a dog barking between my own ears, a barking dog who wouldn't hush. So this was adolescence."[1]

An actor in the spotlight, a princess and her subjects, a boulder and barking dog—you might come up with your own metaphor for this self-indulgent stage in your teen's development. Whatever terminology you want to use, the more pressing issue is, what can you do about it? After all, helping your teen to overcome selfishness is a major goal of spiritual training, a key part of developing Christlikeness. So while it is normal for teens to be self-centered, how can you initiate an attitude adjustment? How can Christian parents help shift their teenager's focus from "me" to "others"?

## The Goal: An "I'm Third" Attitude

Selfishness is not a teenagers-only phenomenon, of course. We've all met plenty of adults who were clearly looking out for number one, pursuing their own agenda with little thought about how others might get hurt in the process. Self-centeredness is indeed a *human* condition, and you only need to read the early chapters of Genesis to see where the problem began.

Obviously, God understands our inclination toward self-inflation. That's why His guidebook, the Bible, is replete with warnings to control our selfishness and drive for self-fulfillment, along with an equal number of admonitions to serve others in humility and love. Consider just a few passages:

*Warnings against selfishness:*
- ■ "Turn my heart toward your statutes and not toward selfish gain" (Psalm 119:36).
- ■ "An unfriendly man pursues selfish ends" (Proverbs 18:1).
- ■ "[Love] is not self-seeking" (1 Corinthians 13:5).
- ■ "The acts of the sinful nature are obvious: sexual immorality, impurity and debauchery; idolatry and witchcraft; hatred, discord, jealousy, fits of rage, selfish ambition . . ." (Galatians 5:19-20).
- ■ "Where you have envy and selfish ambition, there you find disorder and every evil practice" (James 3:16).

*Encouragement to serve others:*
- ■ "Whoever is kind to the needy honors God" (Proverbs 14:31).
- ■ "Whoever wants to become great among you must be your servant, and whoever wants to be first must be your slave—just as the Son of Man did not come to be served, but to serve" (Matthew 20:26-28).
- ■ "Serve wholeheartedly, as if you were serving the Lord" (Ephesians 6:7).
- ■ "Do nothing out of selfish ambition or vain conceit, but in humility consider others better than yourselves. Each of you should look not only to your own interests, but also to the interests of others" (Philippians 2:3-4).
- ■ "Remind the people to be . . . peaceable and considerate, and to show true humility toward all men" (Titus 3:1-2).
- ■ "All of you, clothe yourselves with humility toward one another" (1 Peter 5:5).

Overcoming self-centeredness and learning to serve others are lifelong endeavors for all Christians, but as a parent, you can help your teen to grow in his ability to be compassionate and considerate, humble and helpful.

The teenager who thinks her room is the center of the universe ought to

> *Overcoming self-centeredness and learning to serve others are lifelong endeavors for all Christians.*

**DISCIPLING**

■ ■ ■

## "God First, the Other Fellow Second, and I'm Third."

Out of the sun, packed in a diamond formation and flying as one that day, the Minute Men dove at nearly the speed of sound toward a tiny emerald patch on Ohio's unwrinkled crazy quilt below. It was a little after nine on the morning of June 7, 1958, and the target of the Air National Guard's jet precision team was the famed Wright-Patterson Air Force Base, just outside Dayton.

On the ground, thousands of faces looked upward as Colonel Walt Williams, leader of the Denver-based Sabrejet team, gauged the high-speed pullout. For the Minute Men pilots—Colonel Walt Williams, Captain Bob Cherry, Lieutenant Bob Odle, Captain John Ferrier, and Major Win Coomer—the maneuver was routine, for they had given their show hundreds of times before millions of people.

Low across the fresh, green grass the jet team streaked, far ahead of the noise of the planes' own screaming engines. Judging his pull-up, Colonel Williams pressed the microphone button on top of his throttle: "Smoke on . . . now!" The diamond of planes pulled straight up into the turquoise sky, a bushy tail of white smoke pluming out behind. The crowd gasped as the ships suddenly split apart, rolling to the four points of the compass and leaving a beautiful, smoky fleur-de-lis inscribed on the heavens. This was the Minute Men's famed "flower burst" maneuver. For a minute, the crowd relaxed, gazing at the tranquil beauty of the huge, white flower that had grown from the lush Ohio grasslands to fill the great bowl of sky.

Out on the end of his arm of the flower, Colonel Williams turned his Sabre hard, cut off the smoke trail, and dropped the nose of his F-86 to pick up speed for the low-altitude crossover maneuver. Then, glancing back over his shoulder, he froze in terror. Far across the sky to the east, John Ferrier's plane was rolling. He was in trouble. And his plane was headed right for the small town of Fairborn, on the edge of Patterson Field. In a moment, the lovely morning had turned to horror. Everyone saw; everyone understood. One of the planes was out of control.

Steering his jet in the direction of the crippled plane to race after it, Williams radioed urgently, "Bail out, John! Get out of there!" Johnny still had plenty of time and room to eject safely. Twice more Williams issued the command: "Bail out, Johnny! Bail out!"

Each time, Williams was answered only by a blip of smoke.

He understood immediately. John Ferrier couldn't reach the mike button on the throttle because both hands were tugging on the control stick locked in full-throw right. But the smoke button was on the stick, so he was answering the only was he could—squeezing it to tell Walt he thought he could keep his plane under enough control to avoid crashing into the houses of Fairborn.

Suddenly, a terrible explosion shook the earth. Then came a haunting silence. Walt Williams continued to call through the radio, "Johnny? Are you there? Captain? Answer me!"

No response.

Captain John T. Ferrier's Sabrejet had hit the ground midway between four houses, in a backyard garden. It was the only place where he could have crashed without killing people. The explosion knocked a woman and several children to the ground, but no one had been hurt—with the exception of Johnny Ferrier. He had been killed instantly.

Major Win Coomer, who had flown with Ferrier for years, both in the Air National Guard and on United Airlines and had served combat tour with him in Korea, was the first Minute Man to land. He raced to the crash scene, hoping to find his friend alive.

Instead, he found a neighborhood in shock from the awful thing that had happened. But then Coomer realized that the people felt no resentment as is ordinarily the case when a peaceful community is torn by a crash. A steady stream of people began coming to him as he stood in his flying suit beside the smoking, gaping hole in the ground where his best friend had just died.

"A bunch of us were standing together, watching the show," an elderly man with tears in his eyes told Coomer. "When the pilot started to roll, he was headed straight for us. For a second, we looked right at each other. Then he pulled up right over us and put it in there." And in deep humility, the old man whispered, "This man died for us."

It has been a bold and courageous last act. But it was not an act alien to the nature of John Ferrier. He had been awarded one of the nation's highest medals for risking his life "beyond the call

**DISCIPLING**

of duty" in Korea. And although he hadn't known it, he'd been preparing for this tragic day for years by practicing this most important principle:

> Love the Lord your God with all your heart and with all your soul and with all your mind. This is the first and greatest command-ment. And the second is like it: "Love your neighbor as yourself." (Matthew 22:37-39)

A few days after Johnny's death, his wife, Tulie, wrote the founder of Kanakuk Kamp, Coach Bill Lantz, this letter:

> Coach,
> I went through my husband's billfold last night and found the old worn card which he always carried—"I'M THIRD." He told me once he got it from you. He said that you stressed it at one of your camp sermons. Johnny may have had faults, though they were few and minor, but he followed that creed to the very end. *God is first, the other fellow second, and "I'm third."* Not just on June 7, 1958, but long before that—certainly as long as I've known him. I'm going to carry that same card with me from now on and see if it won't serve as a reminder. I shouldn't need it, but I'm sure I do as I have many more faults than Johnny.

The principle by which Johnny Ferrier lived and died is also the great-est lesson you can teach your teenager. At the heart of making others feel valuable, loved, and accepted is a decision to honor them, even above our-selves.[2]

---

learn that there are billions of lost, needy people desperate for help. The teen who complains about not having the latest and best athletic shoes must understand that millions of people in the world can't afford shoes at all. The child who is accustomed to being waited on must learn the value of serving others (even when it's uncomfort-able or inconvenient). Perhaps most of all, teenagers should come to see that there's tremendous joy in serving God by serving others.

Joe White, director of the Kanakuk Christian youth camps in Branson, Missouri, says a primary goal of his program is to teach kids the "I'm Third" principle. That is, Joe wants every young person who leaves his camp to have an attitude that says, "In every situation and circumstance, it's God first, others second, and I'm third." The camp staff and counselors all strive to demonstrate this principle, which is exemplified by the story they recount of an Air National Guard pilot named Johnny Ferrier, who heroically demonstrated selflessness in a way most of us will never be called upon to do. (See the sidebar on pages 404-6 for a full retelling of this true story. You may want to read it with your teen during a family time and discuss it together.)

The "I'm Third" principle is based on Jesus' teaching in Matthew 22:36-40, when He was questioned by a Pharisee: " 'Teacher, which is the greatest commandment in the Law?' Jesus replied: ' "Love the Lord your God with all your heart and with all your soul and with all your mind." This is the first and greatest commandment. And the second is like it: "Love your neighbor as yourself." All the Law and the Prophets hang on these two commandments.' "

Instilling the "I'm Third" principle should be a primary goal for parents of teenagers. Wouldn't it be wonderful if your teen had an attitude that placed God first, others second, and self third? Wouldn't you feel gratified knowing you're sending your child into the world to serve other people and not self alone? You can do it. Let us offer three suggestions for helping you shift your teen's attitude from selfish to selfless. These suggestions we call "Set the Standard for Selflessness," "Let's Go Servin' Now," and "Send Them into the Real World."

## Set the Standard for Selflessness

When we talk about serving others, we may naturally think first of all the people *out there*—the widow across the street, the homeless folks we pass downtown, the disadvantaged kids in the inner city, the starving children in Ethiopia. Yet the real laboratory for learning to serve is at home, with the people closest to us—family members. These are the people, of course, whom we love dearly but who can irritate us to no end—the people who eat the last of the ice cream, make noise when you're trying to sleep, leave books and papers strewn across the living room floor, borrow your stuff without asking, and forget to tell you about important phone messages. If we can learn to serve, honor, and comfort our family members day in and day out, reaching out to strangers and acquaintances will surely come more easily.

This is no easy assignment, for serving family members means we must do it when we're feeling tired, grouchy, stressed-out, depressed, or plain old lazy. At home, we can't confine our kindness and charity to one morning a week or 10 days during the summer as we might when we volunteer for a periodic or one-time service project. At home, selflessness is a quality honed and hewed every day, morning and night, in good times and bad.

And here's the crux of the matter for moms and dads: You are the ones who set the tone and show the way, leading by example. By far the most important thing parents can do to discourage selfishness and encourage a servant's heart in a teen is to *model* these attitudes and behaviors.

How do kids learn to put others' needs above their own? By watching Dad get up in the middle of the football game to do the dishes so his tired, pooped-out wife doesn't have to.

How do kids learn to serve others in humility and love? By observing how Mom, without any prompting, makes Dad's favorite meal to give him a little boost after a rough workweek.

How do kids learn to love sacrificially? By seeing Mom and Dad take the couple hundred dollars they had set aside for a

## Teens' "Traits of Great Parents," Part 9

- "They listen empathetically to their teens' desires, problems, and fears. They comfort them and help them problem solve as needed. They are willing to be involved in their teens' lives. They actively seek the Lord themselves and are people of integrity. They care."
- "They use teachable moments and always live the way they say you should as a Christian."
- "Parents who like to have fun. Parents who remember what it was like to be a teenager and who can relate to what their kids are going through while still keeping their authority."
- "Patient, confident, consistent."
- "They can say no with compassion, their lives exemplify what they teach, they help their teens be adults, but they also understand that they still need much wisdom."

■ ■ ■

## *Heaven's Celebration of Service*

If heaven keeps a museum, I don't think it will be a grand theater of Christendom's triumphs—a 3-D movie of Satan writhing in inflamed agony, or mock-ups of the mighty empires, from Caesar's to Stalin's, that the man from Galilee smote to rubble, or Constantine's decree to make Christianity a state religion.

I think it will be a small, quiet room filled with ordinary things: a cup of cold water given to a refugee. A laundry basket of clothes washed and ironed for teenagers who never say thank-you. A stack of dishes, rinsed and soaked and cleaned, left by people who never stay around to help. A meal cooked for a sick neighbor. A hundred dollars given to an unemployed man whose giver could hardly afford it. A Samaritan's donkey. A widow's mite. A towel, still damp from wiping feet.

—Pastor and author Mark Buchanan in *Your God Is Too Safe*[3]

weekend getaway and give it, anonymously, to a single mother at church who's having trouble making ends meet.

Michael Tait of the Christian music group dc Talk spoke for many young people who admire their parents' example of servanthood:

> Let me tell you the two most important things I learned from my dad. Number one, love people. That's what he taught, and that's what he did. He cried with people, he laughed with people. Everybody was his friend. He couldn't care less about your race, your nationality, your socio-economic status, whatever. All he cared about was you, your soul.
>
> Number two, live for God and don't get caught up in the things of this world, because they're just fleeting. The world will get the best of you if you let it, so we need to truly live for God.
>
> My dad [a preacher] preached those two things his whole life. And those two things have shaped who I am today. I love people; I realize life is short, God is real and that I need to live for Him.
>
> The man was my hero.[4]

DISCIPLING

*During my sophomore year of high school, I took a mission trip to Monterey, Mexico, with my church youth group. It was an incredibly humbling experience. It was there, staying in homes with dirt floors and no indoor plumbing, that God gave me a healthy disgust for materialism. The people had nothing! But they were so happy and perfectly content. They found joy in their family and in the Lord.*

—*Sarah, 19*

**DISCIPLING**

Often it's not the grand displays of sacrifice that capture the hearts and minds of children but the small, almost unnoticeable gestures of kindness. Simply put, little things go a long way.

Caryl Altmeyer of Spokane, Washington, has four children (ages 8 to 18), in whom she and her husband, Phil, try hard to instill a love for serving others. Caryl often reminds her kids of a memory from her own childhood.

"When I was young," she recalls, "my dad would bring home pies for the family to enjoy. He loved pie, and he liked to bring this treat home to Mom and my two younger brothers. Here's what I'll always remember: If there were two pieces of pie left, Dad would give the bigger slice to me or my brothers or whoever he was serving. He always took the smaller piece for himself. I observed this small act of generosity over and over."

A small act, perhaps, but it left an indelible memory. "It certainly made an impression, probably because Dad had a real sweet tooth, and I knew that deep down he'd prefer to take the bigger portion for himself."

Caryl is handing down this put-others-first approach. "I tell my kids, 'I want to have an attitude like that—unselfish, generous, willing to give someone else the bigger piece of the pie. And I want you to have an attitude like that, too.' "

Perhaps it's not surprising, then, that the Altmeyer clan is big on serving others. Phil is the director of the Spokane Union Gospel Mission, where his kids sometimes help serve the underprivileged. And the Altmeyer family recently spent three weeks in St. Petersburg, Russia, teaching at youth camps and telling young people about their faith in Christ.

■ ■ ■

## There's No "I" in the Lord's Prayer

If you're looking for a simple yet powerful way to reinforce an others-first attitude in your teen, try making the Lord's Prayer a regular part of your mealtime or bedtime routine. Here's why:

You cannot pray the Lord's Prayer and even once say, "I."

You cannot pray the Lord's Prayer and even once say, "My."

Nor can you pray the Lord's Prayer and not pray for one another.

And when you ask for daily bread, you must include your brother.

For others are included in each and every plea,

From the beginning to the end of it, it doesn't once say, "Me."[5]

"Of course, Dad's giving other people the bigger slice of pie was just an example of a lifestyle of unselfishness," Caryl says. "He was the kind of dad who made sure there was milk in the refrigerator for everyone's breakfast and nobody left the house without a few dollars in their pocket. That's an example I'm trying to pass on to my kids."

Just goes to show—you never know who's watching, and you never know how the smallest act of kindness might reverberate through generations.

If you want your teenager to develop a servant's heart, begin

**DISCIPLING**

*I have taken a few short-term mission trips to Mexico that forever changed my life. As I walked through the dumps—what those people called their home—it struck me that I have never known material poverty like this. But then I was struck by the realization that I had once experienced poverty like theirs on a much deeper level: spiritual poverty.*

*I don't think God is concerned that poor people lack big houses and trendy clothes, but He is deeply concerned about the poverty of their souls. The absence of Christ in their lives troubles Him the most.*

*—Mike, 21*

by being a servant to those closest to you—your spouse, your children, and anyone who comes into your house. When an attitude of thoughtfulness and generosity toward others pervades your home, reaching out to those beyond your front door will come naturally.

## Let's Go Servin' Now

Taking on a volunteer project as a family is an excellent way to ease your child into a lifestyle of service. This is especially true for those kids who need a little nudge or hand-holding to get them off the couch and into the world.

A few years ago, Larry and Beth Weeden of Colorado Springs saw an opportunity to encourage their son, Matt, to serve others. Their church sponsored an outreach to a poor part of Oakland, California, where a team would be sent to turn a run-down house into a church youth center.

Over dinner one night, Larry said, "I've been thinking about the church's trip to Oakland next month. I'm excited about it, and I'd love it if we could all go together."

Matt didn't exactly shout, "Great idea, Dad! Sign me up!" But he didn't say no, either. With a little coaxing, Matt agreed to go. Larry, Beth, and Matt spent a week working alongside 25 fellow church members, pounding nails, replacing windows, and putting a fresh coat of paint and a new roof on the youth center.

To be sure, it wasn't a week at the Four Seasons. Long days of dirty, muscle-aching work and nights in a sleeping bag on the

*In high school, I went with my church youth group on several mission trips to various places in the States. At that time, many of the other teens and I were so self-absorbed and thought that our lives were the only thing that mattered. These trips helped show us how different life is for those less fortunate financially and spiritually. And those experiences forced me to move beyond my selfishness and to serve others. Those trips helped create in me a sense of compassion for all of God's children.*

*—Bridgette, 21*

DISCIPLING

floor of a church gym can be challenging. But those are memories Matt is sure to carry with him for years to come.

"Frankly, few of our family vacations have been as meaningful and memorable as that week of hard work," Larry says. "There's something deeply rewarding about giving our time and resources to make a difference in other people's lives. And it was especially rewarding that we could do it together as a family."

Sometimes all that's needed is that first nudge, and the teenager catches a vision for serving others. The following year, when the Weedens' church sponsored a similar outreach, Matt participated willingly even though his mom and dad were unable to.

But maybe your teenager is a zealous, go-getter type who doesn't need parents around for moral support and doesn't require a nudge in order to serve. It's still a good idea to do things as a family. What vivid memories you'll give your kids as they watch Mom and Dad offering their time and energy to help others! Your teen will carry into adulthood images of Mom and Dad serving meals at the homeless shelter, delivering groceries to an elderly shut-in, or taking an underprivileged child out for pizza and ball games with the family.

## Send Them into the Real World

Talk to teenagers, parents of teens, youth pastors, and college students, and all will agree: One of the best things you can do to foster servanthood in young people is to get them out of their comfort zone and rubbing shoulders with the real world. Most often, this means sending your kids on a short-term mission project to another country, but it can also mean serving in a poor area in the United States. The point is to put your teen in a situation where he or she will mingle and mix with people lacking all the luxuries and opportunities most Americans enjoy.

Maybe you've heard church youth group reports when junior highers or high schoolers returned from a cross-cultural outreach project. If so, you have likely heard the kids say things like "That trip was one of the hardest things I've ever done—and also one of the best. I'll never be the same." Or "Those three weeks in Mexico changed my life. I'd heard about people living below poverty

**DISCIPLING**

level, but to be there and see it . . . Wow! That really opened my eyes." Don't rob your kids of the opportunity to be broadened and stretched in this way. Encourage and help them to serve alongside missionaries in the Philippines, teach at camps in Kazakhstan, or build houses for poor people in Guatemala.

Pat and Camilla Cottrell, the parents of 11 kids whom we introduced in the last chapter, make sure an overseas trip is part of their children's spiritual and academic education. "We believe strongly that serving in another culture does amazing things for kids' spiritual development," Pat says. So he and Camilla send each of their children on some kind of mission trip following high school graduation. "It's sort of the completion of their high school education. It caps off the home-schooling we've done and prepares them for college, where they'll be challenged in many ways and forced to stand on their own."

In her first year out of high school, Pat and Camilla's oldest child, Bethany—now a 22-year-old nursing student—spent four months in Moscow, Russia, teaching in a public school, and another four months in Thailand, assisting missionaries.

"Those trips were life-changing in many ways," Bethany recalls. "Getting on a plane by myself and going someplace halfway around the world—that in itself stretched my faith and forced me to depend on God." She also says her cross-cultural experiences gave her insight into life outside the United States. "As much as we may not like to admit it, most people in America, young and old, take for

*While on a summer outreach in the Philippines, I witnessed firsthand how people on the "other side of the world" live. I saw true poverty and a yearning for something more. I also saw people who were not lazy. They worked hard to eat and survive.*

*I learned that summer that we Americans take so much for granted and often don't know what real work is. The Lord has blessed us so much, and many of us just complain, complain, complain. What we should be doing is thanking God on our knees for all He has given us.*

*—Bridgett, 23*

> *When I participated in short-term mission trips, I experienced more culture shock coming back to my country, school, and friends. I remember returning and being very frustrated by people's selfish attitude, ungratefulness, and drive to climb the social ladder.*
>
> *On a more positive note, I also found myself more attentive to the needs of others. I came back with stories of transformation in my life, particularly a stronger desire to give to others.*
>
> —*Lois, 23*

granted all we have here—our religious freedom, our wealth, our opportunities to do just about anything we want. Getting out of our culture for a while gave me more compassion and understanding for what many people around the world experience."

## Putting Others First Creates Harmony

Leonard Bernstein, the famous conductor, was once asked, "What is the hardest instrument to play?" Without a moment's hesitation, he replied, "Second fiddle. I can always get plenty of first violinists. But to find one who plays second violin with as much enthusiasm, or second French horn, or second flute, now that's a problem. And yet if no one plays second, we have no harmony."[3]

Well said. And what's true about the symphony is also true about our homes, churches, neighborhoods, workplaces, and communities: Without servants, without those willing to put others' needs and desires first, there can be no harmony, no unity. As pastor and theologian Alan Redpath has said, "The cause of every discord in Christian homes and communities and churches is that we seek our own way and our own glory."[7]

If you want to raise a teenager to be an adult who promotes harmony, fosters unity, and—most of all—embodies Christlike love, encourage him or her to become a servant. Teach, instruct, model, and demonstrate an "I'm third" attitude. Whether serving family members at home or strangers in a far-off country, your teen will be equipped to speak the universally understood language of Christian kindness and compassion.

# Prescription for Disciple Making

DISCIPLING

Some years ago, author and educator Eugene Peterson published a book on discipleship titled *A Long Obedience in the Same Direction*. That intriguing phrase captures what all Christian parents hope their teen will achieve—a *lifelong* obedience to Christ. A steady march in the direction of holiness and godliness. A persistent, vibrant faith that can't be held back.

If you are a faithful parent who wants to raise a faithful teen, you seek to instill in him a deeply rooted commitment to God that will stand the test of time. If you want your teen to develop a faith that spans a lifetime, you desire to do everything you can to ensure that God's Word and ways are woven into the fiber of her heart.

As you've probably discovered by now, parenting teenagers requires an abundant supply of grit and gumption, tenacity and temerity. Where does this come from? It comes from knowing that raising a godly teen is a *calling*, a commission given to you by God Himself.

Think for a moment about the apostle Paul. Even a quick reading of his New Testament letters reveals a man of single-minded determination. He had a firm sense of mission in his life, and he would not let diversions and distractions keep him from an all-out pursuit of his goal. This is the man who wrote, "One thing I do: Forgetting what is behind and straining toward what is ahead, I press on toward the goal to win the prize for which God has called me heavenward in Christ Jesus" (Philippians 3:13-14).

> *Most often growth occurs in the less significant, more mundane moments of everyday life.*

At this stage of your life, what is the "one thing" you do? What is the one thing that compels you, motivates you, and excites you more than anything else? Our encouragement to every mom and dad is to view the nurturing of your teen's faith as your one thing. During the brief, swiftly passing years when your teen is accessible and responsive to your influence, set as your number-one goal helping your son or daughter become a true disciple of Christ.

In this chapter, we present several ideas—practical, specific, applicable right here and now—to help you guide your teen to an authentic faith. With these ideas, the aim is to root your child so deeply, so surely in her faith, that she will not fall away when Mom and Dad aren't around. Take as many of these strategies as you can and adapt them to your teen's life.

### Teachable Moments: Make Faith Training a Part of Everyday Life

Sometimes kids experience a spiritual growth spurt at big, monumental events: a Young Life rally, a Billy Graham crusade, a week at church camp, a short-term mission trip with the youth group. Those

**DISCIPLING**

## Maximizing Teachable Moments

To make the most of the moment, keep in mind these points:

- *Be available and accessible.* Simply put, if you want to seize teachable moments, you've got to be there when they happen.
- *Don't give a sermon.* Your opportunity to offer a faith lesson will backfire if you preach or lecture. With teenagers, it's best to ask questions and let them answer. Then, if appropriate, express your own opinions.

can, indeed, be powerful times of strengthening commitment to God. But most often growth occurs in the less significant, more mundane moments of everyday life, when Mom and Dad are there to talk about faith and the nitty-gritty stuff of life as it happens.

If we want to help our children grow consistently, we'll take advantage of all those day-in-and-day-out opportunities: driving to school and soccer practice, working together around the house, eating pizza at home on Friday night, throwing the Frisbee around at the park, cleaning out an elderly neighbor's rain gutters. In teachable moments like these, we can talk with our teens about life and love, faith and the future.

This is precisely what the writer of Deuteronomy was getting at when he said, "These commandments that I give to you today are to be upon your hearts. Impress them on your children. Talk about them when you sit at home and when you walk along the road, when you lie down and when you get up" (6:6-7). This concept was so important that it was repeated almost verbatim just a few chapters later (see 11:19).

Do these unspectacular, seemingly insignificant moments of faith building really make a difference? Listen as three college students talk about what influenced their lives during the teen years:

**Bridgette, age 21:**
"I have always been a daddy's girl, and I was the only one who could wake up Dad for church. When I was little, I would gently shake him and tickle him. When I got older, I would crawl in bed beside him and use that time to share my heart with him. Everyone

**DISCIPLING**

---

- *Tell about your own life.* The best lessons you can pass along are the ones you've learned from your own experience—your failures and successes, your hilarious moments and your humiliating ones. Don't be afraid to show your kids your not-so-put-together side; they'll love you all the more for being real.
- *Be on the lookout for lessons waiting to happen.* TV commercials, songs on the radio, news events, activities your child is involved in—all these provide grist for discussion. Train your eyes and ears to be aware of these discussion starters.

else would be rushing to get ready, but Dad and I would lie there for a long time, talking, connecting, and sharing our hopes and dreams. Those times helped me understand so many aspects of my heavenly Father—love, acceptance, gentleness, and compassion.

"My mom did not like to cook much, but when she did, I would go in the kitchen with her and talk. We would share so much about our lives, talking very openly and relating as friends. This didn't occur until I was going through adolescence and I was able to appreciate all she had given to me and to accept her unconditionally. Now she is my best friend."

**James, age 20:**
"Because I didn't have my own car during high school, my parents drove me everywhere—to youth group, baseball practice, friends' houses. I remember that they really tried to use that time—whether it was a five-minute drive or an hour—to talk about things. They could have turned on the news or a game or stayed in their own world like we all do sometimes when driving. But they always made an effort to ask questions and draw me out. If I was coming home from Bible study, Mom would say, 'What did you learn? What do you think about that?' If I was coming home from school, Dad would say, 'Tell me about your friends' or 'What can I be praying about in your life?'

"Recently, I asked my folks about all those drive-time discussions, and they said, 'We decided early on that if we were going to spend hours each week driving you around, it was going to be time well spent.' And it sure was. I stayed connected to my parents talking during all those hours in the car."

**Heidi, age 21:**
"My dad has always been busy with work—not out of choice, but out of necessity and the nature of his job. But every year for our birthdays, he has always taken each of us four kids out to breakfast. As we've gotten older, my sister and I have initiated 'breakfast with Dad' more than once a year. They are treasured times when we talk about life, God, the future. Memories are made in quiet cafés in early mornings.

"Growing up in northern Minnesota was an adventure. We

■ ■ ■

## *Seizing the Moment*

Dr. James Dobson recalls a teachable moment during his son, Ryan's, teen years. The two got up early one morning to hunt, which was one of their favorite father-son activities. They situated themselves in a deer blind, and 20 yards away was a feeder that operated on a timer. At 7:00 A.M., it would automatically drop kernels of corn into a pan below, luring unsuspecting deer.

Dr. Dobson picks up the story:

> Ryan and I huddled together in this blind, talking softly about whatever came to mind. Then through the fog, we saw a beautiful doe emerge silently into the clearing. She took nearly thirty minutes to get to the feeder where we were hiding. We had no intention of shooting her, but it was fun to watch this beautiful animal from close range. She was extremely wary, sniffing the air and listening for the sounds of danger. Finally, she inched her way to the feeder, still looking around skittishly as though sensing our presence. Then she ate a quick breakfast and fled.
>
> I whispered to Ryan, "There is something valuable to be learned from what we have just seen. Whenever you come upon a free supply of high-quality corn, unexpectedly provided right there in the middle of the forest, be careful! The people who put it there are probably sitting nearby in a blind, just waiting to take a shot at you. Keep your eyes and ears open!"[1]

Dr. Dobson couldn't have planned that life lesson. He simply had to be on the lookout for experiences that could illustrate values and insights for living. Such opportunities come about every day. Watch for them and seize them.

heated our house with wood, which meant cutting trees and hauling logs every fall. My dad and my three siblings and I worked side by side, and nobody told us it was hard work and shouldn't be fun. We stacked the cart full of logs, rode on top of the pile, and sang praise songs all the way home. We all made memories and learned the value of hard work without even knowing it."

That line of Heidi's—"Memories are made in quiet cafés in early mornings"—is not only poetic; it's also profoundly true. Each day presents opportunities to explore faith issues and build your relationship with your teen. Grab hold of every opportunity you can.

## Bookend Your Teen's Day

Joe White took literally the admonition in Deuteronomy 6: "Talk [with your children] when you lie down and when you get up" (6:6-7). As much as his schedule (and his kids' activities) allowed, he would begin each day with morning devotions with his kids, and he would end each day by lying down on their beds at night to talk, pray, and memorize Scripture together.

"I set a goal when my kids were young that I would spend time with them individually every night," Joe recalls. "That was a tough goal, because the word *every* is a real taskmaster. Sometimes I was tempted to skip the bedtime ritual, especially when we had company at the house or if I had an early morning meeting the next day. But for the most part, I stuck with it, and those were some of the richest times we had together."

He says the evening times—which he calls "lay by" time, since he would literally lie beside his kids—were especially meaningful. "When kids are tired at the end of a long day, their defenses are down and they're receptive. They become open and vulnerable at bedtime. Night after night, my kids and I would lie next to each other and share our hearts."

Will most parents in our hectic, hustle-and-bustle society be able to have morning devotions with their kids *and* "lay by" time in the evening? Probably not. (Though it would be great if you could!) If you can't do both, pick one or the other—and stick with it. Consistency is the key. Use those times to pray together, read Bible passages, memorize verses, and talk about life. You may find helpful two books authored by Joe White (*FaithTraining* and *LifeTraining*), which provide concise yet meaty devotional material to read through with teens. Whatever you choose to do during those daily times together, they are sure to provide powerful opportunities for relationship building and spiritual nurturing.

## Encourage Your Teen to Join a
## Small-Group Study with Friends

Every parent knows the dangers of peer pressure, but have you considered its benefits? After all, peer pressure cuts both ways; it can be destructive or constructive.

For 12 years, Bill Slocum has led Bible study and accountability groups for teens. The first one started when his oldest daughter, Jackie, was in the ninth grade. She had a group of male friends who wanted some kind of regular time together with other Christian guys. Several of them attended large youth groups, and they felt lost in the shuffle. When Jackie asked her dad if he'd be willing to lead a weekly meeting with them, what could he say? He said (with much trepidation) that of course he'd do it; he'd love to.

So he called 10 of Jackie's friends and invited them to come over every Thursday morning at 6:30 for Bible study, prayer, and mutual encouragement. To his surprise, eight accepted.

More than once, Bill asked himself, "Meet with eight ninth graders every week? What'll I tell them? They won't care what I have to say. They'll think I'm an old fogy." He needn't have worried. Those boys were starved for friends who would help them avoid bad choices and figure out adolescent perplexities, such as girls, siblings, parents, and teachers.

Those Thursday morning gatherings became a highlight of the week for all of them, including Bill. As those eight boys slurped their milk and gulped down doughnuts, Bill would read a short devotional or a Scripture passage, and they would all discuss it for a few minutes. Almost always, though, the most significant part of the meetings was when they talked about their lives. Over time, they became remarkably open with each other. They would say things like "The guys on the football team asked me to go out drinking with them after the game on Friday. I know I shouldn't go, but I want to fit in. What should I do?" The other group members would offer encouragement or advice.

With the exception of one or two boys who moved away (and a few new ones who were added), that same group stayed together through all four years of high school. And when they graduated, Bill started another group with a new crew of boys, this time with his son and his pals. Four years later, yet another group began.

"What I see in those groups is a microcosm of the way the church as a whole is supposed to work," Bill says. "Those kids pray for one another and encourage one another. They ask one another tough questions and keep one another accountable. In a sense, they pressure one another to keep on track with their faith. If someone starts slipping, the others grab him and pull him up. Most of the time, I just provide the kitchen table and a box of doughnuts; the boys keep the group going because they want it and need it."

The Bible is full of admonitions to surround ourselves with fellow believers who will support us and keep us strong. Consider just a few:

- "As iron sharpens iron, so one man sharpens another" (Proverbs 27:17).
- "Carry each other's burdens, and in this way you will fulfill the law of Christ" (Galatians 6:2).
- "Encourage one another daily, as long as it is called Today, so that none of you may be hardened by sin's deceitfulness" (Hebrews 3:13).
- "Confess your sins to each other and pray for each other so that you may be healed" (James 5:16).

Few activities will keep your teen growing in his faith—and out of trouble—more than involvement with a small group of like-minded Christians. Do everything you can to encourage your child to find a Bible study or discipleship group to meet with weekly. Ask your church's youth pastor what's available. Contact a local chapter of Young Life. See if a godly adult in your church will start such a group.

> *Few activities will keep your teen growing in his faith more than involvement with a small group of like-minded Christians.*

If all else fails, take a page out of Bill Slocum's playbook: Launch a group of your own. Sure, it'll require an investment of time and energy, but imagine the dividends it will pay.

## Encourage Church and Youth Group Participation

If being in a small group is one of the best things a teen can do to deepen her faith, participation in a vibrant, lively church youth group runs a close second. Teens need to be involved with other students in fellowship, teaching, service, and good, clean fun.

A father of two teenage girls, ages 13 and 15, said, "When we moved here from another city, the first thing we did was ask around, 'Which church in town has the best youth group?' At this stage, with the girls in the midst of these critical years, I put almost everything behind that consideration. As long as the church preaches the Word of God and its theology is sound, little else matters right now besides finding a place for my daughters to be with other teens who are excited about their faith."

That's a dad who is prudently looking out for his kids' best interests. After all, being involved in a strong church youth program provides teens (and their parents) many benefits, including the following:

1. *A positive alternative to negative environments.* We don't need to tell you that there are endless possibilities for kids to get into trouble and tempting situations. Going to parties, hanging out at the mall, cruising around town in a friend's car—these are the kinds of situations you would love to keep your teen *away* from. Youth group activities can occupy a son or daughter's time and attention in a clean, wholesome environment.

2. *A network of Christian friends and peers.* Yes, we know every youth group has its share of rascals and rebels, and some have their cliques. But your teen is still a lot better off hanging around with kids at church than just about anywhere else. Usually the committed, Christ-focused kids outnumber the apathetic and antagonistic ones.

3. *A chance to be part of something bigger than themselves.* Everyone, especially young people, wants to contribute to something significant, meaningful, and enduring. That's what attracts kids to the idea of a revolution; they want to change the world. Great! Channel all that energy and fervency into Christian ministry. Well-organized, dynamic youth groups offer teens the chance to

DISCIPLING

give themselves to something transcendent, a cause that will have lasting effects.

4. *The reinforcement of values from people besides Mom and Dad.* As we'll point out in the next section, teenagers desperately need other Christian adults in their lives, people who will provide a consistently positive influence. During the years when your son or daughter begins to question what you say—or disregards your views altogether—it's reassuring to know that a youth pastor and adult volunteers are supporting the values you're teaching at home.

As with small-group involvement, steer your teen toward an excellent church youth program. Do all you can to ensure that he or she benefits from this kind of positive input and support.

## Find and Connect Your Teen to a Christian Mentor

It's almost inevitable: At some point during adolescence, your teen will assert independence and pull away from you to one degree or another. He won't seek your input (he might even ignore it when you offer it), and he'll look to other people for affirmation and guidance. That's normal and usually healthy, provided he doesn't follow people who are bad influences.

And that raises a question: Who is your son or daughter going to look to for counsel and companionship? Wise parents see this scenario coming and plan for it by enlisting the help of mentors.

Matt Hannan, a pastor in Vancouver, Washington, realized his son and daughter would reach the stage where they would begin tuning out Mom and Dad and tuning in other adults. He was ready when it happened. Every Saturday evening, after he has preached his last sermon of the night (his large church has multiple services throughout the weekend), Matt and his wife and teenage kids go out to dinner. It's a tradition they all enjoy. But they don't just go by themselves; they go with the same group of Christian friends they've gotten to know well over the years. Occasionally they're joined by missionaries who are home on furlough or friends traveling through the area.

What happens at these weekly get-togethers, besides socializing and relaxing with friends, is informal mentoring. Matt explains: "I give my kids the right not to listen to us and accept our opinions—that's part of growing up. But I also reserve the right to have some say about who they will listen to. At our weekly dinners out, Ben and Amy are surrounded by people I trust, people who will be a positive influence to them. In a sense, this circle of friends is helping to raise our kids."

If informal mentoring works for some teens, others benefit from a more formal, structured arrangement. Kevin Walters of Fort Collins, Colorado, says this: "In the midst of my turbulent teen years, Kurt Davis came along and took me under his wing. I was about 15, and my relationship with my parents was strained—not outright fighting, more like a cold war. Kurt was in his midtwenties and a solid believer. He met with me once a week. Sometimes we'd study the Bible; other times we'd grab a pizza and talk. A couple times he even took me to his parents' mountain cabin for a weekend of fishing. I'd ask him all kinds of questions about friendship and girls and sex, and he never flinched. He gave me straight answers, and he told about his own struggles and weaknesses. He explained how applicable God is to real life. Most of all, he lived it."

Kevin sums up his mentoring experience this way: "I don't know where I'd be today without Kurt's influence and consistency. We ended up meeting together—every week—for three years. That was a huge commitment on his part. He was an anchor during a very stormy time in my life."

"Okay," you might be saying, "I'd love to connect my teen to a godly mentor, but how? Where do I go to sign up for a mentor?" If you are fortunate, your church may have some kind of mentoring or discipleship program. If not, here are a few suggestions for finding a mentor:

1. *Pray.* God wants your teen to be surrounded by positive influences even more than you do. Ask Him to connect your son or daughter with a great mentor.

2. *Explore your network of friends, family members, and fellow church members.* Flip through your mental Rolodex and consider who would be a good match with your teen. Each Sunday, look around for people who could be mentors for your child. In addition, ask your pastor or youth leader to suggest possible mentors.

*3. Seek and you just may find.* You can't expect someone to show up at your door and say, "Hi, I'd like to mentor your son. Here's my résumé, references, and a phone number where I can be reached." No, you or your teen will probably have to go looking.

Christy Smith wanted her son, Eric, to be mentored by a godly man, so she took the offensive. She asked her son's basketball coach, a Christian whom she knew Eric admired, if he would be willing to meet with her son or at least talk with him from time to time. Despite his busy schedule, the coach agreed, and for a couple of years Eric benefited from his coach's consistent input and godly influence.

*4. Start a mentoring program in your church or community.* If all else fails, take the lead and launch a mentoring ministry yourself. You'll help not only your own child but many other teens as well. Begin by discussing the need with your pastor, and offer to help get things started.

However you choose to go about it, encourage your kids to seek out other Christian adults—people who will reinforce the values you've been teaching. Your teens need guidance and instruction from other voices besides Mom and Dad's.

## Hold a Blessing or Rite-of-Passage Ceremony

When Allan Mesko drove his son, Brian, to the Ozark Conference Center about an hour west of Little Rock, the 16-year-old thought he and his dad were simply going to spend the night on the mountain. But Allan had other plans.

They checked in with the couple who manage the camp, and soon this couple's son invited Brian to go for a walk. As the two teenagers strolled down a path, suddenly the headmaster at Brian's Christian school stepped out from behind a tree. Brian's first thought was, *He must be staying at the lodge.*

But after a quick greeting, the other boy returned home. Brian and his headmaster continued walking, the older man explaining that Brian's father had asked him to share some thoughts on the subject of manhood. Bible in hand, he turned to the books of 1 and 2 Timothy and highlighted specific passages relevant to manhood.

After a while, the two came to a teepee, and Brian saw a pair of feet inside. Soon a new escort took the headmaster's place. Walking past ponds and through open meadows, this man talked with Brian about different choices he would face as a man. He also made a statement Brian will never forget: "Brian, maybe one day you'll be doing this walk with my son."

The pair headed into the woods, where a teacher at Brian's school was seated on a bench. His part was to cover the characteristics of manhood. After a while, the two headed back to the lodge, with Brian assuming that the surprises were now over.

They weren't. Four other adult friends were at the lodge waiting for him. Allan grilled some expensive steaks, and the celebrants drank soft drinks out of Mason jars. After dinner, the group gathered in a circle, and each man noted special qualities he had seen in Brian. The young man was speechless.

Allan then presented his son with James Dobson's book *Life on the Edge*, signed by all the men. He also gave his son a plaque, which read: "To my son, Brian Benjamin Mesko, in recognition of your initiation into the community of men. With much love and joy, Dad." To conclude the ceremony, the men gathered around Brian and prayed for him.

Before they left the camp the next morning, Allan and Brian walked the same course Brian had traveled the evening before. The young man repeated what he'd heard and pointed out to his father the key locations. Later, while Brian was occupied with the camp manager's son, Allan drove the same course in his car to take pictures. He later presented the photographs to Brian.

"When I think about that night, I am overwhelmed with joy," Brian says. "I'm so grateful for a dad who would do something like that."[2]

Undoubtedly, that teenager will look back on that ceremony as a highlight of his adolescence. How many grown men and women wish they'd had a community of older, respected people guiding them into adulthood—people who would make the effort to celebrate the passage into manhood or womanhood?

## Types of Ceremonies

Sociologists, psychologists, and religious leaders of all kinds have decried our society's lack of ceremonies that signify the move from

DISCIPLING

childhood to adulthood. Consider this: Between a baby dedication (which the kid won't remember) and high school graduation (when the child is almost out of the house), what ceremonies take place? They are few and far between. Those that do take place are sure to stand out in a teenager's memory for years to come.

In his book *Raising a Modern-Day Knight* (which is must reading for parents with sons), pastor and author Robert Lewis says:

> Ceremonies are those special occasions that weave the fabric of human existence. Weddings. Awards banquets. Graduations. The day you became an Eagle Scout or were accepted into a fraternity. We remember because of ceremony.
>
> Think back upon the significant moments in your life. With few exceptions, the value of those moments was sealed by a ceremony. Someone took the time to plan the details, prepare the speech, and purchase the awards—so you would feel special.
>
> Ceremony should be one of the crown jewels for helping a boy become a man. In many cultures throughout history, a teenage boy is taken through some type of ritual to mark his official passage into manhood. I believe one of the great tragedies of Western culture today is the absence of this type of ceremony.
>
> I cannot even begin to describe the impact on a son's soul when a key manhood moment in his life is forever enshrined and memorialized by a ceremony with other men.[3]

Although Lewis is writing for men and their sons, the same truth applies to girls. Our sons and daughters will benefit greatly from a ceremony held in their honor. Maybe this all sounds great to you, but you wouldn't know how to pull it off. Or maybe you're feeling a little intimidated and uncomfortable. As one dad said, "A man in my church held an elaborate ceremony for his 16-year-old son. It was a huge production involving lots of people, a banquet room, and all the rest. I couldn't do something like that. It's just not me."

Not to worry. The point is to do something—anything—that will honor your child and reinforce the ideals you've been teaching. Here are a few ideas to get your imagination working:

1. *A blessing ceremony.* This could range from the very simple (a few people praying over your teen) to the sophisticated (a meal, a formal blessing, prayers, gifts). Before Ed and Christy Smith's son, Eric, left for college out of state, they wanted to send him off with a blessing. They invited his closest friends and their parents as well as family and church members. All gathered at the Smiths' house for refreshments and conversation, and then the spotlight was focused on Eric. Many of the people talked about qualities in Eric they admired and ways they had seen him grow over the years. Others offered encouragement and advice for thriving in college. The ceremony ended with several people praying a special blessing on his life in the years ahead. For Eric—and everyone involved—it was a deeply meaningful and moving time.

2. *A Christian bar mitzvah (bas mitzvah for girls).* If you've been to a traditional bar mitzvah or bas mitzvah, you know how sacred and inspiring these ceremonies are. A bar mitzvah takes place when a Jewish boy reaches his 13th birthday and attains the age of religious duty and responsibility. The idea here is to weave Christian themes into the Jewish model, which usually involves reciting revered Bible passages, taking an oath or verbal commitment to the faith, commemorating the step from child to adult, and then feasting and partying.

3. *A manhood/womanhood ceremony.* This is the kind of event put on by Allan Mesko, highlighting a milestone in a teen's journey toward adulthood (for instance, age 13, 16, 18—or all of them). It might take place at a conference center, a hotel, a restaurant, or your home. And it might involve your immediate family, a handful of friends and family members, or a large number of people. (See chapter 26, "Marking Milestone Moments," for another example of this kind of ceremony.)

## Characteristics of Memorable Ceremonies

Robert Lewis says that, although ceremonies come in all shapes and sizes, the really good ones share four common characteristics:

1. *Memorable ceremonies are costly.* The more time, thought,

planning, effort, and money you give to a celebration, the more memorable it will be. "Memorability" grows in proportion to cost. The more you give, the greater the impact.

2. *Memorable ceremonies ascribe value.* By setting aside time, making the effort, spending money, and employing meaningful ceremony, we declare the high value of an individual. At the same time, ceremonies ascribe value to the beliefs and morals we hold important. Effective ceremony says, *You are important!* and *This moment is important!* It ascribes dignity and worth.

> *The more time, thought, planning, effort, and money you give to a celebration, the more memorable it will be.*

3. *Memorable ceremonies employ symbols.* Weddings are symbolized by a ring; Christmas, by a star; graduation, by a diploma. Each of these symbols calls to mind a host of pleasant memories. One dad who held a manhood ceremony for his 18-year-old, an avid hunter, gave an expensive compass, which he had engraved on the back: "Direct my footsteps according to your word" (Psalm 119:133). A mom who planned a 16th-birthday blessing ceremony for her daughter gave a nice key chain along with a handcrafted booklet entitled "Keys to a Great Life," in which she compiled advice and encouragement from friends and family members.

4. *Memorable ceremonies empower a life with vision.* The wedding ceremony points to a new life of one rather than two; the graduation ceremony envisions a new career; the fraternity ceremony envisions a new circle of friends; parent-child ceremonies envision a new stage of life. Ceremony marks the transition from one season to another. This fourth characteristic is the most important of them all.

Take the challenge: Hold a ceremony of some kind for your teen. Even the simplest events, when conducted in a spirit of honor and dignity, can be life-changing for a son or daughter. (For more on this subject, see chapter 26.)

## Show How to Think Christianly

Every person, whether he's aware of it or not, has a worldview— a set of values and beliefs about life and God and what's good and bad, important and inconsequential, true and false—that determines how he interprets everything he sees and hears and how he acts and reacts. That worldview is learned over time from parents and other family members, teachers, peers, the media, and whoever else has a chance to influence the person's thinking.

Our goal as Christians, and our desire for our children, is that we learn to think Christianly. That is, the values and beliefs that shape our perceptions of the world, that guide our thoughts and actions, should be those presented in the Bible, reflecting the mind and heart of God. And like our Savior, Jesus Christ—into whose likeness the Father is continually shaping us (see Romans 8:29)—we should apply that worldview to every area of life: work, relationships, ethics, entertainment, politics, and so on.

Instilling a Christian worldview in our teenagers is so important that a separate chapter (chapter 19) has been devoted to it. If you haven't already done so, please read that discussion of the truths that make up a Christian worldview and how you can impart them to your son or daughter.

## Teach the Importance of Evangelism

During family devotions one morning, Pat and Camilla Cottrell of Huntington Beach, California, asked their brood (all 11 of them) to set a spiritual goal for the coming months. The spring school semester was ending, and the more relaxing summer months were around the corner.

"What a great time to challenge ourselves to stretch and grow in some way!" Pat told them.

So as they went around the kitchen table, one child said she'd like to memorize five Bible verses. Another said he was going to read the *Chronicles of Narnia,* by C. S. Lewis. Another child, in early high school, said she was going to try to raise enough money to go on the church's short-term outreach to Mexico. On it went, until at last they came to 17-year-old Jesse, a freshman at a local community college.

"Well, I'm still working on my *last* goal," he said.

Pat and Camilla wondered what that was, since they hadn't set goals together in over a year. They asked him to explain.

"At the beginning of this semester," Jesse said nonchalantly, "I set a goal of witnessing to 42 people on campus. We've only got a week left, and I'm 10 short."

Pat snapped to attention. "You've shared your faith with 32 people this semester?" he asked. "That's incredible!"

Jesse shrugged it off. "Yeah, but I'm still praying I can meet my goal of 42. Seems unlikely, but then there's that all-things-are-possible-with-God verse, so who knows?"

Camilla suggested they all pray about Jesse's goal, which they did. A week later, with classes finished and finals over, the Cottrell tribe gathered around the table again. They were all waiting for a report but wanted Jesse to bring it up. Finally, one of the younger kids said, "Well, Jesse, c'mon. What happened?"

"Forty-two," he said. "I met my goal. I witnessed to 42 people this semester, 10 in the past week."

Wow! If Campus Crusade for Christ drafted students out of college the way the NFL does, Jesse might be a number-one pick. Somewhere along the line, that kid got the message that evangelism is important—he got the message and acted on it.

### Encouragement to Witness

How about your teen? Does he or she know the importance of telling people about God's love and grace? Jesus left no doubt that He intended His followers to spread the good news of salvation:

- "Let your light shine before men, that they may see your good deeds and praise your Father in heaven" (Matthew 5:16).
- "Go into all the world and preach the good news to all creation" (Mark 16:15).
- "You will be my witnesses in Jerusalem, and in all Judea and Samaria, and to the ends of the earth" (Acts 1:8).

Still, many people hear the words *evangelism* or *witness* and their blood runs cold. These words conjure up images of knocking on strangers' doors and debating with them about world religions. Or handing out tracts on the street corner while passers-by tell you to "get lost" (or worse). Some people protest, "I don't have the spiritual gift of evangelism, and I'm no good at it. My gift is encouragement, so I'll just encourage the evangelists while they win the lost."

It's true that evangelism is a spiritual gift, and some individuals are given special ability to speak persuasively to unbelievers about God's love and salvation (see Romans 12 and Ephesians 4). But it's clear from the verses above—and many other biblical passages—that *all* Christians are called to be witnesses for Christ. (A great scripture for your family to memorize is 2 Timothy 4:1-2.) And naturally, this principle should be demonstrated and reinforced by parents. Whether or not your spiritual gift is evangelism, you can model for your teen a heart for the lost *and* some kind of active witness to them.

> *Your teen needs to know that there are hundreds of ways to let our light shine.*

Having said that, your teen needs to know that there are hundreds of ways to let our light shine. Some people, like Jesse, have the ability and boldness to approach people on campus and tell them about Jesus. Others might feel more comfortable inviting a friend to a concert at church. Still others do best at witnessing by serving others. (In the resource list in appendix B, we'll recommend some books that provide lots of ideas and opportunities for evangelism.)

### Guidelines for Witnessing

Whatever form your teen's evangelism takes, some general principles will be helpful. Mike Ross, editor of *Breakaway* magazine, Focus on the Family's publication for teen guys, offers these ideas for effective witnessing in any setting:

*1. Forget "Christianese."* Nobody, especially teens, responds well to churchy lingo and Christian code words. Use your own language, and resist the urge to fall back on clichés and jargon.

*2. Live it.* Your actions really do speak louder than words. How you act when you're in class, on the soccer field, or at your job at McDonald's speaks volumes about your commitment to God. All your words and strategies for winning the lost will be worthless if your life doesn't back up what you say.

*3. Get a partner.* It's no surprise that Jesus sent out His disciples

**DISCIPLING**

to witness in pairs (see Luke 10:1). There's strength in numbers. Having a friend alongside bolsters your courage and provides support.

*4. Show love and compassion to others, instead of treating nonbelievers as a project.* When the religious expert asked Jesus to name the most important commandment, Jesus replied: " 'Love the Lord your God with all your heart and with all your soul and with all your mind.' This is the first and greatest commandment. And the second is like it: 'Love your neighbor as yourself' " (Matthew 22:37-39). That's what will win people to Christ—love. Some people may be won to Christ through debate and intellectual persuasion, but the majority are *loved* into God's kingdom.

*5. Be real with God and others.* Too many teens mistakenly believe that God doesn't want them to be honest about their lives. They think He will be upset if they tell Him how they really feel. But the Scriptures tell us that God does not want you to be superficial—in your relationship with Him, in your relationship with others, or in your own life. In Psalm 51:6, David wrote, "Surely you desire truth in the inner parts; you teach me wisdom in the inmost place."

Be honest about your pain, confusion, or doubt, even with people you're trying to reach with the Gospel. You aren't expected to have all the answers, just a committed, searching heart. The fact is, God desires truth and honesty at the deepest level and wants you to experience His love, forgiveness, and power in *all* areas of your life. Experiencing His love doesn't mean that all your thoughts, emotions, and behaviors will be pleasant and pure. It means that you can be *real*, feeling pain and joy, love and anger, confidence and confusion. It's this kind of honesty that will attract others to the Gospel.

*6. Instead of blending into the crowd, allow the Holy Spirit to touch the world through you.* "Do your best to present yourself to God as one approved, a workman who does not need to be ashamed and who correctly handles the word of truth" (2 Timothy 2:15).

*7. Bathe all your efforts in prayer.* If you want to win your friends and classmates to Christ, the best thing you can do is pray every day for God to draw those people to Himself, to humble them, and to give them an understanding of who He is.[4]

## Show Your Teen How to Disciple Friends

When it comes to discipleship, most teens join groups led by a youth pastor or other older person. But sometimes teens have an opportunity to disciple friends or classmates.

Fifteen-year-old Nate Altmeyer first met Tyler Cummings through a mutual friend. Nate was surprised when Tyler showed up at his church youth group a couple of weeks later, since Tyler had mentioned that he didn't go to church. After the meeting, Nate struck up a conversation, and before long Tyler started firing questions at him: "What did the pastor mean by 'righteousness'? What's salvation? What's a holy ghost?"

Nate answered his questions the best he could, then said, "Tell you what. Why don't you borrow my Bible and read the parts I've highlighted. Then we can meet sometime and talk about what you read. How's that sound?"

"Hey, that'd be great," Tyler said.

And that's what they did. Over Cokes the following week, the two talked through several passages and some basics of Christianity. Tyler had lots of questions, and Nate answered all the ones he could. They met four or five more times, and somewhere along the line, Tyler accepted Christ. Now Nate keeps up with his pal, even through Tyler attends a youth group at a different church.

If your teen expresses an interest in discipling someone, or if you want to encourage him in this direction, keep in mind a few points:

- A goal of discipleship is to help all involved, but especially the less mature believer, to grow in knowledge and understanding of Christ, to develop faith, and to make steps toward Christlikeness.
- Discipling someone else is a great way for your teen to grow and develop his own faith. Here, the cliché holds true: "No one learns more than the teacher."
- This kind of relationship can be one-on-one or in a group setting (see the earlier section on small groups).
- As with virtually every other spiritual pursuit, it's best to lead and encourage your teen by example. It will send a

**DISCIPLING**

powerful message if your son or daughter sees you meeting with someone in a discipling role and hears you talk about how rewarding it is.

Like mentoring, discipleship relationships can be formal or informal (like what Nate did). A more structured form of discipleship usually involves a set meeting time each week over several months, as the participants work through a book or Bible study guide. Going through a book or manual provides a road map for topics that will be important to cover and keeps discussions focused on specific issues and questions. If your teen is interested in discipling a friend or classmate, he can pick up one of the resources we recommend in appendix B.

If, however, your son or daughter prefers a more casual arrangement, talk through key Bible passages and subjects to cover in the discipling relationship. However your teen chooses to proceed, be sure to offer lots of encouragement for his efforts. After all, not all teens care about their friends or their faith enough to pursue an iron-sharpens-iron relationship like this.

## Continually Cast a Vision for Sexual Purity

When it comes to teen sexuality, there's good news and bad news. First the good: A recent survey by the Centers for Disease Control and Prevention showed that, compared to a decade ago, fewer teens are engaging in sexual activity, teens are waiting longer to have sex, and they are becoming involved with fewer partners. In

## A Biblical Blueprint

A good summation of God's advice on sex can be found in 1 Thessalonians 4:1-8. You might want to go through this passage of Scripture with your teen:

- Living a pure life pleases God (verse 1).
- God's will is that we avoid sexual immorality (verse 3).
- God wants us to learn how to control our bodies (verse 4).
- Our methods of controlling our desires must be holy and honorable (verse 4).

1991, 54 percent of teenagers reported ever having sex. That figure dropped to 50 percent 10 years later.[5]

While the decline is encouraging, that still means (and here's the bad news) that half of all teenagers are engaging in sex. Here's more sobering news for people of faith: Christian teens are nearly as sexually active as their non-Christian counterparts. According to a major survey by Josh McDowell Ministries, 43 percent of churched youth had engaged in sexual intercourse by the time they were 18, and another 18 percent had fondled breasts or genitals. Even more troubling, one-third of the youths said they were not able to state that premarital sexual intercourse was morally unacceptable.[6]

All these statistics probably just confirm what you already know: Our culture is saturated with sexual imagery, and the temptation is overwhelming. Unfortunately, many kids give in to their urges. And we hope it confirms something else for you: Moms and dads need to constantly cast a vision for their teen's sexual purity.

Allow us to cite one more research study that supplies more ammunition to dissuade teens from having sex. According to a poll by the National Campaign to Prevent Teenage Pregnancy, 55 percent of boys and 72 percent of girls surveyed regretted their decision to have sex.[7] With your consistent guidance in this difficult area, you can save your son or daughter significant heartache and regret. And when it comes to providing guidance, keep three points in mind:

First, the best way you can instill a sense of importance about

**DISCIPLING**

- How we control our bodies will differ from the methods of unbelievers (verse 5).
- Gratifying our sexual desires outside of marriage offends and detracts from the other person (verse 6).
- We should not take advantage of another person in order to satisfy our sexual desires (verse 6).
- These instructions come from God, not from man (verse 8).
- If we disobey these instructions, we reject God (verse 8).[8]

purity in your teen is to model it. This means being cautious about the kinds of imagery and references you allow into your own mind via the Internet, televi-

> *The best way you can instill a sense of importance about purity in your teen is to model it.*

sion, movies, music, and so on. These days, it's impossible to avoid *all* sexual innuendo or remarks, but it will speak volumes to your teen that you are trying your best to shield yourself (and your family) from degrading messages.

Second, use the teachable moments that we talked about earlier to discuss sexuality. You're bound to see TV commercials or billboards with suggestive messages. Take the opportunity to express your thoughts about what's right and what's wrong with these messages. Encourage your teen to give his or her perspective as well.

Third, reinforcing the importance of sexual purity is a consistent, ongoing process. Some parents are eager to get the "sex talk" out of the way and leave that awkward subject alone. But you need to have an open-ended, running dialogue with your teen. (We'll talk more about this idea in chapter 26.)

### Cultivate Peacemaking Skills

Peacemakers get a bum rap these days. When was the last time a high school handed out awards for "Peacemaker of the Year" or "The Most Valuable Mediator" at graduation? Unfortunately, kids who serve as peacemakers or arbitrators are sometimes looked upon as spineless or gutless, unwilling to go toe to toe in the midst of conflict.

Even in churches and youth groups we don't hear much about peacemaking as a virtue to cultivate in ourselves or our kids. But this was clearly a quality worth developing, according to biblical writers. A quick scan of your Bible's concordance will reveal two dozen or so references to peace and peacemakers. Here are a few:

■ "There is deceit in the hearts of those who plot evil, but joy for those who promote peace" (Proverbs 12:20).

**DISCIPLING**

- "Let us . . . make every effort to do what leads to peace and to mutual edification" (Romans 14:19).
- "Let the peace of Christ rule in your hearts, since as members of one body you were called to peace" (Colossians 3:15).
- "The wisdom that comes from heaven is first of all pure; then peace-loving. . . . Peacemakers who sow in peace raise a harvest of righteousness" (James 3:17-18).

Jesus even singled out people with this quality for special recognition:

- "Blessed are the peacemakers, for they will be called sons of God" (Matthew 5:9).

The implication here is that peacemaking skills are important and admirable in daily life, not just in crisis situations. Teens need to learn how to promote harmony at school, on the job, and at church; resolve disagreements with friends and family members; work together with people they find irritating; and defuse tense situations. Peacemaking is an essential part of Christian life and witness to the world.

The Bible offers numerous practical ideas for living peaceably, including these:

- "When words are many, sin is not absent, but he who holds his tongue is wise" (Proverbs 10:19).
- "A gentle answer turns away wrath, but a harsh word stirs up anger" (Proverbs 15:1).
- "Do not let the sun go down while you are still angry, and do not give the devil a foothold" (Ephesians 4:26-27).
- "Everyone should be quick to listen, slow to speak and slow to become angry, for man's anger does not bring about the righteous life that God desires" (James 1:19).

Does your teen have skills such as these? If so, cultivate them and honor them. If your teen is not a natural peacemaker, work on helping him or her develop in this area. You may want to research

**DISCIPLING**

passages like the ones above and talk about how they apply to everyday life. If your child has a problem with anger or a quick temper, you can find help in a resource like Neil Clark Warren's *Make Anger Your Ally*.

Recently, the Fort Worth *Star Telegram* reported that firefighters in Genoa, Texas, were accused of deliberately setting more than 40 destructive fires. When caught, they stated, "We had nothing to do. We just wanted to get the red lights flashing and the bells clanging."

The job of firefighters is to put out fires, not start them. Likewise, the job of Christians is to help resolve conflict, not start more of it. Encourage your teen to become someone who extinguishes fires of anger and tension.[9]

## Help Your Teen Learn Respect and Reverence for God

If you had to pick one word to describe the prevailing attitude of our culture, what would it be? *Self-centered?* Yes, that would get a lot of votes. How about *irresponsible?* That would be high on the list, too.

Here's one that would certainly make the top-10 list, maybe the top five: *irreverent* (sometimes known as *disrespectful* or *insolent*). Many, if not most, people in our society are irreverent toward others, toward our elected leaders, toward their employers—and, yes, toward God.

Lest we allow a subtle attitude of disrespect and irreverence to infiltrate our hearts, we may want to ponder the words of the apostle Paul: "Since we are receiving a kingdom that cannot be shaken, let us be thankful, and so worship God acceptably with reverence and awe, for our 'God is a consuming fire' " (Hebrews 12:28-29).

Respect and reverence for God and His Word are critical if we want to deepen our faith and the faith of our children. So, where will teens learn to revere God? Two places, primarily: in the home and at church.

### Revering God in the Home

As we've said repeatedly in this book, kids emulate the attitudes and behaviors of their parents. If you treat your relationship with

God and the Bible in an off-handed, cavalier manner, guess what? You're likely to find your teens doing the same. There are many ways to demonstrate reverence for God in the home, but consider two of the most important aspects:

1. *How you talk to and about God.* Are your prayers filled with praise, adoration, and veneration for Him? Although prayers are not necessarily meant to instruct your teen, you can be sure he is soaking in how you communicate with God. When you talk about the Lord at home or in the car, do you refer to Him in ways that show the utmost respect, or are you perhaps a little too casual and nonchalant?

2. *How you respond when others talk about God.* Do you show "righteous anger" when someone uses the Lord's name in vain? Do you say anything when you overhear someone cursing? Do you sit through movies or television shows that degrade the image of God or belittle His authority? Sitting passively by as others disparage God's name demonstrates to your teen that it's no big deal.

Dr. James Dobson has spoken and written extensively on the importance of teaching respect in the home. Some reasons for establishing respectful relationships between parents and teens are obvious, but here's one you may not have considered: "Respect is critical to the transmission of faith from one generation to the next. The child who disdains his mother and father is less likely to emulate them on the things that matter most. Why? Because children typically identify their parents—and especially their fathers—with God. Therefore, if Mom and Dad are not worthy of respect, then neither are their morals, their country, or even their most deeply held convictions."[10]

### Revering God at Church
Sadly, some churches have let the sense of awe for the Lord and His Word diminish. They present God as a buddy, a pal, a chum to take along on field trips or family vacations. While it's certainly true that God desires friendship with us, there's a danger in bringing Him down to our level. We can begin to slide toward irreverence. (Thankfully, the majority of churches maintain a proper reverence for God, and we're grateful for them.)

How does your church do in this area? What attitude toward God does your teen pick up in your church? Matt Hannan, the pastor we mentioned in the mentoring section, is in the habit of having his church members stand when Scripture is read, following the Jewish tradition of showing reverence and holy fear for God's Word. Sometimes he has his congregation, which numbers in the thousands, kneel when they pray during services. Even though his church would be described as informal (definitely not the suit-and-tie crowd), Matt and his staff model an attitude of reverence for God.

When we revere God, we give Him the authority and honor that are rightfully His. Help your son or daughter see that our heavenly Father is worthy of our highest respect.

## Instill a Heart for Missions and Service

In the last chapter, we stressed the point that mission trips are an excellent way to help move your teen's attitude from selfish to selfless. When kids get out of their comfort zone and into the real world, rubbing shoulders with needy people, they're sure to be changed. Although there are numerous opportunities to serve in our own country, let's focus on helping your teen develop a global missions perspective.

A plethora of missions materials exists: books, videos, posters, literature, and so on. Many are free and only a phone call or Web search away. Beyond that are the missionaries themselves, along with their organizations. Here are some ways to link your teens with these resources:

*1. Read missionary stories.* You might read a missionary biography together as part of your family devotions. Most church libraries have some. The stories of Hudson Taylor, Gladys Aylward, and David Livingstone provide a healthy mix of adventure and faith that kids of all ages will enjoy.

*2. Attend missionary meetings.* Mission-minded churches often hold annual conferences, inviting a wide variety of mission speakers to participate. Such events are usually planned with the whole family in mind. Make a tour of the displays, and find a missionary family you'd like to know better.

*3. Have missionaries in your home.* Missionaries return from their fields of service every few years for 6 to 12 months, a period called "home assignment." Take advantage of their presence in your area and invite them over for a meal. Tell them to bring a missions video and their photo album. Allow your kids to ask all the questions they want, and fill in the gaps with queries of your own.

*4. Become pen pals.* With some exceptions, missionaries make the world's best letter writers. Starving for news from home, they love mail. Have your teens write letters to adult missionaries or to their children. Relationships built by mail often last a lifetime. Of course, these days, E-mail is an invaluable tool for keeping in touch with people around the world. Many young people find it easier to correspond via the Internet than to sit down and hand-write letters.

*5. Send a care package.* Choose a missionary family and ask if their country of service has a reliable postal system. Then, if they do, discover their needs and put together a box of items that will thrill them. Consider spices, gourmet coffee, herbal teas, cake mixes, instant puddings, Hershey's Kisses, stationery, Christian music, the latest devotional book, a roll of film—all are possibilities. Include a few family photos, an audiocassette of greetings, and you're set. Involve your teens in everything from picking the items to mailing the box.

*6. Adopt a national.* Some organizations specialize in sponsoring Third World children. There are also missions that support national pastors who otherwise could not minister in poverty-stricken lands. Any missionary would be happy to provide you with photos, prayer requests, and background information about specific people to whom they minister.

*7. Take a mission trip.* With travel more widespread and affordable than ever, seriously consider this option. Whether you do puppet ministry on the streets of Panama City, help build an orphanage in Ivory Coast, or quietly visit with longtime missionary friends in Irian Jaya, your teens will never forget the experience.

*8. Pray for missionaries.* Friends of ours have a photo album of all the missionaries they know. Their six children regularly pore over its pages. Along with the photos, our friends keep the most

**DISCIPLING**

recent prayer requests sent by each missionary. And they pray. If you do nothing else in your endeavor to assist God's work in far lands, this is the road to take. Teach your children to pray for missions, then watch them teach you.[11]

Encourage your teen to look beyond his own neighborhood, city, and country. Help him see that God is at work throughout the world, and we can be a part of the exciting things happening through mission work.

As important as overseas or cross-cultural outreach is, however, let's not forget the innumerable opportunities to serve right in your own community. A teen with a heart for service need not wait for the once-a-year church mission trip. Encourage your son or daughter to volunteer at a soup kitchen, a crisis pregnancy center, a nursing home, or a relief organization in your area. As we suggested in the last chapter, you might consider taking on a service project as a family. Highlight for your teen the importance of reaching out to people both abroad *and* at home.

> *Teach your children to pray for missions, then watch them teach you.*

## Make Sure Your Teen Is Getting Enough Sleep

Sarah is a typical American teenager. Up at around six on weekdays, she hurries to get ready and to inhale a bit of breakfast before running out the door for the drive to high school and her first class, which starts shortly after seven. She goes through her day in a sort of mental fog caused by sleep deprivation, struggling to concentrate on her teachers' lessons and to remember what she studied the night before.

After school, Sarah hustles to another tough gymnastics practice, followed by rehearsal for the school's spring musical. Then, after a quick dinner, she's off to her part-time job at the local Starbuck's. When she gets home mid to late evening, she faces a tall stack of demanding homework that's all due the next day. But that will wait until she has talked with at least a couple of friends on the phone about the day's events.

Finally, eyes barely still open (though she's wishing she hadn't drunk that last latte at work), she stumbles into bed sometime after eleven. She's exhausted, but the caffeine hasn't quite worn off. At last, however, the fatigue wins out and she falls asleep around midnight. In the morning, the cycle will begin all over again.

Sleep experts say most adolescents need eight and a half to nine and a quarter hours of sleep every night. Yet the overwhelming majority of teens (85 percent) get less than that—on average, about two hours less. The result is that most of today's teens are chronically sleep-deprived. Many are so sleepy that they live in "a kind of twilight zone," says adolescent sleep researcher Mary Carskadon. "The term 'zombie' is a pretty accurate description."[12]

What are the consequences of this situation, and why do we take space to talk about teens and their lack of sleep in a guide to mentoring them spiritually? Because being in a state of constant fatigue can directly and seriously harm the quality of a teen's spiritual life.

Consider, first of all, that one of the best ways to grow spiritually is to spend regular time—ideally, every day—in studying the Bible and praying. A daily quiet time is one of the best habits we can instill in our children. But look again at Sarah's schedule, which is typical of many teens' lives. When is she going to fit time with God into her itinerary? Most days, it simply isn't going to happen.

If Sarah does carve out a few minutes to be alone with God and her Bible, what will be the quality of that experience? Sleep loss impairs, among other things, the ability to direct and sustain your attention, the ability to block out distractions, working memory, and the ability to be innovative and flexible in your thinking. A two-hour lack of sleep in one night, for example (and remember that this is the norm for our teens), means that the next day you can expect

- a 20 percent drop in memory
- a 30 percent loss in ability to communicate effectively
- a 75 percent decrease in ability to pay attention
- and a 50 percent drop in judgment and decision-making skills.[13]

**DISCIPLING**

**DISCIPLING**

Thus, not only will Sarah's schoolwork suffer from her lack of sleep but so, too, will any time and effort she puts into developing her relationship with God.

Neither is that the only way in which a teen's spiritual life will be affected. Lack of sleep—even for one night, let alone night after night for months on end—causes an adolescent to feel depressed, moody, irritable, impatient, and angry. It actually alters the way he views life, says sleep researcher Carskadon. "Kids walk around under a gray cloud. Things that are happy and pleasant seem less so. And things that are sad and unpleasant seem more so."

In other words, the emotional roller coaster that teens tend to ride naturally is exaggerated and skewed by lack of sleep. The highs they should enjoy are minimized, while the lows they experience become all the more severe.

Spiritually, this means that a sleep-deprived teen is going to be less aware of God's presence in her life and of the good things He's doing for and with her. To the extent that she *is* aware, she will be less appreciative and less able to enjoy them.

On the other hand, when she's feeling as if the whole world is against her and no one loves her and so she might as well give in to some temptation offered by peers (drugs, alcohol, sex, whatever), the negative feelings will be stronger and the temptation harder to resist. When she does succumb to some enticement, she'll be much more likely to feel as though God (and her parents)

## Teens' "Things I Wish My Parents Had Done Differently," Part 9

■ "I wish we would have had family time. I wish we would have studied the Bible and prayed more together. Later on we started moving more that way, and it affected our family positively."

■ "I wish my parents would have let me question more. If I disagreed or saw issues differently, it was discouraged."

■ "I really wish my parents would have encouraged me to join the youth group at our church even though I didn't want to at the time. I was so involved in sports and every other activity that I didn't see the need. I'm sure the Christian must hate and condemn her. And even if she resists most temptations, she will tend to have a more negative view of God and her parents and life in general.

In short, lack of sleep can do all kinds of direct and serious harm to your teen's spiritual life (not to mention impairing school performance, the ability to drive safely, and so on).

As a parent, here are some things you can do to help your adolescent get adequate sleep:

- Be a good role model. Again, your best input into your child's life is the example you set. Consistently get enough sleep yourself.
- Make it clear to your teen that adequate sleep is as important a need as good nutrition. We tend to want to see our kids involved in as many positive activities as possible, but if your child isn't getting enough sleep, you may need to help him think through his priorities and perhaps cut back. If he starts getting sufficient rest, he will enjoy his remaining activities much more.
- Help her to establish a consistent bedtime routine: a set bedtime, some calming activity (for example, reading a favorite book or magazine) for the last half hour of her day, tending to personal needs (such as brushing her teeth), and so on. Such a routine signals the mind and body that it's time to slow down and sleep.

**DISCIPLING**

support, friendships, and community would have helped me take a stand in front of my nonbelieving friends."

- "If they hadn't been so strict, I may have felt more comfortable sharing with them about things that were going on in my life, and communication perhaps wouldn't have been so awkward. It still sometimes is awkward to talk to them about serious things or spiritual things."
- "I wish they would have told me the importance of finding accountability with someone a little older than myself."

- Keep his bedroom quiet, dark, and cool. He might want to use a fan or other "white noise" generator to block out sleep-disturbing sounds.
- Encourage her to avoid consuming caffeine in the five hours preceding bedtime.
- If he needs a bedtime snack, give him something that contains calcium (for example, a glass of warm milk), since calcium has a mild sedative effect, or something containing tryptophan (for example, turkey, banana, yogurt, whole-grain crackers, or peanut butter), which is an amino acid that also promotes sleep.

Finally, don't assume that being sleep-deprived is just a normal part of the adolescent years. It may seem that way more and more, but it shouldn't be and it doesn't have to be, especially when the consequences can be so severe.

## If Your Teen Moves Away from the Lord

Some of you don't know your teen's whereabouts. Some of you do know, and it shreds your heart. You've come to the local precinct to pick him up. You know about the stuff she's drawing up her nose or holding in her lungs. You've witnessed the explosions, the ranting, the blaming, the tears. You know what it's like to try to say something—anything—to help her see the folly of her thinking, only to find yourself in the crosshairs of her rage.

They're the prodigals of life—the teens who aren't ready for independence but take it anyway. They're the lost boys and lonely girls who have found the safety of home too confining and the house rules too demanding.

Some are card-carrying prodigals, while others are prodigals-in-waiting, young apprentices of the self-destructive lifestyle who are starting to show the telltale signs of wanderlust. And whether they're out of your sight or in your face, whether they're teenagers or old enough to raise a new generation of prodigals, they're never far from your heart.

Jesus told a story in Luke 15:11-32 about a young man who shamed his dad and scorned his family, only to return, hoping to secure a meager job in the family business. In the book *Echoes of His Presence*, author and Bible historian Ray Vander Laan tells us that this story wasn't original with Jesus. Rabbis had told it for centuries to teach lessons on the challenges of good fathering. But Jesus changed the ending. And His editing of the story drew the huge contrast between the heart of God and the wisdom of man.

The original story ended something like this: The prodigal son returns home. Once ushered into his father's presence, he repents of his sin, acknowledges that he is not worthy to be part of the family, and asks to be hired on as a servant. The father not only refuses to welcome his son back but he also shames him for his misdeeds and refuses to give him a job in the family business. He shows his son the door, and people applaud the father for his act of tough love.

> **The truth is, there's a little prodigal in all of us.**

The father in Jesus' story, however, responded very differently. He saw his son a long way off, girded up his robe, and ran out to meet him. He showered him with kisses and tears, and he hugged the breath out of him. When the boy spoke about his unworthiness, the father stopped him midsentence and called for a new outfit and the signet ring to identify him as a son in good standing.

If you've struggled with the pain of a prodigal, take courage from your heavenly Father, who knows what it's like to deal with wayward children. Learn from His lead when that prodigal finally makes his way home.

The truth is, there's a little prodigal in all of us. Someday you're going to make your way toward your heavenly home. When you do, you just might find a gracious Father running to meet you with open arms. And don't be surprised when His precious and faithful Son takes your face in His nail-pierced hands, kisses you, and whispers, "Welcome home."[14] But for now, if your child has moved away from the Lord, what can you do?

*1. Realize that God understands your pain.* The primary theme of the Old Testament concerns a loving Father who continually reached out in love to His children, only to have them repeatedly reject and disappoint Him. God knows what it's like to have children rebuff and refuse Him and go their own way.

**DISCIPLING**

One common characteristic in parents of prodigals is an overwhelming sense of failure. The parents feel these pangs deeply, even though many have done far more to encourage their children than was ever done for them by their own parents. Others live with the genuine guilt of knowing they could have done more when their children were younger. They could have given more, disciplined more, sacrificed more. The more alone we feel in our pain, the more we need to lock our gaze onto the God who knows our hurt, sees our tears, and hears our sighs. The same God who dealt with the failure of the nation of Israel time and again does understand us and offers us daily comfort.

*2. Seek support from others who have shared a similar pain.* Chances are, you know parents whose child has chosen the path of rebellion. Nobody understands like someone who has been there. These people can offer you support, encouragement, and a listening ear. Take a risk and call someone who has been through the anguish of having a teen walk away from the Lord and rejected the family's standards of morality. If you don't know any parents of prodigals, ask your pastor to connect you to one.

*3. Get sound advice and wise counsel.* In addition to seeking encouragement from parents who have been there, meet with your pastor, a youth pastor, or a counselor to devise a plan for rescuing your child. Talk with experts who understand what your teen is going through—and know what might turn him around. There's no sense trying to handle a rebellious situation on your own; listen to those who speak with the voice of authority and experience.

*4. Do all you can to win back your child.* Take appropriate, measured action to turn your teen back toward the light. For instance, if your teen has fallen in with the wrong crowd at school, maybe he needs to be moved to another school. If your teen refuses to participate in your church's youth program because it's "lame" and "boring," investigate alternatives that may be more appealing to him. If your relationship with him is strained, perhaps he would be willing to see a family counselor with you. Or maybe you need to invest more time in rebuilding the relationship using some of the ideas in part two of this book.

In the meantime, continue to witness to your teen with your

godly example. Show her that being in fellowship with God and following His standards is the most satisfying and fulfilling way to live. If she's bothered by "hypocrites" in the church (a common teen complaint), make sure you're not one of them—that your actions match your words and you keep your promises.

5. *Enlist the help of a mentor or other influential people.* Earlier in this chapter, we discussed how mentors often have an over-whelmingly positive impact on a teen's attitude, behavior, and beliefs. An admired adult can also help when adolescents turn away from the Lord. Rebellious teens might be willing to listen to a mentor even as they ignore Mom and Dad's guidance. Muster your reserve army of mentors, coaches, teachers, extended family members, or anyone else who might be able to reach your teen.

6. *Emulate our heavenly Father's unconditional love.* God's love for each of His children is unchanging, enduring, and unwaver-ing, regardless of how badly we blow it. God said, "I have loved you with an everlasting love; I have drawn you with loving-kind-ness" (Jeremiah 31:3) and "Never will I leave you; never will I for-sake you" (Hebrews 13:5). Let this kind of love be your model as you express and demonstrate love for your teen. Communicate to your son or daughter often, "There's nothing you could do that would make me stop loving you."

7. *Pray, pray, pray.* When we're desperate and overwhelmed, prayer can seem like a last resort, a last-ditch effort to ask God to intervene in our child's life. In fact, prayer should be the first and foremost strategy for winning back a wayward teen. Moms and dads of prodigal teens should heed Paul's admonition to "pray without ceasing" (1 Thessalonians 5:17, NASB). This means consis-tently, throughout the day, asking God to protect, guide, and direct your teen—and bring him safely back home, both physi-cally and spiritually.

8. *Never, ever give up.* In chapter three, we talked about the qualities of relentless parents—moms and dads who love their teens with dogged determination and unwavering resolve. (You may find it helpful to reread that chapter.) This is the kind of love parents of prodigals need to summon up from deep within them-selves. No matter how angry or anguished, frustrated or fearful you are, resolve to never stop believing your teen will return.

DISCIPLING

At times, such as when your prodigal does something particularly hurtful, you may find yourself unable to summon such love. If that happens, don't berate yourself for being a bad parent; you're just an imperfect human being, like the rest of us. But take your feelings honestly to the Lord in prayer, and ask once again for His love to fill you, along with His wisdom and patience. Ask Him to help you *act* in love even when you don't *feel* loving. He delights in ministering to parents who are seeking to follow His example.

## A Faith That Lasts

In their book *Guiding Your Teen to a Faith That Lasts*, Kevin Huggins and Phil Landrum wrote:

> Many Christian parents assume that our greatest responsibility is to get our kid to take hold of Christianity, to get him to be a responsible, committed Christian. But what about the kid who has drifted away?
>
> Usually, this kid has, at one time or another, openly taken hold of Christianity. He tried it but decided to give it up. If we say our greatest responsibility is to get our teen to take hold of Christianity, what do we do when he gets disillusioned with that choice?
>
> Getting a teenager to make a commitment to Christianity is not the hard part. The hard part is helping him find in Christianity something that will motivate him to give his life to it.[15]

As you employ the strategies and faith-training endeavors presented in this chapter, your child's love and commitment to God will, we trust, become deeply rooted and steadfast. As you help your teen become a true disciple of Jesus Christ, he will become motivated to give his life in service to God. There are, of course, no guarantees that your teen won't one day wander from the Lord, but providing a solid foundation of belief and understanding of God's Word is the best way to instill a faith that lasts a lifetime.

**DISCIPLING**

# PART 4

■ ■ ■

# Enjoying the End Result

As your older teen prepares to leave home for college, a job, or military service, you can have confidence that key spiritual milestones have been reached and Christlike character qualities have been developed.

# Anticipating Success

Sports psychologists, coaches, and performance consultants encourage athletes to visualize victorious moments—to conjure up in their minds the scene when a glorious triumph is achieved. The athletes are guided through a frame-by-frame sequence in which a heroic feat is replayed over and over like a highlight reel on ESPN. The gymnast pictures herself sprinting fluidly down the runway and vaulting in a flawless display of strength and grace, earning perfect 10s from the judges. The tennis player envisions an exquisite, indefensible serve as the ball rockets over the net and skitters along the centerline. Game, set, and match.

These kinds of visualization techniques have been proved to enhance performance, boost motivation, and reduce fear and anxiety for athletes in virtually all sports. And if this strategy for success works so well in the sports world, it can surely be transferred to other areas of life, including raising teenagers.

For parents of teens, visualizing success means looking ahead to the day when your son or daughter will leave home and anticipating being filled with pride and satisfaction at the young man or woman who waves good-bye to you. It means envisioning your teen as a young adult who is prepared to face the challenges of life, equipped with a solid foundation of faith and armed with an understanding of God's Word. It means expecting to say to yourself as your child leaves the nest, *We had our share of struggles, but that kid turned out okay. Better than okay—he's terrific. I couldn't be more proud.*

Envisioning a positive outcome motivates our action, shifts our thinking from pessimistic to optimistic, and enables us to fix our eyes on the objective before us. It provides a goal to aim for, a finished portrait to work toward. Lest you think all this is just mind games, many research studies have demonstrated the effectiveness of rehearsing an outstanding performance and forecasting a favorable conclusion.

> *Looking ahead with hope and optimism helps to keep today's struggles and tussles in perspective.*

When you expect success, you actually increase the chances of its coming to fruition. Psychologist Neil Clark Warren explains:

> For more than three decades, research evidence has existed showing a close connection between expectation of an outcome and the actual outcome, especially for events in which the individual making the prediction is directly involved. . . . What you expect has a big influence on the final result of whatever your expectations are about. This is true even when your expectations involve someone else's behavior.[1]

Looking ahead with hope and optimism also helps to keep today's struggles and tussles in perspective. Petty problems and disagreements have a way of evaporating when you think forward to when your child is grown. Moms and dads draw courage to press on when they imagine their child's graduation day, wedding day, or some other milestone event. Somehow the current squabble about homework doesn't seem so important when you envision the day your son will load the last box in his car before heading off to college two time zones away.

The fight you had with your daughter last week (what was it about, anyway—the car or curfew or something?) seems trivial when you imagine the day she'll leave for a yearlong mission trip to Zaire.

> *"Long before your child sets foot in his dorm, you'll begin the transition to college-style parent. It's a transition fraught with misgivings and exuberance, with self-doubt and bursts of confidence, with joyful letting go and tearful hanging on. And in case you think these refer only to your child's feelings, they don't. These [emotions] besiege just about every parent along about the second semester of the junior year of high school. That's when the reality sets in that your child—not someone else's this time—will be going off to college."*
>
> —*Norman Gidden*, Parenting through the College Years[2]

Here's one more benefit of anticipating the successful culmination of your parenting efforts: It assures you that the investment of your time, energy, emotion, and money is really worthwhile, even if you don't see tangible results right now.

Family counselor Robin Wall says many of the parents she sees for therapy are frustrated and discouraged by pouring so much into their teenagers' lives with seemingly little to show for it. "Much of what parents do during the growing-up years is groundwork," she says. "By consistently guiding and nurturing their teenagers, they lay a solid foundation that kids can build their lives on. I sometimes tell moms and dads, 'The rewards of your hard work now may not be evident for years. But all your effort is definitely making a difference. And anticipating the satisfaction of a job well done provides motivation and inspiration to keep going even when you want to give up.' "

If you're in the midst of raising a teen or preteen, it might be tough to imagine your child at his high school (or college) graduation receiving a diploma. It may seem far-fetched right now to think about hearing the words "Mom, Dad, I just signed a lease on an apartment. I'll be moving out the first of the month." You may really have to stretch your imagination to picture your daughter becoming a parent herself. But be assured—these events will happen.

Let us encourage you to take a few minutes to envision what it will be like: watching your son pull out of the driveway for the last time and shouting, "I'll call ya" . . . or taking your daughter

**SUCCESS**

to the airport as she heads off to college and knowing you won't see her till Christmas . . . or hearing your son announce that he's been accepted into the Army and he'll be heading off to basic training in a few weeks.

In case you're having a little trouble visualizing the Big Good-bye, when your son or daughter will leave home (along with all the emotions you'll feel at that earth-shaking moment), put yourself in the shoes of a parent who's walked that path:

> *"The greatest gifts you can give your children are the roots of responsibility and the wings of independence."*
> —*Denis Waitley*, The Winning Family[3]

## "I Wish I Could Be with You Forever"

Nancy Rue will never forget taking her daughter, Marijean, to college for her freshman year—about 2,500 miles from home. It's one of those gut-wrenching, heartrending events that stays with a parent long after other, less significant memories recede into the background or disappear from consciousness altogether. As an only child, Marijean had been unusually close to her mom, a writer and educator, throughout the teen years, and both of them knew this transition wouldn't be easy.

The two drove together in Marijean's Jeep from their home in Lebanon, Tennessee, to the Bay Area in California, where Marijean would be attending the University of San Francisco. (Nancy's husband, Jim, who builds stage sets for the country music industry in Nashville, was forced to stay behind.)

As the Jeep rumbled through the endless cornfields of Kansas and vast stretches of desert in Nevada, their conversation drifted toward Marijean's growing-up experiences.

They howled when they remembered the time Marijean was three and she pointed to a rather large woman in the grocery store and shouted, "That lady has big bun-buns!"

They both cringed when they recalled the time Marijean's first date came to pick her up and Jim, a former Navy SEAL, gave the kid his most intimidating glare to keep him in line.

They also looked ahead: What challenges would college bring for Marijean? And what challenges would an empty nest bring for Nancy and Jim?

**SUCCESS**

After three days of driving, they arrived in northern California. They found Marijean's dorm on campus, hauled in boxes and clothes, and took care of administrative details. For a couple of days, the two of them scouted out the campus, located classrooms, bought textbooks, explored San Francisco, rummaged through bookstores, and ate at seafood restaurants.

Finally, the moment both of them had been dreading arrived—it was time for Marijean to take Mom to the airport. They made small talk on the way, chitchatting about Nancy's upcoming writing projects and the novel Marijean was reading. They pulled up to the curb at the Oakland Airport, unloaded Nancy's suitcase, and stood for a moment that seemed frozen in eternity.

At last, Marijean threw her arms around her mom. "Are you going to be okay, Mom?" she asked.

Nancy remembers thinking, *Aren't I supposed to ask you that?*

"Sure," she said. "Of course." But her quavering voice betrayed her.

There they stood, embracing and crying, until it was time for Nancy to catch her plane to Nashville.

"Good-bye, Mom," Marijean said. "I love you. I wish I could be with you forever."

The next several days were tough for Nancy. She settled in at home, told Jim all about the trip, and busied herself with work projects. But she was restless, thinking about her little girl so far away in a huge, foreboding city. At night, she slept fitfully. During the day, she couldn't concentrate on her work.

Hardest of all, waves of grief and loss rolled over Nancy like huge breakers. "I cried and cried like never before," she recalls.

Then, after three days, Marijean called. "Hey, ya'll, I'm having so much fun! We have a posse of, like, six girls, and we go everywhere together. I've seen an opera, and we walked across the Golden Gate Bridge. I drove everybody to Berkeley to buy books because our bookstore is lame. Classes start Monday, and I think I'm gonna be okay."

Amazing how one brief phone call can turn a parent's mood from bleak to buoyant.

"When I got that phone call hearing she was okay, then I knew

## Teens' "Traits of Great Parents," Part 10

- "They love, care for, and respect their teens. They listen and try to understand where the teens are coming from in every situation. They also respect privacy while staying involved. Overall, *love* is the most important thing to show a teen."
- "Understanding and listening, nonjudgmental, strong Christian character."
- "Active parenting—involved; encouraging; flexible with boundaries; healthy relationships in and outside of the family."
- "They have humility to admit when they make a mistake. Praying *with* teens makes a huge statement: 'I care for you, and I want to pray with you. I may not know the perfect answer or solution, but together, we will petition our Father for help.' "

*I* would be okay," Nancy recalls. And finally, she got a good night's sleep.

But that didn't mean her powerful feelings disappeared. A couple of days after Marijean's phone call, Nancy went grocery shopping at the local supermarket. She stopped in the produce section to put something in her cart, and she heard a mother in the next aisle yelling and berating her child.

"All the emotions I'd been dealing with the previous week came rushing to the surface," she says. "I wanted to sprint over to the next aisle, grab that lady by the shoulders, and scream, 'Stop it! That little child of yours is going to be gone before you know it. One day she's sitting in your grocery cart, begging you to buy Apple Jacks cereal, and the next day she's grown and off to college. Gone forever. You can waste these years fussing and fuming at your kid, or you can love her while you have the chance.' "

Four years have passed since Nancy took her daughter to college. And as Nancy looks back, she recognizes a critical component that helped ease that traumatic transition—knowing that she and Jim had raised a great daughter. Even though the letting-go process was painful, Nancy was proud of the person Marijean had become, and that made it all worthwhile.

Jim concurs: "The day Marijean turned 18—the day she legally became an adult—Nancy and I whooped and hollered, high-fived each other, and shouted, 'Yeah, we did it! We made it!' Our excitement came from knowing that we had survived the challenges, all the ups and downs, and our little girl had turned into a terrific young adult."

## Sending Them Off Well Equipped

> *"Forgetting what is behind and straining toward what is ahead, I press on toward the goal to win the prize for which God has called me heavenward in Christ Jesus."*
> *—Philippians 3:13-14*

As Nancy and Jim Rue discovered, seeing your child move out and move on can be daunting—an experience filled with bittersweet emotions. When your time comes, you may suffer a sense of loss, sorrow, and heartache from knowing your child—whose diapers you changed, whom you taught to roller-skate, who used to sit on your lap—is never again going to occupy his or her room on a permanent basis. And if your teenager turns out to be someone you're proud of, you're likely to feel profound satisfaction and gratification. All those years of sacrifice, frustration, and hard work will have paid off in a big way.

Witnessing your child's flight from the nest may be one of the toughest things you'll ever do, but it will undoubtedly be easier if you know he is equipped and prepared to meet the challenges ahead. As psychologist Laurence Steinberg says, "The parent-adolescent relationship is like a partnership in which the senior partner (the parent) has more expertise in many areas but looks forward to the day when the junior partner (the adolescent) will take over the business of running his or her own life."[4]

Indeed, your child is an adult-in-training, an individual who will someday soon stride out of your home and into the world. With this in mind, let us ask some questions to help you think through what kind of teenager you hope to raise and guide into adulthood:

1. As you look ahead, what will bring you deep-down satisfaction when your child leaves home? Knowing that she is going to influence the world in some way? Knowing that he cares about others? Knowing that she has an authentic love for God?

2. Do you tend to evaluate your child on the basis of what he does or who he is? In other words, how do accomplishments and achievements (good grades, athletic success) stack up against character qualities (honesty, servanthood)?

SUCCESS

■ ■ ■

## Helping Your Teenagers Choose a College

■ *Give your children a choice.* Instead of predetermining your teen's university, the best things you can do are to gather and give information, identify and state your boundaries or limitations to those choices, and then offer encouragement and support as a choice is made.

We prayed our high school seniors would be accepted by at least two colleges that were acceptable to us, so the final choice would be theirs. At that stage of growing independence, teens need to have ownership of the decision. Otherwise, they won't buy into it with the same sense of personal commitment.

I've known parents who decide that a certain prestigious college is the only right choice, as if acceptance will become an A on their report card of parenting, then don the sweatshirt of that school or proudly place the decal on the back of the family car.

As parents, our goal should be to help our sons and daughters find a school (or other post-high school choice) that's right for *them*. We don't want to set up a situation for failure by pressuring them into choices that aren't right; we want to help them succeed in a college that matches their abilities and prepares them for the vocation they have chosen.

■ *Gather and file information.* The amount of information that begins to accumulate regarding college choices and applications quickly overwhelms a high school student. At our house, we felt we might drown in a sea of paper, so we offered to bring order to the chaos, and our students gladly accepted the help.

We first set up a system. My husband, Lynn, is the superorganizer in our family, so he got a sturdy, portable file box with folders and started keeping all the information together, but in separate files.

In addition to keeping track of information, we gathered helpful advice by talking with counselors, teachers and other parents. In fact, parenting a child through this stage of life reminded me of parenting an infant through the baby stage. All that talk about feeding and burping seemed deathly boring and unimportant before we had a baby. Then we had a child, and those conversations suddenly became fascinating. The same is true with conversations about leaving home and choosing colleges.

SUCCESS

It all seemed so boring a few years ago, but suddenly, we felt magnetically drawn to those conversations as we shared information and encouragement with other parents. "How is the SAT different from the ACT?" we asked each other. "What do you know about John Brown University?" "How do we know if we qualify for financial aid?"

- *Offer advice.* Because we gathered information, we could pass on helpful advice in the areas where our teens were willing to accept it. For instance, we learned that most colleges don't insist on well-rounded students; they prefer well-rounded classes made up of lopsided students who excel in one or two areas. Most colleges believe that consistently good grades in quality courses are still the best indicators of potential in college; and they especially dislike the choice of "Mickey Mouse" courses during the senior year.

- *Determine and declare limits to the choice.* If we want our students to make the final choice, we need to define our limitations early in the process. For each family, those boundaries will be different. Lynn and I recognized that finding a good college that met the needs of our children for their first year away from home was a high priority and wise investment. We vowed that we would do all we could within our budget to send them to the school that seemed right for them—with a few limitations. We based those limitations on our knowledge of our children—their personalities, strengths, and needs. You may want to actually write out those boundaries. For example: No more that $10,000 a year from *our* pockets; the rest will have to be scholarship money, student loans, etc. No coed dorms. No more than a day's drive from home. No big-city colleges.

- *Consider small schools.* We believe our children need the nurturing, individual attention, and personal challenge found in classes and dormitories at smaller schools, ideally 3,000 students or less. Though some students thrive amidst the stimulation of a large university, we wanted a place where our children were less likely to slip through the cracks, at least for their first year away from home. Both Lynn and I attended large universities where we found ourselves in some classes with 500 other people. Nobody knew if we missed the class; worse, nobody cared. Smaller classes provide an opportunity to know professors personally and to write essay answers to tests (rather than true/false or multiple choice), which teaches students to express themselves and develop their critical-thinking skills.

SUCCESS

- *Liberal arts.* Neither of our older children went through high school with a passionate, clear leaning toward a specific career, so we believed a liberal arts college would best prepare them to become competent, knowledgeable, disciplined people who can write and speak effectively, work well with others, and think critically within any chosen field. We believe a liberal arts curriculum educates for life, not just a specific job.
- *Christian or non-Christian.* This is an important consideration, though we didn't make it a strict limitation. For the first year away from home, we believe that a Christian school offers the most nurturing environment and a proper balance between academic excellence and Christian commitment. But we also believe that when it comes to matters of faith, an 18-year-old faces choices, not requirements. We offered our opinions and information, but we didn't limit their choice to a Christian school.
- *Geographical location.* If our teens desired to go away from home or out of state, we encouraged that choice. We believe, if they are ready, that geographical distance increases their potential to gain independence. If they don't make that adjustment to leaving home now, they'll have to make it at some later date.
- *Cost and budget.* Our children know the total budget allotted for their four years of school. Beyond that, they have to share the responsibility of finding financial aid. The fact is, many of the more expensive private institutions offer more financial aid than public institutions.

## The Final Decision

Our two older children were accepted by both Christian and non-Christian schools. One seemed clear on a choice; the other struggled a bit more. "How do you know God's will?" one teenager asked.

"If it doesn't seem clear, He may care more about the heart attitude you carry to college than the name of the college," we said.

In the end, one chose a Christian college, while the other chose a non-Christian school. In retrospect (because God's will always seems clearer in hindsight), they both appear to be at the schools that are right for them and on the path of growth divinely designed to meet their needs. Both have felt nurtured by their small-school environments, and both seem challenged. (Admittedly, though, the one attending a non-Christian school faces greater adversity and is forced to answer some tough questions, but that student has also found Christian support with various small groups and is stretching toward great growth.)

As I look back, I'm convinced that students can be happy at several different schools and in many different post-high school experiences. Though the decision is important and profoundly shapes the future of the high school graduate, when we surrender ourselves to God, He weaves all our circumstances together for good.

—from Carol Kuykendall,
"Choosing a College—Already?" in *Raising Them Right*[5]

---

3. If you could instill three character qualities in your child, what would they be?

4. How important is it to you that your child gets a college education?

5. Is there an aspect of your child's personality or character that concerns you? How can you help him improve in this area while still under your tutelage?

6. What kind of relationship would you like to have with your child when she becomes an adult?

7. What are your child's greatest strengths, and how can you further develop those through the teen years?

8. When you think about your child's faith, what's most important to you? What kind of beliefs and behaviors do you want your child to carry into adulthood?

Are you starting to get a clear picture of the man or woman you hope your child will grow into? Hopefully, going through this looking-ahead exercise helps to separate the wheat from the chaff in regard to your parenting strategy. That is, focusing on the final result allows you to concentrate your efforts on what's most important while letting go of issues that won't move you toward your goal.

Let us offer one caveat about this envisioning process: As we said in chapter 10, "Appreciating Your Teen's Uniqueness," your child is a distinct individual, not a clone of you. She will inevitably develop goals, aspirations, and interests of her own. She may pursue a career in theater even though *you* think that's frivolous. She may skip college even though education is important to *you*.

Therefore, when considering your role in shaping the person your teen will become, focus on heart and soul qualities, such as honesty, integrity, and humility.

In other words, concern yourself with *who* your child is becoming rather than what he might *do* in the future. (Two chapters from now, we'll offer several checkpoints to evaluate if you're where you want to be in the process of guiding your teen toward spiritual maturity.)

## "How Did These Years Fly By So Fast?"

Parenting is not for the fainthearted, weak-willed, or thin-skinned. As you've no doubt learned by now, it's a tough job. Even when your kids are grown and out of the house, it *continues* to be tough. Neil Warren, the psychologist we quoted earlier, tells about a time when he was struck anew by the realization that his children had grown up—years after the fact—and the gripping emotions he experienced:

> One summer afternoon several years ago, Marylyn and I watched the movie "Father of the Bride," which was filmed near our home in Pasadena, California. Many of you already know the story. A dad and mom go through the excruciating experience of watching their "little girl" fall in love with a systems analyst and prepare for marriage. The film is about the passing of time, the aging of children and their parents, and the enormous emotional challenge for parents as they adapt to their children becoming adults, asserting independence, and leaving the nest.
>
> It was painfully easy for me to identify with the father in this film. With three daughters of our own, daughters we have cherished from the moment of their births, I was a sitting duck for the emotional tug of this story.
>
> Steve Martin played the dad in the movie, and as soon as he learned that his daughter was in love with "this other man," his symptoms began. Threatened with the

## Teens' Advice to Parents About Nurturing Spiritual Growth, Part 10

- "Be involved! Show that you love your teens by spending time with them, even if they push you away sometimes. They need love and encouragement more than anything. Be a role model for them, and show integrity in *all* you do. Make sure you guide them and provide them opportunities to make some deep Christian friendships, whether that be at church or at summer camps."
- "Really try to understand, not judging or being too strict. Be loving and caring, a strong example. 'Don't tell me what to do; show me.' "
- "Be aware, in tune to our moods and emotions. This will allow you to cater to our spiritual need situationally. Practice what you preach. Live a real life plus some. Always live above the expectations of your kids. Its okay to say, 'I don't know the answer' and then help each other find answers to spiritual questions."
- "Don't wait until their teenage years. Begin nurturing spiritual growth at birth. Be open in sharing about times when you struggled and how you found joy after the suffering."

loss of his daughter, he couldn't hold his conscious focus on her as a grown-up. When he looked at her across the dinner table or on the basketball court, he kept seeing her as she was as a seven- or eight-year-old. He suffered, of course, from his unconscious need to keep her small— safely and forever "under the shadow of his wing." He didn't like being reminded that she had become an adult. He was forced to reckon with the anxiety-laden, age-old problem of the inexorable passage of time.

I watched intently as Martin writhed through all his anguish, and I experienced one wave of powerful emotion after another. It suddenly occurred to me that it was only a short time ago—just a few weeks ago, wasn't it?—that our girls were young and impressionable and blissfully playing with Barbies. It was perhaps a couple of days ago that they were rah-rahing as high school cheerleaders, and I'm sure it was just yesterday that we drove each of them off to college.

In reality, they aren't "girls" anymore. They are moms with little ones of their own. "How did these years fly by so fast?" I asked.

SUCCESS

The movie demanded that I recognize all over again the obvious truth: all that we have together with our loved ones cannot be detached from rapidly passing time. There is no *necessary grief* attached to this powerful principle, but to make peace with passing time, we must stay constantly alert, uncommonly focused, and as utterly present as possible at each moment. The only successful antidote for losing time is living and experiencing fully that time *now*—while it is the present.

In that moment, the inspiration I felt gave me a clearer perspective about the vital importance of all my moments, and I was struck by newfound passion to live these moments with maximum personal investment.[6]

## Sow Now, Reap Later

Have you had moments similar to the one Neil Warren described? Even though your kids are not yet grown, maybe you've encountered experiences—giving driving lessons, watching your daughter go off on her first date, teaching your son to shave—that presented incontrovertible evidence that, yes, your little girl or little boy is growing up. He is on a steady march toward adulthood. She is fast becoming a woman.

Hopefully, these awakenings inspired in you, as Dr. Warren said, "a newfound passion to live these moments with maximum personal investment." The time, energy, and care you invest in your teenager *now* will pay dividends in the future. As the apostle Paul wrote, "A man reaps what he sows. . . . Let us not become weary in doing good, for at the proper time we will reap a harvest if we do not give up" (Galatians 6:7, 9). That sowing-and-reaping principle applies to many aspects of life, including raising children.

So as you look ahead, visualizing the kind of adult you want your teenager to become, realize that each day presents opportunities to help turn your dream into reality.

CHAPTER 26

# Marking Milestone Moments

A recent issue of *Parade* magazine, the national publication inserted into millions of Sunday newspapers, featured an article titled "What to Teach Your Kids Before They Leave Home." Subtitled "It would be great if by 18 every person could do the following," the piece presented a dozen areas in which teens should be proficient before launching out on their own:

1. Domestic skills
2. Physical skills
3. Handyman skills
4. Outdoor skills
5. Practical skills
6. Organizational skills
7. Social skills
8. Artistic skills
9. Human skills
10. Orientation skills
11. Recreation skills
12. Survival skills[1]

All these skills would certainly be helpful to a young man or woman setting out into the world, but there's something missing:

What about "Moral skills" or "Ethical skills"? Better yet, how about "Spiritual skills"? Okay, it's probably too much to expect a secular publication to take a strong stand on anything smacking of faith and religion (imagine the letters to the editor). But with such a woeful disregard for integrity permeating our country, it seems as if this should be *number one* on the list. (To be fair, an accompanying piece said that "qualities such as morality and honesty are of overarching importance." But excluding morality and integrity from the top-12 list seems to give the statement short shrift.)

Throughout this book, we've encouraged you to prepare your teens with the very thing the *Parade* article ignored: a strong commitment to faith, values, and morals. We've talked about using regular, planned teaching times as well as those unexpected teachable moments that pop up every so often.

In this chapter, we want to offer ideas for special events or spiritual high points that help to mark your teen's progress on the path toward spiritual maturity. Call them "milestone moments," "memory makers," "power sessions," or whatever you like, the idea is to implement a handful of structured discussions or ceremonies that your teen is sure to remember and carry into adulthood.

What follow are six suggested milestones, along with the ideal age for conducting them.

## Have a "Key Talk" About Sexuality and Purity

(Timing: ideally, by age 14)

We realize the danger in placing this item first: Some parents, recalling their own painfully awkward "sex talk" from adolescence, may quickly turn the page and move on to another topic. Hear us out on two critical points:

First, you know, of course, that our culture is saturated with sexually explicit images, references, and jokes. It seems as if every other television ad contains a sexual innuendo—if not a blatant "sex sells" ploy. Because young people are bombarded with inappropriate, immoral messages, your kids need guidance in this area. If you don't provide information, instruction, and direction, someone else will. It's true that many parents would just as soon

■ ■ ■

## *Is It Ever Too Late for Purity?*

What about those kids who are no longer virgins? Should their parents just forget the idea of a purity talk? Absolutely not! Richard Durfield says he has shared his "key talk" idea with many families over the years, and he's convinced it's a meaningful event for *all* teens, virgins or not.

"Although some kids have jumped the gun," he says, "they can commit themselves to God to remain pure until their wedding day. Teens who have fallen short can become virgins again in the sight of God. Once they're forgiven, it is as though they had never sinned. The Lord tells us in Isaiah 43:25 that 'I, even I, am he who blots out your transgressions, for my own sake, and remembers your sins no more.' "

avoid the subject of sexuality with their kids, but your teen may suffer much emotional, spiritual, and possibly physical harm if you remain silent.

Second, discussions about sex need not be awkward and embarrassing. In fact, they should be positive, upbeat, and candid. Speaking about sex in whispered tones and with vague euphemisms sends the message that sex is bad or shameful, which is clearly not what God intended. What's more, having a milestone event encompassing sex and purity can be a meaningful time of relationship building for you and your teen.

> *If you don't provide information, instruction, and direction, someone else will.*

Teens need their parents' help to withstand the immense sexual temptations they face. What specifically can you do? We think Richard and Renee Durfield came up with a terrific idea.

When their four children were growing up, the Durfields weren't about to give in to the helpless attitude that says, "Well, there's so much pressure on kids to have sex these days, they're bound to give in. There's nothing we can do." Instead, they decided to have ceremony—a private, personal, and intimate time—when each of their children reached an appropriate age.

SUCCESS

■ ■ ■

## Keep Talking

Whew! You made it through "the Talk." You even had a ceremony where your teen committed to remaining sexually pure. Now you can forget about discussing sex with your teen again, right? Sorry, not so fast.

A recent federal survey found that adolescents are most likely to adopt their parents' attitudes about teen sex if Mom and Dad discuss sex-related topics often and seem comfortable doing so. The study involved interviews about communication and sexual attitudes with more than 900 teens and parents in New York, Alabama, and Puerto Rico.

Daniel Whitaker, a psychologist at the Centers for Disease Control and Prevention, says, "A lot of parents are afraid to talk [about sex] because they think they might say the wrong thing. But this study suggests you should try to communicate your beliefs openly."

Even the New York president of the Sexuality Information and Education Council—a group whose Web site lists the "right to express your sexuality safely" as one of its "Teen's Sexual Rights"—says that the study results add to growing evidence that "young people do want to hear from their parents about sex on an ongoing basis—it's not a one-time thing."[2]

During this special occasion, the parents would explain the biblical view of marriage and the sacredness of sexual purity. This is done between a father and son or mother and daughter (same sex is preferable but not mandatory) at a nice restaurant, as befits an important event.

The Durfields also wanted to commemorate the occasion, and they decided to present a specially made "key" ring to the son or daughter. The ring, which symbolizes a commitment to God, is worn by the adolescent during the difficult teen and young adult years. Richard explains the significance of the gift:

> The purpose of a key is to unlock a door, and the ring symbolizes the key to one's heart and virginity. The ring is a powerful reminder of the value and beauty of virginity, of the importance of saving sex for marriage.
>
> The ring also represents a covenant between the child

SUCCESS

and God. A covenant not only obligates us to God, but it obligates God to us. As long as we honor a covenant, God will also honor it. Throughout history, God has blessed those who have remained faithful.

The son or daughter wears the key ring until he or she is married. Then the ring is taken off and presented to the new spouse on their wedding night—that sacred evening when a life of sexual experience begins.

When Richard took his youngest son, Jonathan (15 at the time), for his "key talk," they dressed in their finest clothes and went to a fancy restaurant. Shortly after they were seated, Richard told his son that no question was out of bounds and that if he had been thinking about one of those awkward questions about sex, this was the night to ask it. Jonathan already knew the "facts of life," since his parents had always been open about sexuality. But this was the time to talk it all over and clear up any confusion.

"If something's been bothering you about adolescence or whatever, it's okay to talk about it," Richard told him. "This is a special time for you and Dad to discuss any sexual questions that might still be on your mind."

It didn't take long for the awkwardness to ease and the questions to start coming. Jonathan, who had not been on a date at that point, wanted to know *precisely* what the line was for physical contact with a girl. How far was too far? He thought he knew, but he wanted to hear it from Dad.

"A light kiss is about as far as you can go," Richard explained. "Sexual emotions are very strong, and if you're not careful, you'll do things you don't want to. So you need to avoid anything that leads you up to that point."

The discussion continued throughout the meal, and finally Richard concluded their time by asking Jonathan if he would like to make a pledge of chastity before the Lord. Jonathan said he would. That's when Richard presented his son with the key ring and explained its significance. Then, right there in the middle of the restaurant, father and son held hands and prayed together, asking for God's strength, guidance, and delivery from temptation. They also prayed for Jonathan's future wife.

SUCCESS

Richard says this about that special evening:

My key talk with Jonathan was one of the most memorable and moving experiences I've ever had. It seemed
our hearts were bonded together.

Young people are romantics. They have a real need to
identify their personal self-worth. Wholesome, biblical
thoughts instilled during their tender years open an
avenue for parents to discuss sex with their children. The
importance a parent places on the key talk will greatly
influence the child's sexual behavior prior to marriage.

Obviously, the key ring is a powerful day-in-and-day-
out reminder for the child. The more the child values his
or her virginity, the more the key ring becomes a precious
symbol of the commitment to God and the future spouse.[3]

We highly recommend the Durfields' "key talk" as a milestone
moment early in your child's adolescent years. You can and should
adapt the event to suit your own circumstances and your child's
personality (for instance, some kids might clam up if you try to
talk about sex in a public place). However you choose to approach
the purity and sexuality discussion, make it meaningful and memorable, not just another chat over pancakes and coffee. Go somewhere special, present your child with a nice gift, and talk
positively and affirmatively. (Your gift may or may not include the
design of a key, but it should be something your teen will wear or
at least see every day. And it should remind your teen of his commitment to purity.) Emphasize that God invented sex, and there's
nothing shameful about it when it is enjoyed in marriage.

Skeptics might ask, "Are kids going to resist sexual temptation
just because they make a pledge of abstinence? Do these chastity
commitments really work?" As a matter of fact, they do work.
Researchers with the National Longitudinal Study of Adolescent
Health found that teens who take pledges to remain sexually pure
wait about 18 months longer to have sex than those who don't.

Results of the survey, which included interviews with 9,000
American teenagers, seem to have surprised the researchers. The
University of North Carolina's J. Richard Udry, who helped design

the survey, said, "We were cynical about the likelihood that the pledge would produce [significant results]. But we were wrong."

According to Peter Bearman of Columbia University and Hannah Bruckner of Yale University, authors of the study, "The delay effect is substantial and robust. Pledging delays intercourse for a long time. In this sense, the pledge works."[4]

## Encourage Your Child to Write a Personal Constitution of Core Values

(Timing: ideally, by age 13, with a reevaluation each birthday)

In their book *Leaving the Light On,* authors Gary Smalley and John Trent tell about "constitutions" their families drafted. These were written documents, updated and revised periodically, that formalized the families' rules, codes, and guiding principles. In essence, they were mission statements for the family. When Gary and Norma Smalley's kids were young, their document read like this:

1. We honor Mom and Dad by obeying them.
2. We honor others and our possessions by putting things away after we have used them.
3. We honor friends and family by performing all chores responsibly.
4. We honor friends and family by having good manners and exercising responsibility toward others.
5. We honor God's creation; people and things.
6. God is worthy to receive our highest honor and praise, and His Word is to be honored as well.

These commandments were posted in a prominent place in the home, where each family member would be reminded of them often. And the Smalley clan would regularly evaluate whether they were living according to the ideals they had established. Gary wrote:

> These six guidelines represent the final draft of a Smalley Family Constitution that each of us signed and dated. In a real sense, it was like the constitution of a country. We discovered that having a written, objective set of standards

SUCCESS

greatly contributed to our family's peace, harmony, and security. The children knew from the beginning that violating those limits involved sure and consistent consequences.

Smalley and Trent summarized the constitution idea by saying, "Getting a parenting 'plan' is essential if you want to have a loving home. But so, too, is the need to learn how to define and fulfill our unique mission in life—that captures the vision God has given us to accomplish."[5]

> *A constitution should have two major components: things to leave behind and things to press on toward.*

If a family constitution is an excellent idea (and we certainly believe it is), then individual constitutions are equally worthwhile, especially for adolescents, who are pulled in many directions and face all kinds of temptations. A written document outlining "who I am and how I want to live" provides an anchor in turbulent times.

The best age for drafting a constitution is 13, right on the threshold of the teen years ahead. That is the age—symbolically, at least—when a boy or girl leaves behind childhood and begins marching toward young adulthood. If your son or daughter is already past 13, the 16th birthday is another excellent time. Requiring your teen to write this document before getting a driver's license is great motivation. (Keep in mind that these are suggested ages; your son or daughter can go through this exercise at any time during the teen years.) As new phases of adolescence are reached, your teen should draft amendments to the constitution, such as guidelines in dating relationships, driving a car, conduct on the job, and so on.

What about the contents of the constitution? Whereas the example above contained general, overarching principles that could encompass family members across a range of ages and maturity levels, we recommend a teen constitution be as specific and unambiguous as possible. A constitution should have two major components: things to leave behind and things to press on toward. These categories are based on two of the apostle Paul's well-known verses:

- "When I was a child, I talked like a child, I thought like a child, I reasoned like a child. When I became a man, I put childish ways behind me" (1 Corinthians 13:11).

■ "Forgetting what is behind and straining toward what is ahead, I press on toward the goal to win the prize for which God has called me heavenward in Christ Jesus" (Philippians 3:13-14).

The "leave behind" portion of the constitution contains all the things the teen doesn't want to do, such as drug and alcohol use, breaking curfews, and cheating at school. The "press on toward" section outlines positive pursuits: daily quiet times, church and youth group participation, obedience to Mom and Dad, maintaining sexual purity, serving others, and so on.

Your teen should write the constitution, and then you can discuss it together. Take this opportunity to talk through the significance of each item. This is a "living and breathing" document, one your teen will refer to often over the years, so make sure it's thorough and crystal clear.

Some parents and teens include a third element: consequences if the constitution is broken and rewards if it's maintained. What discipline will be implemented if your son or daughter deviates from the agreed-upon standard of conduct? What is the "prize" for consistently pressing on toward the goal? When all this is spelled out in black and white, there will be no confusion about the appropriate course of action later on.

Once the constitution is agreed upon and approved by you and your teen (it might take a few drafts to finalize it), commemorate it with a celebration, a special gift, a weekend getaway, or extra privileges at home (for example, a later curfew, more phone time, increased allowance). Whatever you do, ensure that writing the constitution is not a chore and a bore; make it a festive rite of passage, a memorable step toward adulthood and independence.

## Teach Your Teen How to Set Goals and Work Toward Reaching Them

(Timing: ideally, by age 16)

Amazingly, some 15-year-olds can state precisely what their college major will be, what their career ambitions are, at what age they want to marry, the kind of person who would be a good mate, and how many children they plan to have (they've probably even researched the highest-rated retirement places). The sureness of their plans is startling, especially since most adults still don't know what they want to be "when they grow up."

The majority of teenagers, however, have a hard time seeing beyond next year (or maybe their next meal). Therefore, one of the best skills you can teach your teen is how to set goals and work toward achieving them. You challenge your child to look ahead, identify precisely what she wants to accomplish in a given area, and establish a plan for progressing toward it. Howard Hendricks has said, "Families don't plan to fail; they fail to plan." It's the same with teenagers—they don't plan to fail; they fail to plan. Instilling the importance of goal setting trains your child to plan for success.

A word of caution: Strive for balance. Some zealous, type-A parents urge their kids to set lofty, sky-high goals: straight A's, student council, the lead in the school play, first violin in youth symphony, and first string on the varsity squad. With goals like that, you might end up with a teen who's driven, compulsive, and perfectionistic—a teen for whom a 3.9 GPA is a failure. Kids who are pushed too hard for too long often succumb to depression, anorexia, excessive anger, and other psychological problems. Or you may destroy your child's self-esteem by setting him up for failure. Set the bar too high and your child might stop trying to jump over it altogether.

On the other end of the continuum are the phlegmatic, go-with-the-flow parents who say, "Goals, shmoals! Just let life happen. Too much planning and organizing robs you of spontaneity." These kinds of parents often produce kids who are unmotivated and unfocused.

Aim for a healthy middle ground. Teach your child to set reasonable, reachable goals—goals that are both challenging and achievable. Consider helping your teen establish goals in areas such as the following:

- *Academics.* Strive for improvement, even if it's just a little nudge upward, over last semester or last year.
- *Finances.* Set a savings account or college fund goal your teen can work toward.

- *Extracurricular activities.* This might be athletics, music, theater, speech and debate, or anything else your teen pursues outside the classroom.
- *Spirituality.* Formulate goals for quiet times, Scripture memorization, evangelism, growth in character qualities, and so on.

This goal-setting exercise might be completed annually (on birthdays, New Year's Day, or at the beginning of each new school year) or less frequently. Be sure to keep up-to-date on what your teen is striving for, and when he or she meets those goals, celebrate in a big way.

## Conduct a Rite-of-Passage or Blessing Ceremony

(Timing: ideally, by age 13 or 16)

One night a few years ago, Phil Altmeyer poked his head into his 13-year-old son's room and said, "Hey, Nate, you and I are going out on Friday night. No one else in the family will be coming. Just us."

"Where are we going?" Nate asked.

"I can't tell you," he replied. "But I want you to get dressed up in your slacks and sports coat."

*What's Dad up to?* Nate thought. *This couldn't be the sex talk. We've already had that.*

When Friday night arrived, Phil and Nate drove from their home outside Spokane, Washington, to the city's downtown area. They pulled into the parking lot of a fancy hotel, and Nate gave a low whistle. Pretty snazzy. As Phil led his son through the hotel lobby, Nate asked again, "Dad, what's going on?"

"Patience, son," Phil said. "You'll see soon enough."

A few seconds later, they walked into a private dining room, where Nate was surprised to see his five uncles and a teacher standing around the table, all dressed in suits and ties.

"Is this some kind of special dinner?" Nate asked.

"It sure is," Phil answered, "and you're the guest of honor."

Nate's expression registered the word "Huh?" so Phil explained: "Nate, you recently turned 13. That means you are well on your way to becoming a man. All these men who you know well, along with me, count it a privilege to encourage you, support you, and teach you as you become a godly, honorable man. Tonight, we're going to share our thoughts on what it means to be a man of integrity, and we're going to pray a blessing on your life."

It turns outs that Phil had read Robert Lewis's book *Raising a Modern-Day Knight*, in which he asserts that boys need a community of older men to guide them into manhood. Lewis argues forcefully that the passage toward manhood should include meaningful ceremonies: "Most men in America today lack a rich, masculine memory because there are no manhood ceremonies. Instead of *lasting* impressions, there are *no* impressions—no powerful, internal portraits etched in memory that call to mind our passage to manhood, no indelible moments that shaped our masculine identity and now compel us to pursue authentic manhood."[6]

With that challenge, Phil had arranged this event for his son. So, after a scrumptious meal, each of the men took turns talking about their lives and highlighting different aspects of manhood—integrity, honor, commitment to God, finding a worthwhile vocation, and so on. Other men who couldn't attend had sent letters to be read. It was a lot to soak in, but fortunately the entire evening was recorded so that Nate could review it all later.

To commemorate the event, Phil gave Nate a specially designed picture, which featured the qualities of manhood Phil is trying to instill in his son. That plaque hangs in Nate's room as a constant reminder of the men who are supporting him and praying for him.

Now 16, Nate says this about his ceremony: "It's something I'll never forget. It was incredible to have all those men I look up to giving me advice and encouragement, and they all planned what they wanted to say and made the effort to come just for *me*. It made me feel really special. It was awesome."

In chapter 24, we provided detailed information about elements of great ceremonies, as well as ideas for ceremonies you might use with your son or daughter (you might find it helpful to review that chapter). Two points bear repeating here:

First, ceremonies that have a strong spiritual and moral theme are often life-changing for teens. These events are mile markers on

> *Ceremonies that have a strong spiritual and moral theme are often life-changing for teens.*

the road to adulthood. Those few teens privileged to have had a ceremony held in their honor often describe them as some of the richest, most memorable experiences of their growing-up years.

Second, our society has a woeful lack of ceremonies that honor our teens and give them guidance and support. Think about it: What rite of passage or blessing ceremonies are held these days? A sweet 16 birthday party? Maybe, but the focus there is usually on fun and games. High school graduation? Yes, but that's at the tail end of the teen years. We strongly suggest you correct this deficiency in your home by holding some kind of ceremony—whether simple or elaborate— that will serve as a tribute to your teen's progress from child to adult.

## Teach Your Teen the Relationship Between Freedom and Responsibility

(Timing: ideally, after a rule is broken, with review as needed)
  "That's not my responsibility!"
  "Why should I be held responsible?"
  "You don't think *I'm* responsible for that, do you?"
  Chances are, you've heard statements like this in the past few weeks, and not just from teenagers. These days, adults are just as irresponsible as young people. Politicians and other leaders have made an art form of blame-shifting and passing the buck. In our society, the idea of responsibility—like its first cousins honor, integrity, and duty—has become outdated and outmoded, a quaint notion of a bygone era.

  If you want your son or daughter to buck that trend and become a responsible adult who handles freedom wisely, now is the time to teach him. In her book *Good Enough Mothers*, Melinda Marshall hits the bull's-eye: "If parents award freedom regardless of whether their children have demonstrated the ability to handle it, children never learn to see a clear link between responsible behavior and adult privileges."[7]

SUCCESS

The relationship between freedom and responsibility is most forcefully taught after an incident of rebellion, when rules have been violated, or some other situation where discipline is called for. When your child mishandles his freedom, he should be held accountable. Consider how two parents approached their sons' abuse of freedom, both involving cars:

Popular speaker and teen specialist Jim Burns recalls how his usually conscientious parents blew an opportunity to teach him the link between freedom and responsibility. Like most teenagers, Jim was excited to get his driver's license when he turned 16. His mom was delighted, too—no more chauffeuring her son around town. But Jim hit a pothole on the road to responsibility. On his first drive-by-yourself date the weekend after he'd gotten his license, he missed his curfew by two hours.

His dad was furious. He immediately revoked Jim's car privileges for four months. However, the next day, Jim's mother asked him to drive to the market to pick up some groceries. He learned that errands were okay, not covered in the driving ban. Then when he needed a ride to a baseball game a few days later, his father said he didn't want to go to the game early. So he threw Jim the car keys and made an exception to the ban. After two weeks, his parents had forgotten about the curfew violation altogether, and Jim was back on the road.

Reflecting on his parents' lax discipline, Jim wrote, "The primary purpose of parental discipline is to teach responsibility. This means consistently helping our children understand that most of life involves choices and consequences."[8]

Joe White's son Cooper ran into his own car troubles early in his driving career. Joe remembers returning home from a trip at 11 at night and climbing into his car in the airport parking lot. As soon as he fired up the engine, his cell phone rang. It was Cooper, who had calculated his dad's arrival time perfectly.

"Hey, Coop, what's up?" Joe asked, sensing the late-night call would bring more than just "welcome home" greetings.

"Well, uh, I got a little speeding ticket," he replied.

"Oh? Just a little one?" Joe said. "How fast were you going?"

Long pause.

"Uh, 80."

"Eighty?" Joe said. "What interstate were you on?"

"Well, it wasn't an interstate exactly," Cooper said. "It was a highway in town."

"What was the speed limit?"

"Fifty-five."

"And you were going 80? That's 25 miles over the limit," Joe said, as if his son didn't know well enough already. "All right. I'll be home soon. We'll talk about it then."

Joe and his wife, Debbie-Jo, had an advantage in meting out fair discipline in this situation. Cooper had written driving regulations into his "constitution of conduct," along with consequences for breaking agreed-upon guidelines. A ticket meant no car use for a month.

Cooper wasn't thrilled by the loss of a privilege, but he knew the rules. In fact, in this case, he had *made* the rules. Joe and Debbie-Jo only had to enforce the consequences and resist the urge to let him slide "just this once." They held firm, and Cooper learned a valuable lesson about freedom and responsibility.

Our intent is not to admonish Jim's parents and applaud Cooper's. We simply want to illustrate the point: It's critical that parents teach their kids that responsibility goes hand in hand with freedom, and moms and dads teach that most forcefully by clearly specifying rules and consequences and then following through when a rule is violated.

### Help Your Teen Understand God's Purpose and Provision in Times of Loss, Adversity, and Hardship

(Timing: whenever such things occur)

Years ago, a TV movie called *The Boy in the Bubble* told the story of a child with a rare immune deficiency that required him to be raised in a ventilated, sanitary, plastic enclosure. He grew up insulated and isolated from the world—that bubble *was* his world. Naturally, with limited contact with the real world, his perspective on life was distorted.

Some parents, with the best intentions, create a kind of bubble around their children to protect them from life's dangers and hardships. Wanting their kids to have a wonderful growing-up

■ ■ ■

## God's Masterpieces Are Stained-Glass Windows

Joe White taught his own teenagers, as well as all the kids who come to the Christian camps he directs, that God uses pain, hurt, and brokenness to mold them into the people He intends. Joe uses the metaphor of a stained-glass window: "The works of art God creates out of His children's lives are not done on canvas, where the paint dries and the picture never changes. No, God takes thousands of little pieces—all our wonderful experiences and all our terrible ones—and solders them together. The result is a beautiful stained-glass window. If you stand close to a stained-glass window, you can see lots of jagged pieces with nicks and scratches. But stand away from the window, let the light shine through it, and you'll see a magnificent mosaic."

experience, these moms and dads rush to resolve problems, alleviate stress, and remove painful circumstances.

There's a big problem with this approach: Kids whose childhood and adolescent years are too cushy and problem-free will be in for a rude awakening when they step into the real world. Life is full of distress and despair, headaches and heartaches. Everyone faces adversity at some time or another. Therefore, wise parents teach their kids how to deal with pain rather than helping them avoid it.

One mother wrote this letter in response to a newspaper column dealing with overprotective parents:

> Being a sheltered child myself, I know what it's like to reach adulthood unprepared for reality. It's like being all warm and cozy and then being dumped into a vat of ice water. It's taken me twenty years to get over that shock and to realize that my parents just loved me too much and couldn't bear to see me get hurt.
>
> I still have an unreasonable fear of people. But getting hurt is what it's all about. How can we ever grow and learn if we aren't hurt sometimes? Mom is not always going to be there to kiss our wounds.[9]

SUCCESS

If parents are too protective, if they shield their child from all hardship, if they raise their child in a "plastic bubble," that kid will leave home an emotional cripple. Woe to that child who is unequipped to handle pain and peril when she leaves the safety of the cocoon.

Worse, sheltered children might be *spiritually* impaired. James told us that God uses tough times to bring about spiritual growth: "Consider it pure joy, my brothers, whenever you face trials of many kinds, because you know that the testing of your faith develops perseverance. Perseverance must finish its work so that you may be mature and complete, not lacking anything" (1:2-4). Lacking spiritual toughness, young people may be blown over by the next strong wind. As the writer of Proverbs said, "If you falter in times of trouble, how small is your strength!" (24:10).

Janice Hanes of Portland, Oregon, takes this issue seriously—and she takes an unusual approach to preparing her teenagers to handle hardship. "I actually pray that God would bring some hard times, even some temptation, into my children's lives," she says. Does this sound mean-spirited, maybe even cruel? Listen as Janice explains: "Before long, my kids will be heading off to college or into the working world. They will face temptation of every kind, and they'll encounter lots of painful situations. I want them to experience some of these things while my husband and I are here to help them through. I believe that's one of the best things we can do as parents—build up their strength so they can withstand trials and trouble when we're not around to prop them up."

> *Wise parents teach their kids how to deal with pain rather than helping them avoid it.*

As you consider how to respond when your child endures hardship, keep these points in mind:

*1. Character counts most.* Nearly 2,000 years ago, the Greek philosopher Seneca said, "Calamity is virtue's opportunity." Nothing has changed since he made that statement. Tough times often stimulate the most spiritual and emotional growth.

One dad in Austin, Texas, said: "My son, Bryce, has always been a gifted athlete—the star of just about every team he's

**SUCCESS**

played on. So when he was benched during his junior year of football, he became angry, frustrated, and depressed. He was clearly a better player than the kid who took his spot at wide receiver. But the coach was apparently trying to teach Bryce a lesson of some kind, though it was never clear what.

"I wanted to march down to the coach's office and have a few words with him. But I didn't. Bryce and I decided to pray and let God take care of it. That was one of the toughest years of Bryce's life, but also one of the best. He learned a whole lot about humility, fairness, patience, and trust in God. It killed me to see him suffer through that miserable season, but he's much stronger spiritually and emotionally because of it. In the end, that's what matters."

Few things are more difficult for parents than watching their kids endure pain. But remember, God may be using the difficulty to shape and perfect your child's character.

*2. Adversity might be preparing your child for greater spiritual service.* The apostle Paul wrote, "Praise be to . . . the God of all comfort, who comforts us in all our troubles, so that we can comfort those in any trouble with the comfort we ourselves have received from God" (2 Corinthians 1:3-4). God has a way of redeeming our most painful experiences. The teen who is rejected by his peers will likely gain a deep sensitivity for outcasts of all kinds. The teen who struggles with an eating disorder will learn firsthand about body image and self-esteem issues. The Lord will often use tough experiences—and the character qualities that come from them—for His service later on.

*3. Teach at the appropriate time.* Nobody in the midst of pain wants to hear a sermon about God's sovereignty or growing through tough times. While wounds are fresh and emotions raw, the best thing you can do is to *be there*. Be there with an arm around your son's shoulder. Be there with a big hug before your daughter goes to sleep. Be there, most of all, with prayer for strength, guidance, and wisdom.

Then when the time is right—days, weeks, or months after a painful event—talk it through with your teen. Help him see any good things that might have come from the hardship. Describe incidents from your own life when you've suffered disappointment and difficulty, and tell what you learned through those experiences. Discuss how God is not the author of evil (rather, Satan is) but that the Lord can use painful circumstances to draw us closer to Himself.

Obviously, you cannot set a time for a milestone discussion about pain and suffering. But you can be prepared to guide your child through hardship when the opportunity comes. Before adversity arises, you may want to read Dr. James Dobson's book *When God Doesn't Make Sense* or Philip Yancey's *Where Is God When It Hurts?*

Let's face it, parents need to utilize all the tools in their tool-box—seizing all the teachable moments and following through on planned-out events—to combat a culture that increasingly champions immorality and irresponsibility. As educator William Kilpatrick wrote, "Parents cannot, as they once did, rely on the culture to reinforce home values. In fact, they can expect that many of the cultural forces influencing their children will be actively undermining those values."[10] The milestones presented in this chapter—along with others you choose to implement—will provide some of the spiritual, moral, and ethical skills your teen needs to stand strong for Christ.

SUCCESS

# Measuring Success

In thousands of homes around the world, there are little lead and ink marks ascending on walls in the hallway or on the backs of kitchen doors. These are not a child's attempt at artistic expression; they're lines parents have made to chart their kids' physical growth over the years.

"See how much you've grown since last year!" dads and moms say to their children as they compare this year's mark with the previous year's. "You sure are getting big!"

Obviously, spiritual growth is more difficult to assess than physical. We can't stand next to a measuring tape to determine how much or how little we've grown. So much of the Christian life involves the heart and mind, and attitudes, thoughts, and perspectives aren't visible. Fortunately, God provides help for gauging our progress. The Bible contains many commandments and admonitions that serve as a kind of measuring stick against which we can evaluate our spiritual growth.

## Checkpoints of a Teen's Spiritual Progress

In the first chapter of this section, we encouraged you to fix in your mind the finished portrait of your parenting efforts—to envision the person you want your child to become by the time he

SUCCESS

or she leaves home. In the last chapter, we suggested a few spiritual milestones you might want your teen to reach along the way. Here, we present several checkpoints for evaluating progress on your teenager's development toward Christlike maturity. We encourage you to take some time to assess how far your child has come—and how far he has yet to go—in his spiritual growth.

Disclaimer 1: The eight checkpoints presented in this chapter are not intended to be the definitive checklist for determining super-Christian status or eligibility for sainthood. In other words, we're not implying that the Christian life can be or should be reduced to an itemized list to check off, an inventory to fulfill. What's more, you may wish to emphasize spiritual qualities not covered in this chapter. That's fine. Use these characteristics as a *starting point* for appraising progress.

Disclaimer 2: When evaluating your child's spiritual life against the points below, keep in mind the adage "Progress, not perfection." Everyone has strengths and weakness, talents and shortcomings. Therefore, your child may naturally excel in some of these areas and struggle in others. The apostle Paul's admonition to "aim for perfection" is balanced by the reminder that "there is no one righteous, not even one" (2 Corinthians 13:11; Romans 3:10). This exercise is meant not to be a report card in which letter grades are assigned to character qualities; it's meant to be a growth gauge that will indicate how your teen is progressing.

The bottom line, then, is that the list below simply provides a way of asking, "Where is my teen on the maturity continuum, and how can I help him to keep moving forward?" At the end of each section, we'll offer some questions to help you think through these areas.

### 1. He Has a Growing, Grace-Based Love Relationship with God through Jesus Christ

"Grow in the grace and knowledge of our Lord and Savior Jesus Christ" (2 Peter 3:18).

In our pragmatic, achievement-oriented culture, it's easy to forget that the heart and soul of the Christian life is a *relationship*. Friendship

> **Friendship with God is the very essence of our faith.**

*SUCCESS*

with God is the very essence of our faith. King David wasn't called the "man after God's own heart" because of the programs he initiated, the military campaigns he waged, or the evangelistic crusades he staged; he was, first and foremost, a friend of God's.

When Jesus walked the earth, He repeatedly emphasized the importance of relationship. "I no longer call you servants," He told His disciples. "I have called you friends" (John 15:15). As theologian Charles Andrews said, "The older I get, the more the wonder I have at those words of Jesus—'I have called you friends.' That one word, *friend*, breaks down barriers of reserve, and we have boldness in His presence. Our hearts go out in love to meet His love."[1]

> *"He who began a good work in you will carry it on to completion until the day of Christ Jesus."*
> —*Philippians 1:6*

Authors Brent Curtis and John Eldredge have called our relationship with God a "sacred romance." They wrote, "Above all else, the Christian life is a love affair of the heart. It cannot be lived primarily as a set of principles or ethics. It cannot be managed with steps and programs. It cannot be lived exclusively as a moral code leading to righteousness."[2]

Curtis and Eldredge remind us of the religious expert who asked Jesus what he must do to obtain real life. Jesus responded by asking, "What is written in the Law? How do you read it?" The man answered by quoting from Deuteronomy and Leviticus: "Love the Lord your God with all your heart and with all your soul and with all your strength and with all your mind" and "Love your neighbor as yourself." Jesus said, in essence, "You've hit the nail on the head" (see Luke 10:25-28).

We read in the Bible, over and over, God's invitation to walk with Him, abide with Him, and be His friend. When our relationship with Him is strong, everything about the Christian life falls into place more easily.

*Assessment:* Do you sense that your teen has a deepening friendship with Christ? Do you see evidence (such as regular quiet times) that your child is pursuing a closer relationship with God? Ask your teen: "How would you describe your relationship with God? Do you feel that it's closer and more intimate now than it was a year ago? Two years ago?"

SUCCESS

## Teens' "Traits of Great Parents," Part 11

■ "They have a strong relationship with their teen."

■ "A willingness to let teens make mistakes; a willingness to give teens freedom when trust is earned; they hold teens accountable in their devotional life."

■ "Flexible, supportive, encouraging, and willing to let teens be independent and make their own decisions."

■ "Discerning, tender, compassionate, accepting, understanding, disciplining."

■ "Great parents have learned to model sacrificial love and can trust God in all circumstances. In a nutshell, great parents are secure."

### 2. She Has a Firm Grip on Scripture

"From infancy you have known the holy Scriptures, which are able to make you wise for salvation through faith in Christ Jesus. All Scripture is God-breathed and is useful for teaching, rebuking, correcting and training in righteousness, so that the man of God may be thoroughly equipped for every good work" (2 Timothy 3:15-17).

In an episode of *The Simpsons*—the popular animated TV series—Bart plops down on the couch next to a Bible. Instantly, he picks it up with his thumb and index finger as if he were holding a dead mouse and tosses it aside while uttering, "Ick!" That two-second vignette, apropos to nothing in the program's story line, speaks volumes about the way many young people view the Bible. If some kids are antagonistic toward the Bible, many more are apathetic toward it, considering it merely a religious relic irrelevant to life in the twenty-first century.

Hopefully, your son or daughter understands that the Bible is God's way of communicating with us, comforting us, and instructing us. Far more than a book of rules and regulations, dusty history lessons and boring genealogies, it is a guidebook for how to live a great life. Pastor and author Mark Buchanan said:

> The Bible is not a book of philosophy—deep thoughts to ponder. It is more like a manual. You don't read a book on kayaking technique simply to ponder the idea. You read it to learn how to kayak.
>
> The book—God-breathed, every word of it—is *useful*.

Useful for what? For propping up overheads? No. For studying ancient languages and customs and cultures of the Middle East? Well, maybe. But that's not what the apostle Paul had in mind. How about for devising certain theological systems? Again, we're wandering off the mark. The Bible is useful for this: shaping and training you to be the kind of person who walks in righteousness and is ready to do good works, God's works, in a fallen world.[3]

Why should your teenager have a firm grasp of Scripture? Because, as Mark Buchanan wrote, it's useful and applicable to our everyday lives. As your teen becomes more and more independent, and as your opportunities to offer hands-on guidance diminish, she will need the internal guidance system God's Word provides. The psalmist wrote, "How can a young man keep his way pure? By living according to your word. . . . I have hidden your word in my heart that I might not sin against you" (119:9, 11). And as your teen faces critical decisions in the years ahead, the Bible, woven into the fabric of her mind and heart, will offer wisdom and direction: "Your word is a lamp to my feet and a light for my path" (Psalm 119:105).

Joe White was so adamant about his kids' being well grounded in the Word that he required them to memorize two books of the Bible before they could get their driver's license at age 16. When they were young, Joe read a magazine article that challenged moms and dads to make Scripture memorization a part of their kids' faith training. Joe admits he was never big on memorizing verses, but reading that article convicted him that he should anchor his children in God's Word—and memorize Scripture right along with them, one verse at a time.

"I knew my kids would grow up quickly," he says, "and I wanted to make sure they had God's Word planted deep within them before they left home. I realized that once they left home, I couldn't be there to keep them on course. But the Bible, hidden in their hearts, could always be there to guide them."

As important as memorization is, understanding what the verses actually mean is even more critical. It's one thing to rattle off verse after verse; it's another thing to grasp the intent and purpose behind the words.

One evening, Caryl Altmeyer of Spokane, Washington, walked past her 15-year-old son's room and noticed him scribbling in a notebook.

"What are you doing, Nate?" she asked.

"I've started writing out a Bible verse or two each day and then rewriting them in my own words," he explained. "Sometimes it's hard to figure out what the verses mean, so it helps if I rewrite them using words I understand."

No doubt Nate's got a good start on understanding what the Bible really means. What's more, since he started this exercise, Caryl has noticed that Nate more frequently asks her or his dad to explain passages that are unclear to him. That's terrific. If he keeps that up, he's going to leave home with an understanding of many of the themes in God's Word.

*Assessment:* Is Scripture memorization important to your child? How much of the Bible has he committed to memory—a few verses? whole books? More importantly, does he understand the principles and rationales underlying the words? Is your teen on pace to have a firm grasp of the Bible's major themes and messages by the time he leaves home?

### 3. She Is Committed to a Clearly Defined Set of Core Values

"If you love me, you will obey what I command" (John 14:15).

There's an old maxim that says, "Aim at nothing and you'll hit it every time." That certainly applies to many people in our society: They've never really identified what they're living for, so they simply go with the flow, riding the currents of prevailing opinions and personal whims.

Sadly, many Christians have never really pinpointed the values and morals they want to live by. Sure, they know it's good to love your neighbor, honor your father and mother, care for widows and orphans, and abide by the "thou shalts" in the Ten Commandments. But they haven't consciously, prayerfully, and introspectively asked themselves, *What kind of person does God want me to be? And how shall I then live?* Call it a set of core

> **Many Christians have never really pinpointed the values and morals they want to live by.**

values, a code of conduct, laws to live by, or whatever—the point is, teenagers ought to know *exactly* what they're living for and the kind of moral principles and belief system they'll base their life on before leaving home. (We'll cover this topic in more detail in the next chapter.)

One college student said this about her parents' instruction regarding specific guidelines for living: "My mom and dad taught me a lot of different values and skills, but they identified four things in particular that they wanted to be *sure* I learned: love for God and His Word; respect for other people; maintaining high standards for honesty and integrity; and discovering my unique gifts and finding a way to use them to serve the Lord. Over and over during my childhood, Mom and Dad reminded me of these four values and showed me how to pursue them. Believe me, I left for college with these goals burned into my heart and mind, and I'm grateful for it."

That's a young lady who knows clearly and unequivocally what she's shooting for. And those are parents who made the effort and took the time to make sure she understood precisely the ideals they wanted her to live by.

*Assessment:* Does your teen know what she's aiming for in life? Can your daughter articulate the values she's living by and why they're important? How would your son respond if you asked him, "What values do you want to serve as your compass in life?"

### 4. He Honors and Loves Parents and Siblings

"Children, obey your parents in the Lord, for this is right. 'Honor your father and mother'—which is the first commandment with a promise—'that it may go well with you and that you may enjoy long life on the earth' " (Ephesians 6:1-3).

Along with all the sacrifices and frustrations, parenthood offers the occasional reward that makes everything worthwhile. Just ask Christy Smith of Spokane, Washington. Her daughter, Carli, came home from school one day and said, "Mom, a lot of my friends talk about how they lie to their parents and sneak around to get away with things."

Christy was wondering if there might be a confession coming,

SUCCESS

but Carli continued, "I just couldn't lie to you, Mom, because I know how much that would hurt you, and I love you too much to hurt you like that."

Wow! Talk about loving and honoring your parents! What a blessing to hear something like that from your teenager!

The teen years are, of course, when kids pull away from parents and move toward independence. That's normal and healthy—they're preparing to stand on their own. But that doesn't mean teens should become disrespectful or disobedient. Even if they disagree with you about household rules or anything else, they can do so respectfully.

*Assessment:* Does your teen show honor and respect to you and your spouse? Is he kind toward siblings? Does she encourage and build up others in the family? Have you seen progress—or regress—in this area since your child hit the teen years?

### 5. She Has an Attitude of Servanthood

"Your attitude should be the same as that of Christ Jesus . . . [who] made himself nothing, taking the very nature of a servant" (Philippians 2:5, 7).

Do you want to help your son to live a fun, fulfilling, meaningful life? Teach him how to serve others. Want to help your daughter to become great? Teach her to become a servant.

In chapter 23, we talked at length about helping to shift your teen's focus from "me" to "others"—to move his or her attitude from selfish to selfless. This concept sounds ridiculous to some teens (and adults) because our society champions and caters to self-indulgence. With so much cultural pressure to be self-serving instead of other-serving, the time to teach your teen the Christlike quality of servanthood is *now*.

How about turning the "me, mine, I" emphasis so prevalent in our society into something positive? Adopt a "serving motto" in your home. Who's supposed to take out the trash? Me. Whose job is it to do the dishes? Mine. Who will clean up the dog mess? I will.

Human nature being what is it, servants aren't often born; they're made. By example and instruction, parents can give their teen's selfish attitude a makeover.

---

**Teens' Advice to Parents About
Nurturing Spiritual Growth, Part 11**

■ "Keep teens accountable in a loving way in their devotions. Let them make mistakes, especially older teens. Have family devotions at the dinner table as often as possible (every night if you can)."

■ "Lead by example! It's so much bigger than *anything* you could ever say."

■ "Don't be naive to what is going on. We are a generation crying out for guidance and love. Don't shy away from your job. Know your teens. Talk to them and discover their passions and struggles. When this line of communication is established, your teens will accept your wisdom and apply it in their lives."

■ "Emphasize how Christianity embraces every part of life and that we should not 'privatize' our beliefs but seek coherency through understanding and application. *Please* emphasize the dangers Christians face today in minimizing their faith in the face of culture's whims!"

---

*Assessment:* On the continuum between "totally self-centered" and "completely selfless," where does your teen fall? Does your teen have the kind of "I'm Third" attitude we talk about in chapter 23? Does he serve others in the family willingly? Is she developing an others-first perspective? Is your son or daughter involved in service projects or volunteer efforts to help disadvantaged people?

**6. He Feels Unconditionally Loved and Equitably Disciplined**
"We have all had human fathers who disciplined us and we respected them for it" (Hebrews 12:9).

For better or worse, children often perceive their heavenly Father to be like their earthly father. If Dad is loving, gracious, and attentive, a young person will likely believe God is the same way. If Dad is harsh, critical, and judgmental, a child will have a similar view of God. As Dr. Ross Campbell explained:

> In order for a teen to identify with his parents, relate closely with them, and be able to accept their standards, he must feel genuinely loved and accepted by them. To lead a teen to the close relationship with God that they possess, parents must make sure that a child feels

unconditionally loved. . . . It is extremely difficult for teenagers who do not feel unconditionally loved by their parents to feel loved by God.[4]

That gives you something to think about, doesn't it? The way you show love and acceptance directly affects your teen's view of God. And what about the area of discipline? We know from Scripture that God disciplines us out of love and always with the goal of causing growth (see Hebrews 12). Although your teen may not like being disciplined at the moment it's occurring, does he know deep down that you have his best interests at heart? Does he realize you're trying—and perhaps sometimes missing the mark—to protect and guide him?

*Assessment:* Would you say your teen feels unconditionally loved by you? More importantly, would your *teen* say she feels unconditionally loved by you? To evaluate this area, you may have to ask your child, "Do you feel there are strings attached to my love for you? Do you feel as if I love you more when you do something good, and less when you do something bad?"

Regarding discipline, does your teen generally believe that the "punishment fits the crime"? That you have listened carefully and attentively to his explanation before disciplining? That you are fair when meting out discipline?

### 7. She Has a Heart for the Lost and a Desire for Christian Ministry

"Serve the LORD your God with all your heart and with all your soul" (Deuteronomy 10:12).

A deepening relationship with God often manifests itself in service toward others. As we grow in Christ, we'll want to serve Him more and more.

A college student named Heidi wrote: "In high school, I went on an outreach to Kansas City. In the mornings, we'd have training in apologetics, and in the afternoons we'd put the information we learned into practice by striking up conversations with people about God. I remember talking to a girl named Michelle underneath a big oak tree in a green park—she was

> *As we grow in Christ, we'll want to serve Him more and more.*

SUCCESS

studying something. My partner and I started talking with her, and she listened patiently. Then she answered, 'That's great for you, but it isn't right for me. Everybody's got their own view of God and religion, and none is better than another. So, thanks but no thanks.' The memory of the emptiness in her eyes as she gave the answer of my generation still haunts me. I will never know what happened to Michelle, but I do know in that moment I saw a glimpse of God's heart, and I wept. From that moment, I have been seeking to understand God's heart more and to be a missionary to my own generation, in my own country."

That's a girl who has a heart for ministry and a concern for people who don't know God. Of course, there are hundreds of ways teens can demonstrate their desire to serve God and reach the lost. Some kids quietly serve in the youth group, doing all the grunt work nobody else wants to do. Others are up-front types, leading worship on Sunday mornings. Still others, like Heidi, go out to campuses and parks, telling people about God's love.

The issue is not *how* your teen is serving God but *that* he or she is, in some way, ministering to people in His name.

*Assessment:* Does your child express concern about the salvation of friends, neighbors, and classmates? Does she reach out to people in a spirit of love and compassion? Is she involved in some kind of ministry as a way of serving Christ?

### 8. He Has Learned to Be Discerning and Filter Opinions through a Christian Worldview

"This is my prayer . . . that you may be able to discern what is best and may be pure and blameless until the day of Christ" (Philippians 1:9-10).

Turn on the TV, open a newspaper, or thumb through a magazine and you'll instantly be reminded that these are perilous times for bringing up kids. Our culture, driven by the media, is saturated with violence, sex, drinking and drugs, and degradation of every kind imaginable.

What's a parent to do? Unfortunately, many parents go to one extreme or the other: They either try to isolate their child from the destructive cultural messages or they take a hands-off approach

*"Then we will no longer be infants, tossed back and forth by the waves, and blown here and there by every wind of teaching and by the cunning and craftiness of men in their deceitful scheming. Instead, speaking the truth in love, we will in all things grow up into him who is the Head, that is, Christ."*

—*Ephesians 4:14-15*

("Oh well, there's nothing we can do about it."). As we pointed out in chapter 20, the better approach is to teach your child to *discern* what's right and what's wrong, what's helpful and what's harmful.

For Al and Jo Janssen of Colorado Springs, teaching discernment is a major focus of their parenting efforts. The Janssens want their three children, ages 12, 16, and 18, to be able to filter all the messages they receive from the media, peers, and authority figures. So Al and Jo frequently help their kids interpret what they're seeing and hearing.

If they hear a radio ad with a sexual innuendo, they might turn down the volume and discuss it. If they watch a TV news segment, they might stop and talk through the slant or spin of the piece, especially if it involves religion or a moral issue. Once or twice a year, Al initiates a "guys' night out," in which he and his boys will grab a burger and see a movie together. (Usually, Al or Jo will have previewed the movie to make sure it's appropriate.) After watching the film, the three of them will talk about what they've seen—the movie's message, the perspective of the filmmakers, and any religious or antireligious themes.

How are you at providing parental guidance? Since the power brokers of our culture seem intent on pushing the envelope of immorality as far as possible, your teen needs the ability to filter input through a Christian worldview.

*Assessment:* How good is your teen at shielding himself from the bad influences of the popular media? Does your teen know how to discern right from wrong? Is your son or daughter equipped and willing to make decisions based on biblical principles?

SUCCESS

## Staying the Course

Like physical growth, our spiritual development occurs rapidly at some times in our lives and more slowly at other times. All of us experience setbacks and strides forward as we seek to become more Christlike. If your teen is progressing by baby steps or giant steps, be thankful. Growth is occurring. If your teen seems stuck in place, or even going backward, don't give up. Keep praying and implementing the strategies in this book. Through God's grace, your child will once again move onward toward spiritual maturity.

SUCCESS

# PART 5

∎ ∎ ∎

# Conclusion

*As the parent of a teen, no feeling in the world can match the deep, abiding joy that comes from knowing that your child—and by God's grace your child's children for generations to come—will spend eternity with you in heaven.*

# The Parent's Cap and Gown

It's graduation day. Caps and gowns. "Pomp and Circumstance." Flashbulbs popping. Camcorders whirring. Applause and cheers. Electricity and anticipation charge the air.

"Who's graduating?" you ask.

No, this isn't your teenager's day to receive the long-sought high school diploma. It's *your* graduation day—the day you stop being a hands-on, always-there parent. The parent who waited up till midnight countless nights to make sure your child got home okay. The parent who listened patiently to all the details of your daughter's crisis du jour throughout junior high and high school. The parent who helped your son navigate the twists and turns, the bumps and potholes, on the road to adulthood.

Yes, today is the day your child moves on. He's no longer your little boy; she's no longer your little girl. Your teenager has reached a new and exciting stage—full-fledged adult. And that means, like it or not, that you'll be moving on to another stage of life, too.

Today, you complete your education (it has been quite an education, hasn't it?). Oh, sure, you'll still be there to provide guidance and support for your grown children. But there's no doubt that the roles and responsibilities have changed. Now you're a hands-off, there-if-you-need-me parent. You'll be there to offer

> *"A wise pastor once said, 'What will it profit a man if he gain the whole world, but lose his own son?' That pretty much lays it on the line. If, at the end of our lives, we've built financial security and purchased nice homes, but our children haven't taken a strong hold of the Lord's hand—what will our lives really have counted for?"*
>
> —Greg Johnson and Mike Yorkey,
> Faithful Parents, Faithful Kids[1]

opinions and recommendations—when asked. You'll be there to share your perspective on career choices and marriage prospects—when asked. And you'll be there to (someday) provide tips on parenting—when asked.

But let's not get ahead of ourselves. After all, it's still graduation day, and you've got one assignment left to complete. You've been asked to give a two-minute "charge" to thousands of fellow parents, soon-to-be-parents, and wannabe parents in attendance at the commencement ceremony.

Wow! How to distill 18 years of parenting experience and accumulated wisdom into a couple of minutes? What will you say? You could talk about the importance of discipline . . . or instilling strong values and morals . . . or guiding children to a fulfilling vocation . . . or helping them choose a life's mate. All those things are certainly important. But after days of reflection and soul-searching, you know what you want to pass along to your eager listeners.

So, after some introductory remarks ("Fellow parents, administrators, teachers, esteemed guests," and all that), you get right down to business:

> If I had to boil down the entire parenting challenge to the essentials—the most critical elements—they would be these: Make sure your child will be in heaven with you for eternity, and do all you can to send your child into the world with a solid, unwavering, genuine faith in God.
>
> Whether your child is a straight-A student or barely

CONCLUSION

scrapes by with C's and D's . . . whether your child is the star of the team or a confirmed benchwarmer . . . whether your child never gets sent to the principal's office or has a reserved seat in detention hall . . . whether your child is offered scholarships to top universities or will be on academic probation at the local community college—what, in the end, does it really matter?

Don't get me wrong: Academic pursuits, moral behavior, discipline and diligence, a sense of responsibility and reliability—these things are vitally important. But in the final analysis, what *really* matters? Faith in God and eternal security. That's it.

You look out on the vast audience and see thoughtful expressions and nodding heads. Good, your words are sinking in. You close your brief discourse with a "parents' paraphrase" of Paul's famous passage in 1 Corinthians 13:

> If I lecture my child about discipline and hard work, but have not taught him to love God, I am only a resounding gong or a clanging cymbal. If I have the gift of parenting and can fathom the mysteries of the adolescent mind, but have not taught my child to understand God's Word, I am nothing. If I give all, even mortgaging my home so my teenager can attend the best university, but have not instilled a genuine reverence for the Creator, I have accomplished nothing.

For this inspired speech you receive a hearty round of applause from the admiring parents gathered there. And as you descend from the dais, you swell with pride that you have not only pinpointed the most significant aspects of parenting but you've also achieved them. Congratulations! Well done, good and faithful parent.

Does that fanciful dramatization ring true for you? Did the words we put in your mouth sound like something you might actually say if asked to address a new class of parents?

Of course, you might want to add a point or two to the speech, some other lesson learned from the parenting school of hard knocks. But we hope that when everything else is boiled down and distilled—when all the triumphs and tragedies, successes and setbacks are steamed away—you would agree that these things rise above all else in importance: that your child accept and own for himself the faith you have passed down; and that someday, after you go to heaven, your child will arrive there, too, to enjoy eternity with you.

This helps to put the parenting task in perspective, doesn't it?

## Authentic Faith: Don't Let Your Kids Leave Home Without It

Joe White asked his daughter Jamie throughout high school to clean her room. He lectured her, scolded her, and nagged her. Nothing worked. Her room remained an unofficial national disaster area. In fact, the more Joe lectured, the messier that room became. As time passed and the accumulation of stuff swelled, Joe dubbed his daughter's room "the Blob."

Jamie, being phlegmatic and easygoing (not at all uptight about something like an untidy room), let the Blob grow. And grow. Piles of papers, letters she'd received, projects she was working on, posters and pictures, dried flowers from boyfriends, programs from who-knew-what events—all of it seeped and creeped out of her bedroom, down the hall, and into the living room.

So, what was a father to do?

Just about when he was ready to take drastic action—call the Merry Maids or a demolition service or something!—a miracle happened. It was around the end of May of Jamie's senior year. Joe walked past his daughter's room, stopped with a jolt, and did a double take. He entered her room (at least he thought it was her room). It was clean—spanking clean. (Big gasp, shock, disbelief.) Most of the things were packed neatly into moving boxes. The posters and pictures were down. The bulletin board was bare. The carpet could be seen. All those years of hounding her to clean her room, and now this!

Just then, Jamie walked in. "Oh, hi, Dad."

## Teens' "Traits of Great Parents," Part 12

- "Consistency, listening ear; open to conversation, not concerned with their agenda but with what the teen is thinking; taking the time to explain their reasoning."
- "Love, passion for God, consistent sacrifice of time and prestige for children's growth."
- "Available, willing to listen, set boundaries, unconditional love, trust, respect."
- "Involvement."
- "Love, spend time with their kids, listen."

It turns out that she was getting a head start on packing for college. She was ready to move out.

Joe thought, *Is this a glorious revelation or a nightmare? Or both?*

"I crawled into her bed, curled up in a fetal position, and cried like a baby because the thing I'd been asking for so long had finally happened," Joe says. "She'd cleaned her room."

So those were tears of joy, right?

Wrong.

"I wished I'd never given a lecture," he recalls. "I wished that her room would've stayed messy the rest of her life—because a messy room would have meant that my girl would be home. And a clean room meant she would be gone."

A few months later, Joe, Jamie, and the rest of the family took all that stuff to college. Dad became a pack mule, lugging box after box, along with furniture and lamps, up four flights of dormitory stairs.

"I didn't grumble or complain—I was too busy crying," Joe says. "As I moved my daughter into her dorm room, I knew I was saying good-bye to her for the next four years—and probably forever."

At the end of that long day, Joe took a few minutes by himself to lean against the car and let it all sink in. Looking back at his daughter's dorm, he felt as if a 300-pound NFL lineman had punched him in the stomach. Where had the years gone? How did his darling baby girl grow up so fast?

"With tears streaming down my face, I realized that Jamie was taking only one possession of significance to college—her relationship with Jesus Christ," he says. "Of all the things I had given her over the years, the things in her new dorm room and the things packed away in the garage at home, only that one thing really mattered: her faith in God."

Driving home that night, with his wife, Debbie-Jo, sitting silently beside him, he still felt a hollow ache in the pit of his stomach. But a strange, soothing joy began sweeping over him as he thought: *No matter what happens to Jamie in college, no matter that her daddy is going to be 600 miles away, that girl is going to be okay because the Word of God and the Holy Spirit will reside within her. Nothing can take those away—ever.*

Joe and his wife weren't surprised when, about two months after college started, Jamie found a group of high school girls to mentor every week. They weren't surprised that many girls sought out Jamie during the next four years to ask her advice, counsel, and prayer. They weren't surprised that she greatly influenced dozens of people during her college career.

"We had passed the baton of faith on to Jamie," Joe says. "That's the greatest feeling in the world for a parent—to know that your child has not only taken on your faith but also owned it for herself. When she left for college, it was painful for Debbie-Jo and me, but we knew she had a solid foundation in the faith and God's Word. Everything else she would do or become was just icing on the cake."

No matter how old your children are, no matter where you are in the parenting process, it's never too early to start helping your kids pack for college.

## Start Planning Your Family Reunion

In the late 1990s, singer Eric Clapton released a song called "Tears in Heaven" that went on to win a Grammy award. Written for his young son who had died tragically, the song asks, "Would you know my name if I saw you in heaven?" Although Clapton has released his share of unwholesome songs through the years, this one challenged many people to think about important issues—to pause and consider where they will end up when life is over.

> *It's hard to imagine anything more terrifying for a parent than to think that your child might not spend eternity with you in heaven.*

For Christians, the assurance of a grand reunion in heaven leaves no question that family members will know our name when we meet them there. Imagine the hugs, kisses, and high-fives, the peals of laughter and squeals of delight, as we come together with those we cherished on earth. Imagine the celebration as we party with ancestors, descendants, and family and friends who shared our faith.

Over and over, Scripture encourages us to look ahead to the day when we'll arrive in heaven:

- "In my Father's house are many rooms; if it were not so, I would have told you. I am going there to prepare a place for you. And if I go and prepare a place for you, I will come back and take you to be with me that you also may be where I am" (John 14:2-3).
- "No eye has seen, no ear has heard, no mind has conceived what God has prepared for those who love him" (1 Corinthians 2:9).
- "In keeping with his promise we are looking forward to a new heaven and a new earth, the home of righteousness" (2 Peter 3:13).
- "He will wipe every tear from their eyes. There will be no more death or mourning or crying or pain, for the old order of things has passed away" (Revelation 21:4).

Most Christians who stop long enough to think seriously about heaven get both wildly excited and deeply concerned—concerned about loved ones who might not be there. Indeed, it's hard to imagine anything more terrifying for a parent than to think that your child might not spend eternity with you in heaven.

As theologian Randall Balmer said, "I suspect that the greatest fear that haunts Christian parents is that their children will not follow in their footsteps, that they will not sustain the same level

## Teens' Advice to Parents About Nurturing Spiritual Growth, Part 12

- "Spend time praying *with*, not just *for*, your teens. Start when they are younger and continue it through adulthood. Not just a quick minute, either, but *time* praying together. Let them know you are real, too!"
- "Make it your number-one priority—even over getting enough sleep that night—to listen and teach. (It has to be number one in your life for that to be an option!)"
- "Be open to your teen's questions and doubts. Teach your kids to think critically."
- "Follow Scripture."
- "Live your life as an example! Kids will pay more attention to your actions than your words."

of piety as their parents—stated baldly, that they are headed for hell rather than heaven."[2]

Sobering words, these.

Fortunately—and that's a *huge* fortunately—you can guide your child in the faith, pray for him consistently, and teach him how to walk closely with God. You can gain assurance that you will not only know each other's names in heaven but also walk arm in arm as you discover the wonders of God's prepared place together. You can, right now, make absolutely sure your child will be a part of the biggest family reunion and the most spectacular celebration history has ever known.

### "Be There to Meet Your Mother and Me in Heaven"

Several years ago, Dr. James Dobson had an experience that shook him to the core of his being—and prompted a weighty conversation with his son, Ryan, who was 17 years old at the time.

Dr. Dobson had been playing an early morning game of pickup basketball with a group of coworkers and friends, and their guest that day was Pistol Pete Maravich, the legendary NBA star. Suddenly, in the middle of a game and without warning, Pete collapsed to the hardwood court. Dr. Dobson was the first to reach him. He made sure Pete's air passage was clear and called for the other guys to help. For about 20 seconds, Pete struggled to take in air, then he stopped breathing altogether. The men started CPR, but they were never able to get another heartbeat or another breath.

As Dr. Dobson recalls, "Pistol Pete Maravich, one of the world's greatest athletes, died there in my arms at forty years of age." (An autopsy revealed a few days later that Pete had a congenital malformation of the heart that he had never known about.)

Later that day, Dr. Dobson, deeply shaken by what had occurred, went home and sat down with his son. He asked to talk with him about something extremely important. Here's what he said:

> *"The question to ask at the end of life's race is not so much 'What have I accomplished?' but 'Whom have I loved, and how courageously?'"*
> —*Geoff Gorsuch*[3]

Ryan, I want you to understand what has happened here. Pete's death was not an unusual tragedy that has happened to only one man and his family. We all must face death sooner or later and in one way or another. This is the "human condition." It comes too early for some people and too late for others. But no one will escape, ultimately. And, of course, it will also happen to you and me. So without being morbid about it, I want you to begin to prepare yourself for that time.

Sooner or later, you'll get the kind of phone call that Mrs. Maravich received today. It could occur ten or fifteen years from now, or it could come tomorrow. But when that time comes, there is one thought I want to leave with you. I don't know if I'll have an opportunity to give you my "last words" then, so let me express them to you right now. Freeze-frame this moment in your mind, and hold on to it for the rest of your life. My message to you is *Be there!* Be there to meet your mother and me in heaven. We will be looking for you on that resurrection morning. Don't let anything deter you from keeping that appointment.

Because I am fifty-one years old and you are only seventeen, as many as fifty years could pass from the time of my death to yours. That's a long time to remember. But you can be sure that I will be searching for you just inside the Eastern Gate. This is the only thing of real significance in your life. I care what you accomplish in the years to come, and I hope you make good use of the great potential the Lord has given to you. But above every other purpose and goal, the only thing that really matters is that you determine now to be there![4]

## A Job Worth Doing Well

We've covered a lot of ground in this book, and we hope you've gleaned from these pages inspiration to persist in the important task of parenting as well as information to assist you in that mission. We also hope the most important themes and messages of this book have burrowed into your heart and mind. A few of the points we highlighted throughout this book include:

- *You can do it.* No matter your background, difficulties from your own childhood, bad choices you've made, or sense of inadequacy, with God's help, you *are* up to the challenge of guiding your teenager to spiritual maturity and responsible adulthood.
- *It's not too late.* If your son or daughter is still at home, you have daily opportunities to strengthen your parent-child relationship and foster spiritual growth in your teen's life.
- *Redeem the time.* The years your child lives under your roof pass incredibly quickly. Don't squander them. Make the most of every opportunity to build a close relationship with your child and to help him grow in his faith.
- *Be intentional.* Helping your son or daughter grow spiritually requires deliberate, thoughtful, planned action on your part. Your child's spiritual development depends largely on your involvement and guidance.

*The years your child lives under your roof pass incredibly quickly. Don't squander them.*

We have taken care to develop these and other important themes in great detail. But all those ideas lead to this point: Do everything within your power to make sure your son or daughter has a relationship with Christ so you can "be there" in heaven together.

Let us add one verse about heaven to those we mentioned above. In 1 Thessalonians, the apostle Paul wrote, "What is our hope, our joy, or the crown in which we will glory in the presence of our Lord Jesus when he comes? Is it not you? Indeed, you are our glory and joy" (2:19-20).

We can almost imagine Paul looking ahead to the day when he would see Jesus in heaven, and his Savior would place a crown of victory on his head. With him there, watching him receive his commendation from the King, are all his children in the faith—the church members of such towns as Thessalonica, Ephesus, Corinth, Philippi, and Rome, as well as Timothy, Silas, and a host of others. They're all there, all the people whom Paul led to Christ or discipled, gathered with him.

> *"You have come to thousands upon thousands of angels in joyful assembly, to the church of the firstborn, whose names are written in heaven."*
> —Hebrews 12:22-23

As a parent, you might imagine a similar scene, standing before Christ with your children beside you. And more: Behind each of your children are their children and their children's children (and on and on). Your lineage is there with you to honor the King of kings and enjoy the riches of heaven with you forever.

Could there be a more thrilling vision for a parent? You can hear Jesus say to you and the ones you love most, "Come, you who are blessed by my Father; take your inheritance, the kingdom prepared for you since the creation of the world" (Matthew 25:34).

Well done, good and faithful parent.

# Questions and Answers: 24 Tough Issues Parents of Teens Face

Have a problem with your teen? This quick-reference guide provides concise answers to vexing questions. For further help with these issues, consult related sections of this book (see index) and additional resources listed in appendix B.

## 1. Alcohol

**So many kids at my son's school use alcohol. What can I do to keep him from getting involved with it?**

Any time teens use alcohol, it's cause for serious concern. Alcohol use is the number-one drug problem among young people.

To prevent your teen from consuming alcohol, try the following:

- *Lead by example.* Your own use or nonuse of alcohol is probably the number-one influence on your teen's drinking. If you drink even occasionally, think long and hard about the message this sends.
- *Educate your teen.* Don't assume your son or daughter knows the effects of alcohol consumption. Even if he or she has heard school or church presentations on alcohol abuse, sit down and have a thorough discussion about it. Your

input may carry the most weight of all the messages he or she has heard.

- *Keep the discussion going.* A one-time talk about drinking is not enough. Check in regularly to see if your teen has any questions or wants to talk about pressure he might be receiving from peers.
- *Assure your teen that not everyone is doing it.* Yes, alcohol use is widespread among teens, but your son or daughter will not be the only one who abstains. Often teens don't really want to drink but cave in because of peer pressure. Don't underestimate how difficult this can be for a young person. Reinforce the idea (perhaps with the help of other parents whose kids are resisting peer pressure) that there are plenty of normal teens who abstain from alcohol use.
- *Listen with restraint.* Let your teenager express his or her feelings on this subject without fear that you are going to dominate the conversation. The only way you're going to get your message across is by keeping the dialogue open.
- *Praise, affirm, and encourage.* When your teen has acted responsibly in a difficult situation, heap on your approval and affirmation.

If you suspect that alcohol is becoming a problem for your teen, consult a youth pastor or counselor and learn how to intervene. Doing so just may save your child's life.

## 2. Anger

**I see my daughter get so upset, apparently for no reason. Why is she so angry?**

Behind anger there is always some kind of hurt—physical pain, disappointment, or sadness. Often this hurt is a reaction to a recent injury—being rejected by a boyfriend, doing badly on a test, or getting into an argument with a classmate. Sometimes the wound is an old one that hasn't healed—divorce of the teen's parents, loss of a sibling, harsh words once spoken by a parent. Wherever there is anger, hurt exists. Look for it.

The catalyst for anger is anxiety. Hidden inside your teen's anger is some form of fear, worry, embarrassment, or apprehension. The anxiety may be harder to uncover than the hurt. One way to do this is to hunt for the "what ifs" in her thinking: "What if nobody likes me?" or "What if I can't handle the workload?" Where there is anger, there is anxiety, and it's usually closely related to how she feels about herself or how others perceive her.

When you mix hurt with anxiety, you get anger. Try to help your teen identify both parts of this formula separately. See if she'll talk out the hurt or disappointment. When it comes to the anxiety, help her challenge the "what ifs" of her thinking. If this challenge proves too formidable, enlist the help of a youth pastor or counselor. The more your teen can manage hurt and anxiety before they get a chance to combine, the less she'll experience flare-ups of anger.

**To avoid outbursts, my son denies his feelings and bottles up his anger. What can I do to help him find healthy ways to cope with these emotions?**

Some teens conclude that anger itself is a sin and never benefit from the valuable service it provides. They may deny or suppress anger in an effort to "be good." That can create more destructive expressions of anger.

The role of anger is similar to that of the gauges on your car's dashboard. Both signal that something is amiss and needs immediate attention. If we ignore or disconnect the Check Engine light, for example, there will be a destructive outcome—despite a few moments of ignorant bliss. Likewise, if we pretend anger isn't present, needs go unaddressed and more hurt will follow.

Anger is powerful and usually uncomfortable, but the Bible doesn't say not to be angry. Rather, it says we shouldn't be quick to anger (Proverbs 14:17), sin in the midst of anger, or allow bitter passions to go unresolved (Ephesians 4:26-32). If we put a lid on anger, it will seep out in the form of negative attitudes, cutting words, depression, or violence.

You can assist your son in his struggle by discussing some of these ideas together, especially if you have unwittingly defined anger as a bad thing. Help your son see how, in an attempt to deny his feelings, he is allowing anger to control him.

Encourage your teen to talk with God about his feelings. He could also write them in a journal as a way to release tension. Or he could talk about them with you or another trusted adult.

## 3. Clothing and Hairstyles

**My son has started wearing some pretty strange-looking clothes. Is this something I should be concerned about?**

Did you wear tie-dyed shirts and bell-bottoms in the 1960s? Plaid pants and platform shoes in the 1970s? Thinking back to your own youthful fashion statements may help put the debate over teen clothing in perspective.

How do you guide your teens toward appropriate clothing styles? Common sense and clear communication are the keys. At times the holey or baggy jeans may drive you crazy, but come back to the main question: Is it worth arguing over? One mom says, "Our rule was, as long as the clothing was not immodest, indecent, or vulgar, it was their choice. The call on immodesty came down to Mom, not to them. They could wear ripped, ugly, smelly clothes if they wanted, but I found peer pressure was a great factor in them keeping their clothes clean."

If you're concerned that your teen's clothes are sending the wrong message to others, sit down and talk about it. Ask questions like these:

- "If you wear a shirt that shows a particular band or product (beer, for example), would people think you are endorsing it?"
- "What do you think when you see a guy wearing his pants way too low?"
- "When you see a girl who's dressed in a provocative or revealing outfit, what thoughts about her go through your mind?"
- "What do you want people to think about you?"

The issues are similar with your teen's hair. In the grand scheme of life, how critical are hairstyles? Find out whether your teen is trying to say something through his or her choice of coiffure. That can serve as the foundation of a meaningful conversation.

In general, issues surrounding a teen's clothing choices and hairstyle can be clarified by answering one question: Is this a matter of preference, or is there a moral issue here?

## 4. Curfews

**I want to set reasonable limits on when my teenager should be in at night. Any ideas?**

Smooth sailing through this region comes as a result of clear communication, honesty, and a willingness to negotiate. Curfew timing is also an opportunity to teach delayed gratification and the concept that being faithful in a small way can lead to more freedom.

Help your teen understand that curfews are not simply a chance for you to regulate him. They promote safety, communication, and a balanced schedule. As you work out curfew times, minimize conflict by keeping these points in mind:

- *Tell your teen to call if she is going to be late.* You don't want her racing dangerously to get home by the appointed time.
- *Don't expect perfection.* Planning and time management are learned skills. Even for a teen who doesn't mean to break the rules, it requires a little practice and experience to learn that things always take longer than you think.
- *If you're parenting with a spouse, discuss your expectations beforehand.* Present a united front when establishing curfews.
- *If your teen shows good judgment, let him propose a reasonable curfew.* If she consistently arrives home at the appointed time, consider easing up on the rules.
- *Be flexible.* Ten minutes late is very different from two hours late. Focus on the spirit of the law, not just the letter.

And what happens if curfew is not met?

The appropriate response should be based on the circumstances and your teen's attitude. Did your teen try to call? Was it a case of irresponsibility or losing track of time? Did a friend's actions cause your teen to miss a ride? You might respond to a first offense with a serious talk. If additional violations occur—or if your teen deliberately chooses to disobey, does not communicate that he will be late, and shows little remorse—you should react more firmly. The next proposed outing should be tagged with an earlier curfew than normal.

## 5. Dating

**Our 16-year-old daughter has started dating. How do we help her keep perspective and avoid trouble?**

Conversations about dating (for parents who don't prefer a "courtship" model) often suffer from unclear terms and expectations. For example, if you express worry about your daughter getting too physical, she may think, *Okay, we won't have sex*. But your concern is probably deeper, desiring that she show self-respect, exercise good judgment, and maintain purity.

State what you mean as clearly as possible. Ask questions to make sure her definitions and expectations coincide with yours.

Help your teen to grasp your reasons for being concerned about dating. Affirm your love for her and your God-given responsibility for her well-being. Let her know you understand her desire for fun, the thrill of romance, and the sense of urgency peer pressure creates. Tell her that you wish to help her avoid unnecessary pain.

Working together, define your family standards for dating, including curfew, conduct, and where your teen is allowed to go and with whom. Set clear boundaries, and make it equally clear that exceeding them will lead to specific consequences.

Finally, encourage your teen to pursue group dating. Social interaction with a group can provide more relaxed fun and foster friendships. Instead of donning a dating face, teens are more likely to be themselves and won't as easily be tempted by physical intimacy.

**My daughter is attracted to a nice boy, but he's not a Christian. How can I help her see the potential danger in pursuing that relationship?**

Once your child is emotionally involved, it's pretty hard for her to hear your concerns. Objectivity disappears. That's why it's best to discuss prior to dating the problem of Christians and unbelievers being unequally yoked.

To address the issue at this point, try the following:

- Read and talk about 2 Corinthians 6:14, which tells us not to become partners with those who reject God. Observe that if the relationship's foundation lacks a shared commitment to Jesus Christ, the whole structure is weakened. Priorities and goals will differ, not to mention moral boundaries.
- Be willing to share positive or negative examples from your own history.
- If your teen is already dating a non-Christian, ask your teen, "How is this relationship helping your walk with Jesus to grow stronger?" Don't buy the "I can witness to him" myth. More often than not, when couples relate at different levels spiritually, the Christian is pulled away from God rather than the other way around. Encourage your daughter to examine herself. If she's honest, she'll see that this relationship can only diminish who she is in Christ. Then pray that such insight will motivate her to make better choices.

## 6. Depression

**How can I tell if my daughter is truly depressed or just moody like teenagers often are?**

You're right to acknowledge that teens can be moody. That's partly due to the physiological changes they're experiencing. But depression can also be passed down between generations, so it's important to know your family's medical history.

The symptoms for clinical depression can be divided into three progressive stages. The more symptoms you see, and the more consistently you see them, the more likely that your teen is truly depressed. Here's the progression:

*Stage one:* Inability to concentrate, withdrawal from friends, impulsive acts, and declining academic performance. If you see these symptoms, encourage your teen to talk openly and honestly with you. Tell her you're concerned about what you've observed and want her to avoid further troubles.

*Stage two:* Acts of aggression, rapid mood swings, loss of friends, mild rebellion, and sudden changes in personality. If you see this pattern, seek immediate outside assistance from a trusted youth pastor or counselor.

*Stage three:* Overt rebellion, visible depression, extreme fatigue, giving away prized possessions, expressions of hopelessness, suicidal threats or gestures. These symptoms require getting professional help right away. If your teen is clinically depressed, she cannot pull herself out of it. She may need to be evaluated for hospitalization. Medication may also be necessary.

Depression is something many teenagers experience. Your teen can recover from it in time with the proper help and encouragement.

## 7. Driving

**We don't think our 16-year-old son is responsible enough to start driving yet. How do we know for sure that we can trust him?**

It's hard to relax and embrace this part of adolescence, no matter how responsible your teen has been. Still, some teens *can't* be trusted with the family car. If there has been a pattern of disrespect toward authority, deceitfulness, secretiveness, drug or alcohol use in the past two years, or ongoing irresponsibility, your hunch not to trust him is probably correct.

If you see this kind of behavior, sit your teen down and list the changes he'll have to make before you'll allow him to drive. Explain that you'll need to see evidence of those changes over the next six to nine months before you'll discuss the topic again. This should be long enough to tell if he's really becoming responsible or if he's just play-acting to get the car. Stick to your guns and don't give in.

Give him a chance to prove himself worthy of your trust. Remind him that being faithful in little things is an important prerequisite to being trusted with bigger matters (discuss Matthew 25:14-30). At the end of the probationary period, assuming you haven't seen any red flags, you can move more confidently into the adventure of teenage driving. Keep in mind, too, that driving is a privilege that you can continue to extend or revoke as needed.

## 8. Drugs

**We are deeply concerned that our son is using drugs but feel powerless to act until we can prove it. What can we do?**

First of all, don't swallow your concerns for lack of proof. The suspicion alone is enough to justify careful intervention. But the goal is to assist your son with life choices, not just to prove yourself right.

If parenting with a spouse, communicate your concerns to him or her—and then to your teen. List the behaviors that fuel your suspicions. What personality changes do you see? Do certain friendships make you uncomfortable? Are grades suffering? What have you heard from an interested teacher, youth pastor, or other adult who observes your son in another setting?

Depending on the feedback you get, you may want to consider a room search for drugs, drug paraphernalia, or a diary or journal that sheds light on the subject. But such action should be taken as a last resort. Only after all else fails should parents risk violating their children's trust in this manner—even when motivated by love and acting in the child's best interest.

If, after being confronted, your teen admits to drug use, develop agreements about what will be done. These should include at least two elements: stopping drug use, and attending counseling as a family in order to develop a strategy to move forward.

If your teen proclaims his innocence and your search is inconclusive, your suspicion may persist. Tell your teen that suspicion is the immediate issue, and let him know what he is doing to create it. If he refuses to cooperate, explain that your mistrust will continue, affecting your responses to him, including your decisions about his freedoms. Let the pressure of your suspicion weigh on your teen over time; some kids just need to see that parents won't give up.

Conduct more research if needed—a school locker check, a meeting with school officials, possibly even drug testing. Contact a Christian counselor for further direction and help.

Throughout the process, pray. Keep assuring your teen that you love him and will continue to watch out for his best interests.

## 9. Earrings, Piercings, and Tattoos

**My daughter wants to put rings through every possible part of her body. I don't want her looking like a heap of scrap metal. What can I do?**

As with clothes and hairstyles, most earrings and other piercings may fit into the personal preference category rather than being a moral matter. Clarify the issues by asking your teen questions like these:

- "Why do you want to have these piercings?"
- "How do you want other people to feel about your fashion statement?"
- "How will you feel about your decision two or five or ten years from now?"
- "How do you think God feels about this?"

Sometimes a ho-hum approach dampens a teen's enthusiasm for this kind of adornment. One mom with two daughters and a son said, "Some things were done just to shock, rebel, and do something that did not have [the parent's] approval. Thus, when my son wanted to pierce his nose—something that grossed me out—I responded with 'How boring. Everyone else is doing that.' His grandparents gave him a similar reaction. The result? No pierced nose. Now, I'm not saying that this would work in every situation, but with all my kids, I explained that I wanted to be sure they were doing it because *they* wanted it done, not because everyone else was doing it."

In the case of tattooing, try to get your teen to see the long-range view. How might your daughter's future husband feel about the flower near her belly button? What might your son's future wife think about that heart on his shoulder, especially if it contains someone else's initials?

If you're concerned for health reasons, explain that piercings can lead to uncomfortable and dangerous complications. Tattooing carries the possibility of contracting Hepatitis B, HIV, or tetanus from the needles and dyes. For more on this subject, see chapter 13, "Overcoming Conflicts."

## 10. Eating Disorders

**My daughter has dropped a lot of weight in the past six months. In fact, she's skinny to the point of looking unhealthy. I think she may have an eating disorder. So what should I do?**

There are two primary types of eating disorders: anorexia nervosa and bulimia nervosa.

*Anorexia nervosa.* Teens with this condition display a preoccupation with dieting and thinness that leads to excessive weight loss through self-starvation. The symptoms include the following:

- distorted body image (she says, "I'm so fat," even though she's thin)
- hair loss
- missing periods
- wearing layered or baggy clothes to hide thinness
- isolation and withdrawal from family and friends
- excessive mood swings and irritability
- inability to concentrate and stay focused on a task
- drop in grades and school performance
- obsession with exercise
- missing meals, often accompanied by excuses (meeting a friend for dinner, going to the library, and so on)

*Bulimia nervosa.* This disorder involves frequent episodes of eating, almost always followed by purging (most often by vomiting or using laxatives). Symptoms include the following:

- use of diet pills, diuretics, or laxatives
- swollen glands or puffy face
- residue or smell of vomit in the bathroom
- leaving the table abruptly after meals
- discolored or decaying teeth
- excessive mood swings and irritability

- isolation and withdrawn behavior
- drop in grades and school performance

If you suspect your teen has an eating disorder, act quickly. Untreated, such a disorder can be fatal. Talk to your doctor or a therapist; don't attempt to correct the problem alone. Eating disorders stem from underlying psychological causes, and you need to focus on the root issues.

## 11. Entertainment

**We've always been very careful about the movies and TV shows we let our kids watch. But lately our son is rebelling against those standards. How can I control what he sees?**

The truth is that you can't. Take the teen who thinks of R-rated movies as a rite of passage. "I've followed your rules all my life when most of my friends haven't," he tells you. "Now that I'm 17, I'm even legal, so what's the big deal? A lot of the shows on TV are worse than that movie, so I'm going to go with my friends— and you can't stop me." If he's intent on seeing that movie, he'll find a way.

As parents, we can only provide a certain amount of protection. We may be able to limit TV use at home and the theaters we attend with our children, but we don't have the same control over the choices our teens make when they're at the cineplex or the homes of friends.

The best approach is to help teens develop their own tools for making God-honoring entertainment choices. For help with that process, see "Teaching Your Teen Media Discernment" (chapter 19).

## 12. Faith and Church Attendance

**My son is suddenly questioning every spiritual truth we've ever taught him. What's going on?**

Challenging principles may simply be the normal process of internalizing them, moving from "what others have taught me" to "what I believe." Teens raised in Christian homes need to develop meaning and understanding to accompany their adherence to the disciplines of faith; the alternative is legalism or empty ritual (see chapter 17 for more on this subject).

Be a good listener. As you listen, try to determine whether a recent event has triggered your teen's challenge. Has he been laughed at by unbelieving friends? Embarrassed by a teacher? Disillusioned by the failure of a trusted church leader? Hurt by the death of a friend? Angered by an incident in which you seemed not to practice what you preach? If possible, talk through these feelings before moving to "proofs" of the Christian faith.

Encourage questions, even if you don't have all the answers. Remember that God accepts our questioning without reprimand (see David's struggles in the book of Psalms, for instance). Explore Scripture together, using reference tools such as a Bible dictionary, concordance, or commentary. Consult books on apologetics for added help (see appendix B).

If your son isn't really interested in finding answers, it's possible that his challenging is a form of passive-aggressive rebellion. In that case, focus conversation on his behavior and the choices he's making. Is his belligerence leading to dangerous actions? If so, you may need to say, "Obey now; we'll discuss *why* later." Continue to listen carefully, pray for him daily, and consult a counselor or youth pastor if things don't improve.

**Getting my daughter to go to church is turning into a wrestling match. She says she's bored and doesn't get anything out of it. How should I respond?**

It's important to maintain the family's commitment to spiritual practices. And church isn't just about what we get out of it. Explain to your teen the "why's" of church attendance, including spiritual growth, worship, service, and building relationships with other Christians.

Listen carefully to your teen's complaints about church or youth group. Challenge her to be specific. Might some of the problems be solved by talking with your church's youth leaders? By moving to a different church? By allowing your teen to be involved in another church's youth program? Would it be reasonable for your teen to drop one church activity in exchange for giving another a chance?

If solutions like these seem like caving in, consider the fact that teens who have negative church experiences are likely to ditch church when they're on their own. If you can prevent that, it may be worth disrupting your status quo.

## 13. Friends

**My daughter has joined a group of friends we disapprove of. What should we do?**

First, recognize that trying to forbid a teen's friendships is usually counterproductive. Unless your daughter is in imminent danger, it's better to challenge her to be more discerning.

Ask yourself what it is about these new friends that concerns you. If possible, host a get-together that allows you to mingle with them and engage them in discussion. (It's always good to get to know your teen's friends.) It could go a long way toward confirming or dismissing your fears.

If you decide that your concerns are over character rather than appearance, bring those issues to your teen's attention. Ask questions like "Did you notice how Damien seems to treat people with disrespect? How do you feel about that?"

Listen to her response. Focus on the behavior or attitude rather than the person. You'll end up talking about what's most critical—your teen and her ability to judge character.

When you need to challenge her thinking, do so in love. When you can affirm her discernment, do so enthusiastically. Nothing will loosen the stranglehold of unhealthy peer relationships better than a supportive parent-teen bond.

## 14. Ingratitude

**My son seems to take an awful lot for granted, as if he's entitled to everything he has and more. How can I help him be thankful for the things he gets?**

Perhaps it's time to take action aimed at helping your son maintain a balance between "needs" and "wants." Here are a few ideas:

- Make thanksgiving to God a regular part of your family's prayer times, going beyond the usual laundry list of requests.

■ Try fasting as a family, spending mealtime talking and praying about the needs of others. But food isn't the only thing you can go without for a set period of time; television, videos, music, or computer use can be sacrificed to gain a deeper appreciation for the things you have.

■ Share a meal with someone less fortunate—an act of charity and hospitality that will help your son appreciate his own prosperity.

■ Donate your time as a family to assist at a local soup kitchen or homeless shelter during the holidays.

■ Adopt a needy family or child through a Christian relief organization.

■ Encourage your teen to join his youth group in a service project or mission trip, particularly if the setting will introduce him to those who have less than he does.

## 15. Irresponsibility

**My teenager doesn't take responsibility for things like keeping his room picked up or getting his homework done. How can I get him to be more conscientious and responsible?**

Let him bear the natural consequences of his actions. Here are examples related to schoolwork:

■ If he's having a problem, offer to help or to get help. If he declines, let it go.

■ If the report card comes back with low grades, limit weekday activities until the schoolwork gets done.

■ If homework is not coming home, call the school to see why.

■ If he continues to abdicate responsibility, let natural consequences take their toll. He may not feel the pinch until he applies to colleges or for scholarships. This can be scary and disappointing for a parent and may even seem insensitive, but it's really just a reflection of who's responsible for the work.

In the case of room cleaning, rewards or penalties may do the trick. If not, you may have to shut the door and let your teen deal with the consequences of living amid a mess.

## 16. Jobs

**We feel it's time our 16-year-old got a part-time job, but he's resisting. Is he just lazy?**

Find out which of the following factors is fueling your son's reluctance to seek employment:

- *Being intimidated by the process.* He's inexperienced and probably has no idea what it takes to get a job. Gently walk him through the steps and remind him of the qualities he has that will make him an asset to an employer.
- *Not recognizing the value of hard work.* This may be especially true for bright teens who are used to succeeding with minimal effort. Explain that hard work is not only a virtue but a lifelong value as well. The Bible is clear that we must work (2 Thessalonians 3:10). We were designed to do so, especially as it honors God and serves others. Discuss the rewards: a paycheck; the satisfaction of helping others; a chance to practice punctuality and self-discipline; and an opportunity to develop skills for problem solving, goal setting, critical thinking, conflict management, and interpersonal communication.
- *Following your example.* Consider the signals your son may be picking up from you about the working world. Do you complain about your job? If so, he may be reluctant to subject himself to the same misery. Try to present a more balanced view of what it's like to work.
- *Downright laziness.* If you've dealt with the other possible causes and your teen still refuses to seek employment, maybe he's just committed to avoiding labor. In other words, yes, he may be lazy. It may be time to tighten the purse strings. Let his need for spending money, car insurance, or other items motivate him to get a job.

## 17. Lying

**I caught my son in a blatant lie. How can I make sure this doesn't become a habit?**

Teens may lie for several reasons: to gain a feeling of independence, to test boundaries, to protect friends, to impress or shock, to avoid getting in trouble, or to gain an advantage over others.

To prevent lying from becoming a chronic problem, take the following steps:

- *Commit yourself to honesty.* If you fabricate or exaggerate a story for effect, or tell a "little white lie" to protect your credibility, your teen is likely to follow suit.
- *Don't label your teen as a liar.* If you say to your son, "You're a liar," he might begin to see himself as one. Believe the best about your teen—and believe that lying is out of character for him.
- *Talk it through.* As calmly and rationally as you can, discuss what motivated the lie. Is it one of the reasons mentioned above? Focus on the issue behind the dishonesty.
- *Go back to basics.* Ask your teen to find and read a few Bible passages about honesty and integrity and to share his reactions with you. Deceit is so pervasive in our society that it wouldn't hurt to have a refresher course on *why* truthfulness is important.

## 18. Music

**I'm troubled by some of the CDs showing up in our home. How do we set a music standard for our teenage daughter?**

You'll find plenty of assistance on this topic in the chapter "Teaching Your Teen Media Discernment" (chapter 19). For now, here are some quick tips:

- As a parent, you have the right to limit what comes into your home. On the other hand, avoid risking your relationship on battles that don't have eternal consequences.
- Clarify what's in and what's out of bounds—and why. Focus on the lyrics rather than musical style. Involve your teen in the process of setting standards; base them on biblical principles and put them in writing.

■ Realize your limitations. You can't control your daughter's music diet for the rest of her life. The goal is to lovingly teach discernment, not simply to enforce a code.

■ If some CDs need to go, offer to replace them with more wholesome ones. If your daughter buys a disc that fails the biblically based standard you've made clear, she can return it or get rid of it. Remind her that if she's ever in doubt, she should check with you *before* buying a disc.

■ Be patient, fair, and keep listening. Remember that you're a spiritual mentor, not the "music Gestapo."

## 19. Money

**We give our son an allowance, but he doesn't seem to handle it very well. We're worried that he'll end up bankrupt when he's on his own. What can we do?**

Your son will have the best chance of learning fiscal responsibility by having to care for himself financially. Begin by putting him on a "living expense budget" rather than an "allowance." Add up the money you would normally spend on him during a year (for clothes, birthday gifts for friends, haircuts, movie tickets, sporting events, and so on). Don't include family event expenses or special gifts you would ordinarily buy him.

Divide that amount by 12 to determine his monthly budget. Every two weeks, give him two weeks' worth of cash. Use a separate envelope for each expense category (including tithe) and mark the amount on the outside.

From this point on, he is responsible for all his expenses. Purchases are still subject to parental approval, but they now come out of his pocket instead of yours. Don't bail him out. Just coach him and help him see the effects of his choices. Let him feel the impact—good or bad—of his financial decisions.

If your son holds a regular job (another great way for him to learn the value of a dollar), set up his own checking or savings account at your bank. Teens are much more careful with money when (1) there's a limited supply, and (2) it's up to them to manage it or suffer the consequences.

## 20. Overinvolvement

**My teenager is involved in too many activities: school, baby-sitting, church, sports. She just can't say no to people, and I'm afraid she's a candidate for burnout. How can I help her find a healthy balance?**

Kids learn by example, and many parents are overcommitted themselves. You may have passed this trait down without realizing it. If so, lead by example; cut back on your own commitments and tell your teen why you're doing so.

Next, sit down with your daughter and review her schedule together. It might help to chart a typical week on a piece of paper. This may be enough to convince her that change is worth considering.

Find out what's behind the busyness. Insecurity can drive teens (and adults) into performance mode and make them reluctant to say no to others out of fear of rejection. Your daughter needs reassurance that her value lies in who she is, not in how many people she pleases.

For younger teens, establish a limit on extracurricular activities, perhaps one sport or club and one type of music lesson at any one time. This rule may be difficult to impose on an older teen, so be flexible.

If all else fails, be there to help your teen pick up the pieces when burnout hits. Finding balance in life is something many people never learn. You can be there to show your teen what went wrong and how to make it right hereafter. (See also the section "Make Sure Your Teen Is Getting Enough Sleep" in chapter 24, p. 446.)

## 21. Parties

**My teen has been invited to a party at a friend's house, which sets off alarms in my mind. I can't keep her locked in her room throughout high school, so what should I do?**

It's an unfair generalization to say that all parties are "dens of iniquity," but parents are wise to be wary when the invitations come. You can minimize the dangers with strategies like these:

■ *Encourage your teen to attend parties sponsored by the church youth group or other Christian ministries.* Problems can occur even in these settings, of course, but your teen is usually far better off when Christian adults are present to monitor the activities.

■ *Find out everything you can about the party your son or daughter will be attending.* Call the school or the adult hosting the party, and discuss what will be going on. Is this nosy? Will your teen accuse you of being paranoid? Maybe. But with teenage drinking, drug use, and date rape so common in our society, it's best to err on the side of caution.

■ *Network with other parents.* Ask them what the scene will be like, based on their experience. At the very least, get to know the parents at whose homes your teen is likely to spend time.

■ *Establish the hour at which your teen is expected home.* Be sure your teen understands the curfew and the consequences for violating it.

■ *Talk through an exit plan with your son or daughter.* If the party starts getting out of hand, how will he or she leave? Agree on a definition of "getting out of hand," too. Assure your teen that she can call you at any time—no questions asked—if she wants to leave the party.

■ *Discuss transportation.* How will your teen get there and get home? Remind her that if she goes elsewhere—for any reason—she's to call you.

■ *Provide alternatives to parties.* Be creative and ask for your teen's suggestions. For example, offer to drive your teen and a few friends to a water park, baseball game, or play. The goal is to satisfy your teen's desire for socializing in a fun, wholesome setting.

## 22. Respect for Parents

**Our teenage daughter doesn't want to be seen with my spouse and me. At the mall, she walks 20 paces behind us. After church, she waits for us in the car. Is this a form of disrespect? How should we handle this?**

This behavior is probably not a sign of disrespect—unless it's accompanied by disparaging remarks toward you, which should not be tolerated. Chances are that your teen is making the normal, healthy move from childhood to young adulthood and doesn't want to be perceived as your "little girl."

Most teenagers want desperately to be adults and resent anything that implies they're still children. Being seen with "mommy and daddy" at the mall or church seems to put them back in the child's role.

What should you do? Wait it out. Unless there is clear disrespect involved, try to accept this behavior as a phase of growing up. In a few years, when your teen accepts herself as an adult and doesn't need to prove it to everyone else, she won't mind walking beside you and being with you.

**I feel disrespected at home. I work my head off picking up after my teenager, but he doesn't seem to care. How can I change that?**

By developing the trait of "honoring." Your teen may not realize that undone chores make you feel so undervalued, so dishonored. Gently but firmly, tell your teen that virtually *everything* he does communicates honor or dishonor, respect or disrespect. Show how honoring works by praising your teen when it's called for.

The result can be an internal motivation to do what he knows will please you—and what will keep him from feeling nagged.

In addition to honoring, make sure you aren't inadvertently encouraging your teen to take you for granted. During the next week, stop picking up after him and see what happens. Over the long term, it probably will be best to let him take responsibility for cleanups—or to let him live with the consequences.

## 23. School and Homework

**Our son has always been a little disorganized, but he squeaked by in grade school. Now that his workload has increased, he seems overwhelmed. How can we help without putting too much pressure on him?**

Some people find it extremely difficult to get and stay organized. That's not an excuse for living in chaos, though. These individuals have to apply themselves more diligently to developing a system for studying. Here are some ideas that might help:

■ *Designate one place to store all the material related to each subject.* Use an organizer notebook or a different folder for each class. The key is to separate subjects, making it easier to find things.

■ *Use a calendar to keep track of all activities and assignments.* Include due dates, exams, holidays, and events that may interfere with completion of homework. Logging all of this information may take some getting used to, but it should help your teen plan ahead and gain more control over his life. Encourage your teen to review the calendar at the start of each week, prioritize the items, and consider current commitments before making additional plans.

■ *Minimize distractions.* Is your teen trying to study while watching TV? Is he overcommitted to extracurricular activities or spending too much time on an after-school job? Is he angry or upset about something? Try to determine what might be making it hard to concentrate on schoolwork. In some cases, a medical condition such as Attention Deficit Disorder might be a contributing factor. If you suspect this, talk with your doctor.

■ *Read a book on time management and organization, or attend a seminar.* You and your teen can apply the principles you learn to improving study habits and work efficiency.

## 24. Sexuality

**My son has been seeing a girl steadily for about six months. She seems like a nice girl, and I'm glad my son is happy, but I worry about how far they might be going sexually. Where do I tell my son to draw the line?**

Setting a physical standard is best done *before* dating begins. Having "the talk" with your son may be uncomfortable, but you need to do that as soon as possible.

Even when both parties accept the biblical view that sexual intercourse outside of marriage is not an option, there are two overriding principles to remember: Stay in control of your body (1 Thessalonians 4:4), and show respect for your body and that of the other person (1 Corinthians 6:20).

Explain to your teen that the romantic process has an order and is progressive. Here's one way to look at the intensifying stages of intimacy: hand-holding, arm around waist, kissing, French kissing, fondling, intimate foreplay, and sexual intercourse.

The first three are "manual." That's when we're in control. The rest are "automatic," when our hormones start calling the shots.

The physical limit needs to be set no further than occasional, brief kissing—the kind that doesn't encourage more. To some this might sound prudish. But if your teen expects to keep control over his body and respect his girlfriend, he should set that limit before natural urges push him further.

Explain that this means no French kissing and no lying down together, even to watch TV or talk. Both activities encourage hormones to kick in, and he'll have to fight the temptation to touch his girlfriend in a sexual manner. He may be able to resist, but why gamble?

In addition, help your teen realize that no matter what that song from *Casablanca* says, a kiss is not just a kiss. It should be a deep expression of love, not simply an act of passion.

If your son admits to already being involved more heavily, help him come up with creative ways to reestablish the limit. Suggest that he explain to his girlfriend that his backing off is a demonstration of love and respect.

How can you enforce these boundaries? You can't; your teen must do that. As a parent, you can guide. He must choose between wisdom and foolishness. Toward that end, encourage him to make a pledge of purity (see chapter 24).

**My husband and I have suspected our 16-year-old has been sexually active. She recently confirmed that. Now what?**

First, address your own emotional reaction privately with your spouse. Give yourself credit for doing something right. After all, if your teen trusts you enough to share such information, the door of communication must be open at least a little. That's critical if you hope to help her rebound.

Second, realize that your daughter has been wounded. Some teens may cover up the hurt, but it's there. She needs to be reassured of your love, especially since she's violated your values. To help you assess the damage, ask:

- Has there been physical trauma? Does she require medical attention?
- Was it a single incident or an ongoing situation? Is it occurring now?
- Is it possible that pregnancy will result? Any evidence of sexually transmitted disease?
- Were relationships damaged, friends lost?
- Is your teen feeling guilt? Did she violate her own standard?
- How has this behavior affected her walk with God?

Ask your teen to assess her own actions. If she justifies or defends herself, it's a signal that continued risk of sexual involvement and consequent pain are likely. If she is genuinely repentant, give her encouragement, reassurance of your love, and the hope of "secondary virginity" by God's grace.

In either case, be steady and self-controlled. An explosive reaction will squelch communication and build emotional barriers between you and your daughter.

This process should also be followed with boys, though their perceptions of the damage done may differ from those of girls. A boy's wounds may be more subtle, but dealing with them is still essential.

A professional Christian counselor can help, especially with teens who are defiant or defensive. The key is to establish in your teen a confidence that you love him or her and will be supportive during this time of restoration.

# Resources for Further Help

*All of these resources were available at the time of printing. Please note that the Focus on the Family booklets and broadcast cassettes are available only through Focus on the Family.*

## Apologetics

### Books

*Baker Encyclopedia of Christian Apologetics* by Norman L. Geisler (Baker). Comprehensive guidebook on key issues, people, and concepts relating to Christian apologetics. Valuable resource for parents, students, and everyday truth-seekers.

*Don't Check Your Brains at the Door* by Josh McDowell and Bob Hostetler (Word). Common myths about God, religion, and life that contradict God's Word are examined. The reader gains confidence to confront the lies that dispute and dilute the truth of God's Word.

*Geek-proof Your Faith* by Greg Johnson and Michael Ross (Zondervan). This challenging, down-to-earth book trains teens to defend their faith. Pro-choice, evolution, and the "safe sex" lie are just a few of the popular debate issues discussed.

*How Now Shall We Live?* by Charles Colson and Nancy Pearcey (Tyndale). Echoing Schaeffer's question "How Shall We Then Live?" Colson explores the state of Christianity in the new millennium. Through true stories of faith, he discusses truth's effects on various topics. A challenge is given to learn to defend the Christian viewpoint.

*Mere Christianity* by C.S. Lewis (Fountain). This is generally considered *the* book on Christian fundamentals. Lewis explores faith's bearing on life, religion, God, the Resurrection, and humankind's place in the universe.

*More Than a Carpenter* by Josh McDowell (Tyndale). McDowell looks at the life of Jesus Christ and examines His claims. He discusses science, biblical records, the apostles, and the Resurrection. The final chapter is McDowell's personal testimony of how the Lord miraculously changed his life.

*New Evidence That Demands a Verdict* by Josh McDowell (Thomas Nelson). Solidly updates the evidence that proves the Bible's claims. At once scholarly and practical, McDowell's book is an authoritative defense of "tried and true" Christianity.

## College

### Books
*As You Leave Home* by Jerry Jenkins (Focus on the Family / Tyndale). Written for parents to give teens, this touching book is a letter to a son expressing love and the difficulty of letting go. Helpful advice to young men and women facing the challenges ahead.

*Dear Graduate: Letters of Wisdom* by Dr. Charles Swindoll (Countryman). This gift book features letters to recent or soon-to-be high school or college graduates, encouraging them to seek Christ in making decisions for their futures. Thirty different topics include priorities, integrity, temptation, generosity, courage, and accountability.

*How to Stay Christian in College* by J. Budziszewski (NavPress). The author exposes some of the challenges and responsibilities a student will encounter in college. This book is an interactive guide to help students face these realities.

*The Fabric of Faithfulness* by Stephen Garber (InterVarsity). Habits, relationships, and beliefs are often solidified during this intense period of life. Garber gives insight into what is actually being learned at college and guides readers to develop ways to be faithful to their core beliefs.

## Communication

### Books
*Bound By Honor: Fostering a Great Relationship with Your Teen* by Gary Smalley and Dr. Greg Smalley (Focus on the Family/Tyndale). Drawn from personal experiences as well as over 5,000 surveyed, father and son offer critical insights for parents on honor in relationships. Also an audio book version.

*Life on the Edge* by Dr. James Dobson (Word). For teens moving closer to being out on their own, this book prepares them with practical principles for making wise life decisions. Dr. Dobson defines dangers to watch for and how to steer clear of life's "potholes."

*Parents Guide to Top 10 Dangers Teens Face* by Stephen Arterburn and Jim Burns (Focus on the Family/Tyndale). Previously titled *Steering Them Straight,* this book helps parents reduce the risk factors of teen crises. Five parenting principles and advice on sex, homosexuality, AIDS, suicide, Satanism, runaways, drugs, eating disorders, spiritual values, and communication.

### Audio Tapes
*Developing Character in Your Children* I,II (Panel, Dr. James Dobson). The Ryun family discusses their concept of courtship as an alternative to dating. Prayer and communication are essential to the development of close family relationships.

*The Parent/Teen Connection* I,II (Gary Smalley, Dr. Greg Smalley, Dr. James Dobson). Gary Smalley and son discuss communication between parents and teens. Their book *Bound by Honor* arose from learning how to deal with conflict without dishonoring each other. Four ways parents can honor their children are outlined.

*What Kids Say When Their Parents Aren't Around* I,II (Dr. Jay Kesler). Kesler elaborates on kids' five common complaints that their parents: don't trust them; "pick on" them; don't listen; are inconsistent; and don't love them.

### Booklets
*How to Keep the Lines of Communication Open with Your Teenager* by Dr. James Dobson. Dr. Dobson explains the ineffectiveness of nagging and suggests positive ways that parents can deal with rebellion.

## Evangelism

### Books
*Evangelism That Works* by George Barna (Gospel Light). This book is a detailed, intelligent manual on how to reach changing generations with the unchanging gospel.

*Fresh Wind, Fresh Fire* by Jim Cymbala, Dean Merrill (Zondervan). Twenty-five years since Pastor Jim Cymbala first received God's call to serve a broken-down church in inner-city Brooklyn, it is now 6,000 members strong—including converted prostitutes, pimps, drug addicts, and homeless. Highly-recommended story of the power of the gospel.

*Keeping Your Cool While Sharing Your Faith* by Greg Johnson and Susie Shellenberger (Tyndale). Short, easy-to-read chapters explain how to share one's faith without being a geek, how to be a friend, and how to deepen one's relationship with Christ.

## For Parents (see also Mentoring/Training)

**Books**
*Bound by Honor: Fostering a Great Relationship with Your Teen* by Gary Smalley and Dr. Greg Smalley (Focus on the Family / Tyndale). Drawn from personal experiences as well as over 5,000 surveyed, father and son offer critical insights for parents on honor in relationships. Also an audio book version.

*Children of Divorce* by Debbie Barr (Zondervan). Research and interviews with single parents provide this book with guidance for helping children of divorce. Discusses grief and how divorce affects children of all ages.

*Confident Parents, Exceptional Teens* by Ted Haggard and John Bolin (Zondervan). Pastors of New Life Church in Colorado Springs give in-depth relevance to the massacre in Littleton, Colorado. Focus is on recognizing the five-step spiral of negativity, the communication wall, and instilling the necessary sense of purpose in kids.

*FaithTraining: Raising Kids Who Love the Lord* by Joe White (Focus on the Family / Tyndale). This book shows parents how to instill a lifelong love for God in their kids through a unique and highly effective approach to Scripture study, memorization, and prayer.

*The Family Compass* by Olivia and Kurt Bruner (Chariot Victor). Practical ideas help parents pass on their faith and worldview to children in a culture void of true Christian focus. Families are encouraged to develop a game plan and find opportunities to live daily the Christian life.

*Helping Your Struggling Teenager: A Parenting Handbook on Thirty-Six Common Problems* by Dr. Les Parrott III (Zondervan). Expert advice on how to respond to teens in trouble. Specific struggles are arranged in alphabetical order, covering questions like "How did this happen?" "What should we do?" and "How could a counselor help?" This book gives tools for handling teen problems.

*How to Keep Your Kids on Your Team* by Charles Stanley (Oliver-Nelson). Defines the role of parents as one of stewardship, making parents responsible to God for their "entrusted talents." Insightful lessons from a father of two grown children, this book shows how to raise loyal kids.

*How to Really Love Your Teenager* by Ross Campbell (Chariot Victor). Campbell gives practical, Bible-based tips on communicating through physical touch and eye contact, handling anger, setting limits, and enforcing consequences. By dealing firmly with love, parents can still affect their child's life regardless of the circumstances.

*How to Speak Alien: Invading Your Teens' World without Invading Their Space* by Michael Ross (Beacon Hill). Gives parents the courage and tact to creatively build rapport with their teenager through communication techniques, unconventional approaches, and unique "invasion" tactics.

*Josh McDowell's Handbook on Counseling Youth* by Josh McDowell and Bob Hostetler (Thomas Nelson/Word). Easy-to-use reference covers everything from simple crises to major teen issues: coping with emotions, relationships, families, sex, abuse, disorders, addiction, school, job, and friends.

*Life Happens: Help Your Teenager Get Ready* by Barry St. Clair (Broadman & Holman). One idea, two points of view. The first talks to teens about how they can find their calling in God's world; the second tells parents how they can help.

*LifeTraining: Devotions for Parents and Teens* by Joe White (Focus on the Family/Tyndale). Powerful, unique daily devotional to help teens and parents build strong, lasting spiritual foundations. Colorful anecdotes, questions, and Scripture memory plan present the gospel in a relevant, transforming way. Also *LifeTraining 2*.

*The Mother-Daughter Connection* by Susie Shellenberger (Word). This book shows mothers that their daughters want to connect. With conversation starters, diary entries, and an in-depth "stuff they gotta know" section, this book helps mothers and daughters survive the teenage years together.

*Parenting Isn't For Cowards* by Dr. James Dobson (Word). Study-guide edition of Dr. Dobson's advice to frustrated parents on the contest between generations, perils of adolescence, and parental burnout. Hope for hurting parents and practical suggestions help you deal with power games, fatigue, and releasing your child.

*Parenting Today's Adolescent* by Dennis and Barbara Rainey, Bruce Nygren (Thomas Nelson). Drawn from experience raising teens and speaking to thousands of parents, this comprehensive guide-book covers peer pressure, sex ed, dating, values, rebellion, and drug abuse and gives a proactive, tested approach to building relationships.

*Raising Sons and Loving It!: Helping Your Boys Become Godly Men* by Gary and Carrie Oliver (Zondervan). Extensive clinical and per-sonal experience gives this book a unique place in helping sons develop healthy, spiritually-centered character. Keys to "emotional intelligence"; cultivating ability to deal with failure, loss, and grief; and other topics are covered.

*Suddenly They're 13: A Parent's Survival Guide for the Adolescent Years* by David and Claudia Arp (Zondervan). Expanded, updated version of *Almost 13* shows how to parent your teen and get through the crit-ical adolescent passage—relationships intact. How to relate, handle fear, eliminate obstacles, and accept change are some of the topics.

*Surviving the Prodigal Years: How to Love Your Wayward Child with-out Ruining Your Own Life* by Marcia Mitchell (Emerald). Designed to encourage hurting parents of rebellious children, this book explores anger, fear, shame, anxiety, rejection, and guilt. Provides real-life testimonies, biblical examples of prodigals and parents, and referral organizations that offer assistance.

*Understanding Your Teenager* by Wayne Rice and David Veerman (Thomas Nelson/Word). Principles and practical advice on raising teens in the changing world of today's youth. This book provides insight into adolescent development and cultural influences.

**Audio Tapes**

*Encouragement for Single Parents* I,II (Robert Barnes, Dr. James Dobson). A helpful discussion for single parents on the subjects of guilt, money, support from the church, role models, sibling rivalry, self-esteem, and overprotection.

*Families That Succeed* I,II (Dr. Jay Kesler). In a prerecorded message, Kesler describes the six common characteristics of families that succeed. He addresses family devotions, unity of parents regarding discipline, and unconditional love.

*Fathers and Daughters* (Dr. H. Norman Wright, Dr. James Dobson). Based on his book *Always Daddy's Girl*, Wright discusses the impact of the father-daughter relationship, especially on future romantic encounters and learning to relate to men.

*From One Mom to Another* (Elisa Morgan). Morgan, president of Mothers of Preschoolers International (MOPS), uses examples from her own experience to encourage mothers. She urges mothers to believe that God has chosen them as the perfect parent for their children.

*Parenting for Fun and Profit* I,II (Ken Davis). With characteristic humor, Davis offers parents the advice contained in his book *How to Live with Your Kids When You've Already Lost Your Mind*. He urges parents to work themselves out of their job.

*Parenting Teenagers* I,II (Dr. Jay Kesler). Kesler relates the two main preoccupations that teens have: adjusting to physical changes and gaining independence from the family. He then lists the 10 most common mistakes parents make.

*Parenting through the Tough Times* (Jim Burns, Steve Arterburn, Dr. James Dobson). Prerecorded stories are played of Burns and

Arterburn working with teens during difficult times, including attempted suicide, bulimia, rape, and rebellion.

*Parents in Pain* (Dr. John White, Dr. James Dobson). This discussion, based on White's personal story of his son's involvement in drugs, is excellent encouragement for parents of problem kids.

*Parents Prepare for Adolescence* I,II (Panel, Dr. James Dobson). Panel members relate their experiences taking their same-sex children on a "Preparing for Adolescence" weekend.

*Releasing Your Grown Child* I-III (Dr. James Dobson). Dr. Dobson talks to parents about the dangers of holding on too long or letting go too soon of children nearing adulthood, and about how to balance power and independence.

*Successful Single Parenting* I-IV (Panel, Dr. James Dobson). This is a transparent and honest discussion by three divorced women and a widower who relate personal experiences. It covers emotions felt, how to help children cope, the Lord's provision, difficulties faced, and advice for other single parents.

*Team Up with Your Kids* I-III (Dr. Charles Stanley, Rev. Andy Stanley, Dr. James Dobson). Guests discuss why parents (even Christian parents) alienate their kids and how reconciliation can occur. Andy Stanley, a youth pastor, tells about his own teenage rebellion and discusses why kids are often angry with their parents.

**Booklets**
*Advice to Single Parents* by Virginia Watts Smith. Relates the changes widowed and divorced women experience when they become single again. She also describes the struggles of a single male parent, the single adoptive parent, and the unmarried parent. A section on helping children through transition is included.

*Five Tips for Parents of Teens* by Dr. James Dobson. Dr. Dobson offers five suggestions to parents for coping with the adolescent years.

*Successful Stepparenting* by David and Bonnie Juroe. Five myths of stepfamilies are addressed: 1) You have to be perfect, 2) Children can adapt easily in stepfamilies, 3) Stepchildren quickly get over loss, 4) A stepfamily can operate like a normal family, and 5) Stepmothers are wicked creatures.

*Teaching Your Kids to Say "No" to Sex.* Developed for the Life on the Edge tour, this small booklet covers the basics for parents to pass on the real "safe sex" message to their teenagers.

*The Strong-Willed Adolescent* by Dr. James Dobson. This booklet offers suggestions for coping with the strong-willed preteen and teenager. It addresses issues of respect, dealing with conflict, and establishing boundaries.

*Woman of Influence: How to Pray for Your Children* by Jean Fleming. The author suggests how to use each sliver of available time to transform the rushed prayer into more-meaningful intercession. She explains how a Christian mother can most strongly influence the lives of her children.

**Magazines**
*Plugged In* (Focus on the Family) (See Media section.)

## For Teens

**Books**
*Answers to Tough Questions* by Josh McDowell and Don Stewart (Thomas Nelson). Concise and persuasive answers to questions often asked by skeptics of the Christian faith. A reader will find questions about the Bible, Jesus Christ, miracles, biblical difficulties, world religions, and more.

*Bondage Breaker, Youth Edition* by Neil Anderson and David Park (Harvest House). Addresses struggles common to teens and how to break the enemy's hold and experience Christian freedom.

*Can I Be a Christian without Being Weird?* by Kevin Johnson (Bethany House). Devotional for junior highers on getting to know God and being a follower of Jesus.

*Catch the Wave* by Kevin Johnson (Bethany House). Shows teens how to affect the world through the power available in prayer and ministry.

*The Construction Zone: Devotions for Building a Faith the World Can't Demolish* by Michael Ross, Jeff Edmondson (Beacon Hill). A "blueprint" for building a faith strong enough to withstand the world's destructive forces. Provides the biblical tools and instructions for using them to answer common "structural" questions.

*Dear Diary: A Girl's Book of Devotion* by Susie Shellenberger (Zondervan). Unique and creative devotional for girls ages 8-12 addressing issues facing young girls today. Provides Bible-based solutions, straight answers, and solutions for everyday life.

*Extreme Teen Bible, NKJV* (Thomas Nelson). This New King James translation gives teens "straight truth," with innovative study helps geared to teen culture, book introductions, and relevant study notes to help teens find God's plan for their lives. Profiles tell stories of amazing young people from Scripture who allowed God to work through them to make an impact on their world.

*Faith Encounter* by Bill Myers and Michael Ross (Harvest House). Engaging, modern 12-week teen devotional on Christ as the model of ultimate life, relationship, truth, wisdom, commitment, freedom, shepherding, love, readiness, mission, sacrifice, and triumph.

*Get Real, Get Ready, Get Going* by Michael Ross (Regal). A training guide for life, with personal stories, discussion starters, devotions, and ideas to help teens share their faith. Four week-long sections give teens seven important areas of spiritual growth, what it means to be a Christian, and how to pursue God's will.

*Getting Ready for the Guy-Girl Thing* by Susie Shellenberger and Greg Johnson (Gospel Light). Mature, intelligent, and honest about worldly influences, this fun book gives teens realistic, biblical advice about romance.

*God Loves Me, So What!* by Guy Doud (Concordia). Teacher Guy Doud helps the reader discover how faith in Jesus Christ affects the choices we make, the way we think about ourselves, and our relationships with family and friends.

*Guys and a Whole Lot More* by Susie Shellenberger (Revell). Great Christian advice from the editor of *Brio* magazine on how to talk to guys, build guy-girl friendships, and learn to accept yourself, your braces, and your body changes. In Q & A form, this book is a guide to what teenage girls are concerned about.

*How to Live with Your Parents without Losing Your Mind* by Ken Davis (Zondervan). Challenges all types of teens to influence their broken or intact families for Christ to effect positive changes. Explains the way parents make decisions, assert authority, and express love.

*If I Could Ask God One Question* by Greg Johnson (Bethany House). Eighty questions and answers on many topics help teens understand the Bible and commit to giving their lives in service to God.

*Jesus Freaks* by dc Talk and the Voice of the Martyrs (Albury). First book by popular recording group dc Talk on examining faith and dedicating yourself to upholding Jesus even in the face of death. Real-life stories give eye-opening information about persecution of Christians around the world.

*Jumper Fables* by Ken Davis and Dave Lambert (Zondervan). Devotional with fun, stimulating stories on such teen issues as how to know God's will, how to find where sex fits in, whether death is the end, how to talk about Christ, why parents say "no," and how to trust God.

*Kids Hope: An Interactive Workbook for Teens in Single-Parent Families* by Gary Sprague and Randy Petersen (Singles Ministry Resources). This book uses personal stories of teens who live with a single parent. Puzzles and surveys help teens sort through common feelings and situations. Chapter 10, "New Parents and New Siblings," is especially for teens who must adjust to a new family.

*Life on the Edge* by Dr. James Dobson (Word). For teens moving closer to being out on their own, this book prepares them with principles for making wise life decisions and steering clear of life's "potholes."

*LifeTraining: Devotions for Parents and Teens* by Joe White (Focus on the Family/Tyndale). Powerful, unique, daily devotions to help teens and parents build strong, lasting spiritual foundations. Colorful anecdotes, questions, and Scripture memory plan present the gospel in a relevant, transforming way. Followed up with *LifeTraining 2.*

*Lockers, Lunch Lines, Chemistry, and Cliques ... 77 Pretty Important Ideas on School Survival* by Susie Shellenberger and Greg Johnson (Bethany House). Youth specialists offer short, helpful suggestions for being successful in high school: teacher-pupil relationships, gossip, cheating, extracurricular stuff, making friends, organization, growth in Christ, and witnessing.

*Man in the Making* by Greg Johnson (Broadman & Holman). Helps teen boys discern the differences between immature and mature decision making. Thirty-five sections address spiritual growth, competition, parents, friends, dating, peer pressure, lust, pride, insecurity, servanthood, contentment, anger, courage, and more.

*Preparing for Adolescence* by Dr. James Dobson (Regal). In this insightful book, topics that trouble teens most are discussed, including inferiority, conformity, puberty, the meaning of love, and the search for identity.

*Reality 101* by Wayne Rice and David R. Veerman (Tyndale). Answers to real-life questions from teens on faith, friends, family, finances, and more.

*Riding the Waves of Life* by Tom Eggum (Longwood Communications). Through personal examples of believers, this book teaches how to ride the waves of life, with encouragement to accept trials as Christ did (with joy) and learn from them.

*Start Where You Are* by Charles R. Swindoll (Thomas Nelson/Word). Swindoll offers wisdom and encouragement for life's passages using four key themes: leadership, success, compassion, and life's trials.

*Stuff You Don't Have to Pray About* by Susie Shellenberger (Broadman & Holman). By paraphrasing biblical stories, this book shows teens how God's Word addresses such contemporary problems as peer pressure, trusting, encouraging, accepting, evangelizing, and more.

*Surviving Adolescence* by Jim Burns (Regal). Written for teens, parents, and youth workers to help teens develop a sense of identity, establish healthy relationships, and make good decisions based on godly wisdom.

*The Teenage Q & A Book* by Josh McDowell and Bill Jones (Word). More than 230 funny, difficult, and downright painful questions of adolescence are answered with simple, biblical solutions.

*The Teen Study Bible-NIV* (Zondervan). NIV translation with introductions to each book, trivia questions, Bible promises, commentary on contemporary issues, and a subject index to teen-related topics.

*Your Place in This World* by Michael W. Smith (Thomas Nelson). Popular Christian recording artist Michael W. Smith asks what you will do with your life and gives the biblical definition of success through personal illustrations.

**Audio Tapes**

*Adolescence: A Notion Called Emotion* I,II (Dr. James Dobson). Six characteristics of surging emotions common to teens: "the human yo-yo," unreliable impressions, teens' "declaration of independence," the "mama's baby" fear, the "age of confusion," and the search for identity.

*Christian Teens: A Challenge to Commitment* I,II (Panel, Dr. James Dobson). Panel discusses proper youth program goals, teens' rejection of church, parental love, what teens need, importance of Jesus over religion, and necessity of convictions.

*Dear Susie, Signed "Typical Teen"* (Susie Shellenberger, Paul Smith, Dr. James Dobson). Encouragement to teens to make Christ preeminent in their lives and withstand cultural pressures. Parents are advised to be watchful of their teens' friends and Internet usage.

*How to Get the Most Out of Life* (Ken Davis). Davis uses humor to convey the importance of enjoying the life God has given you.

*Living and Laughing Together: A Message to Parents and Teens* I,II (Ken Davis). An entertaining message, told from a parent's viewpoint, recounting contradictory phrases, quirks, and humorous incidents in raising children.

*Questions Teens Ask* I-III (Marilee Pierce Dunker, Dr. James Dobson). Dr. Dobson fields questions from three youth groups about the virginity stigma, petting, parents' rules, shyness, spiritual growth, incest, alcoholic parents, and more.

*With Love to Hurting Teens* I,II (Panel, Dr. James Dobson). Features two prerecorded messages by Guy Doud that outline ways to help teens who are struggling with low self-esteem, peer pressure, and difficult situations at home.

**Videos**

*Life on the Edge* video series (Focus on the Family/Word). Seven volumes presented in lecture format, with Dr. Dobson speaking on various issues and pitfalls concerning teens.

Volume 1, "Finding God's Will for Your Life," discusses choosing a career and gives an end-of-life test asking, "What will matter at the moment of death?"

Volumes 2-7: "The Myth of Safe Sex," "Love Must Be Tough," "The Keys to a Lifelong Love," "Emotions: Can You Trust Them?" "When God Doesn't Make Sense," and "Pornography: Addictive, Progressive, and Deadly."

*Masquerade: Unveiling Our Deadly Dance with Drugs and Alcohol* (Focus on the Family). Popular youth speaker Milton Creagh challenges teens to question the "casual user" lie, exposing drug and alcohol addiction in this 30-minute video. Humor, passionate stories, and powerful live interviews show that choices define what teens' lives will become.

*Mind Over Media: The Power of Making Sound Entertainment Choices* (Focus on the Family/Tyndale). Keys for discerning the different messages aimed at teens in the entertainment industry. Interviewing teens, popular musicians, and youth culture experts, this video explores entertainment's effects.

*My Truth, Your Truth, Whose Truth? Discovering Absolutes in a Relative World* (Focus on the Family/Tyndale). This video explores absolute truth, interviewing leading communicators on the critical moral stance necessary for daily decision making. Addresses why it matters when you cheat at school, get high, have sex outside of marriage, or attempt to commit suicide.

*No Apologies: The Truth About Life, Love, and Sex* (Focus on the Family/Tyndale). Thirty-minute video asking teens to compare promiscuity with the value of abstinence.

### Booklets
*Dare 2 Dig Deeper Series* (Focus on the Family). Small yet powerful booklets exploring varied topics: eating disorders, communication, gender identity, sexual abuse, television, sexual purity, drugs and alcohol, popular music, violence in the media, pornography, and suicide.

*Growing Up with Jesus* (American Tract Society). Colorful tract with a "quiz" to determine if a child has asked Jesus to be his Savior. Explains God's promises and instructions for living a life that will please Him.

*Soul Food: Which Nature Are You Feeding?* by Bob Smithouser (Focus on the Family). Teens learn to fill their lives with activities that will feed the spirit rather than the flesh.

*Straight Answers* (Focus on the Family). Taken from Focus on the Family's "Love Won Out" conferences, this hard-hitting booklet gives answers to questions about homosexuality.

**Magazines**

*Breakaway* and *Brio* (Focus on the Family). *Breakaway* (for boys) and *Brio* (for girls) are designed to make the Christian experience come alive for teens. They feature music, sports, advice, humor, profiles, and much more.

*Plugged In* (Focus on the Family) (See Media section.)

*Sharing the Victory* (Fellowship of Christian Athletes). Monthly presentation of events, interviews, and information about FCA ministry, which seeks to influence young people for Christ through the vehicle of sports.

*The Latest* youth bulletin (Tyndale House-Retail Services). This "mini-magazine" by *Brio* and *Breakaway* staff is designed to be offered through youth groups. It compiles the best articles from previous issues into a four-page format.

*Youthwalk* (Walk Thru the Bible Ministries). A monthly magazine of daily devotionals for junior high and high school teens.

## Media

**Books**

*Chart Watch* by Bob Smithouser and Bob Waliszewski (Focus on the Family / Tyndale). Part one gives keys to discernment. Part two provides reviews of more than 400 popular albums in various genres, biographical sketches of artists, and details on content.

*Media-Wise Family* by Ted Baehr (Chariot). Help for parents to equip their children with discernment in choices of movies, television, electronic games, and other media.

### Magazines
*Plugged In* (Focus on the Family). This monthly publication is designed to assist parents in confronting today's trends in music and media. Request through mail or E-mail.

## Mentoring / Training

### Books
*FaithTraining: Raising Kids Who Love the Lord* by Joe White (Focus on the Family/Tyndale). Helps parents raise children of all ages to love the Lord, featuring 365 ways to tell kids you love them without saying the words. Bible studies and devotions are also included.

*Give Them Wings* by Carol Kuykendall (Focus on the Family/Tyndale). Explores the process of helping teens say good-bye to childhood and launch into adulthood, encouraging independence, inspiring faith, and coping with rebellion.

*Let's Make a Memory: Great Ideas for Building Family Traditions and Togetherness* (revised) by Gloria Gaither and Shirley Dobson (Word). A wealth of ideas on how to make family traditions reinforce lasting values in the home. The suggestions include holiday activities, vacation ideas, and relationship builders.

*LifeTraining* by Joe White (Focus on the Family/Tyndale). Devotional tool for parents and children ages 11-18 featuring 260 devotions on Matthew, Luke, John, Acts, James, and Revelation. Can be used in a family setting or individually. "100 Bible Memory Verses Every Christian Teenager Needs to Know" is a great tool.

*Raising a Modern-Day Knight* by Robert Lewis (Focus on the Family/Tyndale). Practical, step-by-step guidance for fathers to lead their sons to biblical masculinity. Illustrates the need for "modern knighthood" and affirmation from father to son.

*The Power of Believing in Your Child* by Miles McPherson (Bethany House). This book helps parents cherish their child as God does, learn how to be free from fear, and have the courage to raise their child according to the promises of God.

*The Sixty-Minute Father* by Rob Parsons (Broadman & Holman). Designed to help men break out of the busyness that interferes with relating to their children. Ten goals for improving fathering and practical advice for applying the principles are offered.

*World Proofing Your Kids* by Lael F. Arrington (Crossway). Real-life illustrations, quotes, and statistics of the modern world, contrasted against the world of Scripture. Ideas and resources to help parents instill biblical values.

**Audio Tapes**
*Building a Child's Conscience* I (Dr. James Dobson). Explores ways parents can develop a child's understanding of right and wrong. Dr. Dobson reads children's definitions of conscience, cites biblical references to the conscience, and gives a checklist for spiritual training that he developed for his own children.

*Christian Teens: A Challenge to Commitment* I,II (Panel, Dr. James Dobson). Panel discusses youth program goals, teens' rejection of church, parental love, what teens need, the importance of Jesus over religion, and the importance of having convictions.

*Developing Your Child's Character* I,II (Dr. Donald Joy, Dr. James Dobson). Children develop rules by watching parents' behavior, so values must be imparted by living them. A discussion of what children need from their parents follows.

*Equip and Challenge Your Children* (Rev. Andy Stanley). Based on 2 Timothy 4:3-7, Stanley portrays the "defensive" posture many parents have in raising children and how to evaluate impact, develop a strategy, and get aggressive in leading children to influence the world for Christ.

*Effective Family Devotions* I,II (Rev. Bruce Wilkinson, Dr. James Dobson). This discussion includes a challenge for parents to commit to regular family devotions, five guidelines for effectiveness, and seven reasons families don't have devotions.

*Getting Behind the Eyes of a Child* I, II (Dr. Darrel Reid, Rob Parsons). Guest host Reid discusses *The Sixty-Minute Father* with author. Ten principles that will help establish good relationships between a father and his children are discussed.

*How to Fall in Love with Your Kids* I,II (Joe White, Dr. James Dobson). Based on *Orphans at Home,* White describes how drastically kids are changing and what they face now. He stresses parental involvement in countering society's influences.

*Raising Kids Who Love the Lord* I,II (Joe White, Dr. James Dobson). White discusses the importance of parents' passing on their faith. He offers advice about building a consistent relationship and tells how he and his children memorize Scripture.

*Teaching Values to Our Youth* (Josh McDowell, Dr. James Dobson). McDowell expresses concern about the lack of moral absolutes among the young and the alarming number of "churched" youth who are unable to distinguish right from wrong.

*The Spiritual Training of Children* II (Dr. James Dobson). This is a challenge to parents to remember the privilege and responsibility of leading children to faith in God and answer their questions about identity, purpose, and values.

**Videos**
*Children at Risk* with Dr. James Dobson and Gary Bauer (Word). Two-part presentation by Dr. Dobson and Gary Bauer at Preston-

wood Baptist Church in Dallas, looking seriously at today's society and what to do to reverse its moral decline.

## Booklets

*A Checklist for Your Child's Spiritual Development* by Dr. James Dobson. Parents concerned about their children's moral development are given a set of six concepts to use in evaluating where children are in their spiritual understanding.

*4 Parents and Teens: Common Ground: A Relationship-building Workbook for Teens & Parents* by Focus on the Family. Activities for parents and teens to deepen their relationship through communication.

*Rebuilding America's Spiritual Foundations* by Charles W. Colson. Colson suggests how family can be the first school of instruction, the building block of society, and the model for godly priorities and reaching out to others.

*Values in the Home* by Dr. James Dobson. This booklet contains a specific plan by which values can be transmitted to children, as well as a list of 40 values Dr. Dobson used with his children.

## Ministries

A.C. Green Programs for Youth
P.O. Box 1709
Phoenix, AZ 85001
602/528-0790
800/ACYOUTH
PR@acgreen.com
www.acgreen.com
Professional basketball star A.C. Green's programs build body, mind, and character and promote sexual abstinence. Disadvantaged boys and girls, 9-15 years old, can be sponsored to attend the week-long summer basketball camp featuring academics, career exploration, and self-esteem counseling. Camps are held in Phoenix and Los Angeles.

Al Menconi Ministries
P.O. Box 131147
Carlsbad, CA 92013
760/591-4696
al@almenconi.com
www.menconi.org
This organization seeks to educate parents and Christian leaders
about today's popular music so they can teach children to think
biblically about media choices.

Christian Encounter Ranch
P.O. Box 1022
Grass Valley, CA 95945
530/268-0877
cem@nccn.net
www.nccn.net/~cem
The ranch is a 16-bed facility for guys or girls ages 16 to 25, located
in the rural foothills of the Sierra Nevada Mountains. Licensed
counselors and pastors focus on psychological, spiritual, and educational development.

Dawson McAllister Association
P.O. Box 26746
Ft. Worth, TX 76126
817/249-6000
800/394-HOPE - for teens in crisis
dmlive@dawsonmcallister.com
www.dawsonmcallister.com
This comprehensive youth resource ministry has study guides,
videos, a monthly magazine called "Teen Quest," and a national
radio show among its services.

Exodus International North America
P.O. Box 77652
Seattle, WA 98177
206/784-7799
www.ExodusNorthAmerica.org
Exodus is a nonprofit, interdenominational Christian organization
promoting the message of "Freedom from homosexuality through

the power of Jesus Christ." Since 1976, Exodus International has grown to include more than 100 local ministries in the U.S. and Canada and more than 135 ministries in 17 countries. A list of current qualified agencies is available on their Web site under the "Find a Ministry" link.

Fellowship of Christian Athletes
8701 Leeds Road
Kansas City, MO 64129
816/921-0909
800/289-0909
fca@fca.org - E-mail
www.fca.org
Presenting Jesus Christ to young athletes and their coaches.

Freedom in Christ Ministries
Dr. Neil T. Anderson
491 East Lambert Road
La Habra, CA 90631
562/691-9128
mail@ficm.org
www.ficm.org
Provides resources and conferences for adults and teens to resolve conflicts and establish a strong identity in Christ. Materials and information also available in Spanish.

JH Ranch
8525 Homestead Ln.
Etna, CA. 96027
530/467-3468
800/242-1224
www.JHRanch.org
JH Ranch exists to foster teens' development in seven key areas: life purpose, problem solving, goal setting, relationships, family, spiritual priorities, and personal standards. Unique outdoor programs, from hiking Mt. Shasta to whitewater rafting and horseback riding, give parents and teens the space to strengthen relationships, foster self-confidence, and deepen their faith in God.

Josh McDowell Ministry
Box 1000
Dallas, TX 75313
972/907-1000
800/222-JOSH - orders
www.josh.org
This ministry outreach of Campus Crusade for Christ published
the "Why Wait?" series on sex, the "Love Test Pendant," and other
materials for teens and parents. Most resources are available in
Spanish.

Navigators
P.O. Box 6000
Colorado Springs, CO 80934
719/598-1212
www.gospelcom.net/navs
International ministry focusing on discipleship of college students,
military, businessmen and women, African Americans, Hispanics,
and local churches.

New Life Clinics Adolescent Program
800/NEW-TEEN
This Christian organization's goal is to help adolescents resolve
conflicts of values, beliefs, and behaviors and develop ways to succeed without drugs, alcohol, and other vices. Group and individual therapy, lectures, worship, prayer, Bible study, and a full range
of medical and psychological services encourage teens to focus on
four areas: overcoming psychological disorders, chemical dependency, compulsive eating disorders, and physical, emotional, and
sexual abuse.

Royal Servants International
Reign Ministries, Inc.
5517 Warwick Place
Minneapolis, MN 55436
612/823-4050
info@royalservants.org
www.royalservants.org

Evangelizing in foreign countries and discipling teens in the U.S. and Canada are the focuses of this organization.

Second Chance Ministry
3505 Houston Levee Road
Germantown, TN 38139
901/368-5683
Located near Memphis, this drug rehabilitation and counseling ministry for youth and their families is directed by Rev. F. Scotty Cassidy, a certified chemical dependency counselor and recovered drug abuser. Long-term treatment (there is a minimum stay of 194 days) is provided for youth aged 15-22 at an affordable cost. The program includes parent and sibling "rap" sessions, individual and family counseling, and a six-month aftercare program to share experiences after leaving. Success rate is 86 percent.

Steve Russo Evangelistic Team
P.O. Box 1549
Ontario, CA 91762
909/466-7060
info@realanswers.com
www.realanswers.com
This ministry for teens, youth leaders, and parents emphasizes training in evangelism, evaluation of rock music and the effect it has on teens, and spiritual warfare seminars. A newsletter, other literature, and tapes are available.

Student Venture
Campus Crusade for Christ
100 Sunport Lane
Orlando, FL 32809
407/826-2450
venture@ccci.org
www.studentventure.com
This high school outreach of Campus Crusade for Christ trains teens in discipleship, evangelism, and leadership. Extensive inventory of resources for youth and youth workers includes a quarterly newsletter for high schoolers, "Venture Out."

Summit Ministries
P.O. Box 207
Manitou Springs, CO 80829
719/685-9103
info@summit.org
www.summit.org
This Christian leadership training center helps young people ages
16 and up to understand how their faith relates to their everyday
lives and how to develop a biblical worldview.

Teen Challenge
National Headquarters—U.S.
National Teen Challenge Inc.
P.O. Box 1015
Springfield, MO 65801
800/814-5729
417/862-6969
tcnusa@ncsi.net
www.teenchallenge.com
Teen Challenge is a Christian drug and alcohol treatment program
with hundreds of centers in the U.S., Canada, Puerto Rico, and 26
other countries, creating mental and emotional balance, social
adjustment, and physical and spiritual well-being. Counseling,
vocational training, and academic instruction are led by others
who have come out of addictive backgrounds with a tremendous
success rate in remaining drug-free.

Teen Mania Ministries
Ron Luce
P.O. Box 2000
Garden Valley, TX 75771
903/324-8000
800/329-FIRE
800/299-TEEN - for information about Teen Mania
info@teenmania.org
www.teenmania.org
This organization equips and trains teens for evangelism and
offers a bimonthly newsletter called "Mandate."

# Notes

**Chapter Two: You Can Do It!**

1. Gary Smalley and John Trent, *The Hidden Value of a Man* (Wheaton, Ill.: Tyndale/Focus on the Family, 1992, 1994), p. 130.
2. Stephen Arterburn and Jim Burns, *Parents' Guide to the Top 10 Dangers Teens Face* (Wheaton, Ill.: Tyndale/Focus on the Family, 1995), p. 316.
3. Joe White, *What Kids Wish Parents Knew About Parenting* (Sisters, Oreg.: Questar, 1988), p. 184.
4. Josh McDowell and Bob Hostetler, *Right from Wrong* (Dallas: Word, 1994), p. 127.

**Chapter Three: Never Quit on a Child**

1. John Trent, *Be There!* (Colorado Springs, Colo.: Water-Brook, 2000), p. 100.
2. Statistics provided by the Barna Research Group (www.barnaresearch.com). Used by permission.
3. This quote is taken from a radio commentary by Dr. James C. Dobson. Used by permission.
4. Nick Stinnett et al., *Fantastic Families* (West Monroe, Louis.: Howard, 1999), p. 13.

5. Quotations and facts provided by *The New York Times* Web site (www.nytimes.com/events/olympics).

**Chapter Four: The Goal of Spiritual Training**
1. Josh McDowell, "Helping Your Teen Say No to Sex," in *Raising Them Right,* ed. Mike Yorkey (Colorado Springs, Colo.: Focus on the Family, 1994), p. 103.
2. George Barna, *Generation Next* (Ventura, Calif.: Regal, 1995), p. 33.

**Chapter Five: The Role of a Mentor**
1. James C. Dobson, *Home with a Heart* (Wheaton, Ill.: Tyndale, 1996), pp. 153-54.
2. Christopher Vogler, *The Writer's Journey* (Studio City, Calif.: Michael Wiese, 1998), pp. 55, 60.
3. Tim Smith, *Life Skills for Girls* (Colorado Springs, Colo.: Cook, 2000), pp. 12-13.

**Chapter Six: The Relationship Is Everything!**
1. Josh McDowell and Bob Hostetler, *Right from Wrong* (Dallas: Word, 1994), p. 123.
2. James C. Dobson, *Solid Answers* (Wheaton, Ill.: Tyndale, 1997), p. 318.
3. Gary and Greg Smalley, *Bound by Honor* (Wheaton, Ill.: Tyndale/Focus on the Family, 1998), pp. 97-98.
4. Ibid., p. 100.

**Chapter Seven: Becoming Your Teen's Biggest Fan**
1. Based on Joe White, *What Kids Wish Parents Knew About Parenting* (Sisters, Oreg.: Questar, 1988), pp. 176-78.
2. Ibid., pp. 151-52.
3. Ibid., pp. 132-33.
4. Ibid., pp. 129, 134.

**Chapter Eight: Learning to Be a Great Communicator**
1. Joe White, *What Kids Wish Parents Knew About Parenting* (Sisters, Oreg.: Questar, 1988), pp. 89-92.
2. Josh McDowell, "The Art of Communication," in *How to Get Your Teenager to Talk to You* (Wheaton, Ill.: Victor, 1988), p. 32.

3. Charles Stanley, *How to Keep Your Kids on Your Team* (Nashville: Oliver-Nelson, 1986), p. 192.

4. Ibid., p. 188.

5. *Focus on the Family Complete Book of Baby and Child Care* (Wheaton, Ill.: Tyndale/Focus on the Family, 1997), p. 524.

6. Gordon McLean, *Too Young to Die* (Wheaton, Ill.: Tyndale/Focus on the Family, 1998), p. 237.

7. McDowell in *How to Get Your Teenager to Talk to You*, p. 29.

8. McLean, *Too Young to Die*, p. 238.

9. Gary Smalley and John Trent, *The Hidden Value of a Man* (Wheaton, Ill.: Tyndale/Focus on the Family 1992, 1994), p. 64.

10. Gary and Greg Smalley, *Bound by Honor* (Wheaton, Ill.: Tyndale/Focus on the Family, 1998), p. 53.

11. Ibid., pp. 63-70.

12. Ibid. pp. 46-51.

13. Gary Dausey, "Communication Killers," in *How to Get Your Teenager to Talk to You*, p. 42.

**Chapter Nine: Finding Time for Your Teen**

1. According to a study by the Mayo Clinic, "Teenagers and Risks," October 1997 (www.mayoclinic.com/home).

2. Joe White, *What Kids Wish Parents Knew About Parenting* (Sisters, Oreg.: Questar, 1988), pp. 144-45.

3. James C. Dobson, *Home with a Heart* (Wheaton, Ill.: Tyndale, 1996), pp. 95-96.

4. From an interview with the actress in *Movieline*, August 2000.

5. Joe White, *FaithTraining* (Wheaton, Ill.: Tyndale/Focus on the Family, 1994), pp. 42-43.

6. White, *What Kids Wish Parents Knew About Parenting*, p. 119.

**Chapter Ten: Appreciating Your Teen's Uniqueness**

1. James C. Dobson, *Solid Answers* (Wheaton, Ill.: Tyndale, 1997), pp. 7-9.

2. Adapted from John Trent and Judy Love, *The Two Trails* (Nashville: Tommy Nelson, 1998).

3. *Focus on the Family Parents' Guide to the Spiritual Growth of Children*, eds. John Trent, Ph.D., et al. (Wheaton, Ill.: Tyndale/Focus on the Family, 2000), pp. 91-94.

4. Andrew Sullivan, "Why Do Men Act the Way They Do?" *New York Times Magazine*, April 2, 2000.

5. George Barna, *Generation Next* (Ventura, Calif.: Regal, 1995), pp. 26-27.

**Chapter Eleven: Giving Grace**

1. James C. Dobson, *Solid Answers* (Wheaton, Ill.: Tyndale, 1997), p. 287.

2. Ibid., p. 288.

3. Charles Stanley, *How to Keep Your Kids on Your Team* (Nashville: Oliver-Nelson, 1986), pp. 187-89.

4. Ibid., p. 200.

**Chapter Twelve: Demonstrating Commitment in Your Marriage**

1. Ross Campbell, *How to Really Love Your Teenager* (Colorado Springs, Colo.: Victor, 1993), p. 19.

2. Mark Galli, *Marriage Partnership*, vol. 8, no. 3, fall 1990.

3. John and Linda Friel, *The Seven Worst Things Parents Do* (Deerfield Beach, Fla.: Health, 1999), p. 37.

4. Norm Wakefield, *Marriage Partnership*, vol. 9, no. 4, winter 1991.

5. Thomas Morell, *Men of Integrity Devotional*, July–August 2000.

6. Charles Swindoll, *Growing Strong in the Seasons of Life* (Portland, Oreg.: Multnomah, 1983), p. 212.

**Chapter Thirteen: Overcoming Conflicts**

1. Charles Swindoll, "Give Me Another Chance," in *How to Get Your Teenager to Talk to You* (Wheaton, Ill.: Victor, 1988), p. 151.

2. Adapted from Gary and Greg Smalley, *Bound by Honor* (Wheaton, Ill.: Tyndale/Focus on the Family, 1998), p. 62.

3. Adapted from YFC editors in *How to Get Your Teenager to Talk to You*, pp. 159-61.

4. James C. Dobson, "Surviving Your Child's Stormy Teen Years," in *Raising Them Right*, ed. Mike Yorkey (Colorado Springs, Colo.: Focus on the Family, 1994), p. 93.

5. *Focus on the Family Complete Book of Baby and Child Care* (Wheaton, Ill.: Tyndale/Focus on the Family, 1997), p. 529.
6. Dr. Allen Johnson, "Mom, I Want a Tattoo" *Christian Parenting Today,* July/August 1998 (ChristianityToday.com).
7. Ibid.
8. Becky Foster Still, "Dressed to Impress," in *Raising Them Right,* pp. 139-41.
9. Mary Manz Simon, Ed.D., "You Want to Wear What?" *Christian Parenting Today* July/August 1999 (ChristianityToday.com).
10. Laura Schlessinger, "Should You Spy on Your Teen?" *Reader's Digest,* July 2000, p. 160.
11. Sandra Picklesimer Aldrich, "Can I Have the Car Keys Friday Night?" in *Raising Them Right,* pp. 120-21.
12. Mike Yorkey, "Charting a Different Course," in *Raising Them Right,* pp. 125-26.
13. Jack Crabtree, "Boyfriends and Girlfriends," in *How to Get Your Teenager to Talk to You,* p. 121.
14. Dobson, "Surviving Your Child's Stormy Teen Years," in *Raising Them Right,* p. 94.

## Chapter Fourteen: Making a Timeless Investment

1. Barry St. Clair and Carol St. Clair, *Ignite the Fire* (Colorado Springs, Colo.: Victor, 1999), pp. 13-17.

## Chapter Fifteen: Creating an "Eager Learner" Attitude

1. Ross Campbell, *How to Really Love Your Teenager* (Colorado Springs, Colo.: Victor, 1981), pp. 25-26.
2. Ibid., p. 27.
3. Barry St. Clair and Carol St. Clair, *Ignite the Fire* (Colorado Springs, Colo.: Victor, 1999), pp. 71-72.
4. Philip Yancey, *What's So Amazing About Grace?* (Grand Rapids, Mich.: Zondervan, 1997), pp. 44-46.
5. Larry Weeden, *Feeling Guilty, Finding Grace* (Ann Arbor, Mich.: Vine, 1998), p. 32.
6. Charles Colson and Nancy R. Pearcey, *A Dangerous Grace* (Dallas: Word, 1994), p. vi.

7. James C. Dobson, "Dare to Discipline in the '90s," in *Raising Them Right*, ed. Mike Yorkey (Colorado Springs, Colo.: Focus on the Family, 1994), pp. 8-9.

8. Joe White, *Over the Edge and Back* (Sisters, Oreg.: Questar, 1992), p. 103.

9. Joe White, *FaithTraining* (Wheaton, Ill.: Tyndale/Focus on the Family, 1994), "A Tribute," p. v.

10. Dobson, "What to Do When Kids Drive You Crazy," in *Raising Them Right*, p. 34.

11. Tim Smith, *Life Skills for Girls* (Colorado Springs, Colo.: Cook, 2000), pp. 110-11.

12. St. Clairs, *Ignite the Fire*, pp. 220-21.

13. *Focus on the Family Complete Book of Baby and Child Care* (Wheaton, Ill.: Tyndale/Focus on the Family, 1997) p. 511.

14. Ibid.

15. Tim Smith, *Life Skills for Guys* (Colorado Springs, Colo.: Cook, 2000), p. 187.

16. Taken from transcripts of an interview with Joe White, June 2000.

**Chapter Sixteen: Helping Your Teen Dream Productive Dreams**

1. George Barna, *Generation Next* (Ventura, Calif.: Regal, 1995), p. 28.

2. Mike Ross, "Ryan's World," *Breakaway*, April 2001 (www.family.org/teenguys/breakmag/).

**Chapter Seventeen: Ensuring Your Child Is a Christian**

1. *Focus on the Family Parents' Guide to the Spiritual Growth of Children*, eds. John Trent, Ph.D., et al. (Wheaton, Ill.: Tyndale/Focus on the Familly, 2000), p. 302.

2. From the "Walk Away" Web site sponsored by the Institute for First Amendment Studies (gemini.berkshire.net/~ifas/wa/stories.html). Please note that Focus on the Family does not endorse this Web site and presents this material for informational purposes only.

3. George Barna, *Generation Next* (Ventura, Calif.: Regal, 1995), p. 75.

4. Gary and Greg Smalley, *Bound by Honor* (Wheaton, Ill.: Tyndale/Focus on the Family, 1998), p. 150.

5. Ibid.

6. Ibid., p. 152.

7. Ibid., p. 154.

8. Dr. William Rowley, *Pacesetter: Rites of Passage* (Colorado Springs, Colo.: David C. Cook, 1987), pp. 8-9.

9. Smalleys, *Bound by Honor*, p. 159.

10. Ibid., p. 160.

11. Ibid., pp. 161-62.

12. Ibid., p. 162.

13. Ibid., pp. 162-63.

14. Joe White, *Over the Edge and Back* (Sisters, Oreg.: Questar, 1992), pp. 99-100.

15. Ibid., pp. 61-63.

16. Ibid., pp. 81-83.

17. Ibid., pp. 94-97.

18. Smalleys, *Bound by Honor*, p. 116.

19. Barry St. Clair and Carol St. Clair, *Ignite the Fire* (Colorado Springs, Colo.: Victor, 1999), pp. 177-79.

20. Smalleys, *Bound by Honor*, p. 117.

21. White, *Over the Edge and Back*, pp. 97-98.

**Chapter Eighteen: Guiding Your Teen Toward Faith-Affirming Friendships**

1. "Teenagers and Their Relationships," Barna Research Group, July 8, 1998 (www.barnaresearch.com).

**Chapter Nineteen: Instilling a Christian Worldview**

1. E. O. Wilson, *The Humanist*, September–October 1982, p. 40.

2. Caryl Matritiano, *Let My Children Go* video recording. Matritiano is an author, international cult expert, and vice president of Jeremiah Films. Call (800) 828-2290 or go to www.jeremiahfilms.com.

**Chapter Twenty: Teaching Your Teen Media Discernment**

1. Newton Minnow, *How Vast the Wasteland Now?* (New York: Gannet Foundation Media Center, 1991) (www.KSU.edu/humec/kulaw.htm).

2. American Medical Association, *ama-assn.org*, March 17, 1999.

3. William J. Bennett, Joseph Lieberman, and C. DeLores Tucker, "Rap Rubbish," *USA Today*, June 6, 1996; Elizabeth F. Brown and William R. Hendee, "Adolescents and Their Music: Insights into the Health of Adolescents," *Journal of the American Medical Association*, September 22, 1989.

4. Artists Rights Foundation, Institute for Civil Society, *Variety*, November 2, 1998; Teen Research Unlimited poll of 13- to 19-year-olds, *USA Today*, December 22, 1998.

5. George Barna, *The Barna Report: 1992-93* (Ventura, Calif.: Regal, 1992), p. 125.

6. Alan Weed, taken from a personal conversation printed in "Raising Media-Wise Teens," *Dare 2 Dig Deeper Parents Series*, a Focus on the Family booklet, 2001, p. 7.

7. Tanya Bell, "Parental Advisory Explicit Content," *The Gazette* (Colorado Springs), Life section, p. 1, September 10, 2000.

8. "Health groups directly link media to child violence" (CNN.com/2000/HEALTH/children/07/26/children.violence.ap/).

9. Personal conversation in "Raising Media-Wise Teens," p. 5; *Billboard*, January 23, 1999.

**Chapter Twenty-One: Learning to Let Go**

1. Dean Merrill, "You Decide," *Focus on the Family*, October 1996.

2. James C. Dobson, *Solid Answers* (Wheaton, Ill.: Tyndale, 1997), p. 322.

3. Ibid., p. 298.

4. George Barna, *Generation Next* (Ventura, Calif.: Regal, 1995), pp. 104-5.

5. Ibid., pp. 98-99.

6. Barry St. Clair and Carol St. Clair, *Ignite the Fire* (Colorado Springs, Colo.: Victor, 1999), p. 74.

7. Merrill, "You Decide."

8. St. Clairs, *Ignite the Fire*, pp. 75-76.

9. Joe White, *FaithTraining* (Wheaton, Ill.: Tyndale/Focus on the Family, 1994), p. 69.

10. *World*, December 18, 1999
    (www.worldmag.com/world/issue/12-18-99/).
11. John Duckworth, *Just for a Moment I Saw the Light* (Colorado Springs, Colo.: Victor, 1994).
12. Tim Smith, *Life Skills for Guys* (Colorado Springs, Colo.: Cook, 2000), pp. 65-66.
13. Janet's story is from the "Walk Away" Web site sponsored by the Institute for First Amendment Studies. (See c. 17, note 2.)
14. Barna, *Generation Next*, pp. 85-86.
15. Ibid., pp. 93-94.
16. Joe White, *FaithTraining*, pp. 66-67.
17. St. Clairs, *Ignite the Fire*, pp. 39-40.
18. J. Budziszewski, "Cloud of Unbelief," from his "Office Hours" column on the *Boundless* Web site (www.boundless.org).

**Chapter Twenty-Two: Finding Time to Train Your Teen**
1. Richard Swenson, "Tame the Time Crunch," *Physician*, November–December 1995, p. 14.
2. Rosalie Maggio, ed., *The New Beacon Book of Quotations by Women* (Boston: Beacon, 1996), p. 502.
3. Ibid., p. 399.
4. Ibid., p. 502.
5. Quoted by Mark Link, *In the Stillness Is the Dancing* (Niles, Ill.: Argus, 1972), p. 11.

**Chapter Twenty-Three: Moving Your Child from Selfish to Selfless**
1. Quoted in *The New Beacon Book of Quotations by Women*, ed. Rosalie Maggio (Boston: Beacon, 1996), p. 9.
2. Gary Smalley and Greg Smalley, *Bound by Honor* (Wheaton, Ill.: Tyndale/Focus on the Family, 1998), pp. 11-14.
3. Mark Buchanan, *Your God Is Too Safe* (Sisters, Oreg.: Multnomah, 2001), p. 217.
4. Mark Moring in *Campus Life* as quoted in "Two Things Dad Taught," *Men of Integrity* newsletter, July 4, 2000 (ChristianityToday.com/moi).
5. *Christian Reader*, vol. 32, no. 3, fall 1992.

6. Ben Patterson, "A Faith Like Mary's," *Preaching Today*, tape 87.

7. Alan Redpath, *Leadership*, vol. 3, no. 2, summer 1982.

**Chapter Twenty-Four: Prescription for Disciple Making**

1. James Dobson, taken from the Focus on the Family booklet *Five Tips for Parents of Teens*, February 1989.

2. Adapted from Robert Lewis, *Raising a Modern-Day Knight* (Wheaton, Ill.: Tyndale/Focus on the Family, 1997), pp. 129-30.

3. Ibid., p. 99.

4. Mike Ross, "Skate Your Witness," *Breakaway*, October 2000 (Family.org/teenguys/breakmag/).

5. *Washington Update*, Family Research Council, July 11, 2000.

6. Greg Johnson and Mike Yorkey, *Faithful Parents, Faithful Kids* (Wheaton, Ill.: Tyndale, 1993), p. 155.

7. "Many Teenagers Regret Decision to Have Sex," Reuters News Service, July 5, 2000.

8. Mike Yorkey, *The Christian Family Answer Book* (Wheaton, Ill.: Victor, 1996), p. 240.

9. This story was taken from PreachingToday.com. It first appeared in *Leadership*, vol. 17, no. 1.

10. James C. Dobson, *Solid Answers* (Wheaton, Ill.: Tyndale, 1997), p. 212. The original quote was found on www.family.org/SolidAnswers.

11. Adapted from Manfred Koehler, "Window to the World," *Single-Parent Family* (www.family.org).

12. Nanci Hellmich, "A Teen Thing: Losing Sleep," *USA Today*, March 28, 2000 (USAToday.com).

13. Focus on the Family, "Healthfocus" employee newsletter, September 2000.

14. Parts of this section were adapted from Tim Kimmel, "Receiving the Prodigals," *Single-Parent Family*, November 1998 (www.family.org).

15. Kevin Huggins and Phil Landrum, *Guiding Your Teen to a Faith That Lasts* (Grand Rapids, Mich.: Discovery House, 1994), p. 19.

## Chapter Twenty-Five: Anticipating Success

1. Neil Clark Warren, *Catching the Rhythm of Love* (Nashville: Thomas Nelson, 2000), pp. 89-90.
2. Norman Gidden, *Parenting through the College Years* (Charlotte, Vt.: Williamson, 1988), quoted in *Family Wisdom*, ed. Susan Ginsberg (New York: Columbia University Press, 1996), p. 202.
3. Denis Waitley, *The Winning Family* (New York: Dodd, Mead, 1987), quoted in *Family Wisdom*, p. 202.
4. Laurence Steinberg and Ann Levine, *You and Your Adolescent* (New York: Harper & Row, 1990), quoted in *Family Wisdom*, p. 177.
5. Carol Kuykendall, "Choosing a College—Already?" in *Raising Them Right*, ed. Mike Yorkey (Colorado Springs, Colo.: Focus on the Family, 1994), pp. 245-48.
6. Warren, *Catching the Rhythm of Love*, pp. 101-3.

## Chapter Twenty-Six: Marking Milestone Moments

1. Marilyn vos Savant, "What to Teach Your Kids Before They Leave Home," *Parade*, March 25, 2001, pp. 20-21.
2. Marilyn Elias, "Chats with Parents Pass Sex Attitudes to Teens," *USA Today*, August 7, 2000 (USAToday.com).
3. Adapted from Richard Durfield, "A Promise with a Ring to It," in *Raising Them Right*, ed. Mike Yorkey (Colorado Springs, Colo.: Focus on the Family, 1994), pp. 143-49. Parents wanting more information about "key talks" should read Richard C. Durfield and Renee Durfield, *Raising Them Chaste* (Minneapolis: Bethany, 1991).
4. Statistics and quotations regarding this study were taken from "Weblog: True Love Actually Does Wait, Study Finds," ChristianityToday.com, January 4, 2001.
5. Gary Smalley and John Trent, *Leaving the Light On* (Portland, Oreg.: Multnomah, 1994), pp. 150-51.
6. Robert Lewis, *Raising a Modern-Day Knight* (Wheaton, Ill.: Tyndale/Focus on the Family, 1997), p. 104.
7. Quoted in *Family Wisdom*, ed. Susan Ginsberg (New York: Columbia University Press, 1996), p. 62.

8. Stephen Arterburn and Jim Burns, *Steering Them Straight* (Colorado Springs, Colo.: Focus on the Family, 1995), p. 212.

9. Ginger Hutton, "Overprotection Harms Children," *Arizona Republic*, April 20, 1987, p. B8.

10. William Kilpatrick, *Why Johnny Can't Tell Right from Wrong* (New York: Simon & Schuster, 1992), p. 252.

**Chapter Twenty-Seven: Measuring Success**

1. Charles Andrews, quoted by Sherwood Wirt and Kersten Beckstrom, *Living Quotations for Christians* (New York: Harper & Row, 1974), p. 80.

2. Brent Curtis and John Eldredge, *The Sacred Romance* (Nashville: Thomas Nelson, 1997), p. 8.

3. Mark Buchanan, *Your God Is Too Safe* (Sisters, Oreg.: Multnomah, 2000), pp. 201-2.

4. Ross Campbell, *How to Really Love Your Teenager* (Colorado Springs, Colo.: Victor, 1993), p. 122.

**Chapter Twenty-Eight: The Parent's Cap and Gown**

1. Greg Johnson and Mike Yorkey, *Faithful Parents, Faithful Kids* (Wheaton, Ill.: Tyndale, 1993), p. xvii.

2. Randall Balmer, *Christianity Today*, vol. 33, no. 16.

3. Geoff Gorsuch, "Journey to Adelphos," *Discipleship Journal*, issue 14.

4. James Dobson, *Life on the Edge* (Dallas: Word, 1995), pp. 271-72.

# Index

# ACKNOWLEDGMENTS

This book represents the dedicated efforts of many people, from its conception and planning, to the extended writing process, through review and editing, and ending with typesetting and proofreading. Focus on the Family wishes to acknowledge and express its gratitude to the following for their invaluable contributions to this work:

**Planning:** Kurt Bruner, Al Janssen, Mike Ross, Susie Shellenberger, Leslie Yeaton, Amy Stephens, Mike Haley, Phil Hildebrand, Jim Mhoon

**Planning, Writing, and Reviewing:** Joe White, Jim Weidmann

**Planning, Writing, and Editing:** Larry Weeden

**Planning and Writing:** Bob Waliszewski

**Research:** Angela Ianniello, Jenny Bellington, Heather Troxell, Livia Stephens, Jill Ritter, Sara Rogers, Kristen Denyes

**Writing:** Lissa Halls Johnson, Keith Wall, Chuck Johnson, Andy Braner, Bob Smithouser

**Writing and Editing:** John Duckworth, Mick Silva

**Editing:** Ray Seldomridge, Eric Stanford

**Interior Design and Typesetting:** Angela Greenwalt

**Reviewing:** Shelly Smith

**Proofreading:** Bonnie Franklin, Jeff Masching, Shana Murph

# Welcome to the Family!

Heritage
Builders®

*Helping You Build a Family of Faith*

We hope you've enjoyed this book. Heritage Builders was founded in 1995 by three fathers with a passion for the next generation. As a new ministry of Focus on the Family, Heritage Builders strives to equip, train, and motivate parents to become intentional about building a strong spiritual heritage.

It's quite a challenge for busy parents to find ways to build a spiritual foundation for their families—especially in a way they enjoy and understand. Through activities and participation, children can learn biblical truth in a way  they can understand, enjoy—and *remember*.

Passing along a heritage of Christian faith to your family is a parent's highest calling. Heritage Builders's goal is to encourage and empower you in this great mission with practical resources and inspiring ideas that really work— and help your children develop a lasting love for God.

\*\*\*

## How to Reach Us

For more information, visit our Heritage Builders Web site! Log on to **www.heritagebuilders.com** to discover new resources, sample activities, and ideas to help you pass on a spiritual heritage. To request any of these resources, simply call Focus on the Family at 1-800-A-FAMILY (1-800-232-6459) or in Canada, call 1-800-661-9800. Or send your request to Focus on the Family, Colorado Springs, CO 80995. In Canada, write Focus on the Family, P.O. Box 9800, Stn. Terminal, Vancouver, B.C. V6B 4G3.

To learn more about Focus on the Family or to find out if there is an associate office in your country, please visit www. family.org.

We'd love to hear from you!

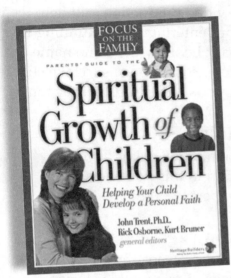

## Mind Over Media

Help your teen understand and expose the subtle and far-reaching power of the media. Hosted by recording artist and national youth speaker Lakita Garth, this MTV-style video production will help teens understand how to make choices about entertainment. Running time: approximately 30 minutes. A paperback book by the same name uses humor, questions, facts, and stories to encourage teens to take charge of what they allow to enter their minds and direct their actions.

## LifeTraining

Cement your teens' spiritual foundation using devotions, encouragement, and inspiration in this power-packed paperback by teen expert Joe White.

## LifeTraining 2

Fortify the faith of your teens and preteens through more parent-teen devotions, hundreds of memorable stories, thought-provoking questions, and a proven Scripture memory plan, with Joe White's *LifeTraining 2*.

## My Truth, Your Truth, Whose Truth?

*My Truth, Your Truth, Whose Truth* challenges your teen to wrestle with the concept of absolute truth. In this eye-opening paperback, Internet chat room participants search for answers to life's deepest questions and discover that absolute truth exists—and that it's found only in Christ. The 30-minute video stimulates deeper thinking and reveals how faith is essential to discernment and decision making, through a captivating mix of teen discussions and thought-provoking apologetics.

Heritage Builders ®

Helping You Build a Family of Faith